The sentence in written English

A syntactic study based on an analysis of scientific texts

CAMBRIDGE STUDIES IN LINGUISTICS

General Editors · W. SIDNEY ALLEN · EUGENIE J. A. HENDERSON · FRED W. HOUSEHOLDER · JOHN LYONS · R. B. LE PAGE · F. R. PALMER · J. L. M. TRIM

THE SENTENCE
IN WRITTEN
ENGLISH;

A SYNTACTIC STUDY BASED
ON AN ANALYSIS OF
SCIENTIFIC TEXTS

RODNEY D. HUDDLESTON

Senior Lecturer in English
University of Queensland

CAMBRIDGE

at the University Press · 1971

Published by the Syndics of the Cambridge University Press
Bentley House, 200 Euston Road, London NW1 2DB
American Branch: 32 East 57th Street, New York, N.Y.10022

Library of Congress Catalogue Card Number: 76–139714

ISBN: 0 521 08062 2

Printed in Great Britain
at the University Printing House, Cambridge
(Brooke Crutchley, University Printer)

Contents

Preface

This book is a substantially revised version of my contribution to *Sentence and Clause in Scientific English*, which was the final report of a research project into the linguistic properties of scientific English carried out at University College London in 1964–7. I would emphasize, however, that the present work is as much concerned with common-core English as with the language of science: see the statement of aims in the Introduction. The original research project was supported by grant Y 5995 of the Office of Scientific and Technical Information. I am deeply indebted to my colleagues on the project: to Dick Hudson and Eugene Winter for their part in the first stage analysis of the corpus, and to Alick Henrici for organizing the computational processing of that analysis. I have also benefited from Dick Hudson's comments on various drafts of the work. Nevertheless, responsibility for the description presented in the book is of course mine.

I should like also to acknowledge my more general indebtedness to Professor Michael Halliday, whose teaching first aroused my interest in English grammar; without his encouragement over the years I should certainly not have come to write this book. Finally I would express my thanks to Cecily McDonald for typing the book, and to my wife for her help with the preparation of the index and the correction of proofs – and for her patience during the writing of the book.

Brisbane, May 1970

TO MY FATHER AND MOTHER

I Introduction

I have had two complementary aims in view in preparing the present book: to give a selective grammatical description of a corpus of some 135,000 words of written scientific English and to investigate certain areas of the grammar of 'common-core' English – the grammar that is common to all varieties of the language (except possibly a few highly restricted ones). The aims are complementary in that it is obviously impossible to give a non-trivial description that will account for the sentences in a given corpus while excluding all sentences of the language that do not occur therein; a text cannot be analyzed in isolation, and the description will be of interest only to the extent that the grammatical categories established have validity beyond the text. On the other hand texts constitute the linguist's primary data and it is salutary to test one's descriptions by confronting them with a sizeable body of such primary data. This is of course not to deny the value of studies based on data derived from introspection: we need to make use of both kinds of data.

The theoretical framework underlying the description is mainly that of transformational grammar. I therefore assume that the syntactic description of a sentence takes the form of a series of phrase-markers, or labelled bracketings, which represent its structure at different levels: the bracketing represents the constituent hierarchy at the given level, and the labelling represents the classification of the constituents. The first in the series of phrase-markers is said to represent the 'deep structure' of the sentence, the last the 'surface structure'; the first is generated by phrase-structure rules, whereas each of the remaining phrase-markers derives from the immediately preceding one in the series by a transformational rule.[1] I should emphasize, however, that

---

[1] Transformational grammar is too well known for it to be necessary to give a summary of it here. The fullest account is in Chomsky (1965); it also figures prominently in several recent textbooks of linguistics, e.g. Lyons (1968), Langacker (1967) and Langendoen (1969). Because of my informal approach, and because the book is intended as a contribution to the grammatical description of English, not to general linguistic theory, I have not felt it necessary to commit myself on such controversial issues within transformational theory as that of the generative or interpretative role of semantics (cf. G. Lakoff, forthcoming, and the references cited there).

I have not attempted to produce a formalized generative grammar: this may be regarded as the long-term goal, but in working towards it we can fruitfully discuss in informal terms what we want the formal grammar to say about the structure of particular sentences or classes of sentences.

The choice of scientific English as the variety for textual study was motivated primarily by practical considerations (though there is also the point that this variety of written English is relatively neglected in the major standard handbooks of Jespersen, Curme, etc.): data on scientific English is likely to be of interest to workers in two of the main branches of applied linguistics, automatic language data processing[1] and language teaching. There is a considerable demand for courses designed to teach this type of English to foreign learners, and although this book itself is in no way intended as a teaching grammar I hope it will be of use to those applied linguists who are concerned with preparing such courses.

I should make it clear that the present work is an exercise in 'descriptive linguistics', not 'stylistics', as these terms are used and contrasted, for example, by Crystal & Davy (1969): a stylistic analysis, in their sense, of written scientific English would seek to isolate those linguistic features which distinguish this from other varieties of English. The difference between my approach and theirs thus has to do with aims and priorities: working in stylistics, they regard the grammatical description as a tool for the differentiation of varieties, for the identification of linguistic features 'which are restricted to certain kinds of social context', and they emphasize that their grammar should be evaluated relative to this aim rather than in terms of its adequacy as a linguistic description – my primary concern, on the other hand, has been to produce as adequate a description as I can, judged simply as a (partial) grammar for its own sake. Because of this emphasis on pure description rather than stylistics I have not attempted to compare the corpus with texts from other varieties of English – the comparison in 5.6 between the relative clauses in my corpus and those in a sample of spoken (non-scientific) conversation is one exception, made possible by the availability of readily comparable data on the latter and included as an illustration of what might be done in a larger-scale study. Until further

---

[1] Cf. the remark of Clarke & Wall (1965: 312) in their 'An economical program for limited parsing of English': 'Perhaps one could hope to select instead the "syntactically most probable" parsing if adequate statistical studies of English grammar were available.'

comparative work of this kind is done one cannot of course tell how far the statistical properties of the corpus reported in the present work are peculiarly characteristic of written scientific English and how far they are generalizable to other varieties; I hope, however, to have provided a solid basis for such comparative study.

As I said at the outset, the description is, naturally, partial and selective. Most of what I have to say relates to the grammar of the clause.[1] The method of presentation I have adopted for the most part is to discuss a given area of the grammar first in general or common-core terms, and then to examine the corpus in the light of the descriptive framework so established. I have not, however, felt it necessary to keep constant from chapter to chapter the relative weight given to common-core and corpus description; thus in the chapter on mood, the textual description occupies quite little space relative to the general discussion, whereas the proportions are reversed in the chapter on the uses of the modal auxiliaries—I have tended to devote relatively more attention to the corpus in those areas of the grammar which are less well understood or where current descriptions are less explicit, such as transitivity (ch. 3) as opposed to complementation (ch. 4).

Full details of the corpus are given in the Appendix. It is made up of 27 texts of 5,000 words each.[2] The texts were taken from three different 'strata', corresponding to different 'levels of brow': the nine 'high' stratum texts come from specialist journals, the nine 'mid' stratum ones from undergraduate textbooks, and the nine 'low' stratum ones from more popular works addressed to the intelligent and well-informed layman. The high and mid texts were also classified according to field or subject matter, the three categories selected being biology, chemistry and physics; it was not found practicable to apply this classification to the low stratum texts. In addition, the corpus was divided into three parts A, B, and C, each being alike in respect of the

[1] The clause may be defined as a simple as opposed to compound sentence; from a distributional point of view simple and compound sentences are virtually identical – wherever a simple sentence occurs it could be replaced by a compound one of the appropriate type – so that while the general category of 'Sentence' appears as a constituent label in phrase-markers, 'Simple sentence' (= clause) and 'Compound sentence' do not. Simple and compound sentences differ in respect of their internal structure: a compound sentence is one consisting of two or more other sentences (typically joined by some kind of conjunction), whereas a clause consists of a subject and predicate (or something similar, depending on one's analysis).

[2] More precisely, each text ends after the orthographic sentence containing the five-thousandth word.

stratum and field classifications, so that each contains one high stratum biology text, one mid physics text, three low stratum texts, and so on. The reason for this division is that certain areas of the grammar have been examined in detail with respect to just one or two parts of the corpus.

Each quoted example is accompanied by a five-digit reference number. The last three digits give the serial number within the particular text of the first clause in the quotation, while the first two digits identify the text – as first digit, 1, 2 and 3 indicate high, mid and low stratum respectively, and as second digit 1, 2 and 3 are used for biology, 4, 5, and 6 for chemistry, 7, 8 and 9 for physics, insofar as the field parameter is applicable. Thus clause 17001 is the first clause in one of the three high physics texts, 22500 is the five-hundredth clause in one of the three mid biology texts, 32050 is the fiftieth clause in one of the nine low texts. The only changes I have made in the quotations involve: (a) occasional omission of irrelevant material, marked by '[...]'; (b) the replacement of a few complex formulae, equations, etc., containing one or more of the relators '=, >, <, ~' by '[R]' ('relation'), with differentiating subscripts where necessary; (c) italicization of the part of the quotation that is particularly relevant to the point being exemplified – the italics of names of plants, etc., of formulae and of Latinisms may be assumed to be the original author's, all the other italics to be mine unless the expression '[*ital. sic*]' indicates otherwise.

As mentioned in the Preface, the present work is a substantially revised version of my contribution to *Sentence and Clause in Scientific English* (Huddleston *et al.*, 1968). The other sections of the latter are (a) 'The Clause Complex' (= 'compound sentence'), by R. A. Hudson; (b) 'Some Aspects of Cohesion', by E. O. Winter; (c) 'Some Quantitative Issues' (which includes a section on the difference between the strata), by A. Henrici. In addition the full set of statistical tables derived from the first stage analysis of the corpus is kept in the Department of General Linguistics, University College, London, and is available for consultation there by interested scholars.

2 Mood

2.1 Mood and illocutionary force

It is important for a number of reasons to distinguish between the grammatical mood of a sentence and the illocutionary force of an utterance (in the sense of Austin, 1962; Searle, 1969). I shall use the terms declarative, interrogative, imperative and exclamative exclusively for types of sentence classified according to grammatical mood, whereas assertion, question, order, exclamation and various other terms will refer to the illocutionary force of different kinds of speech act. The contrast between sentence and utterance (or speech act) in this formulation will suggest that mood is a matter of competence, illocutionary force of performance. But this is not the crucial issue, for we should expect the illocutionary force of an utterance to be largely if not wholly explicable in terms of the semantic–syntactic description of the associated sentence: it is reasonable to require that a competence description should account for at least the illocutionary *potential* of a sentence. My reasons for distinguishing mood and illocutionary force do not therefore depend on the competence–performance contrast; they are as follows:

(a) Firstly there is the practical point that although it is a reasonable requirement that a grammar account for the illocutionary potential of sentences our current descriptions come nowhere near satisfying this requirement. The classification of sentences as declarative, interrogative, imperative and exclamative is quite well-established (which is not of course to say that all grammarians who apply it use exactly the same criteria – or the same terminology) and certainly seems to be valid for some stage in the deep to surface structure progression. Detailed work on illocutionary force is much more recent, and it still remains somewhat programmatic and inexplicit. We do not know what the categories are (the works mentioned above suggest there is quite a large number: suggestion, advice, entreaty, invitation, wager, promise, warning, threat, insult, etc., besides the usual assertion, question, command and exclamation), to what extent they are discrete and mutually exclusive, just what the 'illocutionary force indicators' are (Searle, 1969: 30 ff.) and so on.

It will be expedient therefore to use mood as the basis for our discussion; the use of the terms declarative, interrogative, etc. will make it clear that this classification does not claim to account directly for illocutionary force/potential.

(b) Secondly the domains of the two classificatory systems do not wholly coincide. Consider for example the following sentences:

(i) *a* John didn't know that Bill was coming
   b John didn't know who was coming

As far as the matrix sentences are concerned we shall say that both are declaratives and both are assertions (i.e. would typically be used to make an assertion). But when we turn to the embedded constituent sentences *that Bill was coming* and *who was coming* we see that mood is relevant – the former is declarative, the latter is interrogative – but that the notion of illocutionary force is not applicable, for in any utterance of (i)*a* and *b that Bill was coming* and *who was coming* are not taken as separate speech acts. There are compelling syntactic reasons for grouping together embedded sentences like *who was coming* in (i)*b* and independent ones like *who is coming?*, and this grouping is supported by semantic considerations too: I develop these points in 2.2.3.

This is not to say that the mood system of complement sentences is exactly the same as that of independent sentences. In particular the former does not include imperatives. Thus in *John requested/ordered Bill to leave* it seems to me quite inappropriate to classify the complement sentence (*Bill*) *to leave* as an imperative. Nor is it an 'indirect' or 'reported' imperative: the matrix sentence as a whole may be said to report a request or order, but the latter may have been expressed as an imperative (*leave!*), a declarative (*I would like/I order you to leave*) or, in the case of requests rather than orders, an interrogative (*would you like to leave?*). And what makes the matrix a reported request/order is clearly not the infinitival form of the complement but the presence of the specific verb *request* or *order*: compare *John persuaded Bill to go.* I will leave until later the question of whether the domain of the mood system is the sentence or the clause: for the present I shall continue to discuss it in relation to the more general category of sentence.

(c) Finally there is the phenomenon of echo-questions. Echo-questions are of two main types: 'yes/no' and *wh*. Thus an imperative such as *give him £5* might be 'echo-questioned' as *give him £5?* (yes/no: 'is that what you said?') or *give who £5?* (*wh*: 'who did you say to give £5 to?'). The illocutionary force of these echoes is clearly question not request/command (except insofar as a question is a special kind of request, but this is not relevant to my present point). But to account for the grammatical form of such sentences we need to treat them as both imperatives and interrogatives: the natural way to do this is to distinguish between what we may call basic mood and second-order mood. In basic mood, the terms declarative, interrogative, imperative, and exclamative are mutually exclusive; second-order mood, with terms neutral versus echo-interrogative, cuts across the basic mood system, giving a paradigm such as that shown in table 2:1.

TABLE 2: 1. *Basic and second-order mood*

| | Second-order mood | | |
| | Neutral | Echo-interrogative | |
		yes/no	*wh*
Basic mood			
Declarative	He went with Bill.	He went with Bill?	He went with who?
Interrogative:			
yes/no	Did he go with Bill?	Did he go with Bill?	Did he go with who?
wh	Who went with Bill?	Who went with Bill?	Who went with who?
Imperative	Go with Bill!	Go with Bill?	Go with who?
Exclamative	What a crowd went with Bill!	What a crowd went with Bill?	What a crowd went with who?

The range of elements that can be questioned is greater in echo-interrogatives than in basic ones – *you're intending to what?* can only be an echo, for example. Yes/no echoes are characterized by 'question intonation', but certain types of sentence are ambiguous according as their second-order mood is neutral or yes/no echo. This is so with yes/no basic interrogatives with inverted word-order and rising intonation like *has he finished?* and also with sentences with normal word order and rising intonation like *you're going with her?*. This latter is certainly not necessarily an echo of *I'm going with her*. In its neutral second-order mood interpretation it is probably best treated as an interrogative, since it has the illocutionary force of a question and we could regard the intonation as the illocutionary force indicator. This would be to treat *has he gone?* and *he's gone?* (with 'question intonation') as variants of a single type contrasting with declarative *he's gone* (non-question intonation). One difficulty with this analysis arises with such sentences as *I suppose he's gone?* (again with question intonation). For this is clearly not equivalent to *do I suppose he's gone?* – its meaning is more like that of *I suppose he's gone, hasn't he?*[1]

I shall represent the mood of sentences by means of features assigned to the appropriate S node. This may be regarded as a matter of notational convenience: it avoids the necessity for *ad hoc* constituents like the Q(uestion) and Imp(erative) morphemes of Katz & Postal (1964) or the T(ype) morpheme of Rosenbaum (1968), and I have preferred not to commit myself at this stage to a constituent structure analysis involving abstract performative verbs (cf. R. Lakoff, 1968) – such that all command-imperatives, for example, would have an abstract verb of commanding in the underlying structure. My concern is with the internal structure of the various mood types of sentence and the analysis should carry over whatever means we decide on to represent the mood itself in structural terms.[2]

I shall not deal with echo-interrogatives: all examples will be neutral in respect of second-order mood. Declaratives I regard as the unmarked mood category, and no separate section will be devoted to them: interrogatives, imperatives and exclamatives are characterized by various positive structural properties, declaratives by the absence of all of these.

---

[1] Notice, however, that such a sentence as *do I take it you've finished?* is in effect equivalent to *have you finished?* in the sense that the latter is the question the speaker wants to have answered. It might be possible to formulate rules accounting for the interpretation of various types of sentence in ways that differ from their 'literal' meaning – and in this case we might be satisfied to treat *I suppose he's gone?*, with question intonation, as the interrogative of *I suppose he's gone*, with statement intonation. A similar rule of non-literal interpretation might be envisaged to account for the fact that such sentences as *will you (would you like/care to) help me?* have the illocutionary force of requests; from the point of view of the present analysis, these are regarded as interrogative in mood.

[2] The abstract verb approach would probably give a more satisfactory account of echoes than that suggested above. In such a yes/no echo as *go with her?* there would be two such abstract verbs, one for the interrogative, the other for the imperative. The fact that it is the second-order mood here that correlates with the illocutionary potential of the sentence would be explained by the interrogative abstract verb's being higher in the structural tree than the imperative one, which would be embedded within its complement – cf. 'I ask you whether you request(ed) me to go with her?'

2.2 Interrogatives

2.2.1 Disjunctive interrogatives.

Interrogative sentences are normally subdivided into the two main types exemplified in:

(1) This can be split up into two questions, namely, how thick *can* [*ital. sic*] this layer be, and is this thick enough to do any good? (17464)

Numerous pairs of terms have been proposed for the two classes (cf. Jespersen, 1924: 303), but the terminology is clearly of less interest than the criteria used for distinguishing the classes. It is possible to find three different sets of criteria that have been invoked, explicitly or implicitly, in the classification: one has to do with the presuppositions of the question, a second with the presence or absence of an interrogative word (a *wh*-word), a third with the type of answer expected. These criteria give similar but by no means identical results, so that it is worth considering them in turn.

Consider first then a classification based on the presuppositions of the question: it seems reasonable to suppose that this criterion is implicit in the 'total' versus 'partial' interrogative distinction. Such a sentence as *when did John arrive?* is a partial interrogative in that it presupposes that John arrived and asks only about the time, whereas *did John arrive?* makes no equivalent presupposition and is thus treated as a total interrogative. Notice, however, that in an interrogative like *did John arrive last week?* spoken with contrastive stress on *last week*, John's arrival is presupposed just as much as in the *when* example above. Moreover, in the *wh*-type it is possible to avoid making presuppositions by introducing an *if*-clause: *what, if anything, are you going to tell him?*. Thus although in the simple cases yes/no interrogatives can be regarded as total, and *wh*-ones as partial, we can also find partial yes/no and total *wh*-interrogatives. And while the analysis of presuppositions is undoubtedly of considerable grammatical importance, it clearly involves not just interrogatives but all sentences, irrespective of mood. Thus in such a pair as *did John mow the lawn?* and *John mowed the lawn* with contrastive stress on *John* in both cases, it is presupposed as given that someone mowed the lawn; the declarative gives the new information that John was the someone, while the interrogative asks for new information concerning whether or not it was John (see Halliday, 1967c, for a discussion of this area of the grammar).

There is a sense however in which presuppositions are relevant to the quite different classification of questions into rhetorical versus ordinary? It might be maintained that the answer to a rhetorical question contains *no* new information, which is why it is arguable whether it has the illocutionary force of a question at all: note that Searle (1969: 66) gives as one of the conditions for a (non-examination) question that the speaker does not know the answer, a condition that is clearly not met by rhetorical questions. But I'm not sure how far the rhetorical/non-rhetorical distinction belongs in a grammar of competence, for it raises the difficult problem of 'conduciveness' – cf. Bolinger (1957: 97): 'The devices for creating a conducive or leading Q(uestion), one that shows that a given answer is expected or desired, are intonational, gestural, and verbal. [...] few are determinate enough to make a Q unambiguously conducive without the support of one or more others.'

The presence or absence of a *wh*-word is regarded as a matter of surface structure by Katz & Postal (1964): they claim that there is a *wh*-element in the underlying structure of all interrogatives. I shall return to their arguments below; for the present it is enough to say that as far as independent interrogatives are concerned the presence or absence in surface structure of a *wh*-word correlates quite closely with a significant distinction in deep structure, whether or not this deep structure distinction is itself expressible in terms of the presence or absence of *wh*. To see this let us turn to the third criterion: the type of answer.

The analysis of 'expected', 'appropriate', 'proper' or 'possible' answers belongs of course to the study of competence. In actual performance the addressee may evade the question ('Why should I tell you?', 'I don't know'), challenge the questioner's presuppositions ('When is she coming to Paris?' – 'Who said she *was* coming?'), and so on; nevertheless I take the view that intuitions about linguistically appropriate answers provide as valid data for linguistic analysis as do intuitions about grammaticality, etc.

The most usual classification based on the type of appropriate answer opposes yes/no interrogatives to all others. There are two cases where this classification yields different results from that based on the presence or absence of *wh*. The criteria conflict firstly in the case of Bolinger's (1957: 7) continuation or complementary questions like *his reason being?, and John?, but later?*. The fragmentary nature of the last two is perhaps such that we would not wish to generate them directly, but I see no reason of principle for treating the first as ungrammatical. This type is not exemplified in the corpus, however, and I shall not have anything further to say about it in this study.

The second case of conflict between the two criteria is more interesting. It involves disjunctives, as in:

(i) Will you go now or later?

The *wh* criterion would group this with (ii), the yes/no answer criterion with (iii):

(ii) Will you go?
(iii) When will you go?

And linguists have indeed differed in their treatment of such examples: Bolinger (1957), for instance, adopts the first grouping, putting (i) with (ii), whereas Jespersen (1924: 303) puts (i) with (iii). The similarity between (i) and (ii) is not just that neither contains a *wh*-element in surface structure: they are also alike in having just two possible answers (excluding elliptical variants), whereas (iii) has an indefinite number. It is for this reason that Bolinger classifies the first two as multiple-choice questions. His classification is as follows:

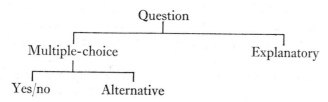

One might argue at this point that such a sentence as:

(iv) Which of his parents does he resemble the more?

is just as much a multiple-choice question as is (ii): (i) may be said to be explicitly multiple-choice, (ii) and (iv) to be implicitly so. This problem can be resolved if we consider the underlying structure rather than the surface structure: there are good reasons for claiming that yes/no interrogatives are explicitly multiple-choice in underlying structure – i.e. that the deep structure contains an explicit *either-or* disjunction just as does the surface structure of (i). The claim is, then, that (ii) has the same deep structure as:

(v) *a* Will you go or will you not go?
   b Will you go or not?

The justification for this analysis as as follows: Firstly it accounts for the synonymy of (ii) and (v). Secondly it provides an explanation for the considerable structural similarities between yes/no interrogatives and overt disjunctives like (i), namely:

(a) Both types lack a surface *wh*-element in independent clauses: this was the starting point for the present discussion.

(b) Both types have *whether* (or its variant *if*) when embedded as a complement, etc. – compare *I don't know whether he's coming* and *I don't know whether it's John or Bill who's coming*.

There is one respect in which overt disjunctives differ distributionally from superficially non-disjunctive yes/no interrogatives, but in fact this also supports the derivation of the latter from underlying disjunctives. Consider the paradigm for concessive interrogatives:

(vi) *a*   He'll be there whoever's giving the talk
    b   He'll be there whether it's wet or fine
    c   He'll be there whether he's invited or not
    d   *He'll be there whether he's invited

All the main types of independent interrogative have concessive counterparts except the plain yes/no class. It seems to me more plausible to regard this gap in the paradigm as due to the blocking of a transformation deleting the negative disjunct from structures like that underlying (vi)*c* rather than as due to constraints on deep structure.

If even plain yes/no interrogatives involve a deep structure disjunction, we can base our classification of interrogatives on the presence/absence of a questioned disjunction rather than the less explicit, less well-defined notion of 'multiple-choice':

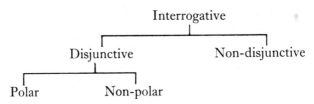

Polar disjunctives are those where the disjuncts differ only as to positive/negative polarity; in non-polars the disjuncts differ in some other respect and are not limited to two – compare:

(2) V_R can be greater than, equal to, or less than zero according to whether the scattered light is displaced towards the red end of the spectrum, is unaffected, or is displaced towards the violet end of the spectrum. (26163)

The treatment of yes/no interrogatives as a special case of disjunctives seems to me much more satisfactory than the converse, namely the treatment of non-polar disjunctives as a special case of yes/no interrogatives. This latter analysis – favoured by Bolinger (1957: 114), for whom disjunctive interrogatives are 'probably a spurious class' – would regard (i) (= *will you go now or later?*) as the sequence of yes/no interrogatives:

(vii) Will you go now? Will you go later?

I find this counterintuitive in that (i) seems to be a single question, not two: it does not raise two matters at once like the type *will you come tomorrow and tell me what you're going to wear*, which Bolinger offers as an analogy. A less impressionistic argument is that (vii) is not in fact a paraphrase of (i) for the examples differ in the presuppositions they make. (i) but not (vii) presupposes that you will go.

Not all interrogatives containing an *or*-disjunction belong to the class of disjunctive interrogatives: this class includes only those where it is the disjunction that is being questioned, that is, those where the possible answers consist of the declarative versions of the separate disjuncts. It has long been known that such sentences as:

(viii) Does he speak French or Italian?

are, in their written form, ambiguous (cf. Sweet, 1891: 174). In one interpretation this is a non-polar disjunctive, such that the possible answers are *he speaks French* and *he speaks Italian*. In the other interpretation it is a yes/no interrogative whose possible answers are *yes, he does speak French or Italian* and *no, he doesn't speak French or Italian*. (My original example *will you go now or later?* was chosen as one where the yes/no reading was contextually rather unlikely, but it is nevertheless formally ambiguous in just the same way as (viii).) In speech the two readings are differentiated by intonation – for a recent analysis see Halliday (1964: 164). Sweet distinguishes between a 'strong' *or*, as in the first interpretation of (viii), and a 'weak' *or*, as in the second: in the terms used above a strong *or* marks a questioned disjunction, a weak *or* a disjunction that is not questioned. It follows of course from the suggested analysis of yes/no interrogatives that the second interpretation of (viii) contains a covert strong *or*, so that its deep structure is the same as that underlying *does he speak French or Italian or does he not speak French or Italian?* A textual example that nicely combines a strong (questioned) disjunction with a weak one is the following:

(3) Whether the animal or man actually responds by moving or speaking is, however, very seldom determined by the actions of a single receptor fibre. (22179)

Formally this sentence is three-ways ambiguous. In the most likely interpretation, the first *or* is weak, the second strong: this meaning can be roughly paraphrased as 'whether it is by moving or by speaking that the creature responds...'. Secondly, the first *or* may be strong, the second weak: 'whether it is the animal or the man that responds...is...'. Thirdly, both *or*'s may be weak implying an additional strong *or* present only in deep structure: 'whether or not the creature responds in one of these ways...'. It is not, however, grammatically possible for both *or*'s to be strong: only one disjunction can be questioned in an interrogative sentence.

What can be said about the deep structure of disjunctive interrogatives? I remarked earlier that Katz & Postal claim that these, like non-disjunctive interrogatives, contain an underlying *wh*. The structure they postulate (1964: 104) for a yes/no interrogative like *did John sleep (or not)?* is as shown in PM(1).

PM(1)

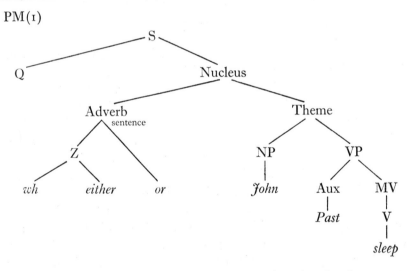

In view of their observation that 'yes-no questions involve the request for a specification of one of two alternatives that are in fact disjunctions of sentences' (100) it is curious that PM(1) does not contain any sentence coordination. The reason for this appears to be their decision to treat *wh-either-or* as a sentence adverb, that is, as belonging to the same syntactic category as the *yes* and *no* that occur in possible answers. But there is no independent evidence for the assignment of *yes*, *no* and *either-or* to the same category – it is indeed difficult to find any environment where *yes* (or *no*) and *either-or* are mutually substitutable: distributionally they are very different. *Either-or* patterns in a very similar way to *both-and*, and traditional grammar was surely right in grouping them together as coordinating conjunctions.

Two main types of coordination are distinguished in the transformational literature: sentence coordination and phrasal coordination (cf. G. Lakoff & Peters, 1969). In many cases what appears in surface structure as a coordination of phrases derives by reduction from a coordination of sentences – thus *John and Mary are French* may be said to derive from the same underlying structure as *John is French and Mary is French*. There are also a number of well-known types where such a derivation is not plausible, e.g. *John and Mary are a pair of criminals*, and in these cases there must be a coordination of phrases, not sentences, in the deep structure. It seems clear, however, that all deep structure phrasal coordination is conjunctive rather than disjunctive: certainly all questioned disjunctions may be treated as involving the deep structure coordination of sentences. Thus the earlier example (i) will be assumed to derive from the same underlying structure as *will you go now or will you go later?* The rule for sentence coordination given by Langendoen (1969: 33) is $S \rightarrow CS^*$, equivalent to $S \rightarrow C(S)^n$, $n \geqslant 2$. The C, coordinating conjunction, may be either conjunctive (*and*) or disjunctive (*or*). Extending to sentence coordination the Lakoff–Peters analysis of phrasal coordination we will posit a 'universal principle' which converts phrase-markers like PM(2) into ones like PM(3).

PM(2)

PM(3)

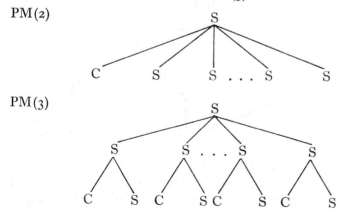

There are further rules that delete coordinating conjunctions where necessary. In English the first conjunction differs in phonological form from the other(s) in the series: *both-and, either-or* (contrast for example the *et-et* and *ou-ou* of French). If there are more than two terms in the coordination the first conjunction must be deleted – at least as far as conjunctive coordination is concerned: *both X (and) Y and Z* is certainly ungrammatical, while *either X (or) Y or Z* seems to be acceptable for some speakers, unacceptable for others.

If we apply this analysis to Katz & Postal's *did John sleep (or not)?* while maintaining their suggestion that *wh* is associated with *either*, we get PM(4) as the remote structure.

PM(4)

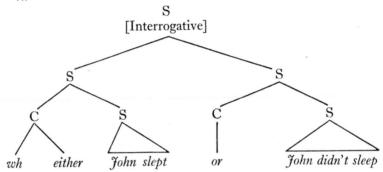

Similarly the structure for (i) *will you go now or later?* will be

PM(5)

S
[Interrogative]

S   S

C   S   C   S

wh   either   you will go now   or   you will go later

(Notice that PM's (4) and (5) are not claimed to be the deepest PM's – they clearly follow the application of the rule converting PM(2) to (3); 'remote' is thus a quite general term meaning 'relatively abstract'.)

What now is the evidence for the *wh*-morpheme in PM's(4) and (5)? Katz & Postal justify an underlying *wh* in yes/no interrogatives by saying that it in fact shows up in surface structure in dependent yes/no interrogatives: *whether* is claimed to be the surface realization of *wh + either*. The absence of *wh* from the surface structure of independent interrogatives would, in this view, be due to a transformation deleting *whether* in appropriate environments. Moreover they point out that in an earlier stage of the language independent yes/no interrogatives with *whether* did occur: this increases the plausibility of such a deletion rule.

There is a further piece of evidence that would seem to lend support to this analysis, though Katz & Postal do not themselves refer to it. *Either* cannot occur in surface structure introducing the first member of a *questioned* disjunction. Consider for example:

(viii) Does he speak French or Italian?
  (ix) Does he speak either French or Italian?

It was noted earlier that (viii) may be read as either a polar (yes/no) or a non-polar disjunctive; (ix) on the other hand is unambiguously polar. These facts can be explained quite naturally if we take PM(6) as the structure of the non-polar reading of (viii), and PM(7) as that of (ix) and of the yes/no reading of (viii).

PM(6)

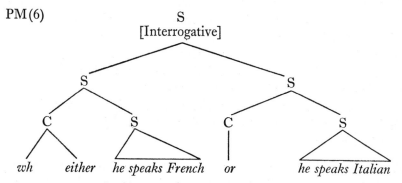

PM(6) cannot lead to (ix) because the only *either* that occurs in it is combined with *wh* into *whether*, which is then deleted. PM(7) on the other hand can lead to either (viii) or (ix) (and several others besides). In both cases S_8 is deleted by conjunction reduction, and the *either* of S_2 is incorporated into *whether* and then deleted. The difference between (viii) and (ix) is due to the fact that the *either* of S_4 is optionally deletable: the two sentences thus differ in just the same way as the

PM (7)

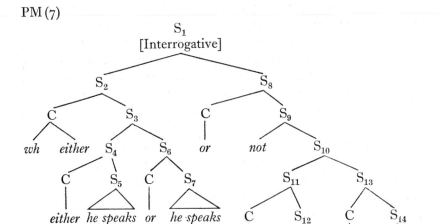

non-interrogatives *John did it or Peter did* and *either John did it or Peter did*. If the *either* of a questioned disjunction were not incorporated into *whether* we should have to say that *either*-deletion is optional for non-questioned disjunctions, obligatory for questioned ones – but this offers no explanation for the stated facts.

The fact that even for speakers who have *either* only in two-membered disjunctions *whether* is not so restricted would not conflict with the suggested analysis, since as we have just seen, it is in any case a necessary part of this analysis that *either*-deletion follow the rule incorporating into *whether* the *either* of a questioned disjunction.

What is difficult to explain under this analysis, however, is that *whether*, unlike *either*, is not restricted to the first disjunct, witness the textual example:

(4) Whether this flora will prove to be very specialized and able to photosynthesize in light intensities which are normally inhibiting in the sea, or whether photosynthesis takes place only at times when the light intensity is low remains to be seen. (32396)

The position of *whether* in the second disjunct here is characteristic of subordinating conjunctions: in a non-subordinate environment, *or* could not be followed by a coordinating conjunction (leaving aside the presently irrelevant case of layered coordination – one coordination within another).

An alternative analysis of *whether* would thus be that it is a complement-izer (subordinating conjunction), like the *that* of declarative complement sentences. This would make interrogative and declarative complements more alike, for it has been argued (e.g. by Rosenbaum, 1967*b*) that all the latter contain a complementizer at some stage of their representation, even if it is not present in surface structure. It would moreover be reasonable to claim that the absence of a complementizer in non-disjunctive interrogatives like *I wonder what he did* was the result of its deletion in the environment of *wh*. And of course in certain environ-ments (see 2.2.4) *whether* alternates with *if*, which is a subordinating conjunction in its other, conditional, use. Compare:

(x) *a* I don't know whether he's coming
   b I don't know if he's coming

The fact that conditional *if* is a subordinator is not irrelevant to the present issue, for the two uses of *if* are intuitively felt to be related (note, for example, that conditional *if* provides an environment for *ever*, which occurs freely in interrogatives but not declaratives: *if he ever comes back, will he ever come back?*, **he will ever come back*).

Neither of the analyses of *whether* is wholly satisfactory. If we derive it from *wh* + the coordinator *either* we have to add an *ad hoc* rule that copies *whether* into the non-initial members of the disjunction; since these already contain the coordinator *or* it is implausible that there should be a rule introducing a second coordinator into them. It is unsatisfactory in other words to treat *whether* as belonging to the same syntactic category as *either*. If on the other hand we treat *whether* as a complementizer we forfeit the explanation provided by the first analysis for the absence of *either* in questioned disjunctions. I know of no way in which we can combine the two analyses to preserve their advantages and avoid their weaknesses; on balance the evidence against taking *whether* as a coordinator seems to me a good deal stronger than that against taking it as a complementizer, and I shall therefore adopt this latter analysis.

In disjunctive interrogatives mood applies to the upper sentence, not to the lower ones – not to the members of the disjunction. In deep structure, in other words, disjunctive interrogative mood is always a property of a compound sentence, never of a simple sentence (clause). But this is not a general characteristic of mood, as we can see from such examples as:

(xi) *a* Come with us or can't you spare the time?

   b Put the light on and then you'll be able to see

   c It's your fault and don't try to deny it

   d I'll mention it to him, or would you rather I didn't?

These all involve the coordination of sentences differing in mood, so that it cannot be the compound sentences that select for mood but only the coordinate members of them, these coordinate members being clauses (except for *can't you spare the time?* and *would you rather I didn't?*, of course). Non-disjunctive interrogative mood may be a property of either a clause or a compound sentence as in (xii) *a* and *b* respectively:

(xii) *a* What's your name and where do you come from?

   b Who stood up and proposed an adjournment?

In the first of these we have a compound sentence consisting of a coordination of interrogative clauses, in the second an interrogative compound sentence – there are two interrogatives in the first, only one in the second.

2.2.2 Non-disjunctive interrogatives. In the most straightforward cases the presuppositions of a non-disjunctive interrogative can be expressed in a declarative sentence differing from the interrogative only in that it has a non-*wh* indefinite instead of the *wh*-word – compare:

(i) *a* Who told you the news?

   b Someone told you the news

It is then reasonable to treat *who* and *someone* as differing only as to the presence or absence of *wh* (whether this is regarded as a morpheme or a feature need not concern us here). Extrapolating from such nuclear instances we might formulate the hypothesis that non-disjunctives in general are characterized by the association of *wh* with some indefinite element. This hypothesis provides a convenient framework for a discussion of the problem of what can be questioned – or more generally, since as we noted earlier not all interrogatives are questions, what elements can have interrogative *wh* associated with them.

The relationship between such clauses as (i) *a* and *b* plays a prominent part in the analysis of Katz & Postal (1964). They explicitly claim, however, that *wh* may be associated with a definite element, and we would therefore do well to consider their apparent counterexample to the above hypothesis before proceeding further. Katz & Postal account for the difference between *which* and *what* by analyzing the former as *wh + the* and the latter as *wh + a/some*; structures for *which book* and *what book* are thus as given in PM's (1) and (2).

PM(1)   PM(2)

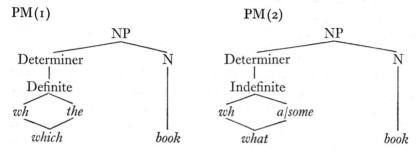

Their *semantic* analysis of the distinction is surely correct: *which* questions a definitely marked domain, *what* an indefinitely marked one (1964: 94). Compare Jespersen (1940: 482): '*which* asks for one (or more) out of a restricted number, while *who* and *what* ask indefinitely.' Consider for example the following sentences from the corpus:

(1) The question then arises as to which part of the plant must be attached for meiosis to occur in the spore mother cells. (11530)
(2) Investigators who have studied sebum are at a loss to imagine what useful purpose it may serve. (35514)

In (1) it is presupposed that the number of possible parts is limited, whereas in (2) the range of possible parts is clearly undefined, indefinite. Or again, compare:

(3) let us apply the above results to a planet going round the sun. In which direction is the force? The force is toward the sun. (27497)
(4) The pressure is increased adiabatically until the ice reaches the melting point. At what temperature and pressure is this melting point? (29155)

In (4) we are concerned with two continua, temperature and pressure: the range of possible answers is therefore necessarily indefinite unless the continua are explicitly or implicitly divided into a fixed or definite number of segments. Direction can in principle also be a continuum, but the use of *which* in (3) indicates that there is only a limited range of possibilities to be considered. The definite domain associated with *which* may be expressed explicitly as in (5) or it may be simply implicit as in (6) and the example given above:

(5) To assist in deciding *which of the two models*, if either, is applicable to hydrogen peroxide, we observe that the dipole moment of the 'easy-chair' model must be zero, whereas that of the 'bath' model [...] is $2 \mu_2 \sin \theta$, (26573)

(6) It is difficult from the structure to say which end is the anterior and which the posterior, (23488)

It does not seem to me, however, that Katz & Postal's syntactic analysis satisfactorily explains this semantic difference between *which* and *what*, for it does not incorporate the notion of domain or range. Moreover, *which* surely involves both definiteness *and* indefiniteness: the set of possibilities is definite, but the selection from this set is indefinite. It is this indefiniteness that the questioner wants to have resolved.

In an interesting discussion of quantifiers Jackendoff (1968) includes *which* in the same class as *some, each, every, few* (and also *all* and *both*, though these differ somewhat from the others): he refers to these as group II quantifiers. He is concerned to account for the paradigms:

(ii) some of the men each of the men which of the men
     some men   each man   which man/men
     some (plural)   each (singular) which (sing. or plural)

Jackendoff proposes two analyses for these forms, eventually preferring the second. In the first, *some of the men* and *some men* have the remote structures in PM's (3) and (4) respectively.

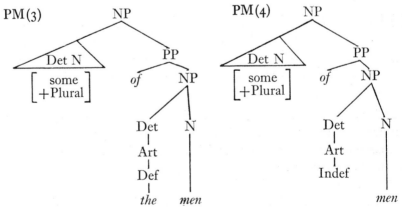

PM(3) yields *some of the men* quite straightforwardly; PM(4) yields *some men* by a transformation that deletes *of* and ensures number concord between *some, each,* etc., and the following noun. In the second analysis, the remote structures are given in PM's (5) and (6) respectively.

PM(5)   PM(6)

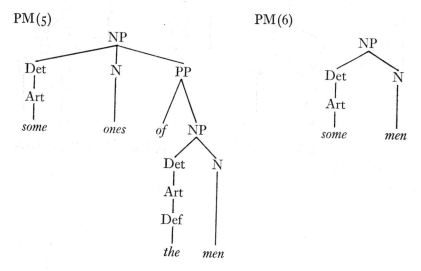

This time *some men* is derived quite straightforwardly form PM(5) while *some of the men* derives from PM(6) by a rule of 'ones-absorption'.

I shall not here attempt to choose between these two analyses but will consider only how the *which/what* contrast could be handled within such a framework: Jackendoff himself does not mention *what*. It is clear that, whichever of his analyses one prefers, some modification will be necessary to account for the fact that the semantic relation of *which book* to *which of the books* is not the same as that of *some books* to *some of the books*. (Nor incidentally, is the proportion *both books : both of the books* the same as *all books : all of the books*.) It is natural to interpret the prepositional phrase in Jackendoff's phrase markers as expressing the domain, in the sense in which this term was used above in discussing *which*. Then we can say that *which* (like *both*) is apparently restricted to domains with definite NP's. *Which book(s)* and *which of the books* would then have the same remote structure: PM (7) if we take the first of Jackendoff's analyses as a basis, PM(8) if we take the second.

PM(7)   PM(8)

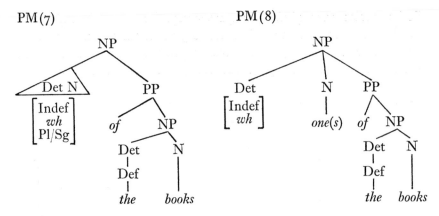

The corresponding structures for *what book(s)* would be respectively
PM's (9) and (10).

PM(9)   PM(10)

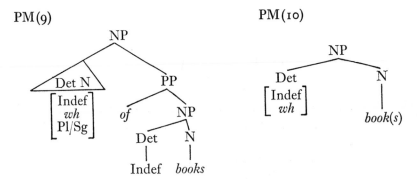

As in Jackendoff's formulation, *of* would be obligatorily deleted with an
indefinite domain – there is no **what of books*, except in a wholly
unrelated sense. But we should have to amend his rules to allow for the
deletion of an *of* preceding a definite NP in the environment of *wh*.

I have argued, then, that the definiteness of the domain explicit or
implicit in interrogative *which* NP's does not in any way conflict with
my hypothesis that *wh* is invariably associated with an indefinite element,
since the definite determiner in these cases belongs in the complement
NP, whereas the *wh* is associated with the determiner in the matrix NP,
and this is indefinite. Having disposed of this apparent counterexample
let us now pursue the question of what elements can have *wh* associated
with them.

Traditional grammarians tended to devote relatively little attention
to this problem, concentrating rather on listing and exemplifying the

various interrogative words. Great progress has been made in recent years, particularly by Katz & Postal (1964) and Chomsky (1968), but many problems remain unsolved and my discussion will be no more than fragmentary. For ease of exposition I shall temporarily leave aside all cases where there is an S node on the path connecting the interrogative S with the *wh*-element – as for example in *what did you say that you wanted?*, where the matrix clause is interrogative while the *wh* belongs in the non-interrogative constituent clause *that you wanted what*.

In the light of the hypothesis that *wh* is invariably associated with indefiniteness, I shall approach the problem by considering the relations between interrogatives and declaratives containing indefinites. In this way we can keep fairly near to surface structure – we need not concern ourselves here for example with the deep structure role of *what* in such clauses as *what happened?* or *what did he do?* for this is not a problem peculiar to interrogatives: the role of *what* is clearly the same as that of *something* in the corresponding declaratives *something happened* and *he did something*. Similarly, the fact that we cannot question the surface direct object in such expressions as *take account of, pay attention to, give rise to*, and so on correlates with the absence of indefinites here: *he took something* is not related to *he took account of it* (see 3.4). The association of *wh* with an indefinite NP functioning as subject, direct object or the object of a preposition would thus seem to raise no new general problems. There is admittedly no declarative equivalent to the type of interrogative exemplified in *what are your gloves doing on my desk?* but this clearly belongs to the realm of 'fossilized syntax' (note that *do* is necessarily progressive here) – and there is no reason to assume that it conflicts in any way with the indefiniteness hypothesis.

With indefinite indirect objects – I restrict this term to (prepositionless) NP's – the relationship between declaratives and interrogatives is a little more complex. Although (iii)*a* and *b* are equally grammatical, *c* seems certainly less acceptable than *d* and would probably be considered ungrammatical by many speakers:

(iii) *a* He lent someone his only copy of the book
    b He lent his only copy of the book to someone
    c ?Who(m) did he lend his only copy of the book?
    d Who(m) did he lend his only copy of the book to?
      (or: To whom...)

If (iii)*c* is ungrammatical, it could be excluded from the grammar by appropriate ordering of the rule shifting *wh* to the left of the interrogative sentence and one transforming the structure underlying (iii)*a* into that of *b*: I assume that the former rather than the latter reflects the deep structure order of elements. The situation is not so simple as this, however, for there are constructions in which the indirect object can be questioned, e.g. those where there is no overt direct object, as in *who did you tell?* and, more problematically, those where the direct object is 'complex': *who did she tell that she was resigning?* The rule for the deletion of *to* (and hence for the creation of indirect objects) will apparently have to be quite complicated.

Consider next the function of attribute, as in *John was tired, the evening was a great success*, and so on. There is no wholly general way of questioning the attribute – we can only question, as it were, a limited range of attributes. Examples are:

(iv) *a* How's John?
     b How was the film?
     c What's the new professor like?
     d What is John?

The first of these asks about John's health – at least in one interpretation, for there is probably a second reading in which it is like (iv)*b*. The latter asks for the addressee's evaluation or opinion of the film: this construction can hardly be used to elicit completely objective information, witness the oddity of:

(v) Question: 'How's the carpet?' Answer: 'It's green.'

(iv)*c* is similar: it too asks for an opinion – rather than a simile. Semantically its relation to such declaratives as *her lecture was like a sermon* is quite tenuous, and we may well feel the clauses contain different *like*'s. (iv)*d* would perhaps most typically be interpreted as a question about John's profession or occupation. None of the interrogatives in (iv) has any very plausible declarative indefinite counterpart: **the film was somehow* is clearly ungrammatical, and *the new professor is like something* allows only for a simile interpretation (it has low acceptability because of the emptiness of the simile, but this is doubtless to be regarded as a matter of performance). The lack of such declarative counterparts makes it difficult to assign a plausible structure to the clauses in (iv), but it does not make them counterexamples to the indefiniteness hypothesis: until an explanatory deep structure is found for them we cannot tell whether they confirm or refute it. Impressionistically it seems highly unlikely that *wh* will prove to be associated with a definite element in any of these examples.

Let us move on now to the adverbial elements in the sentence. The most straightforward are time, reason, and place, questioned by *when*, *why*, and *where* respectively. These correspond to *some time*, *for some reason*, and *somewhere* in the declarative counterparts. One special construction introduced by *why* is exemplified in *why don't you try doing it my way?* This has no declarative counterpart – note that at least in the intended interpretation it does not presuppose that you don't try doing it my way; in its illocutionary force it seems to be a combination of a suggestion and a question: 'I suggest you try it my way; what reasons, if any, have you for not accepting?' In one way it resembles the imperative construction in that the auxiliary *do* is used even when the main verb is *be*: *do(n't) be careful, why don't you be careful?* versus the ordinary interrogative *why aren't you careful?*; but the possibility of having *we, he,* and so on, as subject (*why don't we/they go with her?*). argues against an imperative source. Again we are dealing with partially fossilized syntax, of course: note that the construction is necessarily negative,[1] and non-past, and non-modal.

How, with corresponding *somehow*, may be said to question the manner constituent, though this element is surely much less well understood and defined than time, place and reason. Consider, for example, the wide range of answer types to such a question as *how did he get in?: through the window, with a ladder, by forcing the lock*, etc. Curiously, a classic manner adverb like *noisily* would scarcely make an appropriate answer to the above question, though there are *how*-questions which do take this sort of answer: *how does he drive? – dangerously*. With *know, how* tends to invite a 'because' answer: *How do you know he's still there? – (I know he's still there) because his car's outside*. Semantically *how* does not here question the manner of knowing in the normal static sense of *know*, but rather the way in which the knowing came about: it asks for the evidence on which the knowledge is based.

---

[1] But the negative here does not provide a suitable environment for items like *any, at all, ever,* etc., which can normally occur in negative clauses: thus *why don't you leave until tomorrow?* cannot be interpreted as an example of this 'suggestion' construction.

Besides its manner use, *how* occurs in a modifier relation to gradable adjectives and adverbs and to the quantifiers *many* and *much: how old is he?*, *how much milk have we got?* There is no obvious non-*wh* indefinite corresponding to this use of *how*; Katz & Postal relate it to *somewhat* (which in turn they derive from *to a/some extent*), but the correspondence is not very close. For although *who came?* presupposes that someone came, *how long is the table?* does not, as is well known, presuppose that the table is 'somewhat long'. The long/short antonymy is neutralized with 'unmarked' *how*-questions (as contrasted with marked ones like *hów long is it/hów short is it*: cf. Lyons, 1968: 466–7) but not with the non-*wh* indefinite *somewhat*. *Somewhat* cannot combine with *much*, even in the non-neutralized sense, though it can with its antonym *little*: we have *somewhat little*, but *quite a lot* rather than **somewhat much*. As before, the absence of straightforward non-*wh* indefinites corresponding to the *how* of 'grading' questions does not undermine the indefiniteness hypothesis, for the meaning of indefiniteness is clearly present – it can be contrasted for example with the definite deictic elements in *the table is so long* (accompanied by a gesture indicating the degree to which *so* refers), *he did this much work*, and so on.

Within NP structure we have considered identity questions with *which* and *what* and quantity questions with *how much* and *how many*. Questioning the possessor raises no special problems since *whose book* corresponds to *someone's book*; *John's* can of course be an answer to either *whose book* or *which/what book*. The adjective and relative clause in such NP's as *the red book* or *the book John gave me* cannot be specifically questioned: these are answers to *which/what book?*, but the latter ask for identification of any kind, not just via a relative clause (reduced or unreduced): *this one* or '*Daniel Deronda*' are just as appropriate answers as the above. With indefinite NP's the situation is somewhat different: *a red dress* or *a colourful dress with buttons down the back* are more appropriate as answers to *what sort/kind of a dress?* than to *which/what dress?* The non-*wh* indefinites *some sort/kind of* seem to have become specialized in meaning, so that *what sort of a dress was she wearing?* does not carry the presupposition that she was wearing 'some sort of a dress': the latter has a mildly pejorative overtone absent from the interrogative. This semantic specialization has not affected the definite, deictic *this sort/kind of*, however, which stands in a straightforward relationship to the indefinite interrogative.

There is one final interrogative type I would mention before going on to discuss the occurrence of interrogative *wh* in embedded clauses: it is exemplified in:

(7) Many popular resorts do take the precaution of mincing their sewage [. . .] and thus making it less recognizable when encountered in bathing [. . .]. There remains the unpleasant side effects like the low-tide smell [. . .] and the oily slick on the sea.
   But what of the risk to health? (39157)

Of alternates freely with *about* in this type – cf. the catchphrase *what about the workers?* This construction seems to require a structural analysis in terms of 'theme' and 'rheme' (cf. Halliday, 1968; G. Lakoff, forthcoming), or 'topic' – 'comment': *the risk to health* is the theme/topic and *what* questions the rheme/comment. There is no very close reported analogue to this construction: *he asked about the risk to health* is the nearest, but unlike the *what*-interrogative this does not imply a change of topic: notice that it would be odd to *begin* a conversation with *what about X?*

Let us now turn to the questioning of elements within an embedded clause. Chomsky (1968: 41–7) has discussed in some detail the restrictions that exclude such examples as:

(vi) *a* *What is for him to understand difficult?
    b *Who did he read the book that interested?
    c *Who did he believe the claim that John tricked?
    d *What did John wonder why Bill had read?

I have nothing to add to his analysis of this type of restriction, and there is therefore no need to summarize his explanation in terms of the 'A over A' principle. Instead I would draw attention to a different type of restriction. Consider such a pair as:

(vii) *a* Why do you think John did it?
     b Why do you regret John did it?

The first is ambiguous according as the *wh* is associated with a reason constituent in the matrix ('what makes you think John did it?') or in the constituent clause ('why did John do it, do you think?'). Rough and much simplified remote structures for the two readings are given in PM's (11) and (12) respectively.

PM(11)

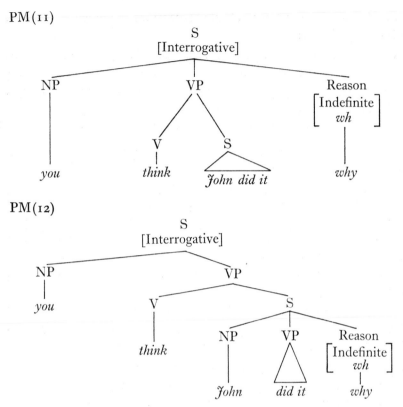

PM(12)

(vii) *b* on the other hand is unambiguous, allowing only the interpretation where *why* questions the reason for your regretting, not the reason for John's doing it. Similarly in (viii) below, the *wh* may belong either in the matrix or the constituent clause (the latter reading being contextually the more likely), whereas in (ix) the *wh* can belong only in the matrix – which is why the examples of (x) are ungrammatical.

(viii) *a*   When do you expect he'll arrive?
      b   How would you say he got in?
(ix) *a*   When did you realize he'd left?
      b   How do you know he got in?
(x) *a*   *Who did you realize had borrowed it?
      b   *What do you know he gave her?[1]

---

[1] It may be that such sentences are acceptable under conditions of contrastive stress: 'What did he give her? – I think he gave her the key and the instruction booklet. – I'm not interested in speculation, what do you *know* he gave her?' In what follows I shall be concerned only with non-contrastive cases.

I am unable to provide a systematic explanation of the restrictions involved here, and must be content with listing some of the factors that appear to be relevant.

(a) The type of complementizer: non-finite complements seem to accept a *wh* more readily than finites (though this is not to say that there are no restrictions with non-finites). Compare for example:

(xi) *a* * ?What do you regret that you missed?
     b What do you regret having missed?
(xii) *a* *Where do you know that he's hiding?
     b Where do you know him to be hiding?

(b) The function of the questioned element: the 'nominal' functions (subject, object, etc.) seem to be more readily questioned than the more peripheral adverbial ones (time, reason, place, manner). Compare:

(xiii) *a* Who did you discover had done it?
      b How did you discover he had done it?

The *how* in the second of these can scarcely be interpreted as applying to the 'doing'. Similarly, while (xi)*b* has a constituent clause *wh*, (xiv) is grammatical only if the *why* belongs in the matrix:

(xiv) Why do you regret having missed it?

(c) The class of verb (or adjective) in the matrix clause: clearly we shall have to mark verbs (and adjectives) according as they do or do not allow an interrogative *wh* within their complement. One will naturally look to see whether this property can be predicted from any other properties, semantic or syntactic, of the lexical items in question. For verbs taking a finite object complement there appears to be a fair amount of correlation with the factive/non-factive distinction (cf. Kiparsky & Kiparsky, forthcoming). Factive verbs like *regret, deplore, resent, realize, know*, etc., involve the presupposition that the proposition expressed in the complement clause is true; non-factives like *believe, say, think, suppose, allege, assume*, etc., carry no such presupposition – compare:

(xv) *a* *He knew he was right but in fact he was wrong
    b He thought he was right but in fact he was wrong

In general non-factives allow a *wh* within the complement while factives do not, but there are certainly exceptions to this generalization. Thus *discover* is factive but allows for the complement subject to be questioned, as in (xiii) *a*. With subject complementation the generalization holds in many cases, but the non-factive adjectives *true* and *false* seem not to allow an embedded *wh*:

(xvi) *a* *Who is it true/false that he meant? (non-factive)
  b Who is it likely/possible that he meant? (non-factive)
  c *Who are you glad/sorry that he invited? (factive)

One way in which the restrictions under consideration here differ from those discussed by Chomsky is that they apply to interrogative *wh*, but not to relative *wh*:

(xvii) *a* *What do you know that she wants most?
  b The thing that I know she wants most

In the construction we have been considering the *wh*-word is shifted from the constituent clause into the matrix; there is also a related construction in which the whole of the complement clause occurs to the left of the matrix verb. Compare:

(xviii) *a* Who do you think will win the election?
   b Who will win the election do you think?
 (xix) *a* What does it appear that he meant?
   b What did he mean does it appear?

The second member of each pair, like the first, is interpreted as a single *wh*-question, not as a sequence of a *wh*-question and a yes/no one. Moreover, only verbs which allow the first type of construction allow the second – though the first type is sometimes the only grammatical one. Thus the ungrammaticality of (xx) follows from that of (x) *a*:

(xx) *Who borrowed it did you realize?

whereas (xvi) *b* has no corresponding type 2 construction:

(xxi) *Who did he mean is it possible?

The ungrammaticality of the latter correlates rather with the fact that the complement of *it is possible* cannot be front-shifted even when the matrix is declarative – compare:

(xxii) *a* *He meant John it is possible
   b Labour will win the election he thinks

All this suggests that (xviii) *a* and *b* are simply thematic variants having the same underlying (cognitive) structure, roughly that shown in PM (13):

PM (13)

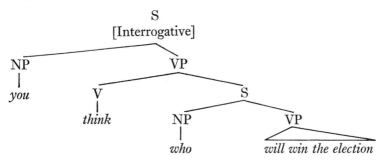

It is not obvious that the presuppositions of the two types are the same: if they differed this would argue against deriving them from the same underlying structure. Thus it might be argued that *when will she come do you think?* differs from *when do you think she will come?* in that in the former the speaker presupposes that she will come, while in the latter he presupposes only that the addressee *thinks* she will come. But I don't think this argument will stand. If we take a more contentful verb than *think*, say *claim*, we can see that the questioner's presuppositions are consistent with – indeed lend further support to – an underlying structure of the type shown in PM (13). Compare, for instance, *when does he claim she'll resign?* and *when will she resign does he claim?* It seems clear that in neither of these does the speaker presuppose that she will resign – only that somebody else ('he') claims she will.

To conclude this section let us return briefly to disjunctive interrogatives, for these exhibit a pattern apparently quite similar to the one we have just been discussing:

(xxiii) Will Labour win the election do you think?

Since this seems to differ from (xviii)*b* only in respect of the disjunctive/non-disjunctive contrast, one might expect its structure to be as shown in PM (14). But though this may well approximate to the structure at some stage in the derivation, it cannot represent the underlying PM. For PM (14) would presuppose that the addressee thinks that either Labour will win or Labour will not win, whereas the correct presuppositions for (xxiii) are that either the addressee thinks Labour will win or he thinks they will not win. Again the difference is easier to grasp if we take another verb than *think*: *is he coming did you say?* involves a disjunction between

PM(14)

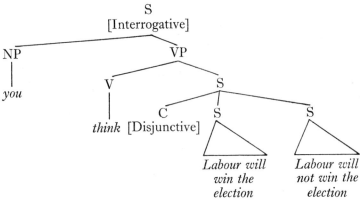

saying he's coming and saying he's not coming, rather than a disjunction within the complement of *say* – it doesn't presuppose that you said 'Either he's coming or he's not coming'. The structure for (xxiii) must therefore be PM(15).

PM(15)

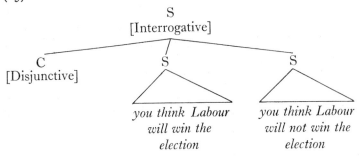

With disjunctive interrogatives, then, the disjunction must always be immediately dominated by the interrogative sentence node: one cannot question an embedded disjunction. There is thus no disjunctive analogue of either of the types of *wh*-interrogative exemplified in (xviii), etc.

The analysis suggested for (xxiii) cannot be extended to the superficially similar clause:

(xxiv) Is John coming do you know?

for this does not presuppose that either you know he's coming or you know he's not coming. Indeed the declarative sentence expressing this presupposition as an assertion is semantically deviant because of the factive nature of *know*: *either you know John's coming or you know he's not coming*. (xxiv) differs from (xxiii) in that the former allows for the possibility of your not knowing, whereas the latter does not allow for your 'not thinking': *I don't know (whether he's coming or not)* is a proper answer to (xxiv), but *I don't think (whether Labour will win the election or not)* is not a proper answer to (xxiii). An alternative analysis of (xxiv) would be to derive it from the same structure as underlies:

(xxv) Do you know whether John's coming?

The relation between (xxiv) and (xxv) would then be the same as in the following pair, where the matrix is declarative:

(xxvi) *a* Is John coming I wonder
      b I wonder whether John's coming

Yet there are difficulties with this analysis. (xxiv) explicitly asks whether John is coming, whereas (xxv) does so at most implicitly. The hearer of the latter will normally infer that the speaker wants to find out whether John is coming and to this extent to reply with *yes I know (whether he's coming)* would be something of an evasion (cf. p. 8, n. 1). Nevertheless, it seems to me that from the point of view of a grammar of competence (xxiv) and (xxv) can scarcely be regarded as paraphrases.

2.2.3 Dependent interrogatives. So far we have been concerned almost exclusively with independent interrogatives, though the point was made in 2.1 that the applicability of mood to dependent sentences is one of the main reasons for distinguishing between mood and illocutionary force. The main constructions in which dependent interrogatives are found are as follows:

   (a) Subject and object complementation (see 4.3.2):

(i) *a How he did it* doesn't matter
   b I don't know *what he wants*

   (b) Preposition + embedded sentence (see 4.4/5):

(ii) That depends on *whether I'm invited*

   (c) Noun + complement (see 4.4) or NP + apposition (see 5.5.1):

(iii) *a* The problem *whether he should resign* weighed heavily on him
    b This problem, namely *whether he should resign*, weighed heavily on him

(d) The concessive construction referred to in 2.2.1 above:

(iv) He'll come *whether we like it or not*

There is no doubt, I am sure, that the classification of all these types as interrogative is correct: their syntactic and semantic resemblance to independent interrogatives demands that they be analyzed as variants of the same category. As evidence supporting this claim we may consider firstly the alternation of 'bound' and 'free' interrogatives in certain environments; secondly the sub-classification of dependent interrogatives, which matches that of the independent type; and finally the semantics of interrogatives.

Bound and free interrogatives differ in two respects: the former but not the latter contain *whether* (or *if*) in the disjunctive class, and the subject–auxiliary inversion rule applies only to the free type. The two types are in free variation in the following environments:

(a) Subject or object of equative *be* (see 3.8):

(v) *a* The problem is what we should do next
     b The problem is what should we do next (?)

(b) Other object complements: in some registers there is also alternation in object complements with verbs other than *be* – *he asked whether he could go* versus *he asked could he go*. The latter is sometimes referred to as free indirect style ('style indirect libre'), as opposed to direct speech, which I am not concerned with here. It is perhaps most characteristic of fictional writing – there were certainly no examples in our scientific corpus.

(c) Noun + complement, and appositional constructions: compare (vi) with (iii) above:

(vi) *a* The problem should he resign weighed heavily upon him
      b This problem, namely should he resign, weighed heavily upon him

The second point is that essentially the same sub-classification applies to dependent as to independent interrogatives: they too show the distinction between disjunctives and non-disjunctives, and within the latter there are the same constraints on what elements the *wh* may be associated with. There are three slight qualifications that must be made to this general statement:

(a) A few verbs/adjectives can apparently take only certain subtypes of interrogative as complement. Compare:

(vii) *a* I was surprised/It's surprising who he takes in
  b *I was surprised/It's surprising whether John did it

Similarly *realize* (and also *aware*, I think) can take only a non-disjunctive – unlike such semantically related items as *know*, *discover*, and so on. With *describe* and *exemplify* it is not easy to decide whether the *wh* complement is an interrogative or an 'independent relative' (for a discussion of this distinction see 5.3), but examples like (1) suggest we must include them among verbs taking interrogative complements – and again the interrogative must be non-disjunctive.

(1) $v = ds/dt$ describes how fast a thing moves, or how far it moves in a second. (27220)

The verb *doubt* is unique, as far as I'm aware, in allowing neither a non- disjunctive nor an overt disjunctive complement:

(viii) *a* I doubt whether he'll come
  b *I doubt whether he'll come or not
  c *I doubt who'll come

It is in fact questionable whether the complement of *doubt* really is an interrogative in deep structure. It differs from clear cases of interrogatives not only in respect of the above restrictions but also semantically: if (viii) *a* included a genuine interrogative it ought to mean the same as *b*, but it clearly doesn't, since the latter is semantically as well as grammatically deviant. Paraphrases of (viii) *a* typically involve a declarative complement rather than an interrogative one: 'I don't think that...', 'I consider it unlikely that...', not 'I don't know whether...', 'it's uncertain whether...'. One could argue therefore that the verb *doubt* (unlike the adjective *doubtful*) takes only a declarative complement; it would then be syntactically irregular not in requiring just one subtype of interrogative complement but in taking the *whether*-complementizer with a declarative complement. It does in fact also take the *that*-complementizer but less readily in a positive declarative matrix than in negative or interrogative constructions: *do you doubt that he'll come?* The difference in meaning between the *that* and *whether* constructions here (if indeed there is any, which is doubtful) is certainly not the same as that found with other verbs: compare, for example *do you know whether he's coming?* with *do you know that he's coming?*

(b) Concessives differ from all other interrogatives in two respects. One is a very minor point which has already been noted: the negative disjunct of a polar disjunctive cannot be wholly deleted. Secondly, in non-disjunctives the morpheme *ever* is obligatory in the *wh*-word – we could not replace *whatever* by *what*, for example, in *I'll come whatever she says*. These *ever*-forms occur also of course in independent interrogatives (*whoever would do a thing like that?*) and perhaps also in 'reported questions' (*?he asked whoever would do a thing like that*), where the effect of the *ever* is to emphasize the indefiniteness, but they are never obligatory and are restricted to colloquial and informal registers. Moreover, in most types of dependent interrogative the *ever*-forms do not occur: **however much you gave him doesn't concern us; *I realized however she had got in.*

(c) There is a third difference between dependent and independent interrogatives which may conveniently be handled here, though in fact it relates to the transformational component rather than to the classification of underlying structures. With subject and object interrogative complements, *who, what*, etc., plus equative *be* can often be optionally deleted, leaving the constituent clause with the surface structure of a definite NP: compare *I'll tell you what the solution is* with *I'll tell you the solution*. A textual example juxtaposing an overt interrogative and a covert one is:

(2) Since we do not know the specific transmitter substance for the vast majority of synapses in the nervous system we do not know if there are many different substances or only a few. (33341)

The overt and covert types can in fact be coordinated, which provides further evidence of their underlying similarity:

(3) The first step [...] is to examine its [*sc.* the brain's] structure in order to discover the components from which it is built and how they are related to one another. (33022)

Koutsoudas (1968: 272) notices the paraphrase relation between:

(ix) *a* Tell me the place where he went
     b Tell me where he went

but he concludes overhastily that the latter in effect derives from the structure underlying the former, or more generally that interrogatives derive from relatives – overhastily because he does not even consider how such an analysis could account for disjunctive interrogatives, multiple-*wh* interrogatives (*who's going where?*) or those containing *how*, especially *how much, how many,* or *how*+adjective/adverb. These problems do not arise if we derive (ix)*a* from *tell me where the place where he went is?* The relation between (ix)*a* and *b* would then be the same as in the following pair: *London is the place where he went, he went to London.* This analysis – unlike Koutsoudas' – provides a simple explanation for the ambiguity of such a sentence as *I know the victim:* 'I'm acquainted with him' or 'I know who the victim is'. Notice that in the latter interpretation it would be semantically absurd to say that *I know the victim* has an animate object (in remote structure).

Finally, let us consider the semantics of dependent interrogatives. Curme (1931: 212) writes: 'The interrogative is used also in indirect questions, i.e. to ask a question in an indirect way, as in *Tell me who did it*, or to report a question indirectly, as in *He asked me who did it*. Our grammarians, however, often regard as an indirect question the subordinate clause of such sentences as "I saw *who did it*" and "We shall soon know *who did it*" [...]. In both examples there is in *who* an element of indefiniteness, but not the slightest suggestion of an interrogation.' Accordingly, on page 244 he treats the complement of (x)*a* as a relative like that of *b*, not an interrogative, like that of *c*.

(x) *a* I told him who did it
   b Give me what you have in your hand
   c I should like to ask who did it

But even if we disregard the structural reasons for treating (x)*a* as an interrogative rather than a relative (discussed in 5.3), we should still want to classify it as an interrogative on semantic grounds. What is common to all interrogatives is that they are concerned with the 'resolution' of a disjunction or of an element of indefiniteness. In a direct question the speaker asks the addressee to resolve the disjunction/indefiniteness: he resolves a disjunction by selecting the appropriate member of the presupposed declarative disjunction (as we have seen, *did John give it to Peter or to Paul?* presupposes that 'John gave it to Peter' or 'John gave it to Paul' – presupposes, that is, the disjunction of possible declarative answers) and he resolves an indefinite element by replacing it by a definite one.[1] But there is no reason to regard it as a crucial property of interrogatives as such that the speaker asks the

---

[1] At least in the nuclear case. Such a question as *who gave you that?* may be answered with *John did* or *someone on the bus did*: the latter must presumably be regarded as a proper answer even though it contains an indefinite pronoun. Nevertheless it seems fair to say that a definite makes a more satisfactory answer than an indefinite.

addressee to resolve the disjunction/indefiniteness. A rough classification of verbs 'and adjectives taking interrogative sentences as complement is as follows:

(a) Verbs of 'asking' – *ask, inquire*, etc. Here the referent of the indirect object is invited to provide the resolution. (We might also include here *wonder* = 'ask oneself'.)

(b) Verbs of 'informing' – *say, describe, explain, inform, tell* (and *answer*, in those dialects where this can take an interrogative complement). These are just as much concerned with the resolution of the disjunction/indefiniteness as are the verbs of asking: the difference is simply that it is now the subject of the matrix verb who communicates the resolution to the indirect object (implicit or explicit) instead of vice versa, but this difference can be explained in terms of the matrix clause structure: it is not relevant to the structure or classification of the complement sentence.

(c) Certain verbs or adjectives expressing mental states or processes (especially the process of discovery) – *determine, discover, find out, note, observe, realize, see, watch; aware, know, understand.*

(d) Certain adjectives expressing certainty – *certain, clear, obvious*, etc., and their antonyms (but not *probable, possible* and so on).

(e) Verbs and adjectives of 'relevance': *bother, care, concern, immaterial, important, matter, relevant* – the relevance at issue being of course that of the resolution of the disjunction/indefiniteness. Concessives would seem to belong under this heading – from a semantic point of view they are like the subject complement of an abstract verb of relevance in the negative: *I'll buy it whatever the price* can be paraphrased as 'it doesn't matter what the price is, I'll buy it' – the more or less fossilized *no matter what*, etc., is of course freely substitutable for concessive *whatever*.

This classification is not exhaustive, nor are the classes necessarily clearly discrete: the aim has been in fact less to differentiate between them than to show what they have in common, namely their semantic compatibility with interrogative complements, where interrogative is interpreted as involving the resolution of a disjunction/indefiniteness. Curme was right in protesting against the classification of (x)*a* as an indirect question. But he drew the wrong conclusions from his observation: instead of treating it as a relative, we need to broaden the characterization of interrogatives so that they cover more than just questions – the question is a special case of interrogative, but not the only case. This lends some support, it seems to me, to the analysis of independent interrogatives (more specifically those with the illocutionary force of a question) as containing an abstract verb of asking in their deep structure. The difference between:

(xi) *a* I ask you who did it
    b I'll tell you who did it
    c I know who did it
    d I don't care who did it

lies in the matrix clauses and there is no reason to give different descriptions to the complements; the similarity of the independent *who did it?* to (xi) *a* rather than the others would follow from the semantic similarity between the *ask* in (xi) *a* and the abstract performative underlying the independent interrogative. Notice that such an analysis would have the effect of making a clearer distinction between illocutionary force and mood – the former being now largely a lexical matter, depending on the choice of matrix sentence verb. It would of course still be necessary to mark *who did it* as interrogative even if it were embedded as complement to an abstract verb – just as it must be marked as interrogative in (xi).

2.2.4 Interrogatives in the corpus. The breakdown of interrogative sentences in the corpus is shown in table 2: 2, where 'free' and 'bound' are used in the sense of 2.2.3 – the subject–auxiliary inversion rule applies only in the former, while the latter, if disjunctive, contain a complementizer (*whether* or *if*).

TABLE 2: 2. *Interrogatives*

	Free	Bound	Total
Disjunctive			
Polar	9	30	39
Non-polar	—	15	15
Non-disjunctive	49	75	124
Total	58	120	178

The free interrogatives can be accounted for under the following headings:

(a) Object of equative *be*, (3 examples), as in:

(1) The next question is how does the mechanism that provides the specific sensitivity of the end organ to its adequate stimulus serve to set up nerve impulses? (22306)

The bound type was also found in this position – compare:

(2) One puzzle is why there are not many more spiral arms as a result of galactic rotation, since the angular velocity is not constant, (34134)

(b) Appositions; in the clearest cases (7 examples) the interrogatives are in the same orthographic sentence as the NP to which they are apposed:

(3) There are certain questions which need to be answered about the surface fauna as soon as possible – how thick are the layers which it inhabits; how stable are these layers in varying sea states; and to what extent is the permanent surface fauna ecologically involved with the transient fauna, and vice versa. (32386)

(There were no analogous examples of bound interrogatives.) There were also three cases (accounting for 8 interrogatives) where the interrogative was in a separate orthographic sentence:

(4) There are also knotty problems to be solved on the other side of the synaptic cleft. What, for example, is the nature of the receptor sites? How are the ionic channels in the membrane opened up? (33357)

And if the concept of apposition is widened so that the first member of the relation may be a sentence (rather than an NP as in the above) we might also include under this heading:

(5) In spite of a considerable amount of research, very little has been learned about the cause or treatment of acne, for which the sebaceous glands are in some way responsible. Why do these lesions occur particularly in young adolescents? Why do they break out on the face, neck and upper torso but not on the scalp or the anogenital areas, where the sebaceous glands are also large and numerous? (35551)

The relationship is probably too loose to be handled formally as apposition. The interrogatives illustrate the kind of knowledge that is still lacking and thus support the previous statement that 'very little has been learned'. It is difficult to say what is the illocutionary force of the interrogatives here; there is a sense in which the author is *citing* questions (questions whose answers, we infer, are currently unknown), rather than *asking* them – we could certainly not claim that they are embedded in an abstract 'I ask you...' construction.

(c) Questions for the student-reader to answer (9 examples); these naturally occurred in the textbook (i.e. mid) stratum, and were generally placed in a special section of the text:

(6) The vapour pressure, in millimeters of mercury, of solid ammonia is given by [R_1] and that of liquid ammonia by [R_2].
  (a) What is the temperature of the triple point?
  (b) What are the latent heats of sublimation and vaporization? [...] (29194)

(d) The remainder (and indeed also some, but not all, of the examples under (a) and (b)) were used as a means of defining the topic of the following sentence or passage:

(7) What is moonlight made of? It is mostly reflected sunlight of course, but is there something more? The answer is yes: the moon gives off some light of its own. The purpose of this article is to review the evidence indicating that there is an indigenous component of moonlight and to propose an explanation for it. (38001)
(8) How much work would be done if we were to turn the object through a very small angle? That is easy. The work done is [R]. (27314)

This use relates to what Halliday (1969) refers to as the 'intratextual' component of language, the organization of the discourse as a message. It bears some functional resemblance to the 'pseudo-cleft' construction discussed in 5.4.1 and exemplified in:

(9) what counts for angular momentum is not how fast it is going *away* from the origin, but how much it is going *around* the origin. [*ital. sic*] (27476)

It may be observed that all interrogatives of type (d) were in the mid and low strata.

  Let us turn now to the bound interrogatives. There was one example functioning as complement to a noun:

(10) The decision whether or not to use live donors must be an individual one for the surgeons concerned. (31261)

(The deletion of *or not* in this type seems to me not wholly acceptable.) The functions of the remainder are shown in table 2: 3; the complement constructions are discussed in more detail in ch. 4.

TABLE 2: 3. *Bound interrogatives*

	Subject/Object complement	Complement governed by preposition	Concessive	Total
Disjunctive				
Polar	24	1	4	29
Non-polar	8	4	3	15
Non-disjunctive	55	13	7	75
Total	87	18	14	119

The *or* in the second member of a disjunction may be deleted if the disjuncts are explicitly numbered, as in:

(11) Two limiting groups of simple mechanisms may be distinguished according as to whether (i) the lattice is in equilibrium with thallium ions which are themselves in equilibrium with thallium in the amalgam and the incorporation of chloride ions into the lattice is rate determining; (ii) the lattice is in equilibrium with chloride ions and the incorporation of thallium ions is rate determining. (16553)

Notice, incidentally, that with *according as* the *to whether* may be deleted, as in the constructed example:

(11') The two groups may be distinguished according as the lattice is in equilibrium with thallium ions or with chloride ions.

The reasons for claiming that *according as* is here followed by an interrogative are both semantic (the synonymy of the constructions with and without the *to whether*) and syntactic (the fact that we could not insert *either* into the first disjunct).

Of the 45 bound disjunctives only 6 had *if* as complementizer (all but one of the 6 being from low stratum texts). *If* is marked *vis-à-vis whether* in that there are certain environments in which only the latter can occur:

(a) In non-extraposed subject interrogatives, as in:

(12) Whether the complex itself is a necessary stage on the reaction path is largely immaterial. (24009)

(Extraposition, the shifting of a sentence to the right of the matrix sentence, is discussed in 4.2.1 and 4.3.2.)

(b) In interrogatives governed by a preposition, as in:

(13) the difference between the two specimens [*sc.* of urine] may offer a guide as to whether or not the peak concentration [*sc.* of alcohol] has been passed. (36296)

If can never immediately precede *or not*, but we could not replace *whether* by *if* in (13) even if we moved *or not* (back) to the end of the sentence.

(c) In an object complement when equative *be* is the matrix verb:

(14) The only alternative is whether or not the avoiding reaction will be produced and only one unit or 'bit' of information passes through the system at a time. (22232)

(d) In complements to nouns (perhaps not an absolute constraint) and appositions.

(e) In concessive interrogatives:

(15) The kinetic form of a reaction is the same, whether reaction occurs through the preliminary formation of a complex, or through a bimolecular or termolecular reaction. (24032)

(f) In infinitival interrogatives, like (10) above.

TABLE 2: 4. *Non-disjunctive interrogatives*

	Head	Modifier	Total
How	37	25	62
What	32	12	44
Which	—	5	5
Where	5	—	5
Why	8	—	8
Total	82	42	124

Table 2: 4 shows the *wh*-items in the non-disjunctive interrogatives: a distinction is made according as to whether *wh* is attached to the head of the NP or to a modifier – determiner in NP structure or the modifier of an adjective or adverb. The only *ever*-forms (6 × *whatever* and 1 × *however*) were in concessive clauses; the following examples also illustrate the possibilities for deletion in this type of construction, equative *be* being deleted in (16), characterizing *be* + anaphorically given subject in (17):

(16) Whatever its chemical nature the meiotic stimulus must be highly specific in its action. (11594)

(17) it [*sc.* 'the doctrine of specific nervous energies'] may be stated in the form that any given nerve fibre, however excited, gives rise only to its own characteristic type of activity in the central nervous system. (22423)

The subject can also be deleted from infinitival interrogatives, as in:

(18) the work of Willard Gibbs in thermodynamics suggested that a form of carbon such as graphite might be transformed into diamond at certain high pressures and temperatures. But *how to define* the exact conditions of this transformation, and *how to build* the equipment to attain such conditions? (38525)

The subjects of *define* and *build* are deleted under the indefiniteness condition – we understand them in the sense of 'one'; the closest finite counterparts of these clauses would have some modal auxiliary – *how was one to define...?*, etc., but I do not know of any independent syntactic evidence that would justify an underlying *be* modal in (18).

2.3   Exclamatives

Exclamative clauses contain one or other of the exclamatory *wh*-words *how* and *what*:

(i) *a* How well she performed!
    b What a marvellous performance it was!

Although all independent exclamatives may reasonably be regarded as exclamations, the converse does not hold – many exclamations contain neither *how* nor *what*. There are severe limitations on what elements may have exclamatory *wh* associated with them, but there is no semantic reason, as far as I am aware, why these should be the only elements about which a speaker may exclaim. But in spite of this poor correlation with illocutionary force, exclamatives form a well-defined mood category. Thus exclamatory *wh* is incompatible with interrogative and imperative sentences:

(ii) *a* *Have you read what a marvellous book?
     b *Pour me how excellent a sherry!

And exclamatives can be syntactically distinguished from declaratives by their limited distribution in dependent sentences – see below.

Exclamatory *how* is from a distributional point of view very like interrogative *how*. Both occur as modifier to gradable adjectives and adverbs, and both occur as manner phrases. Compare, for example:

(iii) E   How clever he is!
     I   How clever is he?
(iv) E   How interesting a film it was!
     I   How interesting a film was it?
 (v) E *How excellent wine it was!
     I   *How excellent wine was it?
(vi) E   How well she sings!
     I   How well does she sing?
(vii) E   How she dances!
     I   How does she dance?

The paradigms are not wholly identical, however. In the first place there is no interrogative counterpart to:

(viii) E How exceedingly subtle she is!

– that is, interrogative *how* cannot modify an adverb that is itself modifying an adjective or adverb. And secondly, it is doubtful whether the difference between the following pair is simply the same as that in the pairs (iii) – (vii):

(ix) E How she resembles her mother!
   I   How does she resemble her mother?

In the interrogative, *how* here means 'in what way/respect', whereas the exclamatory *how* means rather 'to what extent, how much': these seem to be different categories of adverbial. It is not clear whether (vii) E and I differ in this way too.

In all the pairs considered so far the two mood classes have been differentiated by the relative order of subject and verb. But this does not always serve to distinguish them: exclamatives may have 'inverted' order, as in (x):

(x) E How marvellous was the wine!

and there is no order difference when the *how* is within the subject:

(xi) E/I How much remains to be done!/?

In independent clauses the semantic difference between the two types is of course that between an exclamation and a question. What of dependent clauses? In such an ambiguous example as:

(xii) He remembered how long the poem was

the difference in meaning is quite clear because the interrogative *how* (at least in the unmarked case: see the discussion in 2.2.2) neutralizes the *long/short* antonymy, whereas exclamatory *how* does not. Thus the exclamative reading of (xii) presupposes that the poem was long, the (unmarked) interrogative reading presupposes only that it was gradable on the dimension of length. Consider then an ambiguity between an exclamative and a marked interrogative:

(xiii) He remembered how little milk there was left

In both readings he remembered that there was little milk left; the difference is that with exclamatory *how* he remembered that the amount of milk was remarkably small, with interrogative *how* he remembered what the small amount was – he 'resolved the indefiniteness'.

There are two sentences in the corpus that I take to be exclamatives, though both are syntactically ambiguous in the manner of (xii) and (xiii):

(1) A brief examination of a few specific properties of the skin will serve to illustrate how exquisitely it is adapted to its functions. (35195)
(2) It is a tribute to human nature how often relatives and friends of a dying uraemic patient will offer one of their own healthy kidneys, even if there is only an infinitesimal chance of the transplant's success. (31187)

The readings as marked interrogatives would make sense, but it seems more likely that the writers are concerned with the fact that skin is remarkably exquisitely adapted and that people offer one of their kidneys remarkably often, rather than with the determination or resolution of how exquisitely and how often.

Exclamative *what* is more colloquial, informal than *how*. Its syntax is quite different from that of interrogative *what*: the latter operates as determiner or pronominal head in NP structure, whereas exclamatory *what* is a predeterminer – distributionally it is like *such*. Thus exclama-

tive *what a book!* contrasts with interrogative *what book?*. Where the
noun has zero determiner (in count plural, or mass NP's) there will be
no overt difference between predeterminer *what* and determiner *what*:
what books and *what wine* could be either exclamative or interrogative.
The semantic difference is quite clear, for interrogative *what* is concerned with identification, exclamative *what* with quality – compare the
readings of the ambiguous *she remembered what friends she'd had in those
days*. As an interrogative it means that she remembers their identity,
remembers who were her friends; as an exclamative she remembers the
quality of the friendship. (There is also a third interpretation where
what is a relative – she remembered those (few) friends she had in those
days, as distinct from her friends of another period.)

As the examples have shown, exclamatives occur either as independent
clauses or as complement (object or subject) of certain verbs and adjectives. Many of those verbs which take interrogative complements also
take exclamative ones: *discover, forget, imagine, know, observe, realize,
remember, see, show, tell, understand,* and so on. Of the classes mentioned
in 2.2.3 verbs of 'asking' and verbs/adjectives of 'relevance' do not
allow exclamative complements: **he wondered what a lot of people were
there; *what a lot of people were there doesn't matter*. It is difficult to find
clear cases of verbs which take an exclamative but not an interrogative
complement; *exclaim* itself, and *deplore,* may be examples: they certainly
don't readily take interrogatives, though I'm not wholly sure we should
exclude such sentences as, *?he deplored who she'd invited,* or *?he suddenly
exclaimed what the solution was*.

2.4 Imperatives

2.4.1 Second person imperatives.
I shall begin the discussion of
imperatives by dealing with second person imperatives, moving then to
first person plurals and finally to the more problematical case of third
person imperatives. In the second person, we have the following
paradigm:

(i) *a* Come   *b* You come
    c Do come   *d* ?Do you come
    e Don't come   *f* Don't you come

(i) *d* is somewhat marginal: it strikes me as archaic, and I'm not at all
sure that it stands in the same relation to *b* as *c* does to *a*. Leaving aside

these doubts, however, we can account for the six forms in terms of three quite straightforward binary oppositions:

(a) (i) *a–d* are positive, the others negative; the polarity contrast applies to clauses irrespective of mood and nothing further need be said about it, therefore, in the present context.

(b) Within the positive class, (i) *a* and *b* are 'neutral', *c* and *d* emphatic, this category being marked by the presence of stressed *do*; the paradigm could be extended to allow for both neutral and emphatic negatives, differentiated solely by stress. Again the contrast applies to declaratives as well as imperatives: compare *he came* with *he did come*. A minor difference between the two moods is that in declaratives, but not imperatives, an emphatic negative may be marked by a *do* absent from the corresponding unemphatic form:

(ii) *a*   He spoke to no-one about it
    b   He did speak to no-one about it
    c   *Do speak to no-one about it

(c) (i) *b*, *d* and *f* have *you* as overt subject, while the others have no overt subject at all. There is no doubt that the absence of a subject in such forms is best accounted for by a transformation deleting an underlying *you*, as proposed by Katz & Postal (1964). Semantically this explains why they are understood as second person imperatives; syntactically it explains why the reflexive pronoun in such constructions as *wash yourself* is second person.[1] A rather curious alternative analysis of 'short' imperatives like (i) *a* has recently been proposed by Thorne (1966). He claims that the underlying subject of these is *you somebody*, the vocative form of the indefinite pronoun (p. 73). This is not at all convincing. In the first place it implies that (i) *a* and *b* differ in respect of the definiteness of the underlying subject (*you* in the latter deriving from a definite pronoun): this implication I find quite counterintuitive and Thorne gives no evidence to support it. Secondly his proposal depends crucially on a false analogy between *you boys* and *you somebody*. The former is analyzed as in PM (1).

---

[1] Levenston (1969: 43) observes that *yourself* does not occur 'in the words of the song *you must have been a beautiful baby, but baby, look at you now*' and in curses like *damn you*, etc. But *look at* in the first is an idiomatic expression, and the curses, etc., belong to a special construction (discussed in Quang Phuc Dong, 1969): we shall not discard our generalization about reflexivization in imperatives simply because it does not hold for all clauses with a surface structure resemblance to genuine imperative clauses.

PM(1)

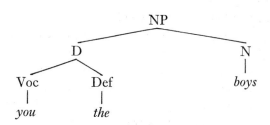

This correctly treats *boys* as the head of the phrase and also accounts for its definiteness. But it is quite improper to ignore the clear phonological difference between *you somebody* and (the relevant reading of) *you boys*. Thus in his example *stop it will you somebody* I see no reason for treating *you somebody* as a constituent: *somebody* is surely here a vocative belonging to the sentence as a whole not just the tag, just as in the declarative *you've finished, haven't you, John?*.

Katz & Postal (1964: 74-9) also treat forms like:

(iii) You will come

as imperatives – or, more precisely, they claim that they are ambiguous between declarative and imperative readings. This claim then constitutes an important part of their justification for postulating an underlying *will* in the structure of all second person imperatives. There are a number of serious difficulties here. Firstly, even if we grant that sentences like (iii) can in appropriate circumstances be used with an illocutionary force something like command, it is doubtful whether the line between prediction and command is clear enough to justify an analysis of (iii) as ambiguous rather than vague – as Lyons (1966: 120) says 'on purely semantic considerations, what reason is there to distinguish sharply between "an imperative meaning" and "a declarative meaning"?' Secondly there is the point raised by Bolinger (1967a: 339): what reason is there for giving special status to *will*? The range of meaning in (iii) is paralleled by that in such a sentence as *you're going to come*. Thirdly we may ask in what way *you* is privileged in this respect. If (iii) can be interpreted as a command, cannot (iv) too be so interpreted?

(iv) You will go in the first car and John will follow in the next

The alleged ambiguity of (iii) is not the only argument used to justify an underlying *will* in all second person imperatives: Katz & Postal also adduce the evidence from tags, as in:

(v) *a* Come early, won't you?

  b Don't come too early, will you?

They do not provide an analysis of tags, but one may envisage two situations in which the surface structure of the tag could provide evidence about the underlying structure of imperatives. It would do so in the first place if we could show that compound sentences like (v) derive from underlying simple sentences by some rule which copied the subject and auxiliary to the right of the VP prior to their deletion in the main clause. In the second place we might maintain that tagged sentences derive from an underlying juxtaposition of two sentences, the fragmentary nature of the tag being due to the deletion of elements from the second that were identical with elements in the first – the reduction would be similar to that applying in coordinate sentences like *John will come early and so will Peter*. In this second approach the tag would reveal the underlying structure of the imperative only if we could show that the subject and auxiliary of the two juxtaposed sentences had to be identical in deep structure.

I have argued elsewhere (Huddleston, 1970*a*) that the first approach leads to insuperable difficulties; the second is much more promising, though even here we cannot impose any identity condition on the auxiliaries of the juxtaposed sentences. If this is correct it is invalid to postulate an underlying *will* in imperatives on the strength of such examples as (v). It is not necessary here to repeat the arguments in detail; for present purposes it is enough to point out that *will* is not the only auxiliary found in imperatives (cf. Bolinger, 1967*a*: 337). Compare, for example: *be quiet, can't you?, just help me lift these parcels in, would you?, let's go, shall we?*. The last of course is a first person plural imperative, but it is nevertheless relevant here in providing additional evidence of the relative independence of the tag auxiliary.

In summary, then, there is no good reason for extending the paradigm of second person imperatives to include such forms as (iii) nor for claiming that (i) *a–f* derive from underlying structures containing *will*.

2.4.2 First person plural imperatives. The relevant paradigm is:

(i) *a* Let's go   *b* Do let's go

  c Don't let's go   *d* Let's not go

The first two are of course positive in contrast with the second two, which are negative; within the positive pair we find the same neutral versus emphatic opposition – *a* versus *b* – that we observed with second person forms. The two negative forms are synonymous: they are stylistic variants.

What makes these forms difficult to analyze is that *let* is to a significant extent syntactically unique: it is the only marker of first person imperatives, and this is moreover its only function, for we cannot for semantic reasons identify the *let* of (i) with that of, say, *he wouldn't let us go*. To avoid confusion I shall refer to the *let* of the latter as *let*$_1$, to that of (i) as *let*$_2$. The contrast between them is illustrated by such ambiguous sentences as *let us go*. With *let*$_1$ this means 'allow us to go'; in this reading *us* cannot be reduced to *'s* and is not necessarily inclusive of the addressee – indeed it will almost invariably be the exclusive first person plural pronoun. With *let*$_2$, the meaning of *let us go* is 'go we' and the *us* can only have the inclusive meaning.

The syntactic uniqueness of *let*$_2$ does not mean that we can make no generalizations about it. There are good reasons for treating it as a verb both in deep and in surface structure. I would argue in other words that the two interpretations of *let us go* are very similar in deep (and indeed also in surface) structure. The similarity of their deep structure may be brought out by the analysis represented in PM's (1) and (2).

PM (1)   PM (2)

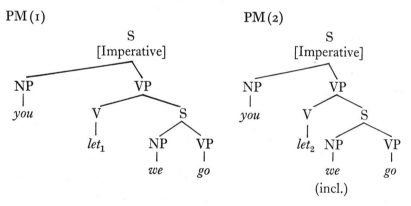

In both, the first person pronoun is subject of *go*, *we* and *go* forming a sentential complement to the main verb *let*. The rule of subject-raising (see 4.2.2/3) shifts the constituent clause subject into matrix object position, which accounts for its being in the accusative case. It is this accusative case which argues against taking *'s* as the subject of the whole clause *let's go* (contrast *may we be spared any more of his tirades*). If *we* is remote subject of *go*, what is the remote subject of *let*? It can't be *we* too, since this would yield *ourselves* rather than *us* as object; the only plausible possibilities are that it is *you* or the constituent clause *we go*. I have opted for the former on semantic grounds. As Jespersen (1940: 469) says, 'the first person plural of the imperative [...] is an injunction to the other(s) [i.e. addressee(s)] to join the speaker in some particular action' – though his paraphrase 'do you as I intend to' does not bring out the potential dependence between your action and mine – cf. *let's get married.* The *let's* form of imperative asks for the agreement/cooperation of the addressee in the proposed action. To postulate an underlying *you* as subject of let_2 is to claim in effect that 'first person plural imperatives' are really a special case of second person imperatives; semantically this seems a very reasonable conclusion.

If *you* is proposed as the remote subject of let_2, one may reasonably ask why we do not attest such forms as:

(ii) *a* *Let's go, will you
    b *You let's go

The absence of the first can be explained fairly straightforwardly. If we adopt the analysis of tags proposed in the paper already referred to, the tag in (ii) *a* will derive from the interrogative structure underlying:

(iii) *Will you let's go?

The ungrammaticality of (ii) *a* would then follow from that of (iii). The latter is ungrammatical because let_2 cannot occur in an embedded sentence; the restrictions on its distribution are more severe than those applying to modals (*can, will,* etc.): modals likewise cannot occur in non-finite constructions, but unlike let_2 they can occur in finite embedded sentences. A further difference between let_2 and the modals is that only the former takes the auxiliary *do* in the negative and emphatic positive.

To exclude (ii) *b* we shall have to make *you*-deletion obligatory in let_2 imperatives. There is some sense in which this is semantically reasonable. With ordinary imperatives the *you* is normally retained only if it is contrastive:[1] *you do it today – I did it last time.* And it is not clear how the need could arise to contrast the *you* that is subject of let_2, since the addressee is necessarily included within the *us* of the complement sentence. For some speakers, incidentally, *you* can be realized overtly in

---

[1] This is not an absolute constraint: we find a *you* that is not contrastively stressed in such clauses as *just you remember where you are!* or in negatives – *don't you do that again.*

the object position in the rather curious construction *let's you and I go*
(*I* seems much more likely than *me* here even with speakers who do not
use *you and I* in all object NP positions).

The negative in (i)*c* and *d* belongs, in remote structure, to the constituent clause rather than the matrix: the speaker is asking the addressee
to agree to a negative proposal – he is not asking him not to agree to
a positive one. (i)*c* is thus closer to the underlying form than is *d*. The
existence of two variants here is due to an optional transformation that
raises a constituent clause negative into the matrix; the fact that this
rule is needed elsewhere in the grammar provides additional support for
the analysis of *let₂* as a deep structure verb taking a sentential complement – compare *I expect not to finish until Tuesday* and *I don't expect to
finish until Tuesday*.

2.4.3   Third person imperative. Although I have argued that *let's go*
is a special case of second person imperative, such an analysis cannot
be extended to sentences like:

(i) If this is what the Prime Minister really believes, let him say so.

(I discount of course the interpretation where *let = let₁* i.e. 'allow'.)
There is no question of this being a command, request, invitation, etc.,
to the addressee, and it would be semantically inappropriate and
syntactically unmotivated to postulate *you* as remote subject. Assuming
then that *let* is here too a verb (I'll call it *let₃*), the underlying structure
will be something like that shown in PM (1).

PM (1)

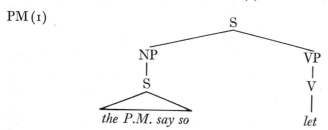

But such a structure remains fairly unilluminating, for *let* differs
strikingly in its syntax from other intransitive verbs taking non-finite
sentential subjects: the pattern exemplified in (i) is an example of
fossilized syntax for which a fairly *ad hoc* treatment seems inevitable as
far as a synchronic description is concerned. The same can be said for
the pattern illustrated earlier in:

(ii) May we be spared any more of his tirades!

The deep structure has *may* as an intransitive verb with a sentential subject. In this case, however, the constituent sentence subject becomes matrix subject, as is usual with modals (see 4.2.2).

It might be questioned whether such sentences as (i) and (ii) are properly to be classified as imperatives. There are no compelling reasons for assigning them to any of the other major mood categories, so the question is really whether they constitute a sub-class of imperatives or an entirely separate class (or classes), say optatives. They have it in common with imperatives that they occur only in independent sentences whereas the other mood categories are also applicable to various types of embedded sentence, as we have already noted. And though (i) and (ii) are not commands or requests, not all second person imperatives are either – cf. such familiar examples as *sleep well*.

When we turn to third person imperatives not containing the special markers *let₃* and *may* we find such examples as the following:

(iii)   God help you
(iv)   ?John give the first lecture and you give the rest
 (v)   *a* Nobody move
        b Don't anybody move
        c Don't move anybody
(vi)   Stand up the boy who said that

In (v) and (vi) the (referent of the) subject is included among the addressees: they are equivalent to 'nobody among you...', 'the boy among you who said that' (cf. Jespersen, 1940: 470) and indeed it might well be maintained that *you* occurs in the underlying structure of such clauses defining the 'range' of the subject (cf. the discussion of *which* and other quantifiers in 2.2.2); since the *you* following *among* (or *of* in the relevant sense) is necessarily plural this analysis would account for the fact that such clauses as (v) and (vi) make sense only if there is more than one addressee. The range-defining *you* is frequently retained in surface structure, of course, as in *one of you open the window*.

In (iii) the subject is obviously not included among the addressees – hence the non-reflexive object *you*. We might wish to regard this pattern as limited to a few more or less formulaic expressions like (iii) itself, *God bless you* and so on. Yet (iv), if grammatical, would seem to suggest that the construction is productive even if quite rare. (I am assuming that there is a constant addressee for both the conjuncts in (iv).) (iv) is admittedly unacceptable for many speakers, but the following is, I think, wholly acceptable:

(vii) You give the first lecture, John the next

– acceptable whether the first conjunct is interpreted as an imperative or a declarative. In the former case the second conjunct must surely itself also derive from an imperative, *John give the next lecture*. This suggests then that the type of imperative exemplified in (iii) must be regarded as still productive in the grammar.

A tentative classification of imperative clauses taking account of the main distinctions I have suggested, is as follows:

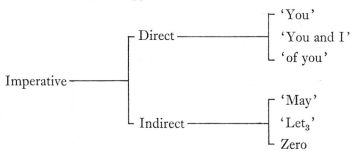

By 'direct' I mean that the addressee(s) is/are directly involved in the action that is commanded, requested, etc.: the addressee is either the subject of this action (the 'you' type, as in *go* and the examples of 2.4.1), or is included within the reference of the subject (the 'you and I' type, as in *let's go* and the examples of 2.4.2), or defines the range of the subject (as in the 'of you' type exemplified in (v) and (vi)). In indirect imperatives there is no such necessary link between 'you' and the subject, though *you* can be subject in the *may* type (e.g. *may you be forgiven*) – I am not sure whether it can also occur as subject within the sentential complement of *let₃* (*?let₃ you be white*, at the beginning of a game of chess, for example.) The label 'zero' for the third subtype, exemplified in (iii), indicates that there is no special marker like *may* or *let₃* and also that the verb occurring with a third person singular subject lacks the 's' that is found in non-imperative moods.

Before closing this section, I would return briefly to the 'of you' imperatives (v) and (vi). The examples illustrate the range of positions that may be occupied by the subject. The position between *don't* and the lexical verb can be occupied only by relatively short noun phrases –

we shall hardly attest *don't the boy who whistled do that again*. Whether this restriction can be made precise I don't know; note that it does not hold – at least in the same form – with interrogatives: *didn't the boy who whistled do it again?* The clause-final subject of (v) *c* and (vi) is distinguished intonationally from vocatives – (as in *stand up, John*) and appositives, (as in *don't move – anybody*). When the subject precedes the verb, co-referential pronouns may be in either second or third person; when it follows, the pronoun is necessarily second person (as observed by Bolinger, 1967*a*: 336):

(viii) *a* One of you lend me his/your jacket
     b Lend me your/*his jacket one of you

Note that the *you* of *your* is co-referential with the subject *one of you*, not with the range-defining *you*: the selection of *your* or *his*(/*their*) depends then on whether or not the speaker 'shifts' addressees, narrowing from plural 'you' to singular 'you' in (viii) *a* and widening from singular to plural in *b*.

The subjects in 'of you' type imperatives are usually indefinite, but (vi) shows that this is not an absolute constraint. Thorne (1966: 77) maintains that the indefiniteness is a matter of deep structure, claiming that (vi) derives from the structure underlying *someone who is the boy who said that stand up*. But there is no syntactic evidence for this, and the semantic argument is faulty: it is not always the case that 'the speaker does not know exactly who he is addressing'. For example in *stay behind all those who got less than 40%*, there is not the slightest implication here that the speaker does not know who got less than 40%. Proper names, however, do not occur as subject in this construction; this does lend a little syntactic support to the suggestion that there is an underlying *of/among you*, for the non-occurrence of proper name subjects would then be a consequence of the ungrammaticality of such expressions as *John of/among you*.

2.4.4 **Imperatives in the corpus.** There were 121 imperatives in the corpus, 36 of the 'first person' type, the remainder 'second person', all with covert *you*. Although in principle the difference is clear between a second person imperative with *let₁* ('allow') and a third person imperative with *let₃* as marker, there is one use of *let* whose interpretation is not immediately obvious – and this use is in fact characteristic of scientific English. There were 9 instances of the type exemplified in:

(1) Let u, v, w be the velocity components along the x, y, z axes of a molecule moving with velocity q, so that

$$u^2 + v^2 + w^2 = q^2 \ (28341)$$

This might seem to be a third person imperative with let_3 since one could scarcely paraphrase such sentences with *allow* instead of *let*. Nevertheless I think the second person interpretation is to be preferred – it belongs to the family of imperatives that a writer addresses to his readers to lead them through the argument. 'Command' is clearly inappropriate as a label for the illocutionary force of this type, and 'request' also seems perhaps too strong: 'invitation' might be better. Other verbs typically occurring in this type are *suppose, assume, consider*, etc.:

(2) *Suppose* there are N molecules per unit volume of gas, and let these be divided into classes, so that all the molecules in any one class have approximately the same velocity, both as regards magnitude and direction. (28176)

The *suppose* here can only be a second person imperative, and its coordination with the *let* sentence thus argues for taking the latter as a second person imperative too. And the let of (1) and (2) can be embedded I think: 'if we let...'; this means that it cannot be let_3.

The two main uses of imperatives in the corpus were:

(a) To further the development of the discussion or argument – the 'invitation' type that we have been looking at. All the 'first person' imperatives belong under this heading:

(3) Let us take the 3 axis in the direction of the magnetic field as usual, and the 1 axis at right angles to the surface of the super-conductor, so that the surface is the 2–3 plane. (18258)

(b) In exercises, in the mid stratum texts:

(4) Discuss theoretically the vibrational spectrum of a linear molecule A–B–A. (26437)

In addition there were the following minor uses:

(c) The hypothetical imperative, equivalent to a dependent *if*-clause (see the discussion of this type in Bolinger, 1967 a):

(5) *Pull the skin* and it will snap back. *Cut out a piece* and the detached piece will contract, whereas the skin around the wound will widen the cut by elastically pulling away from it. (35201)

(d) The appositional imperative, if such it is, of:

(6) there was only one sensible method of amplifying sound – turn it
into an electrical signal, amplify it and turn it back into sound.
(37347)

This might equally be analyzed as an infinitival construction; I have
taken it as imperative on the grounds that in the negative it would at
least be possible to have a form with *don't*.

3   *Transitivity and voice*

3.1   Subjects, objects and cases

Fillmore (1968*a*: 16) makes an important distinction between two different kinds of grammatical relation, or perhaps better, between two ways of expressing grammatical relations in a formal grammar: ' "Pure" relations are relations between grammatical constituents expressable in terms of (immediate) domination. Thus the notion "subject" can be identified as the relation between an NP and an immediately dominating S, while the notion "direct object" can be equated with the relation that holds between an NP and an immediately dominating VP, [...]. By "labelled" relation I mean the relation of an NP to a sentence, or to a VP, which is mediated by a pseudocategory label such as Manner, Extent, Location, Agent.' Thus whereas the symbols, 'Manner', 'Extent', etc., figure directly in phrase-markers, 'Subject' and 'Direct Object' do not – they are definable rather in terms of configurations of nodes within phrase-markers (cf. Chomsky, 1965: 68–74).

Pure relations may be defined at different stages in the deep to surface structure progression. In particular we can distinguish various types of subject according to the stage or level of the phrase-marker to which the constant configurational definition is applied. Thus if we accept that (i) is derived by a passive transformation from (the structure underlying) (ii):

(i) John was interviewed by Peter
(ii) Peter interviewed John

then the subject of (i) will be *Peter* before the passive rule applies but *John* after the transformation. Similarly *John* is the direct object of (i) before passivization, whereas after the rule has applied the clause contains no direct object.

On this basis I shall here distinguish three subject functions, referring to them as the pre-passive subject, the concord subject and the mood subject. The first of these, as the name implies, is defined on the

[61]

phrase-markers which represent the structure of the sentence immediately before the passive rule applies. This formulation does not imply of course that only sentences that are passivized have 'pre-passive subjects': by its place in the sequence of rules the passive transformation defines a level of structure applicable to all sentences. Thus *Peter* is the pre-passive subject of (i) but also of (ii) and equally of sentences like *Peter fell*. Secondly, the concord subject is defined at that level of structure at which the person and number categories of the finite verb are determined: I am assuming that the agreement rule follows more or less immediately after the passive rule – if this ordering is incorrect, 'post-passive' subject would be a better name for what I intend by concord subject. Finally the mood subject is defined on phrase-markers at the derivational stage just before the application of the rules of permutation and subject-deletion associated with the mood categories of interrogative and imperative. In the unmarked case, the subject is the same at all three levels – this is so in (ii) and in (iii) *a* and *b*:

(iii) *a* John went home
     b Did John go home?

On the other hand, the pre-passive, concord and mood subjects may all be different, as in:

(iv) There have already been killed some 500 people

where *there* is the mood subject (compare interrogative *have there been killed*...?); *some 500 people* is the concord subject (note the verb form *have*, not *has*); and the pre-passive subject is understood to be an indefinite pro-form, not expressed in surface structure. In (i) the mood and concord subjects are the same, but differ from the pre-passive, and conversely in (v) the pre-passive and concord subjects are identical but the mood subject is different:

(v) There are some students outside

None of the three could reasonably be called the 'deep subject'. The pre-passive is of course the deepest of the three, but the level of representation at which it is defined is nothing like abstract enough to count as the underlying structure. Whether we define a deeper type of subject than the pre-passive depends on whether we operate in terms of pure or labelled relations at the deepest levels of structure: I shall return to this point later.

Nor can the mood subject, the shallowest of those considered, be regarded as the 'surface subject', since it is clearly not defined on surface phrase-markers.[1] At the surface level I shall take over Halliday's term 'theme' rather than introduce a fourth type of subject, since theme, in the intended sense, is not restricted to NP's. Thus *this book I shall never understand* and *because of the rain I stayed at home* have respectively *this book* and *because of the rain* as theme; both have *I* as subject at all three of the levels I have distinguished. Theme is discussed further in 8.1.

It should be emphasized that the only reason for defining the three types of subject is to facilitate informal discussion of the grammar: they do not figure in any formal statement of the transformational rules, and – unlike such notions as actor on the one hand, and theme on the other – they have no direct semantic relevance.

Because of the different theoretical frameworks it is impossible to make a straightforward identification between any of the above three types of subject and the traditional notion of 'grammatical subject', but on the whole the latter seems to correspond to the concord subject. Thus in *there comes an end to all things* Jespersen (1969: 33), for example, takes *an end* as subject: he speaks of *there* as a 'lesser subject'.

Similarly the traditional notion of direct object (and also that of indirect object) corresponds to a function at the same level of structure as the concord subject: *three men* would not normally be regarded as the ('grammatical') direct object in either *three men were killed* or *there came three men*.[2] Yet the traditional classification of verbs as intransitive or transitive (or ditransitive) is explicable only in terms of whether or not they take an object at a deeper level of structure: in *three men were killed*, *kill* is not being 'used intransitively'. Sweet, who regards the classification as based on the meaning of the verbs, defines the classes as follows

[1] Fillmore (1968*a*: 16) speaks of the surface-structure subject as defined on the '(prestylistic) surface structure'. But it is doubtful whether we can properly speak of a pre-stylistic level of structure. Even if we accept the very dubious dichotomy of stylistic and non-stylistic transformations, it will not be the case that all of the latter precede all of the former. For example, the *there*-rule is presumably stylistic that converts *two men are outside* into *there are two men outside*, yet it precedes the non-stylistic subject–auxiliary inversion rule that applies in such interrogatives as *why are there two men outside?*.

[2] There are in fact difficulties in giving a configurational definition of object that captures the traditional notion. In *he read all night*, for example, *all night* is, at the relevant level of structure, an NP under the domination of the VP, but is not analyzed as an object in classical grammars. The definition would, moreover, have to take account of sequence, since there may be two NP's dominated by the VP; the leftmost would be defined as indirect, the rightmost as direct object, though the definitions would have to apply before the application of the rule permuting pronominal objects to yield *he gave it me*, and so on.

(1891: 89–90): 'Transitive verbs, such as *strike, see, like*, require a noun-word or noun-equivalent in the direct object relation to serve as complement to them, that is, complete their meaning, as in *he struck him; the man saw the boy; boys like jam; I do not like having my hair cut*. Verbs which do not take a direct-object noun-word after them are called intransitive, such as *come, fall, live*.' If verbs are classified for transitivity according as they do or do not take a direct object at the pre-passive level, it is clear that there will be a large amount of overlap between the classes. This indeed is the normal practice in dictionaries, where very many verbs are marked as 'v tr & i'. In grammars, however, it has been implicitly recognized that the pre-passive level is too superficial to yield a semantically insightful classification of verbs: this recognition is reflected in the frequency in traditional grammars of such expressions as 'a transitive verb used intransitively' or 'an intransitive verb used transitively'. A distinction is thus made between basic and non-basic patterns at the pre-passive level. If we adapt the terms transitive and intransitive so that they apply to clauses rather than verbs – according as they contain or do not contain a direct object – then we can interpret this distinction as implying that the transitivity of clauses at the pre-passive level may either reflect their transitivity in underlying structure or else be due to the operation of various transformations which have altered the underlying transitivity. Our task is thus to work back from the pre-passive transitivity to a deeper classification or structural analysis of clauses: in doing so, we may, with Halliday (1968: 182), abandon the single opposition of transitive and intransitive and 'attempt from the start to work towards a set of clause types embodying a full range of possible transitivity distinctions: [a classification distinguishing] the various kinds of process and the participant roles that may be associated with each'.

In this deeper classification it seems clear that the distinction between prepositional phrases and NP's will not be of real significance as such – though it obviously plays a crucial role in traditional accounts of transitivity, where *x consists of y* is intransitive and *x contains y* is transitive. The presence or absence in surface structure of a preposition governing an NP filling one of the 'participant roles' may be due to idiosyncratic properties of the verb or to general rules of preposition-deletion – rules typically involving the thematic organization of the sentence (cf. Fillmore, 1968 a). An example of the latter is found in the familiar contrast between *he gave the book to John* and *he gave John the book*. It is clear that these clauses are alike as far as the 'type of process' and 'the participant roles' are concerned: the difference has to do with such matters as information focus (Halliday, 1967*c*). We can say then that the clauses are alike in respect of transitivity, different in respect of thematic or discourse organization: this is preferable to saying that they are alike in deep structure but different in surface structure – the thematic dimension must certainly be taken into account at the semantic level. The transitivity dimension involves aspects of structure that are relevant to cognitive meaning; the thematic one involves such matters as foregrounding or emphasis, the division of the text into units of information, the distinction between 'given' and 'new' information, and so on – matters which typically affect the order of elements in the sentence and the intonation and rhythm (or punctuation): see Halliday (1967*c*, 1968, 1969). This multi-dimensional view may be constrasted with the 'structuralist' approach exemplified, say, in Fries, who writes (1952: 185): 'To call such expressions as *to the boy* an "indirect object" in the sentence *the man gave the money to the boy* leads to confusion. The expression *to the boy* does express the same meaning as that of the indirect object, but this meaning is signalled by the function word *to*, not by the formal arrangement which constitutes the structure "indirect object". The "subject" in the sentence *the boy was given the money* also expresses the same meaning as that of the indirect object, but we rightly call it "subject", not "indirect object".' From the point of view adopted here, *the boy* has the same transitivity function in all three of Fries' sentences, but different functions in thematic structure; Fries' grammatical description accounts only for the differences, not for the likenesses.

Some of the most compelling evidence for the claim that the structure at the pre-passive level often obscures the underlying transitivity relations is to be found in such paradigmatic contrasts as:

(vi) *a* They quickly sold the book
　　b The book sold quickly
(vii) *a* He opened the door
　　b The door opened
(viii) *a* He marched the prisoners
　　b The prisoners marched

It will be convenient to have a simple term to refer to the verbs entering into such contrasts: I shall speak of them, informally and somewhat loosely, as 'ergative' verbs, since they suggest an ergative organization of the clause (one where a one-place verb, i.e. a verb combining with a single NP, takes an 'affected' element as subject, while a two-place verb takes a 'causer' as subject and an affected element as object) rather than a transitive organization (one where a one-place verb takes an 'actor' as subject and a two-place verb an actor as subject and a 'goal' as object). Ergative verbs are discussed in most of the standard classical grammars, but they have also been given much detailed attention in very recent literature: e.g. Halliday (1967 a, b, c; 1968), Fillmore (1968 a, b, c), Lyons (1968: 350–71), Anderson (1968), Kandiah (1968).

The problem raised by ergative verbs is clearly this: how can we express in structural terms the fact that the pre-passive subject of the intransitive bears, on some level or dimension of structure, the same relation to the verb as the object of the transitive? In (vi), for example, we want to say that *the book* stands in the same relation to *sell* in the two clauses, in spite of its different pre-passive function, and similarly, *mutatis mutandis*, for the pairs in (vii) and (viii) and innumerable other examples. There have been two main approaches to the solution of this problem. On the one hand, we may attempt to show the constant relation by means of deeper, more abstract subject or object elements; on the other, we may express it directly in terms of labelled relations as opposed to pure or configurational ones. I shall consider these two approaches in turn.

The configurational solution will involve either or both of the following mechanisms: (a) the derivation of an intransitive from an underlying transitive by deleting the deep subject and moving the deep object into the initial position so that it becomes the pre-passive subject, (b) embedding an intransitive clause as object of a matrix transitive whose verb is an abstract causative that is transformationally replaced by the intransitive verb of the constituent clause by a process of 'predicate-raising'. The first mechanism might derive *the clothes washed clean* from *someone washed the clothes clean*. This captures the traditional notion 'active in form but passive in meaning': *the clothes washed clean* is active in form in that the verb is active, and passive in meaning in that the concord subject is goal rather than actor – this is shown in the analysis under consideration by having the concord subject derive from the deep object (which is characteristic of passive sentences), not the deep subject; compare Jespersen's category of activo-passives (1927: 347–52) or Sweet's 'passival' verbs (1891: 90). The predicate-raising mechanism might be used to derive *he marched the prisoners* from the rough structure given in PM (1).

PM(1)

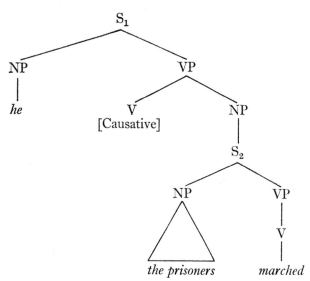

Here [Causative] stands for an abstract semantic predicate with no corresponding lexical verb (cf. McCawley, 1969*a*; G. Lakoff, forthcoming; Postal, 1970). This analysis captures the notion of a transitive use of an intransitive verb: *march* is intransitive in the deep structure but 'becomes' transitive when it is shifted into the matrix sentence.

The first mechanism treats the ergative verb as inherently or basically transitive; the functional identity of the subject of the pre-passive intransitive and the object of the pre-passive transitive is shown by having them both derive from an object at a deeper level. Conversely, the second mechanism treats the ergative verb as inherently intransitive; the identity of the above two elements is shown by having them both fill the role of subject at the deep level.

In principle, either of these mechanisms alone might be used for all ergative verbs, but in practice this would lead to strongly counterintuitive analyses: it seems as wrong-headed to derive *John walked* from *someone walked John* as to derive *Mary washed the clothes* from *Mary caused the clothes to wash* (more properly, from *Mary [abstract causative] the clothes to wash*). Intuition, and the description of traditional grammarians, suggests that with some ergative verbs (such as *wash, build, sell*, etc.) the transitive construction is more basic than the intransitive, whereas with others (such as *walk, march, jump*, etc.) it is the intransitive that is basic, the transitive derived. Jespersen in fact recognized a third class (1927:

332 ff.) containing verbs of change and of motion, where neither transitive nor intransitive is taken as basic: among this class he includes
*move, stir, roll, turn, change, begin, stop, break, drop, improve, burn,
increase, melt* and a fair number of others. Jespersen says of these verbs
that they each have two meanings: '(1) to produce a movement or change
in something, and (2) to perform the same movement or undergo the
same change.' But this is to account for the occurrence of both transitive
and intransitive constructions with these verbs in terms of lexical
polysemy rather than in terms of grammatical structure: it cannot
therefore be considered a viable third mechanism for handling ergative
verbs. Nevertheless, Jespersen's analysis is of interest in that it suggests
a tri-partite division (though without the implication of sharp
boundaries): the basically transitive, the basically intransitive and those
where transitive and intransitive are equally basic. I assume that in the
configurational approach to ergatives that I have been considering, most
of the change and motion verbs will be handled by the abstract causative mechanism, i.e. by predicate-raising (except that, for some verbs,
both mechanisms will be needed: see below) – so that for example the
relation of *the stone moved* to *he moved the stone* will be the same as that
between *the prisoners marched* and *he marched the prisoners*.

   The descriptive validity of the causative mechanism has recently been
called seriously into question in a paper of Fodor's (1970). He discusses
both ergative verbs and suppletive pairs like *kill* and *die*, where the relation of *John killed Peter* to *Peter died* is closely analogous at the more
abstract levels of structure to that of *John marched the prisoners* to *the
prisoners marched*. Fodor presents syntactic evidence arguing that the
object of the transitives cannot derive from a deep structure subject. His
general conclusion is that the derivation of verbs from phrases – *kill*
from '*cause*' to *die* or *melt* (transitive) from '*cause*' to *melt* (intransitive)
– is unsatisfactory because phrases have internal syntactic structure that
enables them to interact with syntactic rules in much more complex
ways than words: an example he gives is the ambiguity of *John caused
Bill to die by swallowing his tongue* (where either *John* or *Bill* may be
understood as the subject of *swallow*) compared with the lack of ambiguity in *John killed Bill by swallowing his tongue*. This raises the much
more general question of the validity of the 'generative' semantics
version of transformational theory, which it is not my intention to discuss
here. The weight of evidence accumulated in support of the predicate-
raising transformation by proponents of generative semantics is such that

Fodor's arguments cannot be regarded as at all conclusive, and it would certainly be premature at this stage to say that the ergative verb constructions are beyond the explanatory range of a configurational subject–object grammar. Nevertheless, there is at least good reason to consider sympathetically the 'labelled relation' approach alluded to above, especially as certain other problems, such as the one-place passive constructions discussed in 3.6.4 below, can perhaps be handled more satisfactorily in this latter approach.

In this type of grammar the constant relation between, say, *window* and *break* in such a pair as *John broke the window* and *the window broke* might be expressed by assigning *the window* the directly labelled function (or 'pseudo-category') 'objective' in both clauses, *John* in the first being labelled 'agentive'.[1] In Fillmore's model relations at the deep level are thus directly labelled by means of phrase-structure rules – these labelled relations he calls 'cases' – whereas relations at later levels are defined by the standard configurational method. The transformational component thus contains rules for the formation of subjects and objects and so on, i.e. rules that yield phrase-markers to which the configurational definitions of subject, object, etc., apply. Such rules may be quite general (e.g. if there is an agentive it will be moved into the pre-passive subject position[2]) or else specific to a given verb or class of verbs (e.g. rules relating to the deletion of prepositions – cf. my earlier remarks about the relative superficiality in many instances of the distinction between NP's and Prep Phr's).

It will be noticed that in this analysis of *John broke the window* and *the window broke*, with *the window* as objective and *John* as agentive, neither the two-place nor the one-place clause is regarded as more basic than the other: there is no sense in which the transitive is derived from the intransitive (with the latter embedded as object to an abstract causative), nor the intransitive from the transitive (by agentive-deletion, etc.). What then of those ergative verbs where one of the transitivity structures *has* traditionally been taken as basic?

---

[1] Objective and agentive are Fillmore's terms; Halliday speaks of affected and causer respectively. The differences are, however, more than terminological since significantly different claims are made about the functional identification of elements in 'action' clauses with those in 'mental process' clauses, and so on (for some discussion of these differences, see Huddleston, 1970*b*).

[2] Fillmore (1968*a*) gives the impression that his subject formation rules by-pass the level I have been calling pre-passive, but it seems to me preferable to retain this level: if we do we can achieve greater generality in the statement of the subject formation rules, and we also keep the passive transformation as a distinct grammatical process.

'Pseudo-intransitives' like *this shirt washes easily* can be handled in a way analogous to that described above in the context of the deep subject/object approach to ergative verbs: we can say that there are two participants present in deep structure, an objective (*this shirt*) and an indefinite agentive which is deleted prior to the pre-passive level of structure. There are two pieces of evidence to support the recognition of such a class of pseudo-intransitives – activo-passives, or 'process-oriented' receptives, to use Halliday's term.[1]

In the first place it is possible to find ambiguities between genuine and pseudo-intransitives: Halliday (1968: 187) contrasts the two readings of *this door doesn't open in wet weather*, which may be a one-place construction (= 'it stays closed') or a two-place one at the deep level (= 'it cannot be opened, e.g. because of the damp'); similarly he observes that *the silver shines* may or may not involve an implicit deep structure agentive – the one-place reading differs only lexically from *the sun shines*, whereas the two-place one means 'it can be made to shine'.

Secondly, there is the evidence of certain manner adverbs and the modal auxiliary *will*. Consider *easily* for example: if we say *John convinced Bill easily* this means 'John had no difficulty in convincing Bill'; but obviously *this shirt washes easily* does not mean 'this shirt has no difficulty in washing' – it is the implicit agentive who has no difficulty. With *well* the situation is different: *this shirt washes well* does not really mean 'one can wash this shirt well'; the adverb *well* expresses some kind of favourable evaluation – in *this shirt washes well* the credit goes to the shirt, not the implicit agentive, whereas in *Mary washed the shirt well* the credit is Mary's. Compare, similarly, *the play read well* (so that it is, in this respect at least, a good play) and *the group read the play well* (they were good play-readers). Yet *this shirt washes well* and *the play reads well* are activo-passives just as much as *this shirt washes easily*; they can perhaps be paraphrased as 'this shirt submits well to the washing process', 'the play lent itself well to the reading process', or something

---

[1] He characterizes the class as follows (1967b: 47): 'This type is especially frequent in simple present tense (*this material washes*), particularly in negative potential, where however the form is *don't/won't* and not *can't: this material doesn't/won't wash;* it is not however restricted to these verbal forms, and may in fact occur with any tense, especially with certain -*ly* adverbs, as in *the clothes washed easily, these books are not going to sell easily*. Underlying all these is a feature of characterization of the process as such, either a qualification of it or a generalization about its feasibility; so that we may call the type 'process-oriented' in contradistinction to the 'agent-oriented' type *the clothes were washed*.

along these lines. It seems clear that these examples involve an implicit agentive just as much as *Mary is washing* and *John is reading* involve implicit objectives, though I am not able to suggest in detail how such activo-passives should be derived: the problem is part of the larger one of giving an explanatory account of manner adverbials.

There are good grounds for claiming that at the level of deep structure the modal auxiliaries *can, will, may, must*, etc., are 'full' verbs (see 4.2.2 and Huddleston, 1969c). In such an analysis *will* is in fact a special type of ergative verb, entering into both one- and two-place constructions. Where it expresses futurity or, more generally, prediction, *will* is a one-place verb taking 'subject complementation'. Thus in the predictive *the rain will destroy the flowers* the one place is filled by the embedded clause *the rain destroy the flowers* (as argued in 4.2.2 this analysis enables us to account for the paraphrase relation between the above example and *the flowers will be destroyed by the rain*). In the volitional sense *will* takes two places; thus in the volitional reading of *John won't escort Mary*, one place is filled by *John*, the other by the embedded clause *John escort Mary* (the fact that there is a direct relation in underlying structure between *John* and *will* explains why this time there is no paraphrase relation with *Mary won't be escorted by John*). Consider now such sentences as *this shirt won't iron*. Obviously this is not attributing volition to the shirt: inanimates don't have volition, and there is surely no personification involved. Yet it seems to me that this is the two-place *will*, the two places being filled by *this shirt* and *someone wash this shirt*. Notice that this *will* – we might call it the *will* of 'submission' – has, like the volitional, but unlike the predictive *will*, a past tense form *would* (in the predictive sense *would* occurs only in 'reported speech' or as an 'unreal' form). Semantically analogous to the *will* of submission, or rather to its negative form *won't*, is the verb *refuse*, as in *the door refused to open*, where it is perhaps more immediately apparent that the verb is a two-place one. What is common to volitional and submissive *will* is that the action expressed in the embedded clause is necessarily agentive – or volitional; it is this which makes one think of these two *will*'s as broadly the same.

It must be emphasized that if such manner adverbs as *easily* and *well*, and in a less obvious way perhaps the *will* of submission, give evidence of an implicit agentive in the examples considered above, then they do so as well with a number of non-ergative verbs. Consider, for instance, *although the tree is an awkward shape the apples will come down quite easily once they are ripe*, or *the light won't come on*, and so on. These seem to imply an unspecified agentive endeavouring to get the apples to come down or the light to come on: *come down* and *come on* are, as it were, the suppletive intransitive alternants of *bring down* and *turn on* respectively (though *turn on* can also be 'used intransitively': *the light won't turn on*).

So much for ergative verbs where the transitive construction is basic: let us look finally at those where it is the intransitive that has traditionally been regarded as basic. We can approach this by contrasting our original examples (vii) and (viii):

(vii) *a* He opened the door
    b The door opened
(viii) *a* He marched the prisoners
    b The prisoners marched

A clear difference is that in the *b* examples *the door* is objective, but *the prisoners* is agentive, where agentive implies some kind of intention or responsibility. How then can we show a constant relationship between *the prisoners* and *march* in (viii) *a* and *b* – assuming we do not postulate any predicate-raising rule? Before answering this directly, let us consider the following examples:

(ix) *a* John moved the stone
    b The wind moved the stone
    c The stone moved
    d John moved

On one dimension the relations of *the stone* to *move* in (ix) *a–c* and of *John* to *move* in *d* are the same: it is the stone/John whose spatial position changes. This common factor may be brought out by labelling *the stone* in the first three clauses and *John* in the fourth as objective. On a second dimension (ix) *a* and *b* differ from the other two in that the process is viewed as involving an external causer: *John* and *the wind* (I am assuming that *c* and *d* are not interpreted as activo-passives). Thirdly the action in *a* and *d* is, we may assume, agentive or intentional: this we may express by analyzing *John* as agentive. To show all the similarities and differences between the roles of the participants involved we need to be able to assign more than one function to certain elements. Using Ag for agentive, EC for external causer, and Ob for objective, the analysis would be:

(ix) *a* John [Ag/EC] moved the stone [Ob]
   b The wind [EC] moved the stone [Ob]
   c The stone [Ob] moved
   d John [Ag/Ob] moved

Returning now to (viii), we can analyze the *b* clause like (ix)*d*, with *the prisoners* now combining the roles of agentive and objective. It might be sufficient to regard (viii)*a* as like (ix)*a* – yet there does seem to be a difference in the functions of *the prisoners* and *the stone*, correlating with their different functions in (viii)*b* and (ix)*c*. We might express this by analyzing (viii)*a* as follows:

(viii) *a* He[Ag/EC] marched the prisoners [Ag/Ob]

Fillmore himself would presumably not countenance this latter solution, given his assertion (1968*a*: 21) that 'the "explanatory" use of this framework resides in the necessary claim that, although there can be compound instances of a single case (through noun phrase conjunction), each case relationship occurs only once in a simple sentence'. In an earlier paper (Huddleston, 1970*b*) I suggested that this restriction may be difficult to justify with certain non-agentive verbs expressing various temporal and spatial relations, such as *X precedes Y, Y follows X, X is to the left of Y, Y is to the right of X*, and so on. A type where it is plausible to postulate two agentives is found in the pair:

(x) *a* John sold Peter the book
   b Peter bought the book from John

Fillmore (1968*c*: 79) specifically argues against taking both *John* and *Peter* as agentives here. He admits the event concerned is one which 'allows more than one individual to be actively or agentively involved', but claims that the agentive role can only be associated with one of them. For him, *buy* and *sell* differ in that they emphasize the contribution to the event of different participants, the 'goal' and 'source' respectively. But this difference of 'emphasis' is surely a matter of thematic organization, which plays no part in Fillmore's definitions of the cases: it could be handled by his notion of 'topicalization'. I see no reason therefore why we should not regard both *John* and *Peter* in (x) as having agentive function: they would be distinguished as source and goal respectively. And similarly, therefore, there would seem to be no reason for rejecting a double agentive analysis of (viii)*a* on general theoretical grounds.

It would be well beyond the scope of the present study to attempt a comprehensive description of the corpus in terms of an analysis of deep structure transitivity relations, whether the configurational or the labelled (case) approach be adopted. As far as case grammar is concerned, much work remains to be done before we can claim to have a reasonably comprehensive list of cases, and there is a pressing need to make more explicit the principles and criteria to be used in identifying case relations across different types of clauses (actions, mental processes, static relations, etc.). In the following sections I shall select for examination just a few of the areas where there are significant differences between the pre-passive and deeper levels of structure.

Because of the large number of variables it proved more useful in textual analysis to consider the behaviour of inivvidual lexical items than to operate in terms of previously established grammatical classes. For this purpose a 'transitivity corpus' was selected; it consists of those clauses in parts A and C of the whole corpus that contained an overt 'lexical' verb as predicator, other than (a) *be*, (b) verbs with less than nine occurrences (in parts A and C). 'Lexical' verb here contrasts with auxiliary – the modal and tense/aspect auxiliaries. In applying the criteria for inclusion in the transitivity corpus I did not attempt to distinguish between homonymy (different lexemes having the same phonological and graphological realization) and polysemy (different uses or meanings of a single lexeme): items alike in realization were at this preliminary stage regarded as tokens of the same verb however different their meanings. The transitivity corpus consists of 5,302 clauses involving 205 different verbs; the full list of these is given in 3.6.6.

3.2 Inherently reciprocal verbs

With the class of verbs which I shall call inherently reciprocal the number of transitivity places filled at the pre-passive level may vary according to the contrast exemplified in the following pair:

(1) *Porpita* is related to *Velella* and also has a float of hard material. *It differs from Velella* in that the float is a disk with numerous air chambers that looks like a cross section of a tree stem. (32173)

(2) These nerve impulses are, as a first approximation, all alike in any one nerve-fibre, but *they differ* in frequency according to the state of affairs at the receptor cell surface. (22174)

Such a verb as *differ* involves a reciprocal or symmetric, relation between two or more terms; at the pre-passive level these terms may be expressed as two separate elements of clause structure, as in (1), or else as a single element, as in (2). In the latter case the one element will normally be plural, though we do find constructions like:

(3) Also, the pattern of onset and loss of symptoms differs in the two groups. (37046)

Here the plurality is expressed in the adjunct *in the two groups,* not in the subject: for present purposes this can be regarded as a variant of *the patterns of onset and loss of symptoms in the two groups differ.*

From a cognitive point of view the two patterns contrasted in (1) and (2) are equivalent. *Porpita differs from Velella* implies *Porpita and Velella differ,* and vice versa. The difference between the patterns has to do with the thematic organization or discourse structure. In the first type the two terms are treated as quite distinct from the point of view of such matters as subject selection, theme selection, 'given' versus 'new' information, and so on, whereas in the second type the terms are treated as equivalent in thematic status. In (1) both terms in the 'differ' relationship had been mentioned in the preceding sentence, but only *Porpita* is pronominalized, clear evidence of a difference in thematic status between them. The example is the beginning of a paragraph whose topic is *Porpita: Velella* had been dealt with in the previous paragraph. In (2) all the terms (these nerve impulses) had again been mentioned before – in the clause preceding *differ,* but without any thematic differentiation among them. I shall therefore speak of the second type as the 'thematically undifferentiated', and of the first as the 'thematically differentiated' variant – in this latter case, the two elements will be 'thematically superordinate' (= subject, in the case of *differ*) and 'thematically subordinate' (= adjunct with *from* as the governing preposition). With some inherently reciprocal verbs the thematically subordinate element may be left unexpressed in surface structure if it is recoverable from the context or from the meaning of the verb – compare *John thinks we should accept and I agree* [sc. with him]; this is of course simply another aspect of the different thematic/informational status of the terms.

The differentiated pattern is 'marked' *vis-à-vis* the other in that it is allowable only if there are exactly two terms (or else two sets of terms, as in *A and B differ from X and Y*); there is no similar constraint on the undifferentiated variant. This suggests then that the latter should be taken as basic, the former being derived from it by mapping the members of a binary coordination onto different places at the pre-passive level (cf. G. Lakoff & Peters, 1969).

There are in fact two subvariants of the undifferentiated pattern, illustrated in the following textual pair:

(4) Now suppose we add the torques τ_i for all the particles and call it the total torque τ. (27543)

(5) Between any two particles the action and reaction are equal, so that when *we add all the equations together*, if any two particles have forces between them it cancels out in the sum; (27087)

These again differ in the number of places filled at the pre-passive level: the difference is in the absence or presence of a 'reciprocal element', realized in (5) as *together*, elsewhere as *with, to, from* or no preposition + *each other* or *one another*. G. Lakoff & Peters (1969: 140–1) argue against deriving (i) from (ii):

(i) John and Bill met
(ii) John and Bill met each other

They derive (ii) from a coordinate sentence construction – *John met Bill and Bill met John*. But such a source will not do for the reciprocal element in examples like *the members of the team met each other*, where there is no coordination between the terms. This suggests that either (i) derives from (ii) or else (ii) from (i). Here I shall leave open the direction of the derivation, noting only that to take (i) as basic would seem to involve treating *meet* as an inherently one-place verb – this is somewhat counterintuitive, and the analysis can scarcely be said to express the reciprocal relation in structural terms.

For most inherently reciprocal verbs (and adjectives too, since items like *different, similar,* and so on, display the same range of patterns as verbs like *differ, add,* etc.,) the reciprocal element is optional, as evidenced by the alternation between (4) and (5). *Resemble* is exceptional in requiring such an element in the thematically undifferentiated pattern: with this verb two places must be filled at the pre-passive level, so that we have *X resembles Y, X and Y resemble each other*, but not **X and Y resemble*. We cannot, of course, have **John and Peter saw*, in the sense 'saw each other', but then *see* is not inherently reciprocal: *John saw Peter* does not imply that they saw each other. Occasionally, however, the reciprocal element can be omitted even though there is no inherent reciprocity in this sense: *in love* is not an inherently reciprocal expression since *John is in love with Mary* does not imply that the love is mutual, yet in *they are in love with each other* (but hardly in *they love each other*) the (*with*) *each other* can be omitted without changing the cognitive meaning.

Some verbs have two slightly different meanings, of which one is inherently reciprocal, the other, not. Thus *add* is inherently reciprocal in the mathematical sense exemplified in (4) and (5), but not in the following:

(6) Either course could add to the energy barrier for oxygenation. (15270)
(7) Perchloric acid was added to the two most dilute hydrochloric acid solutions to bring the ionic strength to that of the I M hydrochloric acid. (16356)

(In (6) there is an object understood: this is a case where it is the thematically superordinate element that is left unexpressed, not the subordinate one, as in the *agree* example above.) We could certainly not paraphrase these as '…add something and the energy barrier' 'perchloric acid and the … hydrochloric acid solutions were added (together)'. The relevant factor in (7) is that there is some kind of movement involving just one term, not both: we take the perchloric acid to the hydrochloric, not vice versa. We can see the same contrast with several other verbs, such as *attach, collide, meet*. Thus *John and Mary collided* implies that both John and Mary were moving, whereas if the collision was between John and something static, say a gate-post, we would expect *John collided with the gatepost*, not (except perhaps humorously) *John and the gatepost collided*. Compare also *he met her off the train* versus *they met at Euston*. Similar considerations might lead one to doubt whether (8) should be treated as inherently reciprocal, but the next sentence but one in the text, quoted here as (9), suggests that it is:

(8) But our success in preparing a monkey's brain as a truly isolated organ allows us to make realistic plans for *joining* a brain graft to the blood vessels of a suitable recipient using existing surgical techniques. (31534)
(9) If the blood vessels of the brain and the recipient can be *joined* satisfactorily, there is no obvious reason why transplanted brain

tissue should not enjoy the same initial escape from rejection by the recipient as heart or kidney transplants. (31538)

This illustrates the frequent difficulty of determining whether two constructions differ just thematically, or cognitively as well. As another example consider the verb *fight*, as in:

(iii) *a* John fought Peter
    b John fought racialism
    c John fought the Germans

(or similar examples with *against* governing the second NP). The first is cognitively equivalent to *John and Peter fought* but *John and racialism fought* is ungrammatical; the third example is intermediate between the first two – we would not expect *John and the Germans fought*, but it is certainly more acceptable than the coordinate version of (iii)*b*. As a final example consider the uses of *agree* exemplified in the corpus:

(10) These values agree favorably with previously reported values. (17005)
(11) Most workers would agree that the use for transplantation of cadaver donors or kidneys that require removal for the donor's benefit – so called 'free kidneys' – is justified. (31255)
(12) the donor may agree reluctantly to give his kidney. (31229)

The first of these has a reciprocal meaning: (10) is simply the thematically differentiated alternant. Where *agree* has a human subject we may distinguish broadly between a 'commitment to belief' and a 'commitment to action' meaning: in the former there is typically (though not necessarily) a finite *that* complement, in the latter an infinitival complement. With the 'belief' sense it is again difficult to distinguish between cognitive and simply thematic differences. Can we say that there is a cognitive difference between *John and Mary agreed that*...and *John agreed with Mary that*...in that the latter necessarily presupposes that Mary expressed her view before John expressed his agreement? (Compare *I agree with Voltaire – Voltaire agrees with me.*) Example (11) is formally ambiguous – it could be interpreted as a thematically undifferentiated reciprocal or as having an underlying *with*: *with me/someone*, or alternatively a *with* governing the complement clause, as in *agree with the proposition that*...In the 'commitment to action' sense, illustrated in (12), the mood subject of the complement clause is usually identical with the pre-passive subject of *agree* (and consequently deleted): *John agreed to come, John and Mary agreed to marry*. We shall not find *John agreed with Mary to come*, though it is perhaps possible to have a *with*-phrase if the complement clause contains *for* plus an overt mood subject: *?John agreed with Peter for them each to give one lecture*.

A few verbs are both inherently reciprocal and ergative. Consider, for example, the following uses of *separate*:

(13) Chromatography on alumina and elution with hexane did not effectively *separate* the olefins although early fractions had lower proportions of 5α-cholest-3-ene than did later fractions. (15322)

(14) The initial reaction is greater in extent than for the unirradiated material, and is not so easily *separated* from the acceleratory period. (16097)

(15) quinone is very volatile with steam and distils rapidly from the action mixture, and *separates* from the cooled distillate as yellow crystals; (25399)

(16) The isomerization, which is comparable to the acid-catalyzed conversion of maleic to fumaric acid, is accomplished by passing dry hydrogen chloride into an ethereal solution of the *syn* form; crystalline precipitate *separates* consisting of the hydrochloride of the *anti* isomer, from which the free oxime is obtained on neutralization with soda solution. (25148)

The first two are transitive at the pre-passive level, the last two intransitive; in (13) the reciprocally related terms are thematically undifferentiated, in the rest they are differentiated. In (15) the differentiation is required because the attribute *as yellow crystals* applies to *quinone* alone, not to *the cooled distillate*; in (16) only one of the reciprocally related terms (the superordinate one) is expressed in surface structure.

Table 3:1 lists the inherently reciprocal verbs in the transitivity corpus. I have not included clauses like (6) where there is no cognitively equivalent undifferentiated alternant. It can be seen from the table that the differentiated pattern is considerably more frequent than the undifferentiated one. Of the latter only five had an overt reciprocal element: *add together* (4) and *connect to one another*. The prepositions given in parentheses are used only in the differentiated pattern, governing the thematically subordinate term (if it is overtly expressed). With *join, to* governs the subordinate term if the superordinate one is pre-passive

TABLE 3: 1. *Inherently reciprocal verbs in the transitivity corpus*

	Thematically		
	Differentiated	Undifferentiated	Total
add (to)	2	11	13
agree (with)	6	1	7
associate (with)	23	1	24
attach (to)	16	—	16
combine (with)	5	4	9
compare (with/to)	5	4	9
connect (with/to)	19	2	21
correspond (to)	22	—	22
differ (from)	9	5	14
distinguish (from)	3	10	13
join (to)	7	6	13
relate (to)	20	1	21
separate (from)	5	9	14
Total	142	54	196

object, but not if it is subject – compare the two instances in the following example:

(17) In the transplantation operation the main artery and vein of the kidney are *joined* to the main artery and vein of the pelvis, just before they reach the thigh, and the kidney is drained via the ureter which *joins* the urinary bladder. (31052)

With *distinguish* the undifferentiated variant may optionally have *between* governing the NP expressing the reciprocally related terms – compare (18) and (19):

(18) Thus the eye includes the rods, sensitive to low intensities of light, also cones of several types, with maximum sensitivity at various wave-lengths, which enable us to *distinguish* colours. (22443)
(19) Experiments with unpolarized neutrons on random domain single crystals are unable to *distinguish* between a simple spiral model and a transverse sinusoidal spin arrangement for the chromium magnetic structure above the low temperature transition. (18449)

The same applies with *connect*, except that here the presence or absence of *between* depends on how many elements there are at the pre-passive levels besides the reciprocally related elements: if there is only one, there is no *between* (*he connected the two wires*), but if there are two, *between* is used, as in the following example:

(20) Thus an ammeter *connected* between the ends of the rod would register the current resulting from this flow of electrons. (37435)

We have noted several instances where one or other of the thematically differentiated terms (usually the subordinate one) may be omitted if recoverable from the linguistic or situational context: with *add* it is possible for all the reciprocally related terms to be left unexpressed, as in:

(21) On the other side of the equation, we get the same thing as though we *added* before the differentiation: (27077)

3.3   Ergative verbs

The general problem of ergative verbs has been discussed in 3.1 above and will not be taken up again here: I shall simply add a few comments about specific verbs. The ergative verbs in the transitivity corpus are shown in table 3:2, which gives the number of occurrences in transitive and intransitive clauses, these classes being distinguished by the presence or absence of an object at the pre-passive level. (I include only those verbs whose 'ergativity' is evident in the transitivity corpus.)

Notes on particular items in the table

(a) *add*. This is ergative only in the mathematical sense. The intransitive column includes the deleted object example (21) of 3.2 plus two activo-passives like:

(1) Thus torques *add* by the ordinary laws of algebra, but we shall later see that this is only because we are working in a plane. (27347)

(b) *begin* and *start*. The intransitive totals include 6 and 4 instances respectively of the split-subject construction, discussed in detail in 4.2.2.

(c) *compare*. Another reciprocal verb; in the intransitive construction the thematically differentiated variant is very much more likely than the undifferentiated – compare (2), intransitive and differentiated, with (3), transitive and undifferentiated:

(2) These observations have been confirmed with the individual epimers by others in our laboratory and *compare* to earlier findings with ring B allylic alcohols. (15307)

TABLE 3: 2. *Ergative verbs in the transitivity corpus*

		Transitive		
	Intransitive	Active	Passive	Total
add	3	8	2	13
begin	14	2	—	16
change	13	6	6	25
collect	2	2	5	9
combine	2	2	5	9
compare	1	10	11	22
connect	1	—	21	22
decrease	5	2	2	9
develop	26	11	14	51
dissolve	2	1	6	9
divide	4	3	4	11
extend	9	4	5	18
fish	2	4	3	9
form	5	14	29	48
grow	25	3	11	39
increase	23	11	7	41
insert	11	1	1	13
move	51	11	1	63
operate	9	1	2	12
pass	14	6	4	24
reduce	4	15	18	37
rotate	13	2	1	16
separate	3	2	9	14
start	10	2	3	15
turn	10	8	1	19
vary	34	2	2	38

(3) The table *compares* the relative cost and weight of various types of engine developing 1000 H.P. (34405)

(d) *fish*. The different patterns are exemplified in the following passage, supplemented by a sentence from a little earlier in the same text.

(4) Clearly it is necessary to have a net which will *fish* away from the ship's wake and other disturbances caused by the passage of the ship through the water. This has been achieved in two ways – firstly by paying out the net from a drifting ship and then hauling it in at a standard speed, and secondly by *fishing* a net from a boom projecting from the ship's side while the ship is under way.

The first method has been used by Russian workers, who have also *fished* surface nets from an anchored ship in a current. [...]

The second method, that of *fishing* alongside a ship using a boom or spar projecting from the ship, has a longer history. (32060)

(5) This [*sc.* the conventional tow net] is a conical bag of fine netting attached to a metal ring and is usually *fished* from the stern of a vessel under way. (32037)

The second and third instances of *fish* are active transitives with *net* as object: (5) is the passive counterpart. The first *fish* in (4) is the intransitive version with *net* as underlying pre-passive subject; I do not see any reason for treating *the net fished* as more basic than *he fished the net*, or vice versa. The other intransitive use, in the last sentence of (4), is clearly different, for the underlying subject is understood as human and indefinite; given the context we might claim there is a deleted unspecified object: it can be interpreted perhaps as 'fishing a net'.

(e) *form*. Two senses of this verb are to be distinguished; they may be distinguished as [± dynamic], as in:

(6) acetophenone condenses to *form* *s*-triphenylbenzene when heated with hydrochloric acid in a sealed tube: (25099)

(7) The tip of the lacinia *forms* a strongly sclerotized hook which is succeeded posteriorly by a double row of strong setae (13010)

The first of these is dynamic in that the formation can be said to take place, whereas the second is non-dynamic – nothing 'happens'. Only the dynamic sense of *form* is ergative, (6) contrasting for example with:

(8) At about three months, for example, hair follicles start to *form* on the head, (35129)

There is no intransitive counterpart to (7), and the 40 instances of non-dynamic *form* have thus been omitted from the table. (6) and (8) do not exhaust the paradigm – a third pattern is found in:

(9) Only stars less than 10^7 years old are closely associated in space with the neutral hydrogen from which they *formed*, (34130)

In terms of case grammar dynamic *form* may be said to take, potentially, an external causer (wich may or may not be agentive), a source (marked by *from* unless mapped on to subject position) and an objective. The active patterns are: *EC forms O from S; EC forms O; S forms O; O forms from S; O forms.* (8) has O alone, (9) – and also (6) if I understand it correctly – has O and S; an example with EC plus O is:

(10) The same muscle action [*sc.* as causes the hair to stand erect] also *forms* the mounds known as goose pimples. (35384)

(f) *insert.* The intransitive use of this verb is unusual in common-core English; it is exemplified in:

(11) It [*sc.* the cardinal abductor] inserts upon the tip of the lateral cardo-process and opposes the adductor by swinging the cardo outwards. (13068)

(g) *pass.* The ergative property of *pass* is exemplified in the following clauses:

(12) Thus, the main functions of the proventriculus in Adephaga are to allow digestive juices to *pass* forwards to the crop whilst preventing food flow to the mesenteron, (13500)

(13) Once food had been *passed* into the dilated pharyngeal region, intrinsic circular muscles would *pass* it back to the large crop. (13280)

(14) In *N. brevicollis*, food is *passed* through the short oesophagus to a large thin-walled crop. (13438)

Pass involves some kind of movement, and the clause may specify the point of departure (typically marked by *from*), the point of arrival (*to* +*crop* in the quoted examples) or an intermediate point (*through the short oesophagus in* (14)). This intermediate point may be realized as a direct object, i.e. as an NP with no governing preposition, as in:

(15) This is because as the cardo-stipital hinge is rotated inwards, the mesal edge of the stipes will encounter the (assumed) resistance of the hump, and this will act as a stop which the stipes cannot *pass*. (13333)

Besides the above three elements, *pass* also takes an objective (the NP whose position changes – *juices* in (12), *food* in (13) and (14), the *stipes* in (15)) and an optional external causer. The 'intermediate point' can only fill the direct object position if there is no external causer, so that the objective fills the pre-passive subject position. We can thus have *it* [*O*] *passed over the hump* [*IP*]; *it* [*O*] *passed the hump* [*IP*]; but not *he [*EC*] *passed it* [*O*] *the hump* [*IP*], (the last is grammatical in a quite different sense, in the pattern of *he passed John the salt*, but this is not relevant to my point for *it* would be 'recipient' and *the hump* objective – see 3.5). This constraint reflects a quite general property of English –

compare Halliday's observation (1967*b*: 44) that 'in "directed action" the roles of actor and initiator are always combined, [so that we do not] have clauses of the type *he washed her the clothes* (meaning "he made her wash the clothes")'. More generally we do not find ergative-type contrasts between NP_1 V NP_2 and NP_0 V NP_1 NP_2, where the deep relations of NP_1 and NP_2 to the verb are constant. The only exceptions to this rule that I have been able to find are the verbs *lose* and *forfeit*, though there may well be a few others: compare *United lost the match* and *this error lost United the match*.

(h) *reduce*. One of the intransitives had an object understood, (16); the others had as subject an element which would be object in the transitive construction, (17):

(16) Similar streaks appear on the body of a person who has gone through repeated bouts of gaining weight and reducing. (35214)

(17) With the 2–3 plane as boundary and the usual choice of gauge for the vector potential, equation (12) reduces to [R]. (18267)

(i) *turn*. This is ergative only when it refers to change of state, as in (18) and (19), or to movement, as in (20) and (21):

(18) exposure to bright light and low moisture may also cause an old thallus to *turn* brick red. (21610)

(19) One of these [*sc.* superstitions] is the notion that a traumatic experience may *turn* the hair gray or white overnight; (35403)

(20) In order to study rotation, we observe the angle through which a body has *turned* (27197)

(21) That is, the amount of work that we have done is, in fact, equal to the angle through which we have *turned* the object, multiplied by a strange-looking combination of the force and the distance. (27321)

The following, however, have not been treated as ergative uses:

(22) this proof that there is no dependence on x_3 in the lowest eigenfunction *turns* on a special choice of the x_1 and x_2 axes, (18215)

(23) We now *turn* to the details of the calculation. (18327)

There is no transitive counterpart to (22); in (23), however, one might argue that there is an understood object which could be subject of an intransitive counterpart – compare *we turned our attention to*...and *our attention turned to*.

3.4   Non-contrastive objects

It is indicative of the relative superficiality of the pre-passive level of structure that there are many pairs of sentences that differ in the number of elements at this level and yet are paraphrases or near-paraphrases. Compare for instance:

(i)   *a*   He attended to what she said
      b   He paid attention to what she said
(ii) *a*   He used it
      b   He made use of it
(iii) *a*   He resembles his mother
      b   He bears a resemblance to his mother
(iv) *a*   The accident occurred at ten
      b   The accident took place at ten

In the second member of each pair the verb + object expresses very much the same meaning as the verb of the first member; in (i)–(iii) the noun object in the second clause has the same lexical stem as the verb of the first. What distinguishes the *b* examples above from ordinary transitive constructions is that they have a greater amount of syntactic cohesion between verb and object, such that these two elements can scarcely be said to be independently variable. There may well be gradience here rather than a clear-cut dichotomy, but the following criteria are valid at least for the nuclear instances:

(a) If the object can be questioned (I discount echo-questions) it is variable independently of the verb, and thus potentially contrastive. Compare:

(v)   *a*   What did he take? He took all the silver
      b   *What did he take? He took part (in the play)

Rather on the borderline are expressions like *have lunch/dinner*, *take* (or *have*) *a bath/shower*, etc., where the object is contrastive within very narrow limits – it can probably be questioned if these limits are established in the situation or linguistic context.

(b) Similarly, if there is a corresponding 'pseudo-cleft' construction (see 5.4.1), this shows that the object is independently variable:

(vi) *a*   What he made was a coffee table
      b   *What he made was use of his knowledge of Sanskrit

(c) Only an independently variable object may be the focus of a negative or of restrictive *only*:

(vii) *a* He held the bottle but not the glass
 b *It held its own but not sway
(viii) *a* He only paid the taxi-driver
 b *He only paid attention

Within the set of close-knit verb–object constructions we can distinguish two degrees of cohesiveness between verb and noun. Where they are most thoroughly fused the noun cannot be modified (by a determiner or adjective), cannot be separated from the verb by such an adverbial element as *however* and cannot be moved to the left of the verb by passivization, relativization or thematization. Thus in:

(1) Link suggested that coronal X rays *give rise* to luminescence on the moon. (38101)
(2) This would have to *take place* before the adducted mandibles started to open. (13278)

give and *rise*, *take* and *place* can occur only in that order, so that we do not attest **rise was given to...*, **rise, which this gave to ...*, and so on. In other cases the pre-passive object can occur to the left of the verb:

(3) If the second assignment is used and *account is taken* of the degeneracy of the transverse modes, poor agreement is obtained. (17178)
(4) An upper *limit* to the thickness is *set* by the absorption of electrons in the conducting layer. (17468)
(5) As we have remarked already, the value of β_A, and hence of the free energy, is a function of the angle the symmetry axes *make* with the axes with μ_{12} zero. (18384)

And while we do not normally find modifers with *rise* and *place* (though perhaps *it gave sudden rise to...* verges on the acceptable) a restricted range of modifiers is permitted with many of the other compounds:

(6) Afterward, when her body returns to its normal size, the skin *makes heroic efforts* to regain its former area, (35208)
(7) This paper describes the preparation and photosensitized oxygenation of 5α-cholest-3-ene (5) and 5β-cholest-3-ene (6), in which the A/B ring systems *bear quasi-enantiomeric relationships* to those in 2 and 1, respectively. (15056)

The object in these cases is nevertheless non-contrastive in terms of the original criteria – the above could not for instance be answers to 'what does the skin make?' or 'what do the A/B ring systems bear?'. (Where the object contains an adjectival modifier this may of course be contrastive, and thus the focus of *only* or a negative: criterion (c) above would therefore need more careful formulation to make it clear that we are here concerned with the contrastiveness of the head noun.)

In many of the cases where passivization, modification and so on, are possible, the noun is a nominalization and the verb little more than a 'prop', which serves as the 'locus' for the marking of tense, mood, aspect, etc. (I borrow the term 'locus' from Lyons, who uses it in a discussion of the copula (1968: 322).) This type accounts for the majority of the non-contrastive objects in the transitivity corpus; among them we may cite: *bear (a) resemblance to, do harm, do work, give the appearance of, give birth, make connexion, make forecasts, make measurements, make a study/studies of, make use of, perform calculations, perform functions, perform operations, set a limit to.*

It is far from clear how such non-contrastive object constructions should be handled at deeper levels of structure than the pre-passive. The fact that the verb and object noun are not independently variable suggests that they should be analyzed in a radically different way from ordinary transitive constructions like *see John, eat meat,* and so on. Two approaches suggest themselves. With the type considered in the previous paragraph, it would seem reasonable to postulate some nominalization transformation, so that (iii)*b* would be derived from (the structure underlying) *a*, and similarly for other pairs. This would account for the synonymity between them, and for the intuition that both members of (iii) are two-place, not three-place, constructions in deep structure. In such an analysis, modifiers of the object noun would derive from underlying verbal modifiers (compare *he used it well* and *he made good use of it*); this is a familiar process, applicable also in certain other types of nominalization: *he cooks well* versus *he's a good cook; he eats a lot* versus *he's a big eater.* Determiners and quantifiers are more difficult: *he bears some resemblance to his mother* is probably to be derived from *he resembles his mother to some extent/degree.*

Such a derivation could not plausibly be extended to expressions like *give rise, take place,* etc., where there is no simple verb cognate. These should doubtless be handled as morphologically complex lexical items or idioms – the noun would thus be present in deep structure, but at a lower place in the constituent hierarchy than ordinary objects, being immediately dominated by V instead of VP. Both the nominalization and idiom analyses are necessary, I think: the former cannot handle all cases but a transformational approach is preferable to a lexical one for the quasi-productive type with a verbal 'prop' like *do, make, perform* and a few others.

3.5 Ditransitives

At the pre-passive level a clause will be said to be ditransitive if it contains two objects. Where neither is a pronoun, the first (leftmost) of the objects at this level is traditionally referred to as indirect, the second as direct. Normally the meaning of the indirect object function is something like 'recipient' or 'beneficiary', and in a case grammar it would presumably derive from a deep structure case labelled in some such way. In the rules relating the deep and pre-passive levels of structure there is usually a choice between making the recipient or beneficiary into an indirect object by deleting the underlying preposition and keeping the preposition so that the recipient/beneficiary appears as an adjunct to the right of the (direct) object: this is the familiar contrast between *he gave the book to John* and *he gave John the book*. The choice between these patterns involves the thematic organization of the sentence, the rightmost position being normally the focus of new information (see Halliday, 1967*c*).

There are in fact strong grounds for recognizing recipient and beneficiary as distinct elements at the deep level. In the first place they may combine syntagmatically, as in *will you pay John his wages for me?* or *could you return these books to John for me?*, with *John* as recipient and *me* as beneficiary in both examples. Secondly a clause may be ambiguous according as the indirect object is interpreted as recipient or beneficiary. Thus in *will you sell us these shares?*, *us* may be understood as recipient, meaning 'to us' or as beneficiary, 'for us' (in the latter reading the sentence might be addressed to the speaker's broker). One way of characterizing the difference between the two functions is to say that the beneficiary is process-oriented, the recipient goal- or object-oriented: the process is carried out for the beneficiary, the object is for the recipient. This correlates with the fact that the latter can occur only with an inherently three-place verb (which is not, however, to say that the direct object must be expressed – it isn't, for example, in *I told him*), whereas there is no such constraint for the beneficiary (witness *he died*

4

for his country). The typical prepositions associated with recipient and
beneficiary are respectively *to* and *for*, but the preposition cannot be
taken as a wholly reliable guide, since we need to treat some *for*-phrases
as recipients. I would argue, for example, that *John bought the portrait
for Mary* is ambiguous according as (*for*) *her* is recipient or beneficiary:
in the former reading John made Mary a gift of the portrait, in the latter
he was simply acting as her agent or representative, buying the portrait
on her behalf (presumably with her money). The two types of *for*-
phrase co-occur in *will you buy some flowers for my wife for me?*, which
might be said by a busy executive to his secretary: the flowers are for
the wife, but the buying is for the executive. It is extremely rare for
both recipient and beneficiary to be realized as indirect objects in the
same clause – *will you teach me my daughter French?* might be regarded
as an example of such a construction. A beneficiary cannot be realized
as an indirect object unless it is followed by a direct object; thus we can
have *he wrote me* [*beneficiary*] *my German essay* or *he wrote me* [*recipient*]
a letter, but in *he wrote me* only the recipient interpretation of *me* is
possible.

Having distinguished these two elements I shall have nothing further
to say about the beneficiary, which is not relevant to any of the ditransitive clauses in the corpus. Among the verbs taking a recipient there is,
firstly, a sub-class of verbs of communication: *tell, ask, explain, say,
mention*, etc. The recipient may be realized as an indirect object with the
first two, but hardly with the others; the underlying preposition is *to*
with all the items except *ask*, which takes *of* (*he asked the time of me*).
Among the non-communication verbs we may distinguish: (a) those
with *to* as underlying preposition: *give, hand, leave* ('bequeath'), *pass,
pay, return, sell, take, throw*, etc. – with all these the preposition is
optionally deletable; (b) those with underlying *for*: *book, buy, cause, get,
keep, leave* ('cause to remain'), *make, procure, save* ('keep'), etc. – again
the preposition is optionally deletable; (c) those where the recipient is
always realized as an indirect object: *save* (as in *I'll save you the trouble*),
spare. The negative component in the meaning of *save* and *spare* makes
'recipient' a somewhat inappropriate label – but it is found also with
deny and *refuse*, which can take an overt *to*, and thus belong in class (a).
With classes (a) and (c) the 'recipient' may readily be mapped into subject position by passivization; with class (b) this possibility varies according to the dialect, and also, I think, according to the particular verb in
question: speakers vary in their acceptance of *she was bought a new hat*

while *we were caused a lot of trouble* seems more generally acceptable.

There were few recipients in the transitivity corpus, and fewer still
ditransitive constructions. The clearest verbs taking an overt or covert
recipient were *afford, allow, give* and *offer*. Table 3:3 shows their distribution between the following patterns:

(a) Active with recipient as indirect object:

(1) Most of the region lying mesal to this joint and posterior to the base
of the lacinia is covered by an extensive arthrodial membrane *which
allows the maxilla considerable motility*, especially in anterior–posterior movements. (13032)

(b) Active with recipient as adjunct (with overt *to*):

(2) they [*sc.* the 'empty' floats] *offer settlement to barnacle larvae*, and
perhaps to early larvae of the gastropod mollusc *Ianthina*. (32169)

(c) Active with no overt recipient:

(3) It is a tribute to human nature how often relatives and friends of
a dying uraemic patient will *offer one of their own healthy kidneys*,
even if there is only an infinitesimal chance of the transplant's
success. (31189)

(d) Passive with recipient as subject:

(4) they [*sc.* the following parameters] *are given the same labels* as in
the previous paper (18104)

(e) Passive with recipient as adjunct (with overt *to*):

(5) but this does not fully explain the protection *afforded to the brain by
low temperatures*. (31511)

(f) Passive with no overt recipient:

(6) The fishermen have suggested that the shade *given by a floating
object* and the presence of small fish which could act as food for the
larger ones are the attracting factors, (32330)

There were no examples of passives with recipient as indirect object, as
in *the money was given John*, nor of clauses containing a recipient but no
(pre-passive) direct object, like the *I told him* mentioned earlier.

It will be noticed from the table that the proportion with specified

4-2

TABLE 3: 3. *The principal recipient verbs*

	Active			Passive			
	Recpt obj. (*a*)	Recpt adj. (*b*)	No recpt (*c*)	Recpt subj. (*d*)	Recpt adj. (*e*)	No recpt (*f*)	Total
afford	—	—	13	—	2	2	17
allow	2	—	20	—	—	3	25
give	13	2	80	2	—	47	144
offer	2	1	5	—	1	2	11

recipient is quite small – about 13 %. It is doubtful in fact whether it is appropriate in all cases to postulate an unspecified recipient with these verbs in clauses of types (c) and (f). In (3) and (6) it is reasonable to do so; the chief doubt is with *give* in its frequent use with an equation, formula, etc., as direct object, as in:

(7) The best fit to the experimental curve *gave*: A = 11.1 ± 0.1, [...]
    (17132)

Perhaps an unspecified (human) recipient analysis is valid here, though it is striking that none of the many examples of this use of *give* contained an overt recipient; the meaning of *give* here is very similar to that of *yield*, which is a two-place, not a three-place, verb.

We may end this section with comments on two verbs which take recipients but do not enter into the ditransitive construction. In the 'give' meaning of *present* there is a thematic contrast between the cognitively equivalent patterns *NP₁ presents NP₂ with NP₃* and *NP₁ presents NP₃ to NP₂* which is analogous to that we have been considering between *NP₁ gives NP₂ NP₃* and *NP₁ gives NP₃ to NP₂*, so that it is reasonable to take the NP₂ in the *present* constructions as recipient: it is a property of this verb that either recipient or objective must lose its preposition but they cannot both do so. In the textual examples, however, the recipient was in all cases left unspecified:

(8) Experimental evidence is presented from HgTe and a Bi-Sb-Te-Se alloy on the usefulness of the method. (17443)

With the 'exhibit' sense of *present* the *NP₁ presents NP₃ to NP₂* pattern did occur, though it is arguable whether NP₂ is recipient here – there is certainly no contrast with a *NP₁ presents NP₂ with NP₃* pattern:

(9) the brightness of the moon sometimes varies in a way that cannot be accounted for simply by changes in the moon's distance from the earth or by its librations, which cause it to present slightly different areas of its surface to the earth at different times. (38040)

With *provide* we find the two patterns NP_1 *provides* NP_2 *with* NP_3 and NP_1 *provides* NP_3, exemplified in:

(10) I should like to express my gratitude to E. E. Anderson for providing me with the magnetization data and to V. J. Folen for providing the crystal of YIG and several stimulating discussions. (17429)

NP_2 is recipient, NP_3 objective, so that with this verb the rules are that if a recipient is expressed it is necessarily realized as object (at the pre-passive level), the objective retaining its preposition *with*, but if no recipient is expressed the objective is realized as object.

3.6   Voice

3.6.1   Active transitives with no passive counterpart. In the simplest cases the relation between structures at the pre- and post-passive levels is as exemplified in:

(i) *a*   John killed Peter
    b   Peter was killed by John
(ii) *a*   John died
     b   *Was died by John

With intransitives, passivization cannot occur and so there will be no difference in structure at the two levels. With transitives, passivization is optional; if it is applied the pre-passive subject and direct object become adjunct (with *by* as the governing preposition)[1] and subject respectively at the post-passive, or concord, level, and *be* + *en* is introduced into the auxiliary. Such an account of voice is much oversimplified, and I want here to discuss some of the qualifications and corrections that need to be made; I shall not attempt an exhaustive coverage – in particular, I shall have nothing to say about the question of the effect of quantifiers on the cognitive equivalence of active and passive, as in

---

[1] The *by*-adjunct is often referred to as the 'agent' – this term is quite different from 'agentive', used in 3.1 etc., as the name of a 'case'; in particular, not all agent NP's derive from underlying agentives.

Chomsky's well-known examples *everyone in the room knows at least two languages* and *at least two languages are known by everyone in the room.*

In the first place there are transitive actives with no acceptable passive equivalent. In some cases there may be a quite general explanation for the absence of a passive. Passivization does not normally take place where pre-passive subject and object are identical – i.e. we do not normally find reflexive agents: *John knew himself to be in the wrong* but **John was known by himself to be in the wrong.* This constraint does not hold if there is contrastive stress on the reflexive agent: cf. Halliday's (1968: 189) *he was supervised by himself:* (with *himself* as agent: we are not of course concerned with the 'on his own' interpretation). The same principle applies where the pre-passive object contains a possessive determiner that is coreferential with the subject: *Mary's briefcase was lost by her* (i.e. Mary) is unacceptable if there isn't contrastive stress on *her* – and indeed rather marginal even if there is. Similarly inherently reciprocal verbs do not normally allow passivization. Thus **'house' is meant by 'maison'* or **nine is equalled by three squared* are ungrammatical whereas *that isn't what was meant* and *the world record was equalled by Smith,* with non-symmetric meanings of the same verbs, are perfectly normal. However, the acceptability of passives with symmetric verbs seems to be subject to some degree of dialectal variation (cf. Halliday's *Mary isn't resembled by any of her children,* 1967*b*: 68).

Mary hated/liked/loved/preferred/wanted John to play the piano hardly allow passivization with *John* as concord subject – in contrast to similar clauses containing *expect, intend, request, require* and so on. With *hate, like,* etc., it may be possible to correlate the lack of a passive with some semantic property of the verbs; but this will certainly not always be possible. *Have,* for example, is necessarily active when it means 'possess' though the verb *possess* itself can occur in the passive:

(1) *E* is the mean energy possessed by each of the molecules in 1 cc. of gas (28460)

As R. Lakoff (1968: 22–3) observes, *have* must simply be marked as an exception in that it blocks the passive rule; this is apparently an idiosyncratic property of the verb, not predictable from any of its other properties. *Have* was the most frequent item in the transitivity corpus, and all 229 occurrences were indeed active. The constraint is absolute, however, only for one of the two main uses of *have,* for we can attest passives like *dinner can be had at any reasonable time, the last word was had by Mary.* The two uses I have in mind are distinguished by whether or not the auxiliary *do* is required in the interrogative, negative, etc. It is the use where *do* is required that allows passivization – compare *at what time do you have dinner?*, **at what time have you dinner?*, *at what time can dinner be had?*, versus *how much money does John have?*, *how much money has John?*, **how much money is had by John?*.

The tables in 3.6.6 group the verbs in the transitivity corpus according to the proportion of active to passive occurrences.

3.6.2 Pseudo-passives and passives of ditransitives.

'Pseudo-passive' is the (not very happy) term used for the construction where the concord subject derives not from a direct object but from the object of a preposition: here then we have a thematic contrast between active and passive with sentences that are intransitive at the pre-passive level: compare

(1) In the first place these artefacts give us a set of standards to which we can refer. (22162)
(2) This number is frequently referred to as *Loschmidt's number*, (28251)

The only verbs in the corpus entering into the pseudo-passive construction were *refer* and *account*. They are typical of the construction in that the prepositions are determined by the verb (*refer to, account for*) rather than being contrastive and lexically meaningful – though as far as constituent structure is concerned they are nevertheless bracketed with the NP, not the verb. Chomsky (1965: 105–6) observes that with the ambiguous *John decided on the boat* passivization is not possible if *on the boat* is locative ('John was on the boat when he made his decision'), but is possible where *on* is non-contrastive ('John chose the boat'); it is obvious that the underlying relationship of *the boat* to *decide* is quite different in the two cases, and this difference may well be reflected in different bracketings at the pre-passive level, as Chomsky's proposals would imply. However, not all pseudo-passives are of this type: the preposition is in some cases lexically contrastive. The object in prepositional phrases of time, duration, manner, reason, etc., cannot become the concord subject of a passive: **the first day of term was eloped on,* **a couple of hours were read for, *enthusiasm was sung with, *the rain was remained indoors because of;* but with some place and perhaps instrumental prepositional phrases, passivization does seem possible: *that bed hasn't been slept in for years, that chair mustn't be sat on, this cup has been*

drunk out of, ?this blade has already been shaved with twice. The acceptability of a passive with a locative phrase depends in large measure, I
think, on whether the action not only occurs at the stated place but also
affects that place: a cup that has been drunk out of needs washing, to
say that a bed has been slept in may suggest that the sheets need changing, and so on. Notice, for example, that one would be more likely to
accept *the bed had been slept in* than *the village had been slept in, the home
doesn't look lived in* than **Reading is lived in by* *100,000 people;* we might
not reject *the village, small as it was, had been slept in by no fewer than
eight monarchs,* but again we would probably interpret it as implying
that the village had been affected, in the sense of having some kind of
distinction conferred upon it.[1] It is not clear how such facts should be
handled; in the 'case' approach to deep structure discussed in 3.1, where
underlying relations are 'labelled' rather than 'pure' and multiple functions are allowed for, we might say that in the deep structure of such
a sentence as *that bed has been slept in, that bed* fills two roles, affected
and locative (more precisely the locative would be *in that bed*): it would
then be the affected role that was relevant to passivization.

If at the pre-passive level there is a direct object as well as a prepositional phrase, the direct object, but not the object of the preposition,
may become the concord subject by passivization:

(i) *a* Bill was referred to them
    b *They were referred Bill to
(ii) *c* John was decided on the boat
    b *The boat was decided John on
(iii) *a* Wine had been drunk out of the glass
    b *The glass had been drunk wine out of

Similarly, with three-place verbs like *blame, present, provide,* etc., where
there is a choice as to which underlying preposition is deleted to yield
a direct object, it is only the NP whose preposition has been dropped that
may become concord subject of a passive – compare:

---

[1] It is relevant at this point to mention a type of exception to the rules governing which
elements interrogative *wh* may be associated with. I referred in 2.2.2 to Chomsky's
observations about the constraints on associating *wh* with embedded elements
(Chomsky, 1968: 41 ff.); he excludes for example, **who did they intercept John's
message to?* Yet such a sentence as *which departments should we invite the heads of?*
seems at least marginally acceptable, suggesting an interpretation whereby 'inviting
the head of' is something one may do to a department—to afford it some measure of
recognition or status, for example.

(iv) *a*   He blamed the error on John
    b   The error was blamed on John
    c   He blamed John for the error
    d   John was blamed for the error
    e   *John was blamed the error on
    f   *The error was blamed John for

With ditransitives it is normally the indirect object that is mapped onto the concord subject in the passive. Of the three types:

(v) *a*   John was given the money
    b   The money was given to John
    c   The money was given John

the first two are a good deal more usual than the third – Halliday (1967*b*: 56) explains this in terms of the comparative rarity of *someone gave John the money* in the reading where *John* carries the tonic stress and is thus the focus of new information. (v)*b* derives from (*someone*) *gave the money to John:* in accordance with the observations made in connection with (i)–(iv), it is the only passive version of that clause (which is not ditransitive). However, (v)*c* is not ungrammatical, so that we must allow for two passive versions of (*someone*) *gave John the money:* I do not see any non *ad hoc* way of generating (v)*c*. This type is more readily acceptable when the underlying preposition is *to* than *for:* such sentences as *the car was bought John, *a new dress was made Mary* can probably be excluded as ungrammatical; similarly with verbs like *envy* and so on, where there is never a preposition at the pre-passive level, only the indirect object may become concord subject: *she was envied her good looks, *her office was envied her, I was saved a lot of trouble, *a lot of trouble was saved me.*

3.6.3   Statal passives. Jespersen (1931: 92–3) makes a distinction between 'conclusive' and 'non-conclusive' verbs; with the former the 'action is either confined to one single moment, e.g. *catch, surprise, awake, leave, end, kill,* or implies a final aim, e.g. *make, bring about, construct, beat*', whereas non-conclusive verbs denote 'feelings, states of mind, etc.; the activity, if any such is implied, is not begun in order to be finished. As examples we may mention *love, hate, praise, blame, see, hear*'. With conclusive verbs he goes on to distinguish two kinds of passive (1931: 98–9): a passive of becoming and a passive of being. These terms can be misleading (for reasons which will emerge) and I shall consequently use Curme's (1931: 443–7) 'actional' and 'statal' respectively. The contrast is illustrated in the ambiguity of such sentences as *his bills are paid*. As an actional passive this corresponds to the active (*someone*) *pays his bills* (it is likely, but not necessary, that the actional passive and the corresponding active here will be interpreted as having habitual aspect); the statal passive reading on the other hand expresses the result of a past action: he (or someone) *has* paid them.

Although Jespersen's conclusive/non-conclusive distinction may be relevant at some point in the discussion of passives, I think that the primary division must be between dynamic and non-dynamic verbs, where the former express actions or processes, the latter states or relations. A considerable number of verbs may of course be ambiguously dynamic or non-dynamic: e.g. *understand* ('to reach or have an understanding'), *surround, separate, form* and so on – *the army quickly surrounded the village* is dynamic whereas *high mountains surrounded the lake* is non-dynamic. This overlap obviously does not invalidate the distinction in any way. I will begin by considering the passives of dynamic verbs, for it is here that we have the contrast between the actional and statal types.

The difference in meaning between the two kinds of passive is clear from such ambiguous examples as *his bills are paid*, discussed above; how can the difference be represented in structural terms? I have been assuming so far that an actional passive and its active counterpart, such as (i)*a* and *b* respectively:

(i) *a* The wall was painted by John
     b John painted the wall

derive from a common structure at the pre-passive level: if the optional passive rule is applied to this structure we get *a*, if it is not we get *b*. This assumption may have to be amended. The common structure accounts for the cognitive equivalence of (i)*a* and *b*, but it is doubtful, as remarked earlier, whether thematic differences in general or the particular thematic difference between the clauses in (i) can be satisfactorily regarded as simply a question of surface structure: they certainly have semantic relevance. And secondly, there are well known difficulties in ensuring that the passive rule yields the correct derived constituent structure: this was one motivation for the proposal (eg. Katz & Postal, 1964: 72; Chomsky, 1965: 104) that passives contain in deep structure a Manner constituent dominating *by* plus a dummy element Passive, which is replaced by the (pre-passive) subject by means of the passive trans-formation.[1] But these doubts do not undermine the main part of the assumption: we can still say that before the application of the passive transformation the structures of (i)*a* and *b* are, if not identical, at least alike in that *John* is subject and *the wall* direct object.

As for statal passives, there are good grounds for saying that these have essentially the same structure as copulative sentences with adjec-tival attributes, such as *John was tired*. This is the analysis proposed, for example, by Palmer (1965: 68); he distinguishes between the actional *they were married last year* and the statal *they were married when I last saw them* by taking the former as an ordinary passive clause and analyz-ing the latter as containing lexical (i.e. non-auxiliary) *be* plus a past participle functioning as adjectival complement.

The following factors support an analysis of this kind:

(a) The statal passive, unlike the actional, has no direct active coun-terpart. *He pays his bills* corresponds to the actional reading of *his bills are paid*; the statal reading has a past time or perfective component which is absent from *he pays his bills*. Palmer's analysis of statal passives makes *be* the main verb so that the tense selection applies to this *be*, not to the participial verb; this description thus goes some way towards capturing the meaning that the concord subject is in the state resulting from the action associated with the participial verb.

(b) In statal passives the participle may be coordinated with an adjective:

(1) The cell-wall of Gram-negative organisms is very thin and made up of two electron-opaque layers separated by a less dense layer to give a total thickness of about 100 Å. (12209)

Since coordination is normally possible only between elements of like function, examples such as this lend strong support to the proposed analysis.

(c) The pro-form *so*, which is used to refer to adjectival attributes, may also be substituted for the participle of a statal passive, as in:

(2) These motions are generally directed towards the plane but are not entirely so. (34250)

---

[1] This particular proposal is scarcely satisfactory: to categorize *by John* in (i)*a* as a manner phrase fails to explain why it cannot be questioned by *how* (Lyons, 1966: 122), and why it can combine non-coordinately with a genuine manner phrase, as in *the wall was skilfully painted by John*.

So is not a possible substitute with actional passives: **the first liquid was heated and the second was so too.*

(d) The participle of a statal passive has the further property in common with adjectives that it may combine with the negative prefix *un-*: this is not possible with actional passives. Thus whereas *the manuscript was finished* is ambiguously actional or statal, *the manuscript was unfinished* is unambiguously statal. (The prefix in *to undo, untie*, etc., is of course a different one from that under consideration here.)

(e) In statal, but not actional, passives *be* commutes with most if not all copulative verbs – witness:

(3) Since light tends to *become polarized* when it is reflected, this finding suggests that moonlight at its brightest includes some light that is not reflected sunlight. (38058)

(4) These invaginations are stacked 5–15 high to form the chromatophores and *remain attached* to the plasma membrane by a tubular stalk. (12428)

(5) The only facts about acne that *seem definitely established* are that there is a hereditary disposition to it and that it is connected in some way with diet and with the activity of the androgenic hormones. (35557)

The fact that the notion of copulative verb here may be a fairly superficial one (*John seems tired* deriving for example from, roughly, *for John to be tired seems*) does not affect the present argument, whose aim is to demonstrate the functional similarity between adjectives and statal passives, as opposed to actional ones.

Notice that the dynamic, or change of state, component in (3) does not conflict with its analysis as a statal passive, for it is attributable to the lexical meaning of *become*: the participle is just as much statal in (3) as in (4) and (5). (It is clear then that some qualification needs to be made to Palmer's account: otherwise his use of colligability with *already* as a criterion for distinguishing statal from actional passives may be misleading.) The attribution of the dynamic component to *become* rather than to the passive verb is supported by the fact that *become* may be followed by the passive participle of a non-dynamic verb:

(6) as the neighbouring cells continue growth they [*sc.* the carpogonia] eventually *become surrounded*. (21263)

Since *surround* can be either dynamic or non-dynamic the point can perhaps be made more clearly with such a constructed example as *the professor's political views soon became widely known.*

To say that a statal passive has the structure of a copulative sentence does not of itself explain the relationship between actional and statal passives. Up to this point I have been concentrating on the differences in the proposed structural treatments. Yet they obviously have also a good deal in common: whether we interpret *his bills are paid* statally or actionally there is, on some dimension or level of structure, a constant relationship between *his bills* and *pay*. How can we amend our analysis so as to account both for the similarities and for the differences between the two types of passive? Two possibilities suggest themselves, according as we in effect take the statal or the actional as the basic pattern. To take the statal as basic would presumably involve postulating an abstract inchoative or causative matrix verb in actional passives; thus the actional reading of *his bills are paid* would derive from a structure very much like that of *it comes about that his bills are paid*, where the subject position is filled by a statal passive. (This seems to be the analysis favoured by G. Lakoff & Peters, 1969: 137, though they do not specifically discuss the contrast between statal and actional passives.) This proposal suffers from a number of interrelated weaknesses. If an actional passive contains an embedded statal passive as subject of an abstract inchoative, there will be presumably an embedded statal passive in the underlying structure of *active* sentences – and indeed Lakoff & Peters treat *John married Mary* as involving *it for John and Mary to be married* (statal) as subject of a *come about* pro-form. Since there are many actives with no passive equivalent this would seem to produce quite unwarranted complexity. There is moreover the obvious point that morphologically the participle is clearly a derived form – the derivative nature of the statal passive is particularly clear with such statal 'pseudo-passives' as *everything was now accounted for.* Furthermore from a semantic point of view it seems that even in the statal reading of *his bills are paid* some unspecified agent is implicitly involved.

The alternative approach would take the actional passive as basic; this would imply that the adjective-like participle of the statal passive was the surface residue of an embedded clause. The structure of *his bills are paid* in the statal sense might thus be roughly as in PM (1).

PM(1)

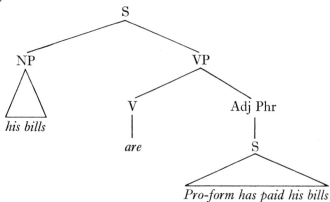

Pro-form has paid his bills

This too suffers from a serious weakness, in that it will be necessary to impose severe restrictions on the structure of clauses embedded to function as adjective phrases: the pre-passive subject for example must be a subsequently deleted pro-form since *by*-agents *are* not found in statal passives: *his bills are paid by his father* is unequivocally actional. Similarly we should have to rule out many types of adverbial element: we do not wish to say, for example, that *his bills are now paid* is structurally ambiguous according as the *now* originates in the matrix or the constituent clause. I do not think, however, that such restrictions invalidate a structural analysis along the lines of PM(1), since similar restrictions have to be stated in other places of the grammar: e.g. when *begin* and many other verbs take a non-finite complement, it is not possible for both matrix and constituent clause to contain a time adverbial – only the matrix may (cf. Huddleston, 1969c).

The distinction between actional and statal passives was motivated in part by the need to account for ambiguities in passive clauses containing dynamic verbs. The first thing to note about the passives of non-dynamic verbs is that they do not exhibit any equivalent ambiguity – compare, for example:

(7) However, very little is known about these layers despite their accessibility. (32003)

Consequently, we shall not wish to assign two different grammatical descriptions to such clauses. Assuming that we do not have here some third type of passive, should (7) and its kind be equated with the statal or the actional passive of dynamic verbs? This question is of course to be settled on syntactic grounds: the terminology adopted in the discussion of dynamic verbs should not prejudge the issue.

There are two respects in which the passives of non-dynamic verbs resembles the actional rather than statal passive of dynamic ones. In the first place there may be a *by*-phrase corresponding to the pre-passive subject:

(8) Two circular horizontal discs of radius 5 cm. and distance apart 1 mm. are separated by a layer of oil of viscosity 1.01 C.G.S. (28079)

Secondly we do not find the covert past tense or perfective component that we noted in the statal reading of *his bills are paid:* thus (7) does not differ in underlying tense or aspect from the active *(we) know very little about these layers.*

On the other hand the passive participle of a non-dynamic verb shows all the functional similarities to an adjectival attribute that characterize statal passives: it can coordinate with an adjective, take the *un-* prefix, be replaced by the pro-form *so* and occur with the full range of copulative verbs. The last two properties are exemplified in:

(9) the clubbed hairs are firmly attached to the follicles and will remain so after the skin is tanned. (35366)

It is difficult to see how these facts can be accounted for other than by treating the passives of non-dynamic verbs as statal. (In the light of this decision the terms actional and statal may be retained as semantically appropriate.) The fact that there is no tense/aspect difference from the corresponding active will be handled by omitting the *have*-element that was postulated in PM(1) for dynamic verbs. Notice that if we agree to take perfective *have* as a main verb, as suggested in 4.2.2, it will follow that the main verb of all clauses embedded as attribute to form a statal passive will be non-dynamic (since *have* itself is clearly non-dynamic), whereas all actional passives will contain dynamic verbs.

There is a small sub-class of dynamic verbs which do not – or do not readily – take a statal passive. *John was killed* will normally be interpreted actionally rather than statally – though it is perhaps just possible to contextualize statal passives with this verb: *now that three of them are killed it only remains to deal with the ringleader himself.* Better examples are thus *hit, strike, slap*, mentioned in this connection by Fillmore (1967: 18–19); we might also add *blame* and the sense verbs in Jespersen's list of non-conclusive verbs.

All the actional passives in the corpus have *be* as the passive auxiliary. The *get* of more informal registers is, I think, to be regarded as a variant, at least in some uses. I would thus treat *it got established* as an actional passive, even though *it became established* is statal (with a dynamic copulative verb). The syntactic justification of analyzing *get* and *become* in these different ways involves the verbs mentioned in the previous paragraph: although we can readily have *he got killed/hit/struck/slapped*, we do not find *he became killed*, etc. This correlates, I think, with a semantic difference: *become*, unlike *get*, implies coming to be in the state expressed in the following verb.

3.6.4 Passives with no 'by'-phrase.

In the most straightforward cases that we began with, an actional passive and its active counterpart differed only in thematic arrangement of the same set of transitivity elements; in particular the concord subject of the active and the 'agent' of the passive (the NP governed by *by*) both derive from the pre-passive subject. However, a large majority of the passive clauses in the corpus do not contain any such *by*-phrase (detailed figures are given in 3.6.6). How can we explain its absence?

In many examples it can be argued that there is an agent understood: no specific mention is made of it because it is assumed to be recoverable from the context (linguistic and/or situational). This type can be described formally by the familiar agent-deletion transformation, which suppresses *by* + NP provided the latter is a pro-form. In most such cases in the corpus the covert agent is understood to be (or to refer to) the writer or experimenter – usually in fact one and the same. Where the writer is reporting a series of actions carried out by the same person(s), to specify the agent for each would involve a degree of repetition that is generally regarded as stylistically undesirable. This factor of course is likely to have favoured the selection of passive rather than active voice. The following passage is a paradigm example of this aspect of scientific style: an account of experimental work in which the researcher fills the role of pre-passive subject for a considerable sequence of actions without being overtly specified in any of them.

(1) The working electrodes of thallium amalgam were in the form of segments of spheres of known size formed on the upturned end of a capillary. The capillary was *fed* from a micrometer actuated syringe and the cell was *designed* so as to permit a rapid response of the working electrode to step pulses of the applied potential. The subsidiary electrode was a helix of platinum wire surrounding the working electrode and a silver/silver chloride electrode was *used* as reference. The potentials are *expressed* as overpotentials with respect

to the appropriate reversible potential of the thallium amalgam/thallous chloride/chloride ion electrode in the same solution as that surrounding the working electrode. The value of this potential could be accurately *measured* with respect to the silver/silver chloride electrode by first forming a thin layer of thallous chloride on a pool of thallium amalgam.

Samples of the deposits for electron diffraction and microscopy were *prepared* on a small pool electrode by applying a square pulse of the desired overpotential. The falling edge of the pulses actuated a polarized relay which switched the working electrode out of the circuit. The solution was *drained* under a hydrogen atmosphere, the deposits were *washed* with water and methanol and *dried*. A film of formvar was then *cast* on the deposit and this was *reinforced* by a film of collodion. All the operations were *carried* out using hypodermic syringes by inserting the needles through serum caps mounted on the cell. Sections of the deposits were then *mounted* on grids, the collodion backing being *dissolved* off. The micrographs and diffraction patterns were *taken* by transmission.

Thallium amalgams of the following concentrations were *prepared*: 30, 10, 3.0, 1.0, 0.1 atoms %. The three most concentrated amalgams were *made* by electrolyzing a solution of thallous sulphate for a measured time using a stabilized constant current and a weighed quantity of mercury as cathode. The solution and amalgam were *stirred* with purified nitrogen. The two most dilute amalgams were *made* by using a known quantity of thallous sulphate and electrolyzing until the solution was free from thallium ions. The amalgams were *removed* from the preparation cell and stored under hydrogen. The formation of thallous chloride was *examined* using five solutions of hydrochloric acid of concentration 5, 2, 1, 0.5 and 0.1 M, and also in a 1 M solution of potassium chloride. Perchloric acid was *added* to the two most dilute hydrochloric acid solutions to bring the ionic strength to that of the 1 M hydrochloric acid. All solutions were made in triple distilled water and the A.R. chemicals were twice *recrystallized* and then *heated* at 500 °C. The mercury was *distilled* twice under vacuum and the acids were constant boiling mixtures.

The potentiostat *used* in these measurements was a modification of one which has been *described* but with an increased sensitivity and improved frequency response. It was *used* in conjunction with a modification of a pulse generator. All the kinetic measurements were *made* as follows: the potential of the working electrode was *held* at − 100 mV with respect to the thallium amalgam/thallous chloride/chloride ion potential; a first pulse was *applied* to switch the potential to the reversible value and the specific adsorption of chloride ions was *allowed* to go to completion; thallous chloride was then *formed* by applying a second pulse. By using this procedure the effects of the current, caused by the specific adsorption process, on the current–time transient due to the formation of the first monolayer were *removed* as far as this was possible. All current–time transients were *measured* oscillographically. The related problem of the kinetics of the specific adsorption of chloride ions will be *discussed* elsewhere. (16314)

(The passage also includes eleven non-finite active clauses where the subject is deleted but understood to refer likewise to the experimenter.)

A second large class of instances involves the generalized human 'one' or 'people', as in:

(2) The reasons for the association are not understood. (32329)
(3) Most of the work has used similar techniques of fixation, dehydration and embedding in resin and *it could be argued* that the methods themselves are creating similarities between the two groups, (12042)

Thus the closest active version of (3) would be something like *one could argue that*... The passive here contains no less information than the active, for *argue* in this sense belongs to the class of verbs that must have a human subject at the pre-passive level.

Verbs which do not imply a human subject at this level (or, more precisely, a human agentive at a deeper level) present more of a problem in the passive. In some cases at least the only plausible explanation for the absence of an agent is that there is no corresponding participant involved in the process, etc., that is, there is no agent understood. There are numerous examples in the corpus where this seems to apply; I quote as many as 10 since I am aware that some are perhaps open to different interpretations. (Compare also the discussion in Mihailovič, 1967.)

(4) I should emphasize that results like those shown in Figure 4 are obtained under conditions far *removed* from practical applications. (37494)
(5) We know nothing of the cerebral patterns or how they are *established*. (22099)
(6) The pores, which range in diameter from 60 to 600 Å, may be randomly *arranged* as in *Mastigocladus laminosus* (12152)
(7) Recently Helen W. Dodson and E. Ruth Hedeman of the University of Michigan have pointed out an apparent correlation between the particle fluxes *associated* with solar activity on the one hand and the lunar cycle on the other. (38473)
(8) By applying the laws to probability, Maxwell showed that it is possible to calculate the law according to which the speeds of the molecules would be *distributed* at any temperature. (28308)
(9) The similarity between the fine structure of the outer gelatinous slimy layers of the two forms is probably *based* on the chemical

nature of the layers and their reaction to the preparative techniques of electron microscopy. (12106)

(10) *Cicindela* (adult) feeds in this way, and here the setae in the proventriculus are *reduced*. (13549)

(11) In this genus, which is restricted to warm waters, the young coenocyte consists of one large vesicle whilst the old one becomes *divided up* into a number of multinucleate segments. (21449)

(12) The outer lobe is a two-jointed palp-like appendage which is characteristic of most of the Adephaga, and is *attached* immediately mesal to the base of the palp. (13016)

(13) If we wish to study the motion of such a body, and agree to ignore the motion of its center of mass, there is only one thing *left* for it to do, and that is to *turn*. [*ital. sic*] (27174)

The majority, though not all, of these are statal passives but this does not affect the point at issue. It may be helpful to consider such constructions in the light of what was said in 3.1 about ergative verbs. With ergatives we were concerned with contrasts at the *pre*-passive level within such pairs as *the book sold/they sold the book* or *the stone moved/they moved the stone;* here we are concerned with contrasts at the *post*-passive level within such pairs as *the problem was solved/they solved the problem* or *the pattern was established/they established the pattern.* I suggested that of the apparently one-place constructions with the ergative verbs, some derived from deeper two-place constructions (e.g. *the book sold*), while others were inherently one-place (e.g. *the stone moved* – at least in one interpretation). I would argue that the same applies with one-place passives: some derive from two-place constructions at the pre-passive level (e.g. *the problem was solved*), whereas others are one-place constructions at that level (e.g. (4)–(13)). With neither the ergatives nor the passives is the distinction always easy to draw in practice, but there seem to be enough clear examples to justify the distinction nevertheless.

In a case grammar we can handle the inherently one-place passives (like *how the cerebral patterns are established*) by treating the one-place, i.e. the concord subject, as an affected or objective case which is mapped onto the direct object at the pre-passive level; passivization would then map it onto the concord subject, as with ordinary two-place passives. There would be no subject at the pre-passive level – and consequently no *by*-phrase at the post-passive. Passivization would thus apply obligatorily in such constructions, to satisfy the general requirement of English that the concord subject position must be filled (even if there is subsequent deletion). It is not clear how inherently one-place passives can be handled in a grammar whose functions in deep structure are configurationally defined subjects and objects, etc.: I do not see how one could avoid setting up two quite distinct passivization rules, one applying to (inherently) one-place constructions and having the effect simply of adding *be + en* to the auxiliary, the other applying to two-place constructions and operating in the normal way.

3.6.5   Instrumentals and related elements. We were concerned in the last section with passive sentences containing no *by*-phrase; where there is such a phrase we are faced with the problem of determining whether it does in fact derive from the pre-passive subject. Thus Chomsky (1957: 89–90) contrasts two readings of *John was frightened by the new techniques* according as it derives from the structure underlying *someone frightened John by the new techniques* (i.e. someone used the new techniques to frighten John) or from *the new techniques frightened John* (i.e. John was frightened at the idea of the new techniques). Both types of *by*-phrase are found in:

(1) The crystal we used was grown by a flux method by Folen.
    (17352)

The two types are often distinguished as instrumental versus agent, but these terms are more appropriately used for a distinction that is separate from, but not unrelated to, the question raised above. Whatever the terminology used, we need to keep apart, then, these two questions: firstly, does the *by*-phrase derive from a pre-passive subject or from what we may refer to as a pre-passive adjunct? and secondly, does it derive from a deep structure agentive or instrumental (where agentive and instrumental are regarded as labelled relations or cases, in deep structure)? The two questions are distinct inasmuch as a pre-passive subject may itself derive from an underlying agentive or from an instrumental. This point is made by Fillmore (1968a: 25), who contrasts *John opened the door* and *the key opened the door*, the syntactic difference between *John* and *the key* being demonstrated by the fact that they cannot be coordinated, yet can be combined non-coordinately: *John opened the door with the key*. The following textual examples might similarly be regarded as having instrumental subjects:

(2) Treatment of monoolefins with molecular oxygen can produce allylic hydroperoxides. (15021)

(3) Radio studies of neutral hydrogen are now greatly increasing our understanding of the structure and dynamics of our Galaxy; (34010)

(4) At the extremities two transducers convert at one end an A.C. electrical input to a sound wave and at the other convert the amplified sound back to an electrical signal again. (37481)

(5) A programme of investigation designed to study the surface eco-system will yield results of both economic and zoological interest. (32367)

Such an analysis enables us to relate them systematically to, for example, (2′), (3′) and so on:

(2′) We can produce allylic hydroperoxides by (the) treatment of monoolefins with molecular oxygen.

(3′) We are now greatly increasing our understanding of the structure and dynamics of our Galaxy by means of radio studies of neutral hydrogen.

The ambiguity of Chomsky's *John was frightened by the new techniques* is thus not introduced by the passive rule: it is present also in the active version, *the new techniques frightened John.*

It follows that for some passives containing an instrumental *by*-phrase and having an agentive understood there will be two possible derivations from a single source, according as the covert agentive is deleted before or just after passivization. Consider, for example, the paradigm:

(i) *a* We solved the problem by inviting John
   b Inviting John solved the problem
   c The problem was solved by inviting John

If we confine ourselves to interpretations where *inviting John* is instrumental, it is apparent that *c* may be derived from either *b* or *a* (or something very like it); in the former case the agentive is deleted before the pre-passive level, in the latter it is deleted after the passive rule has mapped it into the adjunct position. Such structural ambiguities are of course found only where the main verb is one that allows an instrumental pre-passive subject; thus in the following example the understood agentive is unequivocally deleted *after* passivization:

(6) Intuitively this curve can be seen to be the stable curve by the following argument. (18072)

Not all instrumental adjuncts are governed by the preposition *by*: *through*, *with* and *by means of* are also commonly found, as in:

(7) Transmission interference fringes from 2690 to 320 cm⁻¹ for InAs and from 1330 to 320 cm⁻¹ for CdTe have been analyzed with classical dispersion theory to obtain the room-temperature dielectric constants. (17001)

(8) The correctness or otherwise of this interpretation can only be obtained through a better knowledge of its phylogenetic history and the reproductive processes of other members of the group. (21491)

(9) The molar entropy of gaseous acetylene at atmospheric pressure is found directly by means of the usual equations: (26549)

Except in some special constructions involving *with* (see below), these prepositions mark the phrase as unambiguously instrumental rather than agentive, and it is probably reasonable to say that where they occur in passive clauses the phrase derives from an adjunct at the pre-passive level, not from the subject. We should also include under the same heading certain *-ly* adverbs, as in:

(10) All current-time transients were measured oscillographically. (16382)

(11) Thus pontellid copepods and one or two species of decapod crustacea possess a pigment which has been extracted and examined spectroscopically. (32258)

The meaning here is obviously 'with or by means of an oscillograph/spectroscope', not 'in an oscillographic/spectroscopic way'.

In introducing the agentive/instrumental distinction earlier I merely showed the need for a distinction of this type and illustrated the two cases with clear-cut examples. Let us now look at it in a little more detail. Fillmore (1968a: 24) defines agentive as 'the case of the typically animate perceived instigator of the action identified by the verb', and instrumental as 'the case of the inanimate force or object causally involved in the action or state identified by the verb'. Applying these definitions to:

(ii) *a* John opened the door
   b The wind opened the door
   c The key opened the door

we analyze *John* as agentive, *the wind* and *the key* as instrumentals. I have suggested elsewhere (Huddleston, 1970b) that this obscures an important difference between (ii)*b* and *c*, namely that under normal interpretations the latter but not the former presupposes an implicit agentive. I proposed limiting instrumental to the type found in (ii)*c* where there is this presupposition; *the wind* in *b* would then be some kind of 'non-agentive force' or 'external causer' (cf. 3.1 above).[1] Although I think that this analysis is sound in principle, it is not always easy to apply in textual studies because it may be unclear how far, how directly and how relevantly there is some human agent involved in the process: this is not really a new problem, but rather a further facet of the one considered in 3.6.4.

Let us look at a few textual examples, some clear-cut, others border-line. First:

(12) The stable solution is obtained by comparing the free energies which in this case are just the entropies. (18065)

(13) Solving (5) gives as $\alpha \to 0$, $\gamma \to 1/\alpha$ [...] (18075)

(14) Because piezoelectricity is a two way process *increasing the charge increases the compression and rarefaction in the crystal*, and increased mechanical stress in the crystal produces an increased amplitude of the sound wave. (37469)

Where an embedded *ing*-clause governed by *by* has no overt subject, we may be fairly sure that it is an instrumental, as in (12). The covert subject of *compare* here is human, and understood to be identical with the implicit agentive of *obtain*. The situation is different when the *ing*-clause is functioning as subject of the matrix, as in (13) and (14). In the former there is again a human pro-form understood as subject of *solve*, but the embedded clause *solving (5)* is not an instrumental: there is no human agentive understood in the matrix clause. In (14) *increasing the charge* is probably to be taken as an instrumental since we could have:

(14′) we increase the compression and rarefaction in the crystal by increasing the charge.

The *because*-clause in (14) is of some interest here: it gives the reason why the effect of increasing the charge is to increase the compression and rarefaction – the fact that the reason clause is thus closely linked to the instrumental will probably have favoured the thematic upgrading of

---

[1] This view of instrumentals would fit in better with G. Lakoff's (1967) treatment: he derives instrumentals from complex sentences with *use* as main verb, the deep subject of *use* being then the presupposed agentive.

the latter that is involved in its selection as subject, though this is not to say that (14′) would be unacceptable if we added the same *because-*clause. If on the other hand there were a reason clause more directly related to the agentive, the latter could not be suppressed:

(14″) we increased the compression and rarefaction in the crystal by increasing the charge because we wished to verify that increased mechanical stress in the crystal produces an increased amplitude of the sound wave.

Here it would not make sense to delete *we* and make *increasing the charge* the subject.

The next example is more difficult:

(15) Amalgamated tin and hydrochloric acid in alcohol at the reflux temperature removes one oxygen and produces desoxybenzoin, while amalgamated zinc and cold alcoholic hydrochloric acid eliminates both oxygens and gives the unsaturated hydrocarbon stilbene. Desoxybenzoin can be made also from phenylmagnesium bromide and benzyl cyanide or by the Friedel and Crafts reaction of phenylacetyl chloride with benzene (68–72% yield). (25325)

In the second sentence we infer a human agentive involved in the 'making' of desoxybenzoin – but how far does the same apply to the 'producing' of the same substance in the first sentence (note the *also* in the second sentence)? The first sentence contains four very similar clauses, of which the last – the one with *give* as main verb – could not be reformulated in such a way that *we* was subject and *amalgamated zinc and cold alcoholic hydrochloric acid* adjunct: for this reason we would probably not wish to posit a covert agentive for any of the four clauses – yet it is difficult to draw a sharp line between such constructions and (14), for example.

The following examples illustrate the range of patterns entered into by the verb *show*:

(16) We shall *show* that the lowest value of the eigenvalue $\mid \alpha \mid$, and therefore the highest values of H_{c2} and H_{c3} is found when $k_3 = 0$, as in the isotropic case (18189)

(17) The pressure curves obtained from (4) and (5) are *shown* in the figure. The pressure curves *shown* *show* that the ordered solution obtained from (5) touches the disordered solution (4) at the point [R]. (18059)

(18) A subsequent analysis [. . .] *showed* that the sublattice magnetizations could be accounted for very well without any need to postulate large intrasublattice interactions (17302)

(19) Grundon, Henbest and Scott obtained 65–81% of cholest-4-ene
(4), *shown* by infrared analysis to contain a small proportion (<
10%) of 5α-cholest-3-ene (5). (15070)

(20) Table 1 *shows* a comparison of the above dielectric constants with
previously reported values. (17134)

(21) Although his personality was well preserved and he had never had
psychiatric treatment, he *showed* many of the cardinal symptoms of
schizophrenia. (37148)

(16) is quite straightforward: the subject *we* is clearly an agentive; and
in (17) the two passive instances of *show* may reasonably be understood as having implicit human agentives. The third example of *show* in
(17) and those in (18) and (19) are less obvious; notice first of all that we
can say:

(18′) We showed by a subsequent analysis that. . .
(19′) By infrared analysis they showed the cholest-4-ene to contain. . .

We might then argue that *a subsequent analysis* and *by infrared analysis*
are instrumentals. We can distinguish two slightly different uses of *show*
in such cases: in one the agentive uses the analysis to demonstrate what
he already knew (cf. *we can show this to be true by means of the following
argument*), with *show* thus equivalent to 'make you/someone see'; in the
other use, the person doing the analysis may himself learn from it. Both
uses can be expressed, I think, in either of the forms *NP [agentive]
showed by analysis that* and *analysis showed that*. . . But in the second
sense we can also find

(18″) A subsequent analysis showed us that. . .

which is scarcely paraphrasable as the contextually rather unlikely *we
showed ourselves by a subsequent analysis that*. . . For this reason it does
not seem valid to posit an implicit agentive in (18″), and this in turn
casts doubt on the appropriateness of doing so in (18) and (19). Example
(20) could also be rephrased with an overt agentive as subject, but
table 1 would typically be governed in the adjunct position by the locative *in* rather than the instrumental *by (means of)*. We can see from (21)
that this kind of locative subject with *show* does not necessarily presuppose an agentive: there is certainly no covert agentive in this last

example, yet it could be replaced with *symptoms* as subject (pre-passive) and *he* as locative adjunct (*in him*).

This type of locative pre-passive subject was quite common in the corpus. With a number of verbs we may postulate the following paradigm:

(iii) *a* NP_1 V_{act} NP_2 in NP_3
    b NP_2 V_{pass} by NP_1 in NP_3
    c NP_2 V_{pass} in NP_3
    d NP_3 V_{act} NP_2
    e NP_2 V_{pass} by NP_3

where NP_1 is agentive, NP_2 objective and NP_3 locative. A near-minimal contrast between *c* and *d* is exemplified in:

(22) this article describes some of the results obtained, particularly on the flotation of galena with xanthates. (32422)
(23) The work described in this article is pointed in a different direction, however: (38500)

Verbs in the transitivity corpus displaying such contrasts are: *analyze, consider, describe, examine, illustrate, report* and *show* – and we might also include *assume* and *say* in view of such examples as:

(24) Maxwell's deduction of the law for the distribution of velocities is not very satisfactory, because it assumes that the three velocity components are independent. (28404)
(25) We take Newton's law of action and reaction to say, not simply that the action and reaction are equal, but also that they are *directed exactly oppositely along the same line* [*ital. sic*] (Newton may or may not actually have said this, but he tacitly assumed it), (27556)

With all these verbs (except for *show*, whose more complex array of patterns was discussed above) we may say that there is an agentive present in deep structure, whether or not it is expressed at later levels of structure. There is a further set of verbs allowing a locative to be mapped onto the pre-passive subject without there being any necessary implication of an underlying agentive, as in:

(26) We have now dealt with the physical chemistry of molecules containing one, two and three atoms, (26445)
(27) Denoting M/m, i.e. the number of molecules contained in 1 gram-molecule, by N_m, we have [...] [R], (28238)

Verbs of this type in the transitivity corpus were *bear, contain, dissolve, support,* and also – if we allow ourselves to extend the notion of locative somewhat – *include* and *involve:*

(28) its [*sc.* quinic acid's] conversion to quinone involves dehydration, decarboxylation and oxidation. (25354)
(29) The accompanying formulas indicate the steps involved in the application of the method to the preparation of an intermediate of use in the synthesis of certain alkaloids. (25232)

A further difference between these verbs and the *analyze* class is that these are inherently locative (in the relevant senses).

In some cases there may apparently be two locative elements, as in:

(30) It [*sc.* the nudibranch mollusc *Glaucus*] is very buoyant and apparently contains bubbles of gas within the body cavity; (32211)

But this can be accounted for in terms of 'narrowing': *within the body cavity* is a narrower specification of place than *the nudibranch mollusc Glaucus*: we can say that *within the body cavity of the nudibranch mollusc Glaucus* is a single locative constituent on the transitivity dimension of structure, which is split into two by the thematization of just a part of it.

Of the five forms given in the paradigm (iii) the last is scarcely possible with verbs of the *analyze* class: there were certainly no examples in the corpus. It is found, however, with some (but not all) of the inherent locative class; the following example contains a close juxtaposition of patterns (iii)*c* and *e*:

(31) the hull of the hydrofoil boat is *supported on* legs carrying foils or wings which provide lift in the same way that an aircraft's wings provide lift in the air. In contrast the hull of the hovercraft is *supported* above the surface *by* a bubble or cushion of air. (34318)

A further class of verbs take an element which bears some resemblance to an instrumental, but which nevertheless cannot be identified with this case. Typical of the class are *cover* and *fill*, which enter into a range of patterns illustrated by the following textual examples:

(32) The bulb is filled with hydrogen at an initial pressure of 86 cm. of mercury, density 13.6 gm. per c.c., (28054)
(33) The destruction of the old threads in the centre of the ball results in a cavity which may become filledwith water, gas, or mud. (21355)

(34) The chloroplast is band-like and often does not fill the entire cell,
(21049)

(35) This axis [...] bears much branched laterals that normally grow
out in tufts, the short cells composing the laterals being almost
wholly filled by one entire chloroplast containing a single pyrenoid.
(21012)

The paradigm is very similar to that given in (iii), except that *with*
replaces *in* (none of the *fill*-clauses contained an overt agentive). NP$_3$ –
the element governed by *with* in the analogue of (iii)*c* – I shall refer to
informally as a 'pseudo-instrumental': it cannot be equated with a
genuine instrumental since the two cases may combine, as in *he filled it
with acid with a pipette*. Nor does the pseudo-instrumental presuppose
an agentive: there is clearly no agentive understood in (33)–(35), though
one might argue for one in (32).

There are several verbs very like *fill* and *cover* except that the pseudo-
instrumental element is not so closely associated with the preposition
with: I have in mind such verbs as *surround, attach, join* and *relate* (the
last three have the added complication of being symmetric verbs).
Because the pseudo-instrumental may, but need not, combine with an
agentive there will often be difficulty in deciding whether there is a
covert agentive, especially in passives where *by* governs the pseudo-
instrumental:

(36) Studies were made on kidneys removed from dogs, placed in
polythene bags *surrounded by ice*, and then reimplanted in their
original donors. (31279)

(37) Each sclerite has the same shape as a palpal segment and *is surrounded by a flexible arthrodial membrane*. (13109)

(38) It is to be observed that the distance between the carbon atoms in
cyanogen, where *they are joined by a univalent bond*, is almost the
same as the inter-atomic distance in the diamond lattice.
(26533)

(39) Two vessels of equal cross-section, α, *are joined near their bases by
a horizontal narrow tube* of length *l* and internal radius *r*. (28014)

These verbs may be either dynamic or non-dynamic (cf. the discussion
of statal passives and ergatives above); if there is an overt or covert
agentive only the dynamic interpretation is possible, though the converse does not hold: the dynamic sense does not presuppose an agentive
(e.g. *the water quickly surrounded the mound he was standing on*). In (37)

and (38) there is certainly no deleted agentive, but in (36) we may assume that the ice must have been put around the bags by some human agency. If we treat (39) as having a covert agentive the passive must be taken as statal, so that the meaning would be roughly 'in the state resulting from somebody's joining them by means of a tube', but it is very questionable whether the original factor of human agency is really relevant to the interpretation of (39). The following example emphasizes the similarity of pseudo-instrumentals to instrumentals in that the governing complex preposition is *by means of*:

(40) The young plant is originally attached by means of a much reduced prostrate system together with rhizoids from one or two basal cells. (21006)

There is no agentive understood here and the clause is probably best treated as one of those passives where there is no subject at the pre-passive level.

In this section I have been considering various elements, deep structure cases, which at the pre-passive level occur sometimes as subject, sometimes as object: instrumentals, locatives and psudo-instrumentals. Similar contrasts are found with the purpose element associated with such verbs as *need* and *require*. The principal patterns are:

(iv) *a* NP_1 requires NP_2 Purpose
   b Purpose requires NP_2
   c NP_2 is required by NP_1 Purpose
   d NP_2 is required Purpose

(There is no possibility of the purpose element being governed by *by*.) Examples:

(41) The best solution, however, would be to choose a material of higher electron mobility, which would *require* a lower applied electric field for the electrons to reach the velocity of sound. (37562)

(42) To obtain a gain of 45 dB per centimetre *requires* careful selection of a suitable cadmium sulphide crystal; (37528)

(43) A minimum electron concentration is *required* to ensure an adequate coupling between the electron stream and the sound wave to be amplified. (37513)

Again, patterns (iv)*b* and *d* may or may not have a deleted agentive – compare:

(44) Nevertheless, under other conditions, quartz, silicates, fluorides and oxides of metals can be floated with equal success by use of fatty acids, traces of metallic salts being *needed* to activate the minerals if they do not themselves provide suitable cations. (32495)

(45) This [*sc.* a rigid body] means an object in which the forces between the atoms are so strong, and of such character, that the little forces that are *needed* to move it do not bend it. (27165)

In (44) there is an unspecified human agentive, the same as is understood in the *floated*-clause (note the agentive-presupposing instrumental *by use of fatty acids*); but in (45) it is simply *to move the object* that needs the forces.

This by no means exhausts the lists of elements having alternative functions at the pre-passive level; I conclude this section with a few more examples from the corpus of the same phenomenon, but without attempting to fit them into any general types. First there is the contrasting pair:

(46) *Work-up gave* a yellow oil (0.91 g.) whose infrared spectrum showed that 5β-cholest-3-ene, cholest-4-en-3β-ol, and cholest-4-en-3-one were the principal components. (15520)

(47) The product was oxidized with chromium trioxide in acetic acid at 50–55° for 20 hr. and *gave on work-up* a crude oil containing considerable ketonic material. (15364)

Finally, consider the unpaired examples:

(48) This is easily demonstrated by the apparatus shown in Fig. 18–4 where a weight M is kept from falling very fast because it has to turn the large weighted rod. (27612)

(49) In the simpler parts of the nervous system a motor response may be produced when impulses are set up in relatively few afferent fibres. (22474)

The *because*-clause of (48) could be replaced with little or no change of meaning by *by the fact that*...or *by its having to*..., and the *when*-clause in (49) differs little from *by the setting up of impulses*. The grammatical relevance of such replacements and similarities is demonstrated by the fact that it would be difficult to supply a pre-passive subject for *keep* and *produce* while maintaining everything else constant – the closest active counterparts of the quoted examples would thus have to have the subject position filled by such expressions as *the fact that it has to turn*..., *the setting up of impulses* and so on.

3.6.6 Verbs in the transitivity corpus. Table 3:4 shows the relative frequencies of active and passive occurrences of the verbs in the transitivity corpus. At this stage an attempt was made to distinguish between radically different meanings or uses of a given form: meanings with less than nine occurrences were discarded. A rough gloss in a footnote indicates either that the item in question occurs more than once in the table, with different meanings, or that some instances not covered by the gloss have been excluded from the table.

The table is divided into five sections, one each for the groups of verbs whose percentage of passive occurrences is 0, 1–25, 26–50, 51–75, 76–100. Within each group the arrangement is alphabetical.

The explanation for the columns in the table is as follows:

(*a*) Total number of occurrences of the verb.

(*b*) Total number of active occurrences.

(*c*) The number of actives with no overt object (except that for present purposes a 'zero' relative counts as an overt object).

(*d*) Actives whose mood subject is human.

(*e*) Actives with no overt mood subject (except that for these purposes subjects deleted by coordination reduction count as 'overt'). Thus the *study-* and *try-*clauses in (1) count for this column (and so would the *reproduce-*clause except that it is excluded by the minimum of nine occurrences limitation), but the *grow-*clause in (2) does not:

(1) there has been considerable interest in studying simple models of such a gas in order to try to reproduce the same behaviour analytically. (18004)

(2) In some species rhizoids develop at the base of the branches and grow downwards (21021)

(*f*) The number of actives containing an instrumental *by* + NP.

(*g*) The number of actives containing an instrumental *by* + *ing*-clause.

(*h*) Total number of passive occurrences.

(*i*) Percentages of passives.

(*j*) Passives containing *by* + human NP.

(*k*) Passives containing *by* + non-human NP in instrumental or causer function.

(*l*) Passives containing instrumental *by* + *ing*-clause.

(*m*) Passives where there is some implicit human agent(ive) understood (irrespective of whether there is or is not an overt instrumental). As I have argued in 3.6.4/5, there are many cases where it is difficult

TABLE 3: 4. *Verbs in the transitivity corpus*
(a) Percentage of passives: 76–100

| | Active | | | | | | Passive | | | | | |
| | Total | −O | Hum S | −S | by NP | by ing | Total | % | by Hum | by Non-Hum | by ing | Impl Hum |
Total (a)	(b)	(c)	(d)	(e)	(f)	(g)	(h)	(i)	(j)	(k)	(l)	(m)
arrange 10	2	—	2	1	—	—	8	80	—	—	—	2
associate 24	—	—	—	—	—	—	24	100	—	—	—	—
attach 16	—	—	—	—	—	—	16	100	—	3	—	1
attribute 9	1	—	1	—	—	—	8	89	—	—	—	8
compose[a] 15	2	—	—	1	—	—	13	87	—	—	—	—
connect 22	1	1	—	—	—	—	21	95	—	3	—	2+
convert 20	4	—	1	1	—	—	16	80	—	—	—	—
cover 11	2	—	—	—	—	—	9	82	—	2	—	0+
cut off 13	1	—	—	—	—	—	12	92	—	3	—	—
derive 17	—	—	—	—	—	—	17	100	—	1	—	7+
discover 11	2	—	2	1	—	—	9	82	2	1	—	7
distribute 10	—	—	—	—	—	—	10	100	—	—	—	0+
fill 9	2	—	—	—	—	—	7	78	—	1	—	0+
illustrate 16	2	—	1	1	—	—	14	88	—	2	1	11
know 62	13	1	13	3	—	—	49	79	—	—	—	49
need[b] 17	3	—	2	—	—	—	14	82	—	—	—	7+
regard 23	4	—	4	1	—	—	19	83	—	—	—	19
relate 21	4	—	4	3	—	—	17	81	—	—	—	1
store 11	2	—	—	—	—	—	9	82	—	1	—	6
Total 337	45	2	30	12	—	—	292	87	2	17	1	120+

[a] All the passive clauses contain an *of*-phrase, where *of* governs the pre-passive subject: compare *the short cells composing the laterals are almost wholly filled by one entire chloroplast* (21012) and *the thallus* [...] *possesses a main axis composed of large barrel-shaped cells* (21007).
[b] Excluding the *need* which takes an infinitival complement.

(b) Percentage of passives: 51–75

| | Active | | | | | | Passive | | | | | |
| | Total | −O | Hum S | −S | by NP | by ing | Total | % | by Hum | by Non-Hum | by ing | Impl Hum |
Total (a)	(b)	(c)	(d)	(e)	(f)	(g)	(h)	(i)	(j)	(k)	(l)	(m)
achieve 20	8	—	2	3	—	1	12	60	—	5	2	9
activate 11	5	—	—	2	—	—	6	55	—	4	—	—
add 31	14	3	8	3	—	—	17	55	—	—	—	17
analyze 9	4	—	3	2	1	—	5	56	—	1	—	5
apply[a] 30	9	—	9	6	—	—	21	70	—	—	1	19

TABLE 3: 4 (b) (*cont.*)

	Total (a)	Total (b)	-O (c)	Hum S (d)	-S (e)	by NP (f)	by ing (g)	Total (h)	% (i)	by Hum (j)	by Non-Hum (k)	by ing (l)	Impl Hum (m)
call[b]	38	18	—	18	—	—	—	20	53	—	—	—	20
carry out	11	4	—	2	—	—	—	7	64	2	—	1	5
collect	9	4	2	2	2	—	—	5	56	—	—	—	5
combine	9	4	2	2	2	1	—	5	56	—	—	—	5
conduct	12	4	—	2	2	—	—	8	67	—	—	1	7
deduce	10	3	—	3	2	—	—	7	70	—	—	—	7
describe[c]	45	17	—	12	4	—	—	28	62	12	—	1	16
detect	17	7	—	6	3	—	—	10	59	—	3	—	9+
determine[d]	28	9	—	8	7	—	1	19	68	1	3	1	18
determine[e]	11	5	—	—	2	—	—	6	55	—	6	—	—
discuss	23	8	—	8	4	—	—	15	65	2	—	—	13
dissolve	9	3	2	—	1	—	—	6	67	—	—	—	6
do[f]	13	6	—	—	1	—	—	7	54	—	2	—	—
emit	16	7	—	—	—	—	—	9	56	—	3	—	—
employ	9	3	—	3	1	—	—	6	67	2	1	—	3
establish	15	4	—	—	1	—	—	11	73	—	1	—	6
examine	26	10	—	9	4	—	—	16	62	—	2	—	16
expect	17	5	—	5	1	—	—	12	72	—	—	—	12
expose	14	5	—	1	3	—	—	9	64	—	—	—	5
find	170	85	—	81	21	—	—	85	50	1	2	1	84
form[g]	48	19	5	2	9	—	—	29	60	—	7	1	1+
identify	16	6	1	5	1	1	—	10	63	1	4	—	8+
introduce	15	7	—	4	4	—	—	8	53	1	1	—	4+
investigate	11	4	—	3	2	—	—	7	64	1	—	—	6
isolate	21	9	—	9	2	—	—	12	57	—	1	—	12
join	13	6	1	1	4	—	—	7	54	—	2	—	4+
make up	13	5	—	—	2	1	—	8	62	—	1	—	—
measure	41	20	—	11	8	1	2	21	51	—	3	2	20
mention	9	3	—	3	—	—	—	6	67	—	—	—	6
observe	61	17	—	17	2	—	—	44	72	1	—	—	43
obtain[h]	71	24	—	23	8	2	1	47	66	2	7	3	45
perform	19	9	—	1	1	—	—	10	53	1	—	1	9
place	12	5	—	3	—	—	—	7	58	—	—	—	7
prepare	20	5	—	5	5	—	—	15	75	—	9	1	15
push	18	6	1	1	3	—	—	12	66	—	1	—	—
record	21	8	—	8	2	—	—	13	62	1	1	—	11
reject	10	4	—	3	1	—	—	6	60	—	1	—	0+
remove	15	6	—	1	2	—	—	9	60	—	—	—	8
replace	21	10	—	7	5	5	—	11	52	—	11	—	0+
report	22	8	—	4	2	—	—	14	64	2	—	—	12
resolve	9	3	—	1	2	—	—	6	67	—	—	—	6
separate	14	5	3	—	—	—	—	9	64	—	6	—	2
solve	9	3	—	3	2	—	—	6	67	1	1	—	5

TABLE 3: 4 (b) (*cont*).

	Total (a)	Total (b)	−O (c)	Hum S (d)	−S (e)	by NP (f)	by ing (g)	Total (h)	% (i)	by Hum (j)	by Non-Hum (k)	by ing (l)	Impl Hum (m)
								Active → **Passive**					
support	17	7	—	—	1	—	—	10	59	—	9	—	—
test	9	3	—	3	2	—	—	6	67	—	1	—	6
treat	19	5	—	5	4	—	—	14	74	—	—	1	11
understand	19	7	—	7	5	—	—	12	63	—	—	2	12
use	126	60	—	49	45	—	—	66	52	4	1	—	60
Total	1302	525	20	363	201	12	5	777	56	35	100	19	600+

a 'administer, make use of'; excludes the 'be applicable' sense.
b 'name, refer to by name'.
c 'give description of'; excludes the use in *the molecule describes a distance*.
d 'ascertain'.   e 'fix', 'be the decisive factor in regard to'.
f Verbal prop (3.4), as in *do harm*, etc.   g In the dynamic sense (3.3).
h 'get'; excludes the intransitive *obtain*, 'be valid, apply'.

(c) Percentage of passives: 26–50

	Total (a)	Total (b)	−O (c)	Hum S (d)	−S (e)	by NP (f)	by ing (g)	Total (h)	% (i)	by Hum (j)	by Non-Hum (k)	by ing (l)	Impl Hum (m)
								Active → **Passive**					
accompany	14	8	—	—	3	—	—	6	43	—	6	—	—
account	18	13	13	4	5	—	—	5	28	—	4	—	1+
amplify	10	7	—	6	6	—	—	3	30	—	—	—	0+
assume[a]	27	16	—	15	9	—	—	11	40	—	—	—	11
believe	17	11	1	11	2	—	—	6	35	—	—	—	6
calculate	33	20	—	20	11	—	1	13	39	1	1	1	12
cause	44	31	—	—	6	—	—	13	20	—	12	—	—
compare	22	11	1	8	7	—	—	11	50	—	—	—	10
confirm	12	6	—	—	—	—	—	6	50	1	5	—	0+
consider[b]	47	34	—	33	14	—	—	13	28	—	—	—	13
cool	15	8	2	5	5	—	—	7	47	—	—	1	7
define	21	14	—	7	5	—	—	7	33	1	—	—	6
demonstrate	15	10	—	5	1	—	—	5	33	2	1	—	3
develop	51	37	26	5	—	—	—	14	27	—	2	—	3
distinguish	11	7	3	5	2	—	—	4	36	—	2	—	2+
divide	11	7	4	3	2	1	—	4	36	—	—	—	0+
evaluate	11	6	—	6	6	—	—	5	45	—	—	2	5
exert	12	6	—	—	2	—	—	6	50	1	4	—	—
explain	17	12	—	10	9	—	1	5	29	—	2	—	0+
extend	18	13	9	3	3	—	—	5	28	2	—	—	1
fish	9	6	3	4	3	—	—	3	33	—	—	—	3

TABLE 3: 4 (c) (*cont.*)

		Active						Passive				
Total (a)	Total (b)	−O (c)	Hum S (d)	−S (e)	by NP (f)	by ing (g)	Total (h)	% (i)	by Hum (j)	by Non-Hum (k)	by ing (l)	Impl Hum (m)
fit[c] 11	6	—	3	4	—	—	5	45	—	—	—	5
follow 38	26	15	2	2	—	—	12	32	—	11	—	—
give[d] 144	95	—	14	25	—	1	49	34	3	19	—	26
grow 39	28	25	—	4	1	—	11	28	1	1	—	10
heat 11	7	2	7	6	—	—	4	36	—	—	—	4
hold[e] 10	7	—	—	5	—	—	3	30	—	—	—	1
involve 27	17	—	—	5	—	—	10	37	—	—	—	—
keep[f] 17	10	—	6	9	—	—	7	41	—	—	—	7
leave 15	10	—	1	2	—	—	5	33	—	—	—	1
lose 15	11	—	4	2	—	—	4	27	—	1	—	—
maintain 18	12	—	3	4	1	1	6	33	—	1	1	4
make[g] 61	33	—	16	10	—	—	28	46	4	—	1	20
make[h] 25	13	—	10	4	—	—	12	48	—	6	3	12
neglect 11	6	—	6	5	—	—	5	45	—	—	—	5
note 22	16	—	16	8	—	—	6	27	1	—	—	5
offer 11	8	—	2	1	—	—	3	27	—	—	—	3
predict 10	6	—	2	2	—	—	4	40	—	3	—	1+
present 13	9	—	2	5	—	—	4	31	—	—	—	4
produce 99	58	—	2	10	—	—	41	41	—	18	—	3+
pull 11	8	2	1	2	—	—	3	27	—	—	—	—
reduce 37	19	5	6	7	—	1	18	49	—	2	1	9
refer[i] 17	10	10	5	—	—	—	7	41	—	—	—	7
reflect 10	5	—	—	—	—	—	5	50	—	—	—	—
require 33	17	—	2	1	—	—	16	48	—	—	—	1+
say 28	18	—	16	6	—	—	10	36	—	—	—	10
see 58	38	1	38	5	—	1	20	34	1	1	—	19
set up 16	9	—	1	4	—	—	7	44	—	1	—	1
show 157	115	—	32	8	—	—	42	27	1	3	—	38
study 31	23	—	22	9	—	—	8	26	5	—	1	3
surround 16	10	—	—	5	—	—	6	28	—	4	—	0+
take[j] 22	14	—	14	3	—	—	8	36	—	1	—	8
take[k] 11	6	—	6	1	—	—	5	45	—	—	—	5
take[l] 11	7	—	—	—	—	—	4	36	—	2	—	—
think 13	7	3	7	2	—	—	6	46	—	—	—	6
write 22	13	—	12	3	—	—	9	41	—	—	—	9
Total 1525	980	125	408	270	3	6	545	36	24	113	11	310+

[a] 'make the assumption' (mental activity); excludes the use in *the anemones can assume a sedentary existence.*

[b] Excluding the transitive intensive use (3.7).

[c] In the mathematical sense, e.g. *the parameters that were used to fit the curve.*

[d] Excluding its use as a verbal prop (3.4).

[e] Excluding its use as a verbal prop (3.4), as a transitive intensive (3.7) and in the 'hold good' sense.

[f] 'maintain'.
[g] Verbal prop (3.4).
[h] 'construct'.
[i] 'allude'.
[j] 'measure'.
[k] 'consider'.
[l] With a measure of time as object.

(d) Percentage of passives: 1–25

	Total (a)	Active						Passive					
		Total (b)	−O (c)	Hum S (d)	−S (e)	by NP (f)	by ing (g)	Total (h)	% (i)	by Hum (j)	by Non-Hum (k)	by ing (l)	Impl Hum (m)
affect	17	13	—	—	—	—	—	4	24	—	3	—	—
afford	17	13	—	—	1	1	—	4	24	—	3	—	—
allow	26	23	1	2	10	—	—	3	12	—	—	—	3
approach	11	9	3	1	1	—	—	2	18	1	—	—	1
bear[a]	15	12	—	—	1	—	—	3	20	—	—	—	—
carry	19	16	—	—	8	—	—	3	16	—	—	—	—
change	25	19	13	3	3	—	2	6	24	—	1	—	0+
choose	20	18	—	18	14	—	—	2	10	—	—	—	2
constitute	11	9	—	—	2	—	—	2	18	—	—	—	—
contain	86	80	—	—	25	—	—	6	7	—	—	—	—
decrease	9	7	5	—	1	—	—	2	22	—	—	—	0+
ensure	12	10	—	1	3	—	—	2	17	—	1	—	—
exhibit	9	8	—	—	—	—	—	1	11	—	1	—	—
form[b]	40	39	—	—	9	—	—	1	3	—	—	—	—
include	24	19	—	3	3	—	—	5	21	—	—	—	4
increase	41	34	23	5	7	—	—	7	17	—	—	—	5+
indicate	57	44	—	2	7	—	—	13	23	—	5	—	7
insert	13	12	11	1	3	—	—	1	8	—	—	—	—
make[c]	21	17	—	3	3	—	—	4	19	—	2	1	3
move	63	62	51	5	19	—	—	1	2	—	—	—	—
operate	12	10	9	1	4	—	1	2	17	—	—	—	1
pass	26	22	14	4	7	—	—	4	15	—	—	—	1
penetrate	12	10	3	—	—	—	—	2	17	—	2	—	—
point out	11	9	—	9	—	—	—	2	18	2	—	—	—
possess	31	30	—	2	3	—	—	1	3	—	1	—	—
prevent	18	16	—	5	11	—	—	2	11	—	—	1	2
provide	46	42	—	6	5	—	—	4	9	—	2	1	1+
put	11	9	—	8	2	—	—	2	18	—	—	—	2
reach	24	22	—	2	4	—	—	2	8	—	—	—	1
receive	11	9	—	—	5	—	—	2	18	—	1	—	—
represent	36	31	—	1	5	—	—	5	13	—	4	—	3
retain	14	12	—	3	1	—	—	2	14	—	1	—	—
rotate	16	15	13	—	2	—	—	1	6	—	—	—	—
start	15	12	10	4	4	—	—	3	20	—	—	—	2+
suggest	57	48	—	16	5	—	—	9	16	1	1	—	6
suppose	10	9	—	9	6	—	—	1	10	—	—	—	1
take[d]	31	27	—	6	2	—	—	4	15	—	—	—	4
turn[e]	11	10	8	—	1	—	—	1	9	—	—	—	1
vary	38	36	34	4	2	—	—	2	5	—	1	—	2
Total	966	843	198	124	189	1	3	123	13	4	29	3	52+

[a] 'carry'; excludes verbal prop (3.4) and 'give birth' sense.
[b] In the non-dynamic sense (3.3).   [c] 'render' – the transitive intensive construction (3.7).
[d] Verbal prop (3.4).   [e] 'revolve'.

(e) No passive occurrences

	Total (a)	Total (b)	−O (c)	Hum S (d)	−S (e)	by NP (f)	by ing (g)
acquire	9	9	—	2	2	I	—
act	32	32	32	—	7	—	I
agree	9	9	6	3	—	—	—
appear	72	72	72	—	2	—	—
apply[a]	13	13	13	—	—	—	—
arise	38	38	38	—	3	4	—
become	67	67	67	6	—	—	—
begin	16	16	14	3	I	—	—
come	19	19	19	4	7	—	—
consist	39	39	39	—	6	—	—
contribute	10	10	6	—	—	—	—
correspond	22	22	22	—	3	—	—
depend	39	39	39	—	—	—	—
differ	14	14	14	—	—	—	—
enable	9	9	—	—	3	—	—
enter	9	9	3	I	4	—	—
exist	19	19	19	—	2	—	—
fall	12	12	12	—	3	—	—
function	17	17	17	—	I	—	3
get[b]	12	12	—	10	I	—	I
give[c]	31	31	—	—	7	—	—
go	31	31	31	4	4	—	—
have	203	203	—	53	13	—	I
have[d]	26	26	26	12	2	—	—
help	22	22	—	—	4	—	—
hold[e]	10	10	10	—	—	—	—
imply	9	9	—	I	I	—	—
lead	36	36	26	3	6	—	—
lie	36	36	36	I	6	—	—
live	11	11	11	I	6	—	—
mean	13	13	—	—	—	—	—
occur	79	79	79	—	5	—	—
proceed	15	15	15	3	4	I	—
range	11	11	11	—	6	—	—
remain[f]	32	32	32	2	4	—	—
result	26	26	26	—	5	—	—
return	10	10	10	2	—	—	—
reveal	16	16	—	—	I	—	—
rise	10	10	10	—	—	—	—
seem	46	46	46	3	—	—	—
serve	13	13	—	—	—	—	—
suffer	14	14	10	10	2	—	—
survive	10	10	5	I	—	—	—
tend	9	9	9	—	—	—	—

TABLE 3: 4 (e) (*cont.*)

	Active						
				Hum		*by*	*by*
	Total	Total	−O	S	−S	NP	*ing*
	(*a*)	(*b*)	(*c*)	(*d*)	(*e*)	(*f*)	(*g*)
travel	16	16	16	1	5	—	—
try	11	11	—	9	6	—	—
undergo	18	18	—	2	4	—	—
work	17	17	16	9	8	—	—
yield	14	14	—	—	3	—	—
Total	1272	1272	857	146	147	6	6

a 'be applicable'.   b 'obtain, receive'.
c Verbal prop (3.4).
d 'must' – in this sense *have* takes infinitival subject complementation (4.2.2).
e 'be valid'.   f In the intensive use (3.7).

(f) Summary of active clauses

	Number of occurrences				Percentages			
			Hum				Hum	
	Total	−O	S	−S	Total	−O	S	−S
	(*b*)	(*c*)	(*d*)	(*e*)	(*b*)	(*c*)	(*d*)	(*e*)
Table (a)	45	2	30	12	100	4	67	27
Table (b)	525	20	363	201	100	4	69	38
Table (c)	980	125	408	270	100	13	42	28
Table (d)	843	198	124	189	100	23	15	22
Table (e)	1272	857	146	147	100	67	11	12
Total	3665	1202	1071	819	100	33	29	22

(g) Summary of passive clauses

	Number of occurrences				Percentages			
			by				*by*	
		by	Non-	Impl		*by*	Non-	Impl
	Total	Hum	Hum	Hum	Total	Hum	Hum	Hum
	(*h*)	(*j*)	(*k*)	(*m*)	(*h*)	(*j*)	(*k*)	(*m*)
Table (a)	292	2	17	120	100	1	6	41
Table (b)	777	35	100	600	100	5	13	77
Table (c)	545	24	113	310	100	4	21	57
Table (d)	123	4	29	52	100	3	24	42
Total	1737	65	259	1082	100	4	15	62

to decide whether there is a deleted human agentive; only the clear cases are counted in column (*m*), but a '+' indicates that there are also some borderline examples.

For the corpus as a whole the percentage of passive clauses was 26.3.

3.7 Attribution

There are a number of respects in which verbs and adjectives are syntactically alike, and it has been suggested in several recent works (e.g. G. Lakoff, 1966; Lyons, 1966, 1968; Fillmore, 1968*a*) that they should therefore be regarded as belonging to the same deep structure category, 'verb' or 'predicate'. What they have in common is that various classificatory dimensions apply equally to verbs and adjectives. The principal dimension mention in the literature is that contrasting stative and non-stative predicates, where only non-statives occur in imperatives and with progressive aspect, etc. (thus *know the answer, open the door, *be tall, be careful* – cf. G. Lakoff, 1966). Properties we have had occasion to deal with in the present study that apply to adjectives and verbs alike are:

(a) Both are classified according as they may or may not take an embedded complement clause as subject, object, etc., and if so, what the mood of the clause is. Thus *sleep* and *old* do not take clausal complements, *insist* and *probable* take declaratives but not interrogatives, *remember* and *certain* take declaratives or interrogatives (see 2.2.3 and 4.3).

(b) Verbs and adjectives may alike be inherently reciprocal or symmetric (see 3.2 and G. Lakoff & Peters, 1969). Thus the adjectives *different, equal, similar*, etc., display the same range of patterns as verbs like *differ, resemble, agree*, discussed earlier.

The same classificatory dimensions apply in fact to nouns (see 4.4 and Chomsky, forthcoming) – and indeed to certain idomatic Prep Phr expressions – compare:

(1) Investigators who have studied sebum are at a loss to imagine what useful purpose it may serve. (35514)

where *at a loss* is functioning as a 'two-place predicate'.

If verbs and adjectives belong to the same deep structure category, we shall expect the underlying phrase-markers of such sentences as *it emerged that he spoke Greek* and *it was true that he spoke Greek* to be essentially the same, differing only in the lexical item realizing the predicate, with the *be* of the second sentence thus introduced transformationally. This analysis has not been adopted in the present study, however, mainly because *be* is certainly not the only copulative verb – and there is also the point that *be* is certainly to be regarded as a deep structure verb in some of its uses (e.g. in identification constructions, 3.8, or in the progressive, 4.2.2). 'Attribute' has thus been recognized as a distinct element of structure, which may be realized by an Adj Phr, NP, Prep Phr or by an embedded statal passive (3.6.3).

The system of classification we used in textual analysis was based on the more detailed study by Halliday (1967*b*). On one dimension clauses are classified as attributive or non-attributive according to the presence or absence of an attribute element. Secondly, clauses are classified as intensive or extensive according as they are or are not inherently attributive. With inherently attributive verbs the attribute is obligatory, with extensive verbs (more precisely with those that allow an attribute at all) it is optional. The contrast between intensive and extensive attributive clauses may be seen in such a pair as *he grew angry* and *he grew tall*. The first is more or less equivalent to *he became angry*, whereas the second would be better paraphrased as 'he grew, and thereby/in the process became tall' or 'he became tall by dint of growing'. Thirdly, the normal transitive/intransitive classification depends on the presence or absence of an object; normally in a transitive clause it is the object, in an intransitive the subject, that is the 'attribuant', i.e. the element to which the attribute applies. Within transitive clauses the intensive/extensive contrast distinguishes, for example, *he made her angry* and *he painted the fence blue*. In the first there is no underlying verb–object relation between *make* and *her* (the clause does not assert that he made her) whereas in the second there is such a relation between *paint* and *the fence* (it *is* asserted that he painted the fence).

These three dimensions yield six classes of clause, exemplified as follows:

(i) *a* He grew angry [Intrans/Intens/Attrib]
    b He made her angry [Trans/Intens/Attrib]
    c He grew tall [Intrans/Extens/Attrib]
    d He painted the fence blue [Trans/Extens/Attrib]
    e He grew [Intrans/Extens/Non-attrib]
    f He painted the fence [Trans/Extens/Non-attrib]

Nothing more need be said here about non-attributive clauses; the other four classes will be considered in turn with examples from the transitivity corpus.

(a) *Intransitive intensive clauses.* The most common verb found in this construction was naturally *be*; the verbs in the transitivity corpus were:

| appear | 2 | look | 2 | prove | 6 | seem | 18 |
| become | 67 | make | | remain | 32 | turn | |

The morphology of the attributes was: Adj Phr (86), statal passive (25), NP (12), Prep Phr (6). Examples:

(2) exposure to bright light and low moisture may also cause an old thallus *to turn brick red.* (21612)
(3) The pelt of such an animal *makes a good fur piece* only if it is taken during the resting period, (35366)
(4) In very dry places the rhizoid may be abbreviated to such an extent that the plant *looks like a Chlorococcum.* (21605)
(5) the fact that it [*sc.* the couvade syndrome] often affects those who, except during the critical period of their wives' pregnancies, *remain in good physical and mental health* does not, as a general rule, allow a ready explanation in terms of mental disease. (37158)

With *appear, look, prove* and *seem* it is possible to insert *to be* before the attribute: we thus have an alternation between such pairs as:

(ii) *a* This much seemed to be clear
   b This much seemed clear

It is therefore natural to derive (ii)*b* from *a* by deletion of *to be.* (ii)*a* is itself analyzed as taking infinitival subject complementation (4.2.2), so that the remote subject of *seem* in both members of (ii) will be *for this much to be clear.* There are no similar grounds for postulating a covert *to be,* and thus an embedded clause as remote subject, with the other copulative verbs – *become, make, remain, turn.* Nor is there any paraphrase relation with these analogous to that holding between (ii)*b* and *it seemed that this much was clear,* which is an obvious instance of subject complementation.

The assignment of *make* to the class of intransitive intensive verbs is somewhat problematical: an important difference between it and the other verbs is that with *make* the attribute (if such it is) can normally only be an NP. (Jespersen, 1927: 369, notes *make merry, bold, free,* but adds that other adjectives are hardly possible.) There is admittedly an obvious difference between *she made a pretty dress* and *she made a good wife*, with only the former being passivizable and the latter being semantically similar to the clearly intensive *she became a good wife*. But if we treat examples like *the cushion made an effective barrier* as intensive, should we not also include verbs like *constitute, form,* and so on, in the same class? The line between object and attribute becomes quite hard to draw in such cases. Notice also that example (3) bears some resemblance to an activo-passive; is there a systematic relation between it and (3')?

(3') One can make a good fur piece of/from/out of the pelt of such an animal only if it is taken during the resting period.

(b) *Transitive intensive clauses.* The verbs in the transitivity corpus were:

call	38	keep	8	maintain	set	2
consider	2	leave	2	make	21	turn
hold						

(6) This subsection includes all structures outside the plasma membrane considered responsible for the rigidity of the microbial cell. (12108)

(7) Holding all other parameters constant, the resonant frequency 3920 cm^{-1} could be varied $\pm$ 100 cm^{-1} before a significant error was introduced into the parameters used to fit the curve. (17116)

(8) The initial reaction leaves the face it has traversed, at least notionally, covered with a nickel monolayer. (16155)

(9) The invention of the transistor made the job easier but did not disturb this established pattern. (37354)

(10) just as external force is the rate of change of a quantity *p*, which we call the total momentum of a collection of particles, so the external torque is the rate of change of a quantity *L* which we call the *angular momentum* [*ital. sic*] of the group of particles. (27435)

(8) contrasts with such an example as *John left the room angry*: in the latter it is the subject, *John*, that is attribuant, and the clause is moreover extensive, for John is said to have left the room, so that the attribution is secondary to the leaving; in (8) on the other hand it is the object that is attribuant and the clause is intensive, for there is no leaving process independent of the attribution.

With *consider* there is again alternation between forms with and without *to be*: *he considered it safe/it to be safe.* Similarly with *make*, *be* is optional: *they made it (be) an offence to drive with more than this much alcohol in the blood*, though often the form with overt *be* sounds somewhat unnatural (as in *?he made it be clear that he wanted to leave*) and it is doubtful whether such a pair as *he made them respectable* and *he made them be respectable* are exactly synonymous. If we postulate an underlying *be* with transitive intensive verbs we shall be treating them as two-place verbs in remote structure, with one of the places, the objective, filled by an intransitive intensive clause – this corresponds to Jespersen's notion of a 'nexus-object', except that he does not distinguish between intensive clauses, where such an analysis is appropriate, and extensive ones, like (i) *f*, where it isn't (since it fails to express in remote structure a direct relation between the main verb and the surface object).

The syntax of *call* is quite complex and difficult to handle. Confining ourselves to constructions where, at the pre-passive level, there are three places filled besides the verb, we find such examples as:

(iii) *a* John called her a cab
    b John called her stupid/a fool
    c John called her Mary
    d John called her names

Leaving aside the well-known facetious interpretation, *a* is quite straightforwardly a ditransitive construction, with *her* as recipient (3.5), the clause being equivalent to *he called a taxi for her*. *b* appears to be quite like constructions with *consider*: we might argue that there is object complementation with both verbs, deletion of *be* being optional with *consider*, obligatory with *call*. But let us look at the contexts in which *b* might (truthfully) be uttered. In the first place it could be used to report John's saying that she was a fool (in the second or third person 'you are/she is a fool'). Secondly to report John's addressing her as *(you) fool*. Thirdly, to report that he spoke of her as a fool – his actual words might have been *the fool has missed the train*, with *the fool* referring to 'her'. It is only in the first use that there is a close resemblance to *consider*, but the object complement analysis is probably valid for them all: there is in all of them an attribuant–attribute relation between *her* and *a fool*. (iii) *c* could mean that John christened her Mary or that he addressed her or referred to her as Mary. Here it is a good deal less clear that *Mary* is attribute – note that if there is a *be* understood here it is the extensive equative *be* rather than the intensive one (see 3.8). However, the use of the substitute forms *so*, as in (11), does lend support to the attribute analysis:

(11) *Urospora* is of interest because the zygote first produces a *Codiolum* stage (so called after the alga it resembles), which is considered to be diploid, (21439)

(iii) *d* is equivalent to *John insulted her* and there seems to be no relation of attribution or identity between *names* and *her*: the example would seem to belong to the non-contrastive object type of construction discussed in 3.4.

A few of the verbs listed above are 'ergatives' in the sense of 3.1: *keep, turn* and possibly *prove* (though with this last it is arguable whether the transitive and intransitive uses involve the same verb: compare *he proved her wrong/she proved wrong*). It would of course be inconsistent to say that there was a deleted *be* in the transitive but not in the intransitive. Thus if we say that *he kept her quiet* has *she + be + quiet* as an embedded complement, we must also recognize the same complement in *she kept quiet*. Notice moreover that since *keep quiet* is an acceptable imperative, there must be a direct relation between *she* and *keep* in remote structure. Thus both *he kept her quiet* and *she kept quiet* will be two-place constructions in remote structure, one place (agentive) filled by *he/she*, the other (objective) by the intensive clause *she be quiet*. *Turn* differs from *keep* in that, at least in the intransitive pattern, it is normally non-agentive: thus if *it turned red* has an underlying *be* it will be within a subject complement: *[it be red] turned*.

(c) *Intransitive extensive clauses.* The only clear cases in the corpus were two instances of *grow* with *long* and *coarse* as attribute:

(12) Another common misconception is the one that shaving causes the hair to grow increasingly coarse. (35411)

We also included the following example with *hold*:

(13) There has been much criticism of this law and there are exceptions to it, but it still *holds good* as an approximation (22391)

This is somewhat marginal inasmuch as *good* and one or two near-synonyms are the only adjectives that can occur here, and the meaning is scarcely changed if we omit the *good* – compare:

(14) This is true only for ideal gases, and so the laws will *hold* for real gases within varying degrees of closeness, which depend on the extent to which the gas approaches the state of a perfect gas. (28277)

(d) *Transitive extensive clauses.* Again the extensive attributive construction was very rare, the only verbs involved being *find* and *obtain*, as in:

(15) The plants are confined to well-aerated fresh water though they have also been *found growing* on fish living in stagnant water, (21088)

(16) Selected fractions were brominated and two dibromides were *obtained pure* by chromatography (15085)

Find is one of the verbs that can take an attribute in both intensive and extensive clauses – compare Halliday's (1967b: 77) *he found her attractive* (intensive, = 'considered her attractive') and *he found her unconscious* (extensive, since he found her – in a state of unconsciousness). (16) contrasts with (17), where the attribute is realized as a Prep Phr:

(17) attempts to obtain the other olefins in pure form by crystallization were unsuccessful. (15324)

3.8 The verb 'be'

Apart from its use as the passive auxiliary, as a modal (see 7.7), and as marker of progressive aspect, *be* occurs as main verb in three principal types of clause.

(a) Its most frequent use – accounting for about 70% of its occurrences in the corpus – is in intensive intransitive clauses, as discussed in 3.7 and exemplified in:

(1) Skin is a remarkable organ (35004)

(b) It occurs also in extensive intransitive clauses, as in:

(2) This axis is primarily for support, (21012)
(3) Vegetative reproduction is by means of fragmentation, (21063)
(4) In the disk forms the carpogonia originate as terminal bodies on the outside of the disk, but as the neighbouring cells continue growth they eventually become surrounded and appear *to be* in the older part of the thallus. (21263)

Here *for support, by means of fragmentation* and *in the older part of the thallus* function not as attributes but as purpose, means and place adjuncts respectively; *be* is here replaceable by such clearly extensive verbs as *exist, take place, be situated* and so. The *there*-transformation (discussed in 8.2) often applies to clauses of this class, especially when there is no adjunct present:

(5) There are three main groups of photosynthetic bacteria. (12309)

  (c) Finally it occurs in extensive transitive clauses, as in:

(6) It is true that the stubble after shaving feels rough, but the reason *is* simply that the soft, tapered ends of the hairs have been cut off; (35416)

(7) The equation of these points *is* the usual $p = 2nt\tilde{v}$, where p *is* the order number, n *is* the index of refraction, t *is* the sample thickness, and $\tilde{v}$ *is* the wave number. (17078)

(8) Man's most obvious sign of age *is* the dry, wrinkled, flaccid skin that marks his late years. (35178)

I shall refer to the *be* of this type of construction as the equative *be*. Following Halliday (1967*b, c*) the post-verbal NP here is taken, not as an attribute as in (1), but as an object (Halliday's 'extensive complement'). The difference in meaning between types (a) and (c) is fairly clear: the intensive construction characterizes the subject, whereas the extensive one involves the identification of one term by another. However, *pace* Fries (1952: 179) the difference is not 'signalled' by the contrast between Adj Phr's and NP's – the former are normally attributes, but the latter occur freely as attributes or objects. Unless we allow for this we shall be forced to treat *he's a fool* as identifying even though it is equivalent (in its most likely interpretation) to *he's foolish;* and we shall not be able to account for the ambiguity in Halliday's *the result was a failure*, which may mean either that the result was unsuccessful (with intensive *be*) or that a failure resulted (equative *be*).

The grammatical justification for assigning different descriptions to the intensive and equative constructions depends on the 'reversibility' of the latter; (8) for example contrasts with:

(8′) The dry, wrinkled, flaccid skin that marks his late years is man's most obvious sign of age.

In determining the nature of this reversibility it is useful to begin by distinguishing three different effects that may result from reversing the sequence of two items in a construction.

Firstly, the reversal may not affect the grammatical structure at all, so that both expressions contain the same structural elements in the same order, the difference residing only in the selection of lexical realizations of the two elements. This is the case with such a pair as *John saw Mary* and *Mary saw John*. These differ in cognitive meaning of course, but this is because *see* is a non-symmetric verb: if we had chosen *resemble* instead the expressions would have been cognitively equivalent.

Secondly the two expressions may contain the same structural elements (realized by the same items) but in a reversed order. This type of reversal is exemplified in *the second experiment was more successful* versus *more successful was the second experiment*. In both of these *more successful* is attribute and *the second experiment* is mood subject (notice that the interrogative version of the second clause is not **was more successful the second experiment?*). This type of reversal is effected transformationally: in this particular example two interrelated rules are involved (see the discussion of marked theme in 8.1).

Thirdly, the reversal may change the value or function of one or both of the items permuted, as with *the three normal children* versus *the normal three children*. These are probably best regarded as containing different *normal*'s: the first is an ordinary adjectival attribute, contrasting for example with *abnormal* (compare *the three children who are normal*), whereas the second is a kind of post-determiner commuting with only a small set of items such as *same, very, former*, but hardly *abnormal*, etc. As with the first type of reversal, there is here no transformational relationship between the two expressions.

Which of these three types provides the model for the contrast between (8) and (8′)? The third seems clearly inappropriate – there is no reason to suggest that the two clauses contain different elements in remote structure. If we apply the interrogative inversion test, it is clear that both (8) and (8′) have the leftmost NP as mood subject, for their respective interrogative counterparts are *is man's most obvious sign of age the dry, wrinkled, flaccid skin...?* and *is the dry, wrinkled, flaccid skin... man's most obvious sign of age?* Are we to say therefore that (8) and (8′) differ in the grammatically trivial way that *John saw Mary* and *Mary saw John* differ? Since (8) and (8′) are cognitively synonymous this would mean treating equative *be* as a symmetric verb, like *resemble*. Although this seems *prima facie* a reasonable conclusion, we can see that it is inadequate by considering such a pair as:

(i) *a* What I told him was what she wanted to know
   b What she wanted to know was what I told him

Each of these is ambiguous (as written), and in the same way: meaning either that she wanted to know what I told him or that I told him what she wanted to know. This ambiguity can be accounted for by postulating two different functions or cases, an 'identifier' and an 'identified', such that in the first interpretation *what I told him* is the identifier, *what she wanted to know* the identified, and vice versa for the second interpretation. (We would expect identifier and identified to be special instances of more general deep structure cases, but I shall not consider this question here.) In the original examples (8) and (8'), the only semantically plausible interpretation has, in both cases, *man's most obvious sign of age* as identified and *the dry, wrinkled, flaccid skin that marks his late years* as identifier, though from a purely formal point of view they are presumably both ambiguous according to the direction of the identification, just like (i). The important point to establish here then is that in the equative *be* construction we must recognize distinct identifier and identified functions, and allow either to be mapped onto the subject; equative *be* is not symmetric.[1]

If we leave aside cases of intonationally marked contrast and constructions in which the identifier is a pronoun, we shall expect the nuclear stress to fall on the identifier:

(ii) *a* What I can't stand is his **arrogance**
     b His **arrogance** is what I can't stand

Since the normal position for the nuclear stress in clauses in general is (other things being equal) at the end of the clause, we may regard the identified-as-subject type, (8) and (ii)*a*, as basic, the identifier-as-subject type, (8') and (ii)*b*, as 'marked' – and as deriving from the basic construction by a transformational rule permuting identified and identifier. The basic construction was very much the more frequent in the corpus, as can be seen from table 3: 5 below.

In textual analysis the identified-as-subject construction was normally quite easy to recognize: the difficulty was rather in distinguishing be-

---

[1] In his much more detailed analysis of the equative construction Halliday introduces another pair of functions, 'value' and 'variable', such that the identified may coincide with value and identifier with variable – an 'encoding' construction, or vice versa, a 'decoding' one. Notice that there are two types of answer to such a question as *who's the Senior Proctor*, exemplified in *the Senior Proctor is Dr Smith* and *the Senior Proctor is the Officer responsible for student discipline*. Both of these have *the Senior Proctor* as identified (and subject); Halliday's analysis enables us to distinguish them as encoding and decoding respectively.

tween the marked equative and the intensive constructions, especially when the second NP was definite. Thus in:

(9) The only epineustonic animals are five species of *Halobates,* which are the only insects which live in the open ocean. (32225)

the first clause is clearly a basic equative: it identifies the epineustonic animals; the second clause (*which are...*) is probably intensive, characterizing *Halobates,* but could also be interpreted as identifying the insects which live in the open ocean (compare (10) below). Of the following examples, (10)–(12) were analyzed as marked equative, (13)–(15) as intensive:

(10) In addition to these main components, there are two minor categories. One of these is the Epineuston – animals that live entirely on the surface; the various insect species of *Halobates are* the sole representatives of these. (32152)

(11) To assist in deciding which of the two models, if either, is applicable to hydrogen peroxide, we observe that the dipole moment of the 'easy-chair' model must be zero, whereas that of the 'bath' model [...] is $2\mu_2 \sin \theta$ [...]. The observed dipole moment of hydrogen peroxide [...] lies nearer to that of water [...] than to zero; and one is tempted to conclude that the planar bath model *is* the correct one. (26578)

(12) C. L. Perkins in 1919 had the idea of using as collectors, in place of complex oils, sparingly soluble organic compounds that would be relatively easily oxidizable. Diphenyl thiourea *was* one of several substances specifically cited. (32512)

(13) It [*sc.* the skin] plays a major role in regulating blood pressure and directing the flow of blood. It embodies the sense of touch. It *is* the principal organ of sexual attraction. (35016)

(14) Hydrogen *is* the most abundant element in the universe. It is the major constituent of most stars and the regions between them. (34001)

(15) Since absorption of electrons increases with increasing atomic number, a good heat conductor with a low atomic number is needed. This *is* one reason for choosing aluminium for the conducting layers. (17468)

In deciding on the most plausible interpretation we considered what was the most likely location of the nuclear stress: in (10)–(12) it would probably fall within the subject, and this reading fits the interpretation as a marked equative, the subject being the identifier of the post-verbal element. (11), for instance, is telling us which the correct model is, not which the planar bath model is, and similarly for (10) and (12). In (13)–(15), on the other hand, it makes more sense in the context to put the stress at the end of the clause. In (13) the *be*-clause is one of a series of clauses listing the properties and characteristics of skin: skin is the point of departure for the information of the clause. (14) is the beginning of an article; we would not expect any discourse to begin with a marked equative construction since the identifier will normally precede the identified only if the latter is 'known' or informationally 'given', as in (11). If (15) had been preceded by, say, *why is aluminium used?* the *be* would be interpreted as equative, but in fact it is only in the *be*-clause that the choice of aluminium is mentioned.

Although there is a tendency for the NP's in equative *be* constructions to be definite, indefinites are also found; thus the identified in (16) and the identifier in (17) are indefinite:

(16) Another feature that changes abruptly at this same minimum point is the location on the solar disk of sunspots and other disturbances. (38079)
(17) The principal constituent of such radiation is protons. (38202)

In the textual examples the identified element was normally realized by an NP or by an independent relative clause (see 5.4.1). There was a wider range of realizations for the identifier; compare:

(18) One significant fact that emerges from the available data *is* that not one of the recorded lunar brightness phenomena occurred simultaneously with a solar flare or any other major solar disturbance. (38388)
(19) The usual habitat of this order *is* on the gills of fishes where they often live isolated. (23312)
(20) The usual method of obtaining TO(Γ), the transverse optical mode at the zone center, *is* by analyzing measurements of the residual ray reflectivity band with the aid of classical dispersion theory. (17014)

(Again it is the reversibility of the elements that distinguishes (19) from an intransitive clause containing a locative adjunct.) There are certain types of expression which can occur as identifier but never as identified

– for example embedded declarative clauses with *that* as complement-izer, as in (18), embedded interrogative clauses, as in *whether anybody else was involved is the question we've got to solve,* and various other types of subordinate clause, such as that introduced by *because* in *why he was late was because he was feeling ill.* Interrogative *wh* can likewise only be associated with the identifier.

In the following example the elements are reversible only if the pronoun *that* or something equivalent is inserted before the *of*: I have assumed that some such form has been deleted.

(21) One unexpected discovery of hydrogen-line radio-astronomy was of the high-speed motions in the centre of our Galaxy. (34228)

There may occasionally be ambiguity between transitive and intransitive uses of extensive *be*. This occurs for example in *the rumour was that he was resigning.* In the transitive (i.e. equative) reading *that he was resigning* is identifier, *the rumour* identified (with *the* therefore anaphoric) – it answers the question *what was the rumour?* In the intransitive reading, the meaning is 'there was a rumour that he was resigning': in remote structure the subject is *the rumour that he was resigning,* the *that*-clause being shifted subsequently to the right of *be* by extraposition (4.2.1). In this latter reading *be* is syntactically like such a verb as *spread,* which could readily be substituted for it. We find this same type of ambiguity in the textual example:

(22) It may *be* that the greater conformational flexibility of ring A has some influence (15157)

The *it* might here be anaphoric, referring to some such NP as *the cause*: in this case *be* would be equative with *it* as identified; in the context there is in fact no such anaphoric reference – in remote structure the *that*-clause is dominated by the subject NP.

The corpus contains one *be*-clause that does not fit readily into any of the types we have been considering:

(23) to remain in a favourable state is in general to be inactive (22580)

The infinitival clauses cannot be reversed here (without changing the cognitive meaning), and an infinitival clause is not the sort of expression that occurs as identified: the *be* is therefore not equative. Yet I know of no clear cases where an infinitival clause functions as attribute, which casts some doubt on the analysis of (23) as an intensive clause. I would be inclined to take it as a two-place non-equative extensive; syntactically *be* is here somewhat like *involve, entail,* etc., some of the very small class of verbs which can take both subject and object complementation (in the sense of 4.1), as in *finding it involved emptying the whole drawer.*

Table 3: 5 shows the number of overt occurrences in the corpus as a whole of the three main types of construction involving *be* that have been discussed in this section (example (23) is not included). The high frequency of the equative type is doubtless a distinctive feature of scientific English.

TABLE 3: 5. *The verb 'be'*

	Number	Percentage
Intensive	2758	70
Extensive intransitive		
+*there*	243 ⎫ 380	10
−*there*	137 ⎭	
Extensive transitive		
(i.e. equative)		
unmarked	733 ⎫ 788	20
marked	50 ⎭	
Total	2926	100

4 Complementation

4.1 The principal types of embedded clause

It is customary to distinguish two kinds of sentence recursion, conjoining and embedding: these correlate quite closely with the traditional notions of sentence coordination and subordination respectively. Conjoining and embedding can be distinguished in terms of underlying phrase-markers: conjoined sentences are immediately dominated by an S node, embedded sentences by some node other than S (typically NP). If we leave aside various types of 'adverbial clause' (in particular those introduced by such subordinating conjunctions as *although*, *because, if, since, so that* and so on) the remaining embedding processes are of three main types: relativization, comparison and complementation.

The distinctive characteristic of relative clauses is that they contain an element, normally an NP, that is identical with an 'antecedent' in the matrix sentence: there is no such identity constraint in complementation. A familiar contrast is that between such a pair as *the report that he received* and *the report that he received bribes*, the first involving relativization, the second complementation. In the first *that* is a relative pronoun with *report* as antecedent: there is a verb–object relation between *receive* and *that*. In the second example the object of *receive* is *bribes*, with *that* being simply a subordinating conjunction or 'complementizer'. The same contrast can be found with non-finite clauses: compare *an opportunity to take* and *an opportunity to take it*. The latter exemplifies complementation, whereas the former contains a reduced relative clause, with *opportunity* the antecedent of the underlying object of *take*.

Comparative clauses are also distinguished from complements in that their structure is constrained in such a way that it resembles the structure of the matrix sentence in certain respects. Rather than attempt here to make this precise, I shall merely illustrate the structural resemblance between constituent clause and matrix with a very simple example. In *John was more subtle than Bill* the underlying structures of the two sentences are roughly *John was Degree subtle* and *Bill was Degree subtle*, where *Degree* represents a class of modifiers, including *very, rather, surprisingly* and so on. In the matrix *Degree* is realized by *more*+the comparative sentence; in the latter the Degree element is not apparent in surface structure, but must be assumed to be present in deep structure.

Relatives and comparatives will be discussed in the following two chapters: here I shall examine certain aspects of complementation. Complement sentences have been characterized so far in purely negative terms: they are embedded sentences (other than the 'adverbial' clauses that I am leaving out of account) which do not exhibit the structural constraints that identify relative and comparative clauses. This is not to say that there are no constraints on the structure of complement clauses: with *try* for example the subjects of the constituent and matrix clauses must be identical (*I tried to escape*, but not **I tried for John to escape*), but these are particular constraints, related to particular lexical items and do not serve to characterize any general type of construction.

Complementation embraces a wide range of patterns, not all of which can be dealt with in the present study. Most attention will be paid to what I shall call subject and object complementation, i.e. constructions where the complement is dominated in remote structure by the subject or object NP. Strictly, both the following types involve subject complementation: *the news that he was leaving surprised me, that he was leaving surprised me*. For presentation purposes, however, it will be convenient to leave aside until 4.4 all cases where the NP, whatever its function in the clause, has a substantival head: the terms subject and object complementation as used in 4.2 and 4.3 will thus refer exclusively to cases where the NP dominating the complement has *it* as its underlying head. Complementation has been discussed in great detail by Rosenbaum (1967*b*) and this chapter owes a great detail to his analysis (cf. also my review of his work, Huddleston, 1969*b*).

4.2 Some general problems of subject and object complementation

4.2.1 Extraposition. Consider first the contrast exemplified in each of the following pairs:

(i) *a* It surprised me that he came
   b That he came surprised me

(ii) *a* It's an offence to drop litter
   b To drop litter is an offence

Rosenbaum has argued that the members of each pair derive from a common remote structure; in the case of (i) this is essentially that shown as PM(i).

PM(i)

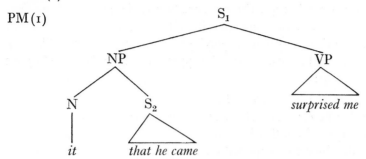

(This is certainly not the deepest structure, but it is deep enough for present purposes.) In the derivation of (i) *a* the complement clause S_2 is shifted to the right of the matrix VP by a transformation that Rosenbaum calls 'extraposition': *it* is then left as the subject of the matrix clause S_1. In (i) *b* extraposition is not applied, but a later transformation then obligatorily deletes the *it*.

It is important to distinguish extraposition from a later and quite different transformation which may nevertheless have a similar effect on the surface structure. It applies, for example, in the derivation of:

(i) *c* It surprised me, that he came

This is distinct phonologically from (i) *a*; in terms of the phonological analysis put forward by Halliday (1963, 1964, etc.), (i) *c* is characterized by tone 13, so that typical intonation patterns for (i) *a* and *c* might be respectively:

(i) *a′*   1 ∧ it surprised me that he **came**
    c′   13 ∧ it **surprised** me that he **came**

(i.e. a fall on *came* in *a′*, and in *c′* a fall on *prised* and a slight rise on *came*). Halliday refers to the pattern of *c* as 'substitution', but to avoid this perhaps confusingly general term I shall speak of it as 'pronoun apposition'.

Extraposition and pronoun apposition differ in two respects. Firstly, extraposition moves some designated element to the rightmost position in the matrix clause, whereas pronoun apposition involves copying the element in that position and then pronominalizing the original. Or, since 'shifting' or permutation probably is to be described formally in terms of the elementary operations of adjunction and deletion, we should perhaps say that extraposition copies an element into final position and then deletes the original, while pronoun apposition copies an element into final position and then pronominalizes the original.

Secondly, what is copied in extraposition is the post-head modifier of an NP, whereas in pronoun apposition it is the whole NP (the rule may in fact be slightly more general, applying to certain types of Prep Phr too). Derivations for (i) *a* and *c* will thus be approximately as shown in (iii) and (iv) respectively:

(iii) *a* it that he came surprised me
   b it that he came surprised me that he came
   c it surprised me that he came
(iv) *a* it that he came surprised me
   b that he came surprised me
   c that he came surprised me that he came
   d it surprised me that he came

The copying adjunction part of extraposition transforms (iii) *a* into *b*, the deletion part then yields *c* (= (i) *a*). In (iv) extraposition does not apply, so that the *it* is deleted producing (iv) *b*; the copying adjunction part of pronoun apposition transforms this into *c*, which then becomes *d* by pronominalization. (It is not clear that the transformations as described above yield the correct surface structures. Given the phonological difference between (i) *a* and *c* we would expect them to have somewhat different structures, and in fact the rules do yield different structures since *that he came* is not dominated by NP in (i) *a* although it is in *c* – but is this the correct analysis of the difference?)

There are two pieces of evidence to support this account of the difference between extraposition and pronoun apposition. In the first place, consider the data from other constructions than subject complementation. Examples of pronoun apposition are:

(v) *a* He's gone, John
   b They've finished, the Smiths

(With the meanings *John has gone, the Smiths have finished;* (v) *b* is to be distinguished from *they've finished the Smiths* with *the Smiths* as object, from *they've finished, John* with *John* as vocative, and finally from *they've finished, the bastards,* whose analysis is obscure in the intended interpretation – it could also be taken as the pronoun apposition form of *the bastards have finished*). The adjunction rule in (v) seems clearly to involve the whole subject NP: there is, for example, no reason to derive (v) *a* from *he, John, has gone.* Examples of extraposition on the other hand are:

(vi) *a* The rumour spread that he was resigning
     b More people came than we had expected
     c The man didn't arrive who(m) we'd all come to hear
     d The man came, from the Gas Board

(This last is to be read//1 ˄ the/**man**/came//1 ˄ from the/**Gas**/Board// – in spite of the comma, it is not read with the tone 13 of pronoun apposition; the example is from Halliday, 1961: 255, who constrasts it with//1 ˄ the/man/came from the/**Gas**/Board//, where there is no extraposition, *from the Gas Board* here being simply a locative, not part of the original subject.) In the first of these it is a complement clause that is extraposed, in the second a comparative, in the third an ordinary relative and in the last a reduced relative: in all of them it is the post-head part of the subject NP that is copied to the right of the VP.

The derivations suggested in (iii) and (iv) enable us to generalize this account of the difference between extraposition and pronoun apposition from examples like (v) and (vi) to the subject complement constructions of (i).

The second piece of supporting evidence is that with certain verbs, such as *seem*, extraposition is obligatory, so that we have (vii)*a* but not *b* – or *c*:

(vii) *a* It seemed that he was ill
     b *That he was ill seemed
     c *It seemed, that he was ill

This example shows that extraposition must precede pronoun apposition: in this way the two ungrammatical sentences can be handled with a single statement, namely that extraposition is obligatory; if the order was reversed we should need one rule to exclude (vii)*c* (namely that pronoun apposition couldn't apply with *seem*) and a second to exclude *b* (namely that extraposition must apply).

Extraposition of the subject post-modifier can in principle apply whatever the structure of the VP. Intensive examples like (viii) thus follow the pattern illustrated above:

(viii) *a* It's odd that he came so late
     b It's been nice seeing you
     c It's important for John to get there on time

With non-finite complement clauses the mood subject may be deleted if indefinite or if identical with an NP governed by *for* (or occasionally *to*) in the matrix; since we find both *for John to get there on time is important* and *to get there on time is important for John* it follows that (viii)*c* is structurally ambiguous according as *for John* belongs in the matrix clause as adjunct or in the constituent clause as complementizer + subject.[1] Prepositional and complementizer *for* co-occur in *it was important for John for Mary to win*.

In all the examples considered so far extraposition has shifted the subject post-modifier to the right of the VP; Rosenbaum has shown, however, that the rule should be generalized to cover objects as well, though the underlying *it* of object complementation is rarely retained in surface structure (but cf. *I doubt it that he'll come*). Additional support for this generalization comes from the fact that extraposed relatives and comparatives may originate in object NP's:

(ix) *a* He gave all the money to charity that he had won in this way

   b He gave more money to charity than he could really afford

We may note in passing that pronoun apposition likewise generalizes to object NP's, as in *I've seen them, the Smiths*.

In the above discussion I have been following Rosenbaum in taking the *it* of *it surprised me that he came* to be introduced in the base rather than transformationally. There are, however, grounds for doubting whether this is correct: I shall return to this question in 4.4, continuing in the meantime to assume an underlying *it*. (If *it* is not present at the stage when extraposition applies we can nevertheless still differentiate in general terms between the latter and pronoun apposition by saying that extraposition copies a Sentence constituent and pronoun apposition an NP constituent.)

4.2.2 The split-subject construction. If we assume that at some stage in their derivation all non-finite complement clauses contain a mood subject, then three main construction types may be distinguished according to the subsequent derivational history of the subject. In the simplest – but rarest – case the mood subject is retained in that function, as in:

(i) *a* He was waiting for John to come

   b I'd prefer for you to see her

---

[1] In the latter case I see no reason for regarding *for John* as a constituent. R. Lakoff (1968: 27) treats it as an NP, but her argument – that in many languages the complementizer corresponding to *for* appears as a case inflexion – seems quite irrelevant to the surface structure of English.

Secondly, it may be deleted, as in:

(ii) I expected to leave
(iii) He persuaded John to come

(Here I shall be concerned only with deletions that are conditional on the mood subject NP being identical with some NP in the matrix clause – subject in (ii), object in (iii) – as distinct from the deletion of indefinites as in *it's an offence to drop litter*.) Thirdly it may be shifted or 'raised' from the constituent clause into the matrix, as in:

(iv) The weather seemed to improve
(v) He expected John to come

Superficially (ii) resembles (iv) and (iii) resembles (v), and it will be convenient to discuss subject-raising by contrasting these two pairs in turn: in this section I shall deal with the difference between (iv) and (ii), in the next with that between (v) and (iii).

To analyze (ii) in terms of subject-deletion and (iv) in terms of subject-raising is to claim that in the former there are two deep structure occurrences of *I*, whereas in the latter *the weather* belongs in remote structure not to the matrix, but to the constituent clause. Remote structures for (ii) and (iv) will thus be essentially as shown in PM's (1) and (2) respectively (no attempt being made to represent tense).

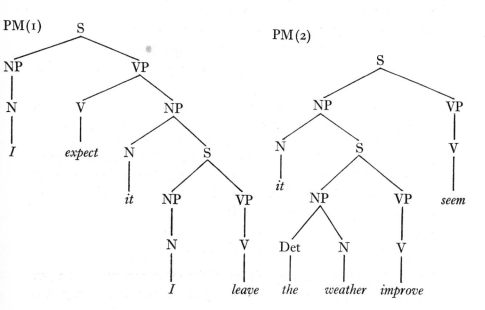

The main justification for attributing such radically different underlying structures to these examples is that it enables us to account for the different effect of a change of voice in the constituent sentence. Compare for example:

(vi) *a* John expects to escort Mary
      b Mary expects to be escorted by John
(vii) *a* This argument seemed to convince Bill
      b Bill seemed to be convinced by this argument

Clearly (vi) *a* does not bear the same relation to (vi) *b* as (vii) *a* does to (vii) *b*. The latter pair may be regarded as paraphrases: they differ only in terms of thematic organization, and the relation between them is the same as that between *this argument convinced Bill* and *Bill was convinced by this argument*. This means that there cannot be a subject–verb relation between *this argument* and *seem* in the remote structure of (vii) *a*; if there were there would have to be the same relation holding between *Bill* and *seem* in (vii) *b* – but then there would be no way of explaining how sentences with different underlying subjects came to be paraphrases. (The argument here holds whether we describe the deep grammar in subject/object terms or in terms of labelled cases.)

As further support for the claim that the remote structure subject of (vii) *a* and *b* is *it* + [*this argument convinced Bill*] we may note that they have equivalents with finite complements:

(viii) *a* It seemed that this argument convinced Bill
       b It seemed that Bill was convinced by this argument

where it is clear that there is no direct relation in remote structure between *seem* and *this argument*/*Bill*. But this is not the crucial argument, for there are a number of verbs (such as *tend*) which enter into the pattern of (vii) without having finite equivalents in the pattern of (viii).

Unlike the sentences in (vii), those in (vi) are not paraphrases, and the difference between them is due to the fact that here there *is* a remote structure subject–verb relation between *John* and *expect* in the one and *Mary* and *expect* in the other. This explains why the second member of the following pair is ungrammatical:

(ix) *a* John expected to receive a prompt reply
     b *A prompt reply expected to be received by John

The deviance is due to the violation of the selectional rule that *expect* takes a human (or at least animate) subject in remote structure. Just as the examples of (vii) were matched with sentences containing finite complements, so too are those of (vi):

(x) *a* John expects that he will escort Mary
   b Mary expects that she will be escorted by John

Here too the finite versions reflect more directly the underlying relations and support the analysis of *expect* as a two-place verb in (vi). As before, however, this is not the main argument for the analysis, for there are verbs (such as *want*) which take non-finite but not finite object complementation.

I expected to leave (= (ii)) and *the weather seemed to improve* (= (iv)) are thus distinguished structurally as follows. In remote structure (ii) has *I* as subject and *it* + [*I to leave*] as object as in PM(1); the second occurrences of *I* and *it* are transformationally deleted so that the infinitive immediately follows the matrix verb. Example (iv) is intransitive in remote structure, with *the weather to improve* as complement to the subject pronoun *it*, as in PM(2); the complement is shifted to the right of the VP *seemed* and the constituent clause subject *the weather* is then shifted into the matrix to take over the matrix subject function. (Rosenbaum achieves this by a 'pronoun replacement rule': the subject from the complement clause replaces the *it* that, in his account, is introduced in the base.)

I have illustrated subject-raising with the extensive verb *seem*; the transformation applies also with a few adjectives, i.e. with intensive matrix clauses, as in:

(xi) John is likely to succeed

This is derived in the same manner as (iv): the remote subject is *it* + [*John to succeed*], the complement is extraposed and then *John* is raised into the matrix as subject by the pronoun replacement rule· Again the justification lies in the paraphrase relation between such pairs as *John is likely to know the answer* and *the answer is likely to be known by John*. Some of the adjectives concerned take finite subject complements: *it is likely/certain that John will come;* others take only the infinitival construction with subject-raising, e.g. *bound, liable, apt* (in the sense of 'liable' not 'appropriate': *we're liable to forget her, she's liable to be forgotten, *it's liable that we will forget her*). As further support for the proposed analysis, it may be added that the infinitival clause cannot be omitted; thus whereas (xi) is grammatical, **John is likely* is not (except perhaps by ellipsis), and though *John is apt/bound/liable* are grammatical they involve different senses of the adjectives from those where there is subject complementation. And just as it was necessary to distinguish *the weather seemed to improve* from *I expected to leave* and so on, so must we distinguish (xi) from such constructions as:

(xii) *a* John is (too) young to beat Paul
    b John was clever to beat Paul
    c John was keen to beat Paul

In all of these there are two occurrences of *John* in remote structure, one belonging in the matrix as subject/attribuant of the adjective, the other belonging in the constituent clause as subject of *beat*: it is clear that they are not paraphrasable as *Paul is (too) young to be beaten by John*, etc. In (xii)*a* the constituent clause is (part of the) modifier to *young*, and it is plausible to suggest that it is governed by the preposition *for* in remote structure (cf. *he's (too) young for that*). No fully satisfactory analysis has yet been found for (xii)*b*; semantically the non-finite clause functions as some kind of reason element – but a reason that relates to the assertive modality of the main clause rather than to the action (if any) expressed therein, the type of reason element in, for example *John has left because his room is locked* ('that's how I know') as distinct from *John has left because he was unwell* ('that's why he left'). The type of reason element I have in mind here is incompatible with imperatives, and there is of course, no imperative counterpart to (xii)*b*. Many examples of this pattern have variants of the form *it was clever of John to beat Paul*. In (xii)*c* we shall probably again say that there is an underlying preposition (*on* in this case, but *for* for many adjectives, such as *eager*, *willing*, etc.), but the Prep Phr clearly is not a degree type modifier as in (xii)*a*; if we treat adjectives as belonging to the same underlying category as verbs, it will probably be best to say that *keen* in (xii)*c* is a two-place 'predicate' expressing a relation between *John* and *on* + [*John to beat Paul*]. The constituent clause of this type has been included under object complementation for the purposes of this chapter. A more detailed discussion of the adjective and infinitive construction can be found in Lees (1960), Bolinger (1961) and Rosenbaum (1967*b*: ch. 6).

The analysis proposed for the sentences with *seem, be likely*, etc., is essentially the same as that put forward by Jespersen (1940: 319). His formula for *she happened to notice it* is $\frac{1}{2}$S V $\frac{1}{2}$S(IO): 'the notional subject is *she*...*to notice it*'. The only items Jespersen lists as taking such a split subject (assuming an active matrix clause) are *happen, chance, be sure*, *be certain, be likely,* with *seem* and *prove* as 'doubtful cases'; in another work (1969: 47) he also includes *fail.* Rosenbaum (1967*b*: 121) has *appear, chance, happen, seem* and *turn out* as the verbs taking infinitival subject complementation. But in addition to the items in Jespersen's and Rosenbaum's lists (including *prove,* which is, I think, a clear case) there are several other quite common verbs belonging in the same class (cf. Huddleston, 1969*b*: 19): *begin, start, continue, cease, come* (*it came to be regarded as*), *get* (*it soon got to be understood that...*), *tend* and *have* (in the obligation sense: *we have to finish it/it has to be finished*). There are also a few verbs entering into the same pattern except that the complement clause has an *ing*-form verb rather than an infinitive: *begin, start, continue, keep, finish* and *stop,* as in *the weather began improving* and so on.

With some of these verbs, however, we must distinguish two uses. There is a difference, for example, between:

(xiii) *a* The storm began to frighten her
    b John began to open the door

The split-subject analysis is valid and necessary for the first of these, which can be paraphrased as *she began to be frightened by the storm,* but there is no equivalent paraphrase for *b,* where there does seem to be a direct relation in remote structure between *John* and *begin.* The first example asserts that a certain event or state of affairs began, namely the storm's frightening her; the second asserts similarly that an event, John's opening the door, began, but we also understand John to be the initiator of the action. The difference between the examples in (xiii) thus matches that between such a pair as *the meeting began* and *John began the meeting* with *begin* an 'ergative' verb in the sense of 3.1. Thus (xiii)*a* will be analyzed as a one-place construction with a split subject, whereas the analysis of *b* will depend on how we handle ergatives: in one approach we will say that there is an abstract causative with *John* as subject and *it* + [*John to open the door*] + *began* as object, in the second approach considered in 3.1 we will treat (xiii)*b* as a two-place construction with *John* as pre-passive subject and *John to open the door* as object, with a derivation like that of *I expected to leave* (= (ii) above).

The other 'aspectual' verbs listed above behave like *begin* in entering into both constructions: *start, continue, keep, cease, finish, stop.* So too, I think, do *appear* and *seem,* except that these occur in the two-place construction only if they have contrastive stress:

(xiv) Couldn't you just *appear* to go out?

On the other hand none of the adjectives – *likely, certain,* etc. – are found in the two-place pattern (except with quite different meanings). Notice in this connection that none of them can occur as the predicate of an imperative: in imperatives (more precisely the 'you' type of 2.4) there is a direct relation between *you* and the predicate. The ungrammaticality of **be likely to see her* is thus due to the fact that *likely* cannot take *you* as remote subject.[1]

I have argued elsewhere (Huddleston, 1969c – cf. also McCawley, 1969b) that the modal and tense/aspect auxiliaries should be analyzed as 'full' verbs in remote structure – in spite of surface structure differences, we need to show the underlying syntactic similarity between such pairs as *he may have left/he seems to have left, she was writing/she continued writing, I must finish by six/I have to finish by six,* and so on. I shall not repeat in detail the arguments for this analysis: suffice it here to say that the main justification is that auxiliaries are like full verbs as far as 'deep' tense selection is concerned. Thus just as *John intended coming tomorrow* involves two tense selections, a future associated with *come* (more precisely with the clause whose verb is *come*) and a past associated with *intend,* so in *John was coming tomorrow* we have future (*come*) in past (*be*). Similarly, *John may have done it yesterday* has a past tense associated with *do* and a present with *may*: compare *it is possible that John did it yesterday.* Perfective *have* is more difficult: it may be either a full verb in deep structure, as in *I have seen him* ('past in present') or else be simply the realization of a past tense selection: in *John may have done it yesterday* there are two, not three, tense selections.

If this analysis is accepted, then most of the auxiliaries also belong to the class of verbs entering into the split-subject construction, for they satisfy the criterion of 'voice-neutrality', (to coin a short name for the property discussed above) witness the paraphrase relations between (xv)*a* and *b* and between (xvi)*a* and *b*:

(xv) *a* John is painting the wall
       b The wall is being painted by John
(xvi) *a* John may have seen the accident
       b The accident may have been seen by John

---

[1] *Be sure to see her* is not a counterexample, since it is not the imperative version of *you are sure to see her.* It seems in fact to have no close independent declarative counterpart: this can be seen from the ungrammaticality of **I told him to be sure to telephone as soon as he got home and he was* (sc. sure to do so), compared with *I told him to be early and he was. Be sure to* also has a variant with *and* instead of *to.*

Some of the modals are like *begin* in entering into both one- and two-place constructions, but the meaning of the modal is different in the two cases: as observed in 3.1, for example, *will* takes the one-place split-subject construction in the predictive sense, but when it expresses volition it takes the two-place construction with complement subject deletion.

There is one final type of split-subject construction which merits attention – the type exemplified in:

(xvii) This problem needs studying more carefully

The exact derivation of this is far from clear; the two points about which we can be most certain are, firstly, that *this problem* is understood as the pre-passive object of *study*, and secondly, that it is understood as the mood subject of the same verb. Evidence for the latter point is that the pre-passive subject may be expressed in the form of a *by*-phrase adjunct (*this needs reconsidering by the executive committee*), and also that it is not possible to insert a mood subject NP between *needs* and *studying* in (xvii). It seems then that the constituent clause has undergone a transformation whose effect on the pre-passive subject and object is the same as that of the passive rule. I would suggest in fact that the constituent clause undergoes passivization in the ordinary way, and then a later rule simply substitutes *ing* for *to* + the passive auxiliary. In this way we account for the fact that the construction of (xvii) is possible only with passivizable verbs in the constituent clause (**a degree needs having by all applicants*). This replacement rule is of course quite *ad hoc*, but so would be an '*ing*-passivization' rule, distinct from the ordinary passive. Moreover, such an '*ing*-passivization' rule could not apply on the transformational cycle with the constituent sentence as domain, since it is dependent upon the matrix containing *need, require, want* or *deserve* as main verb – yet surely a rule permuting the pre-passive subject and object of a sentence would be expected to apply on the cycle with that sentence as domain.

Of the four verbs just listed, the first three, I think, are one-place verbs, the last two-place. Thus (xvii) involves subject-raising, whereas *John deserves punishing* has the constituent clause subject deleted (under identity with *John*). (xvii) is thus systematically related to:

(xviii) *a* This problem needs to be studied more carefully
        b We need to study this problem more carefully

Notice also the near-paraphrase with the obviously one-place construction *it is necessary that this problem be studied more carefully*. The one-place nature of *require* is more problematical: I cannot find a convincing pair to match (xviii); it is of course a two-place verb in *I require that it be finished to-day*, but this is a different sense from that found in *the patient requires nursing/to be nursed*.

4.2.3 Further remarks on subject-raising.

Let us now return to the contrast between the other pair of superficially similar non-finite constructions introduced at the beginning of the previous section, namely:

(i) *a* He persuaded John to come
    b He expected John to come

I claimed that in (i)*a* the mood subject of the complement clause is deleted, there being thus two deep structure occurrences of *John*, whereas in *b* there is only one *John*: it belongs originally in the complement sentence but is raised by the pronoun replacement transformation to become direct object of the matrix verb *expect*. Remote structures for the two examples are thus approximately as shown in PM's (1) and (2) respectively:

PM(1)   PM(2)

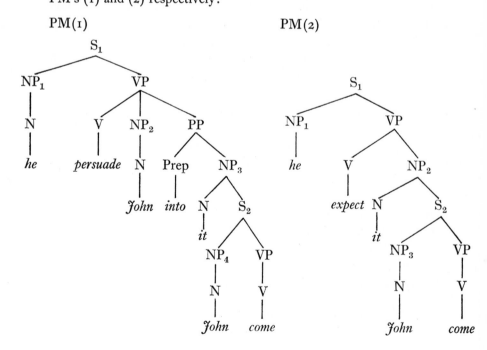

The *into* in PM(1) is postulated on the basis of such sentences as *he persuaded John into it*, etc.; there is a general rule deleting prepositions when they immediately precede an infinitival complement. NP_4 in PM(1) is deleted under identity with NP_2 and *it* is subsequently deleted too. In (i)*b* subject-raising takes place in the way described in the previous section; thus PM(2) undergoes extraposition taking S_2 from under the domination of NP_2, and NP_3 then replaces NP_2 (i.e. *it*), yielding the derived structure PM(3).

PM(3)

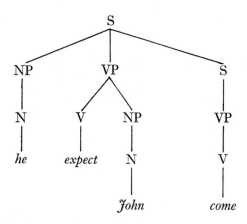

There are two sides to the justification of this analysis; we must first defend the remote structures PM(1) and PM(2), and then the surface structure PM(3). We may begin by reviewing a number of important syntactic differences between *persuade* and *expect*.

(a) As Chomsky (1965: 22–4) has observed, a change from active to passive voice in the complement clause has a different effect according as the verb is *persuade* or *expect*. Chomsky's well-known example is:

(ii) *a* I persuaded a specialist to examine John
    b I persuaded John to be examined by a specialist
(iii) *a* I expected a specialist to examine John
    b I expected John to be examined by a specialist

This type of contrast played a prominent part in the justification of the analyses proposed in the previous section, and we can draw the same kind of conclusion from it here. Since (iii)*a* and *b* are paraphrases there cannot be any remote structure verb–object relation between *expect* and the NP which follows it in surface structure, *a specialist* and *John* respectively. Conversely, we can explain the fact that (ii)*a* and *b* are not paraphrases by postulating two underlying occurrences of *a specialist* in the former and *John* in the latter – one as (pre-passive) object of *persuade*, the other as (mood) subject of *examine*.

(b) With *persuade* but not *expect* there are selectional restrictions between the matrix verb and the following NP (cf. Rosenbaum, 1967*a*: 112). Thus:

(iv) *a*   I persuaded John to build a house
      b *I persuaded a house to be built by John
 (v) *a*   I expected John to build a house
      b   I expected a house to be built by John

The deviance of (iv)*b* is due to the fact that *persuade* requires an animate object; we could not explain the difference in well-formedness between (iv)*a* and *b* unless we took *John* and *a house* as their respective remote structure direct objects.

(c) A third criterion – one which proved useful and easy to apply in textual analysis – is the possibility of having unstressed *there* as surface object:

 (vi) *a*   He persuaded a friend of his to be at the station
       b *He persuaded there to be a friend of his at the station
(vii) *a*   He expected a friend of his to be at the station
       b   He expected there to be a friend of his at the station

This *there* is introduced transformationally: the rule converts such structures as *a man was at the door* into *there was a man at the door*. *There* is always introduced in the mood subject position, never in the object position: *I saw a man at the door/*I saw there a man at the door* (the latter is probably acceptable with stressed locative *there* but this is irrelevant to the argument). This explains the difference in grammaticality between (vi)*b* and (vii)*b*. In (vi) there are two deep structure occurrences of *a friend of his:* the first has object function and thus cannot be replaced by *there* (nor can it be deleted). In (vii)*b* the *there*-transformation applies before the rule shifting the complement clause subject into the matrix object position (this is why the subject-raising rule applies to the *mood* subject). The rules must apply in this order since the *there*-rule applies in the transformational cycle whose domain is the complement sentence, while the subject-raising rule applies in the cycle with the matrix sentence as domain.

(d) Chomsky also points out the different patterns of alternation with finite clause complements:

(viii) *a* I persuaded John to give the lecture
     b I persuaded John that he should give the lecture
(ix) *a* I expected John to give the lecture
     b I expected that John would give the lecture

The paraphrase relation between the second pair does lend some support to the analysis expressed in PM (2): it is clear that in (ix)*b* there is no verb–object relation between *expect* and *John*. (viii)*b* has relatively little relevance to the point at issue, however, since it is certainly not a paraphrase of (viii)*a*: to persuade someone to do something is to get him to agree to do it, whereas to persuade him that he should do something is only to get him to accept that he ought to, which is quite a different thing. A better example illustrating the three-place nature of *persuade* would be *I persuaded John into giving the lecture*. However, since there are some verbs which allow only one type of complement, this point (d) is of less general relevance than the others considered.

Just as a few verbs, such as *begin, continue* and so on, enter into both the one-place and the two-place constructions contrasted in the previous section, so we can find verbs which enter into both the two-place and three-place constructions contrasted here by means of the *expect* and *persuade* examples. Consider, for example, the following sentences containing *order*:

(x) *a* I order you to return the money
  b ?I order the money to be returned by you
  c I ordered the photographs to be destroyed
  d I ordered that the photographs be destroyed

I interpret (x)*a* as a three-place construction with a direct relation in deep structure between *I* and *you*: I give the order to you. *Order* is thus here patterning like *persuade*, and this explains the deviance (if such it is) of *b*. The third example is obviously different: I did not give my order to the photographs – the sentence is equivalent to *d*, and in neither of them is there more than one deep structure occurrence of *the photographs*. In these last two examples, therefore, *order* is patterning like *expect*. Although it is not easy to determine the grammaticality of certain examples, the syntax of *order* (in the relevant sense: I am not concerned here with *he ordered a taxi/a bottle of Beaujolais*, etc.) seems to be more or less as follows: There are three inherent roles associated with the verb – the giver of the order, the recipient of the order and the content of the order; the first must be a human NP, the second animate (and normally human too), the third *it* + a complement clause. When *order* is used as a performative, as in (x) *a* and *b*, the giver and recipient are respectively first and second person. The recipient may optionally be left unexpressed. If it is not expressed the complement clause may be finite, as in *d*, or infinitival as in *c*; in the latter case the subject-raising rule applies, shifting the complement clause subject into the matrix object position. If the recipient is expressed the complement can only be infinitival (I take *I order you that*...to be ungrammatical) and its mood subject must be identical with the recipient, and consequently deleted.

As a second example consider the syntax of *allow* on the basis of such sentences as:

(xi) *a* He wouldn't allow there to be any dancing
    b He wouldn't allow his coat to be sent to the cleaners
    c He wouldn't allow John to go with them

The first two of these present no problems: they are clearly two-place constructions to which the subject-raising rule has applied. But it seems possible to interpret the third in two ways, paraphrasable as:

(xii) *a* He wouldn't give John permission to go with them
    b He wouldn't give permission for John to go with them

In the first, but not the second, reading there is a remote structure verb–object relation between *allow* and *John*; we might take *John* in this reading as an indirect object, so that the pattern would be like that of *he allowed John another turn*. I think we are justified in treating (xi) *c* as a genuine syntactic ambiguity; this makes *allow* syntactically similar to *order* (except that *allow that*...is scarcely possible in the permission sense of *allow*), which is a very plausible conclusion.

Even *expect* itself may enter into a three-place construction as in:

(xiii) *a* I expect it of you that you will support your mother

(a clear example of extraposed object complementation). It may be then that we should treat the first of the following as structurally ambiguous in the same way as (xi) *c*:

(xiii) *b* I expect you to support your mother
    c I expect the weather to improve

The second of these is clearly a two-place construction with the characteristics discussed earlier in this section. We can perhaps distinguish between two senses of *expect*: in (xiii)*c* it means roughly 'regard as likely', whereas *a* means something like 'I regard it as your duty to support your mother'. This 'duty' sense is the contextually more likely interpretation of (xiii)*b* and in this interpretation we will postulate two occurrences of *you* in deep structure – but we must allow for an interpretation of *b* in which it differs only lexically from *c*.

To summarize this part of the discussion I would say that there is plentiful and compelling syntactic evidence to support the proposed remote structure difference between a three-place construction such as underlies *I persuaded John to come*, with two occurrences of *John*, and a two-place construction such as underlies *I expect the weather to improve*, with just one occurrence of *the weather*. The distinction is for the most part clear-cut, but there are a few cases where it becomes somewhat blurred owing to the fact that a few verbs (*order, allow, permit, expect* and doubtless some others) enter into both types of construction. This leads to a good deal of formal structural ambiguity though the corresponding semantic ambiguity may be fairly slight. But this blurring of the distinction in no way undermines the validity of the analyses differentiating the two constructions.

It remains now to justify PM(3) as the derived structure of *he expected John to come* (in the 'regard as likely' sense). One aspect of PM(3) in fact strikes me as rather questionable, namely the claim that the infinitive is not part of the matrix VP. But there are strong reasons for treating *John* as the direct object of *expect* at the pre-passive level of structure:

(a) If the NP in question is identical to the matrix subject NP it is reflexivized, as in *he expected himself to get the job*. In general reflexivization does not take place when the second NP is dominated by an S node that does not also dominate the first NP (cf. Chomsky, 1965: 145–6):

(xiv) *a* *He expected that himself would get the job
    b *He expected that they would give himself the job

(b) It may become the mood subject of the matrix under passivization: *He expected John to come* ~ *John was expected to come*. (The latter is thus a further type of split-subject construction.)

(c) Pronouns are in the accusative, not nominative, case: *I expected him/*he to come*.

(d) Intuitively the NP plus the complement clause VP does not form a single constituent in surface structure. Less impressionistically, we may note that *John to come* does not behave as a single constituent in respect of any transformation, as far as I'm aware. Compare:

(xv) *a* *John to come was expected
    b *John to come I expected
    c *What I expected was John to come.[1]

(e) Finally there is the point about 'gapping' made by R. Lakoff (1968: 37), who observes that only the first of the following pair is grammatical:

(xvi) *a* I believe that John is rich, and Bill that Arthur is poor
    b *I believe John to be rich, and Bill, Harry to be poor

The rule of verb-gapping 'deletes the main verb in the right-hand member of two conjoined sentences, under identity with the verb in the left-hand sentence. But if in the superficial structure of the right-hand sentence there are three constituents, verb-gapping cannot take place.' Lakoff thus treats the ungrammaticality of (xvi)*b* as due to a violation of the same rule as excludes *I gave John a nickel and Bill, Harry a dime.*

There is thus strong syntactic evidence supporting the subject-raising rule. One thing it does not account for is the deviance of (xvii)*a* (in contrast to the well-formedness of *b*):

(xvii) *a* *I expected John quite confidently to give the lecture
     b I persuaded John quite easily to give the lecture

where the adverbs modify the matrix verbs, not *give*. But there is a good deal of idiolectal variation and uncertainty in assessing the acceptability of sentences containing adverbs in such positions, and we should probably not attach too much weight to the evidence of (xvii) in the present connection.

To clarify the textual description in 4.3 let us here briefly summarize the principal non-finite constructions considered in this and the preceding sections:

(a) One-place construction, complement subject retained in constituent clause:

(xviii) It's usual for John to do it

(b) One-place construction, complement subject raised into matrix (yielding 'split-subject'):

---

[1] With *ing*-constructions however, this is not so clear, for we find sentences like *all I could hear was Leo mowing the lawn* (where *mowing the lawn* is not a reduced relative).

(xix) *a* John seemed to like it
    b The weather began to improve/improving
    c She was working
    d He may be dead
    e I have seen her
    f He is likely to win

(c) Two-place construction, complement subject retained in constituent clause:

(xx) *a* Peter preferred for John to come
    b I dislike John's being so punctual[1]

(d) Two-place construction, complement subject deleted under identity with matrix subject:

(xxi) *a* I expect to leave
    b I won't answer
    c I enjoy going to the cinema

(e) Two-place construction, complement subject raised into matrix, as object:

(xxii) *a* I expected it to rain
    b I hate him being so late

(f) Three-place construction, complement subject deleted under identity with matrix object:

(xxiii) I persuaded him to go

Some, indeed probably all, of the 'transitive intensive' clauses of 3.7 are to be regarded as special cases of pattern (e). Thus in *she considers John too ambitious*, *John* is subject in remote structure of the adjectival predicate *too ambitious* and is consequently raised into matrix object position. The constituent clause verb *be* is also deleted, which has the effect of raising the attribute into the matrix too.

4.2.4 Object-raising. Lees (1960: 217) draws attention to the relationship between such sentences as:

(i) To convince the man is hard (for us)
(ii) The man is hard (for us) to convince

---

[1] Again I am not certain that the *to* and *ing* types are entirely parallel. In terms of surface structure is not *John's being so punctual* a possessive determiner plus head construction rather than subject plus predicate?

and suggests that the latter be derived from (the structure underlying) the former. In terms of the rules proposed by Rosenbaum this can be achieved by a process of object-raising, analogous to the subject-raising of 4.2.2. The remote structure for (i) and (ii) would be roughly *it + [for us to convince the man] + is hard*; if extraposition does not apply, *it*-deletion yields (i). If extraposition is applied an optional object-raising rule replaces the *it* by the constituent clause object, which thereby becomes subject of the matrix. The object concerned may be the object of the verb or of a preposition, as in *John is easy to get on with, he's easy to be intimidated by*. Unlike subject-raising, object-raising appears to be always optional.

Just as we distinguished between superficially similar constructions involving subjectless complement clauses, some having had the subject raised into the matrix, others having had it deleted under some identity condition, so must we distinguish (ii) from the superficially similar examples:

(iii) *a* John's (too) young to send to school
      b The cake is ready to eat

In (iii)*a* the complement clause (governed by underlying *for*) is a degree modifier to *young* – or, if *too* is present, is part of the degree modifier. There are two occurrences of *John* in remote structure, one as subject of *be young*, the other as object of *send*: the second occurrence is simply deleted. The same applies to *b*, except that here *for + it +* the complement is not a degree modifier. These examples of object-deletion thus parallel the subject-deletion of *John is (too) young to beat Paul* and *John was keen to beat Paul* respectively (= (xii)*a* and *c* of 4.2.2 – there is no object-deletion equivalent to the third type of subject-deletion discussed there, exemplified in *John was clever to beat Paul*). However, the evidence for distinguishing between one and two underlying occurrences of the relevant NP is stronger in the subject type of 4.2.2 than in the object type under consideration here, where there is nothing analogous to the 'voice-neutrality' test. The criterion for distinguishing (ii) from (iii) is that the former, but not the latter, has a variant like (i), which clearly involves subject complementation. Intuitively one feels more satisfied with the object-raising analysis in those cases where the infinitive cannot be deleted (or replaced by a Prep Phr) except in ellipsis or with a change in the meaning of the adjective: it does not seem to be the case for example that the relation between *the cake is ready to eat/ice*, etc., and *the cake is ready* is the same as that between *John is hard to convince/please*, etc., and *John is hard* (excluding cases of ellipsis, as in *Peter is easy to convince but John is hard*). But with some adjectives deletion is possible:

(iv) *a* To solve this problem is simple
 b This problem is simple to solve
 c This problem is simple
(v) *a* To buy such a watch is expensive
 b Such a watch is expensive to buy
 c Such a watch is expensive

Are we justified in saying that there is a direct subject–'predicate' relation between *this problem* and *simple* in the remote structure of (iv)*c* but not of *b*, and similarly, *mutatis mutandis*, in (v)? (One might almost be inclined to regard (v)*a* as a back-formation from *b*.)

The only verb I'm aware of that allows object-raising is *take* with a time expression typically filling the object position. The following paradigm seems to be unique to this item:

(vi) *a* It took an hour for John to read the letter
 b The letter took an hour for John to read
 c It took John an hour to read the letter
 d The letter took John an hour to read
 e It took an hour to read the letter
 f The letter took an hour to read
 g John took an hour to read the letter

John in *c* and *d* can hardly be regarded as raised from the constituent clause: this would require a wholly new type of subject-raising rule. I would treat *take* as a three-place verb, with one of the cases – the one that is mapped onto the indirect object *John* in *c* and *d* – optionally omissible. Then in *c* and *d* the constituent clause subject is deleted under identity with this indirect object, whereas in *e* and *f* it is deleted under the indefiniteness condition. *Take* is unlike other items in allowing either object-raising, as in *b*, *d* and *f*, or subject-raising as in *g*.

There is apparently also just one item allowing object-raising from an *ing*-clause, namely *worth*. Compare:

(vii) *a* His new book is worth reading
 b It's worth reading his new book

Worth belongs to the class of two-place predicates, differing from most other adjectives in that no preposition is required before the second NP:

the stamp is worth £5. If the object NP is unexpressed extraposition is obligatory:

(viii) *a* Reading his new book wasn't worth the effort/while
     b *Reading his new book wasn't worth

Worth differs from other items allowing object-raising in that the rule can apparently apply only if the complement clause subject is deleted under the indefiniteness condition – compare (vii)*a* with:

(ix) *His new book is worth your reading

4.2.5 Infinitival and participial complements. In surface structure there are four distinct non-finite verb forms found in complement clauses:

  (a) The *to*-form or 'full infinitive':

 (i) *a* I prefer for him to come
    b He seemed to be ill

  (b) The zero-form, plain stem, or 'bare infinitive':

 (ii) *a* I made him go
    b He can't swim

  (c) The *en*-form or past participle;

(iii) *a* I had it repaired
    b He has finished

  (d) The *ing*-form or present participle and gerund;

(iv) *a* I don't like John('s) coming so often
    b I saw him coming
    c He is coming
    d He needs helping

The morphemes *to* and *ing* are classified by Rosenbaum (1967*b*: 24) as 'complementizers' – a term that also covers *that*, *for* and Poss, the genitive suffix exemplified in (iv)*a*. The complementizers are said to be introduced by transformational rules rather than in the base.[1] With all the non-finites that he deals with either *to* or *ing* is introduced in this way. (In fact all those with *to* also have *for* introduced, all those with

---

[1] But see Bolinger (1968), who shows that in many cases *to* and *ing* constructions have consistently different meanings.

ing have Poss, but I shall not here be concerned with this aspect of the question.)

In some cases it is reasonable to postulate the introduction of *to* even where the surface structure has a plain stem: this is so when the presence or absence of *to* (in surface structure) depends on the voice of the matrix sentence – compare *they made him come* versus *he was made to come,* or *they heard him laugh* versus *he was heard to laugh.* Here we will say that *to* is introduced into the complement of *make, hear,* etc., but is subsequently deleted if passivization does not take place. But there are some verbs whose complement always has the plain stem – the following modal auxiliaries: *can, may, will, shall, should, must, dare, need;*[1] and also *have* (in the pattern *he had them repair the bridge*) and *let* (in all three of the uses distinguished in 2.4). Of these only *let*$_1$ (i.e. *let* in the sense of 'allow') can be passivized, and even then the passive is somewhat rare and perhaps marginal; but certainly *they were let leave early* is more grammatical than **they were let to leave early.* With these verbs I can see no justification for postulating a *to*-complementizer at any stage in the derivation.

One use of the *en*-form is with perfective *have,* as in *he has finished* I suggested above that in some of its uses, in particular when it is finite, perfective *have* is a remote structure one-place verb, taking subject complementation – i.e. its remote subject NP dominates *it* + S. Since the embedded clause necessarily has past tense we might take *en* as the past tense marker; however, *seeing* also has past tense in *I remember seeing it,* but is not marked by *en.* We may therefore prefer to regard *en* as a complementizer of very limited distribution.

The second use of *en* is in passives. I have not treated simple actional passives like *he was killed* as involving complementation, and consequently *en* is not analyzed as a complementizer in these cases.[2] In such contrasts as:

(v) *a* He saw them win it
    b He saw it won (by them)
(vi) *a* He had them repair the bridge
    b He had the bridge repaired (by them)

---

[1] *Dare* and *need* do occur with the *to*-complementizer but in such cases they differ syntactically from the modal auxiliaries in requiring *do*-support in the negative, interrogative and so on.

[2] R. Lakoff (1968: 43) mentions a proposal by Postal that the passive auxiliary *be* is a deep structure intransitive verb taking subject complementation, but gives no discussion of this analysis.

(vii) *a* He got them to repair the bridge
    b He got the bridge repaired (by them)

the difference between the *a* and *b* members of each pair is a matter of voice, not of complementizers – the presence of *en* in the *b* examples is determined by passivization of the constituent clause. We may assume then that the *b* examples are derived by the deletion of the passive auxiliary *be*, with the consequent deletion of the complementizer *to* in the case of (vii)*b*; in the light of the earlier remarks about the plain stem form, *to* will also be assumed to have been deleted in both members of (v). With *have* and *get* deletion of the passive auxiliary *be* is obligatory; with *see* and other sense verbs deletion is normal, but forms with overt *be*, such as *I saw them be beaten*, etc., cannot, I think, be wholly ruled out. (vi)*a* and (vii)*a* are paraphrases, except that the *have*-construction is formally ambiguous in a way that the *get*-one is not: (vii)*a* is thus a paraphrase of one reading – the more likely one – of (vi)*a*. *Have* may be agentive or non-agentive, but *get* can apparently only be non-agentive if the constituent clause is passive. Thus of the following examples:

(viii) *a* He had someone steal his car
    b He had his house burnt down
    c He got his hair singed
    d He got someone to steal his car

the first three may be agentive ('he brought it about') or non-agentive ('it happened to him'), but the last allows only the agentive interpretation.

Get + past participle without an intervening NP is more difficult to analyze. We must in fact recognize a number of different sources for the one surface structure pattern:

(a) *He got killed* is equivalent to the actional passive *he was killed*, from which it differs only stylistically, *get* begin more colloquial (none of the passives in the corpus had *get* as auxiliary). *He got killed* and *he was killed* should presumably have very similar underlying structures and derivations; in particular, if there is no complementation in the latter, I see no reason why there should be in the former. (*Get* does differ from *be* in requiring the *do* auxiliary in the negative and interrogative forms, etc., but this difference is not relevant to the question of complementation.)

(b) In *I'm going to the hospital to get X-rayed*, *get* will be understood as agentive. This type can be subsumed under the pattern of (vii)*b* if we allow for the subject of the constituent clause to be deleted under identity with that of the matrix. This deletion is optional, for we also have *I got myself X-rayed*. The presence of the reflexive pronoun makes the clause more clearly agentive. Nevertheless *get* + past participle without the reflexive is itself more readily interpreted as agentive than is *be* + past participle; it seems to me, for example, that in the pair:

(ix) *a* He ordered John to get sacked
 b He ordered John to be sacked

the normal interpretation of the first is that the order was given to John that he get himself sacked, whereas the second is likely to be understood as 'he ordered that John be sacked' (cf. the discussion of *order* in 4.2.4). We cannot, however, altogether exclude an agentive interpretation of *be*-passives, especially in the negative; if we did we should be unable to explain their use in imperatives like *don't be seen, don't be misled* and so on, which are often paraphrasable with *allow*: 'don't allow yourself to be misled'. Such agentive *be*-passives cannot be regarded as ordinary actional passives, i.e. as differing from an active only in terms of thematic structure; they must surely involve complementation just as do the agentive *get* passives.

(c) In one interpretation, doubtless the most likely, *John got dressed* means much the same as *John dressed*. In this interpretation *John got dressed* is again agentive, but it differs from type (b) in that John is understood to have dressed himself rather than to have been dressed by someone else. Intuitively I interpret the *dressed* here as a statal passive, but I cannot find clear syntactic evidence to support this.

In discussing the two examples of (v), namely *he saw them win it* and *he saw it won by them* I suggested that the different forms of the constituent clause verb are due simply to the voice contrast: we do not need to say that *see* takes two different complementizers. The same applies, *mutatis mutandis*, to the pair:

(x) *a* I watched them play
 b I watched them playing

Again it is not a question of *watch* taking different complementizers: the difference between *play* and *playing* is one of aspect, non-progressive versus progressive, so that we may derive the second example from the structure underlying *I watched them be playing*, by obligatory deletion of *be* (cf. the 'telescoped progressive' of Fillmore, 1963). Given that the progressive auxiliary *be* is here being treated as a main verb, remote structures for the above examples will be as shown in PM's (1) and (2) respectively.

PM(1)

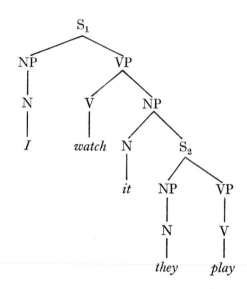

PM(2)

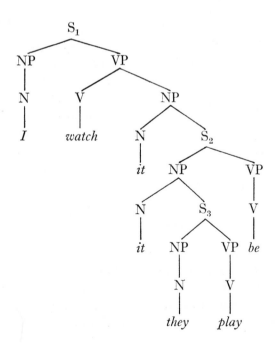

The *ing* of (x)*b* is thus a complementizer, yet it is determined not by the *watch* of S_1 but by the covert *be* of S_2.

It is not easy to determine just which verbs allow (or rather require) the deletion of a progressive *be*, but two criteria may be suggested. Firstly, is there a contrast between an *ing*-form and an infinitive (with or without *to*), as in (x)? If only the *ing*-form is possible I would be very reluctant to postulate an underlying progressive *be*. It is admittedly the case that verbs do impose constraints on the structure of their complement clauses (some require the complement to be agentive, others to have a subject identical with the matrix subject and so on), but nevertheless it would be an unusual type of constraint if a verb required that the main verb of its complement clause be progressive *be*. I know of no case where there is firm enough evidence to warrant such a constraint. There may well be a 'progressive' meaning in many *keep* + . . .*ing* constructions, for example, but this can be accounted for in terms of the meaning of *keep* itself without postulating an underlying *be*: *be* is after all not the only verb whose meaning has to do with aspect. The second criterion is perhaps more conclusive: can the *ing* be suffixed to verbs which do not normally occur in the progressive aspect? If so, we shall not assume a deleted *be*. Thus, to return to *keep*, *it kept being Mary who knew the answer* and *she kept having stomach ache* are quite normal, whereas **it was being Mary who knew the answer* and **she was having stomach ache* are not. The only clear cases of verbs taking a 'telescoped progressive' would thus seem to be: (a) the sense verbs *feel, hear, watch, see*, etc. (and the last only in the meaning 'discern by sight', as distinct from 'discern mentally' or 'call up picture of, imagine': in *I can see him owning half the cinemas in the country before he retires*, the *ing*-complementizer is determined by *see* – there is no underlying progressive *be* here); (b) *have* and *get*, as in *he had them sweep the floor/sweeping the floor, he got it to work/working*. The class is thus apparently the same as that which allows or requires the deletion of passive *be*.

4.3 Subject and object complementation in the corpus

4.3.1 Preliminary delimitation. In this section I shall examine the various types of construction found in the corpus where a complement clause is immediately dominated by a subject or object NP with *it* as head – 4.4 deals more briefly with cases where there is some noun as head. I have taken object in a very wide and therefore fairly superficial

sense. For the purpose of this chapter, for example, I have not distinguished between verbal and adjectival predicates, so that in *I know that he's coming* and *I'm sure that he's coming* the *that*-clause counts as an object in both cases. Clauses governed by prepositions – such as the *ing*-clause in *it is capable of measuring such quantities* – have not been included: again these are taken up briefly later in the chapter; the criterion of exclusion here was the presence of a preposition in *surface* structure: the fact that the NP dominating the complement in *I persuaded John to go* may well be governed by a preposition in remote structure has been ignored. Clauses with 'adverbial' function, such as purpose, result, etc., have not been regarded as object complements (though assignment to these categories is not always straightforward); the infinitival clauses in the following sentences are, for example, beyond the scope of the present chapter:

(1) A limiting crystallite size must exist for this to be true. (16268)
(2) Thus hair growth is a matter of alternate growing and resting periods, with new hair arising periodically to displace the old. (35360)

Nor are clauses forming part of a compound modifier to an adjective or adverb regarded as object complements. This excludes cases like the *that*-clause in (3) or the infinitival one in (4):

(3) This [*sc.* the spore-mother-cell cytoplasm] had been so densely granular that the nucleus was not clearly discernible. (11326)
(4) Individual hyperfine components in crystals are sufficiently narrow to allow resolution of two sextets from the two naturally occurring europium isotopes. (14558)

The second of these is to be distinguished from (5), which is included:

(5) In fact, a potential difference of 70 millivolts is just sufficient to maintain the observed disparity in the concentration of chloride ions inside the cell and outside it; (33170)

The adjective *sufficient* is a two-place predicate, with the second place here taken as an object; in a comprehensive analysis we would obviously hope to account for the systematic relationship between the constructions exemplified in (5) and (4), but this has not been attempted in the present study.

In addition there is one type of subject complement and one object complement construction that are not included in the account of non-finites in 4.3.3. The analysis of the modal and aspectual (*be/have*) auxiliaries as main verbs (4.2.2 above) was not adopted until after the textual analysis had been completed: they are thus not included among the items taking subject-raising (or, in the case of one or two of the modals, such as *dare* and volitional *will*, subject-deletion). Object complements with no verb, more precisely with copulative *be* understood, as in *he finds her incomprehensible*, have also been excluded: see 3.7 above. However if there is complementation within the attribuant this has been counted as subject complementation; thus in:

(6) the flow of some sodium ions through the membrane opens the gate further and makes it easier for others to follow. (33201)

for others to follow is taken as a subject complement, but *it easier for others to follow* has not been counted as an object complement. This is doubtless a little inconsistent, but was motivated by (a) the difficulty of knowing when to postulate a covert *be* in intensive constructions and the practical need to avoid too abstract a description in textual analysis; (b) the fact that in all respects relevant to 4.3.3 *for others to follow* is like a subject, not an object, complement. (There were, moreover, only 7 instances of such constructions, so that the figures are scarcely affected by this inconsistency.)

Where a complement consists of a coordination of clauses, as in (7), it counts as only a single token of complementation:

(7) They found that the formation of bacteriochlorophyll ran parallel to the morphogenesis of the thylakoids and that the content of bacteriochlorophyll and number of thylakoids were related to the intensity of the illumination. (12415)

Finally the second sentence of the following example was excluded from the account of non-finite object complements:

(8) The origin of this term [*sc. moment*] is obscure, but it may be related to the fact that 'moment' is derived from the Latin *movimentum*, and that the capability of a force to move an object (using the force on a lever or crowbar) increases with the length of the lever arm. *In mathematics 'moment' means weighted by how far away it is from an axis.* (27410)

This belongs to the special register of talking about language, in particular stating meanings or definitions: it cannot be generated by the normal rules of the language, and I have not set up an *ad hoc* pattern to deal with it.

4.3.2 Finite complements. Tables 4: 1 and 4: 2 give the figures for subject and object complements classified on two dimensions, according to the mood and function of the complement; in table 4: 1 the functions are defined at the pre-passive level, and in table 4: 2 at the mood level.

TABLE 4: 1. *Finite complements classified as to pre-passive function and mood*

	Declarative		Non-declarative		Total	
	No.	%	No.	%	No.	%
Pre-passive object	571	85	68	87	639	85
Pre-passive subject	105	16	10	13	115	15
Total	676	100	78	100	754	100

TABLE 4: 2. *Finite complements classified as to mood function and mood*

	Declarative		Non-declarative		Total	
	No.	%	No.	%	No.	%
Mood object	493	73	57	73	550	73
Mood subject	183	27	21	27	204	27
Total	676	100	78	100	754	100

I shall begin by listing the matrix 'predicates' (verbs and attributes) occurring with the various types of finite complement, and then go on to deal with extraposition, and the complementizers in declarative clauses.

(a) Predicates in an active matrix with a declarative object complement (493 examples):

agree		consider	4	establish		forecast	
assume	18	demonstrate	6	estimate		forget	
be	56	determine		expect		guess	
believe	12	discover	2	fear		hear	
conclude	9	emphasize	4	feel	4	hold	
confirm	4	ensure	8	find	40	imagine	

imply	8	point out	7	require		sure	2
indicate	23	predict	3	reveal	9	surmise	2
inform		presume		say	15	suspect	
insist		prove	6	see	20	teach	
know	5	provide	2	show	88	tell	
learn		recognize	2	speculate		think	5
mean	10	recommend	2	state	4	verify	
note	15	record		stress		vow	
notice	3	recount		suggest	50		
observe	6	report		suppose	12		

The 56 *be*'s were of the equative type. Only *inform*, *teach* and *tell* occurred with a recipient. All the predicates were verbs, with the exception of *sure*. Examples:

(1) An important consequence of this model *is* that the nuclei are not arranged at random, but along linear imperfections. (16178)
(2) My colleague on R.R.S. *Discovery*, M. V. Angel, *informed* me that the body breaks the surface, though the finger-like processes do not. (32211)
(3) We are not *sure* that the glowing spots Greenacre and Barr saw were manifestations of exactly the same phenomenon represented by the bright areas on our photographs; (38275)

(b) Predicates in a passive matrix with a declarative object complement (78):

accept		emphasize	2	observe		remember	
appreciate		estimate		point out		report	2
argue		expect		postulate	2	rule out	
arrange		find	9	realize		see	3
assume	5	hope		recall	2	show	13
believe	2	know	6	recognize		state	
conjecture	2	note	5	recommend		suggest	9
demonstrate							

Examples:

(4) It will be *recalled* that, because these molecules are homonuclear, they are non-polar, and consequently do not exhibit a pure vibrational spectrum. (26265)
(5) That the disease is a very old one in Egypt is *shown* by the discovery of *Schistosoma* eggs in the kidneys of mummies of the twentieth dynasty (1250–1000 B.C.). (23425)

(c) Predicates in an active matrix with a non-declarative object complement (57):

ask		discover		inquire	2	suggest	
be	4	explain	3	know	3	tell	5
consider		figure out		note		test	
decide		find out	3	observe		understand	2
define	2	illustrate		say	2	visualize	
describe	2	imagine		see	5	wonder	
determine	6	indicate		show	4		

All the complements were interrogative, except that of *illustrate* (quoted as (1) of 2.3). Example:

(6) We have to *explain* why there are ninety-odd naturally occurring elements, ranging from hydrogen to uranium, the latter being 238 times as heavy as the starting material. (39291)

(d) Predicates in a passive matrix with a non-declarative (interrogative) object complement (11):

describe	establish	see	3
determine 2	know 3	show	

(7) It is not yet *known* whether temperatures below 10°C are harmful to the central nervous system, (31505)

(e) Predicates taking a declarative subject complement (105); these may be further subdivided into verbs and attributes (adjectives, etc.). The verbs were:

appear	3	happen	seem	7
be	6	lead to the conclusion	turn out	2
follow	16	make sense		

Apart from *make sense* these are all intransitive, and *sense* is of course one of the non-contrastive objects discussed in 3.4. All the *be* examples included the modal *may*. Examples:

(8) Rather, it *may be* that detachment from the plant, with the consequent exclusion of the meiotic stimulus, is responsible for the developmental failure. (11269)

(9) So it *makes sense* that the amount of twist, or torque, is proportional both to the radial distance and to the tangential component of the force. (27403)

(10) That separate spin resonance spectra can be observed for these two species *leads to the conclusion* that they are well separated in the form of loose ion-pairs rather than as centrosymmetric units similar to the monomer described by Becker, Lindquist, and Alder. (14512)

The adjectives, etc., functioning as attribute with a subject complement were as follows; the first column gives factives, where the truth of the constituent proposition is presupposed, the matrix thus expressing some comment about it, and the second gives the non-factives, where there is no such presupposition. (See Kiparsky & Kiparsky, forthcoming; the distinction could have been applied to verbs too – I make it here to facilitate comparison between the adjectives taking finite and non-finite complements.)

Factives		*Non-factives*	
amazing		apparent	3
curious	2	clear	11
interesting	2	evident	8
an interesting fact		likely	11
mysterious		plausible	
relevant		possible	8
significant		our postulate	
suggestive		probable	8
surprising		true	3
a tribute to...		essential	2

(11) Moreover, it is *suggestive* that at the points of arrival of input channels in the cortex there are numerous stellate cells, whose influence may be to spread activity widely from any point. (22086)

(12) That the skin survives these daily torments is a remarkable *tribute* to its toughness. (35175)

(13) It is *evident* that the various laws, deduced above and confirmed by experiment, are true only within the limits imposed by the assumptions made in the deductions. (28269)

(14) Since no granules are found in the chloroplasts of controls or of plants kept in the dark before or after fumigation, it is our tentative *postulate* that the granules found after PAN fumigation are not related to those reported in the literature. (11181)

Formally this last example is ambiguous according as the *be* is extensive or intensive; I have taken it as intensive, as this makes much more sense in the context: the writer is not identifying his tentative postulate, but simply making it.

(f) Predicates taking a non-declarative subject complement (10):

certain	2	doubtful	2	a tribute to...
clear	4	immaterial		

The complements to the adjectives are interrogative, that to the NP an exclamative (= (2) of 2.3).

(15) Just why the brain should be so tolerant is not *clear*. (31404)

Extraposition. Of the 204 examples of mood subject complementation all but 8 have the complement extraposed, with *it* therefore filling the matrix subject position: the non-extraposed pattern is thus very much marked *vis-à-vis* the *it*+extraposed complement pattern. Four of the eight examples have been quoted above, as (5), (10), (12) and (15); I will quote one further example:

(16) The main relevance of such complexes to chemical kinetics lies in the possibility that the forces responsible for the formation of complexes are also operative in the transition state, and thus play a part in determining the rate of reaction. Whether the complex itself is a necessary stage on the reaction path is largely immaterial. (24004)

The difference between the extraposed and non-extraposed patterns has to do with the thematic organization of the sentence or discourse, and it is not difficult to suggest thematic reasons for the order of elements in all the non-extraposed examples. (10) has a very long matrix VP, which itself contains a *that*-clause; to extrapose the subject complement here would produce a sentence that was virtually impossible to read with the intonation and rhythm characteristic of extraposition: it could of course be read with pronoun apposition intonation, but this is a stylistically much more informal construction – it is not used at all in the corpus. This example (10) contrasts nicely with (8) and (9), where the VP is very short. In (5) the VP is also long, containing as it does the pre-passive subject in the form of a *by*-phrase: we may assume that the passive was selected here in order to bring the pre-passive subject into clause final position, the normal position for 'new' information (example (3) of 2.2.1 is similar); the passives with extraposition, on the other hand, either have no *by*-phrase, as in (4), or else a short one.

In (12) and (15) the complement clause contains an anaphoric reference to the preceding sentence; in (15) the content of the complement is given, the informationally new material being in the VP, so that again the information pattern is the normal given + new (as before, the reader is referred to the work of Halliday for a detailed discussion of 'given' and 'new'). In (12) *these daily torments* is given in that the previous sentences have been detailing them ('stretching, scraping, gouging, soaking and burning') and the fact of the skin's survival is taken for granted as obvious, and treated as given information: the informationally new material is again expressed at the end and thus naturally carries the tonic stress, marking it as the main information focus. In (5) and (10) there is also anaphoric reference in the complement, but the constituent clauses as wholes cannot be regarded as given: normal readings would divide each into at least two information units.

Finally in (16) there is an explicit contrast between the relevance of one factor and the irrelevance ('immateriality') of another: the final position of *immaterial* makes the contrast clearer. If extraposition had been applied it would have been more or less necessary to insert a *but* or *however* (or something similar) in order to convey the intended meaning.

Complementizers. The only clear declarative complementizer found in the corpus was *that*, though there were two border-line cases. One contained *if*:

(17) Now it would be nice if we could write Eq (18.3) as the total mass times some acceleration. (27098)

It might be argued that this is a case of subject complementation with extraposition of the *if*-clause. But there are two ways in which (17) differs from standard subject complementation. Firstly, the *if*-clause could occur to the left of *it*, as marked theme; this might sound unusual in the case of (17) itself, but if we replace *be nice* by something more contentful the result is more obviously acceptable:

(17′) If we could write Eq (18.3) as the total mass times some acceleration it would make things a lot simpler.

This pattern is out of the question with *that*-clauses: **that he's coming it's probable* (this may be acceptable as a type of pronoun apposition structure with copying to the left rather than to the right – as in *John, he's gone*, for example – but this is intonationally quite distinct from (17′)). Secondly, when the *if*-clause is thematized in this way, *it* is replaceable by *that* or *this*. These pro-forms clearly refer to the content of the *if*-clause (less the *if* itself of course). These facts suggest that the *if* of (17) is not a complementizer but the ordinary conditional conjunction, and a plausible remote structure for the example would contain both an *if*-clause and a *that*-clause as subject complement: *it + that we could write*...*would be nice if we could write*..., with pronominalization reducing the complement to *it*.

The second doubtful case is:

(18) We have now dealt with the physical chemistry of molecules containing one, two and three atoms, and have observed how mathematical difficulties accumulate as the molecules become more and more complex. (26445)

The manner component in *how* is somewhat attenuated here, so that it is not clear whether the independent clause equivalent of the complement is the interrogative *how do mathematical difficulties accumulate* or the manner-less declarative *mathematical difficulties accumulate*. *How* can certainly occur as a complementizer in declaratives, as in *he told us how he had a brother in Moscow* where there is scarcely a plausible manner interpretation (cf. R. Lakoff, 1968: 69, who also includes *when* and *where* – and *if*), but as this use of *how* is more characteristic of colloquial than formal registers, we counted (18) as an interrogative.

Although *that* is in principle optionally deletable in most types of object and subject complements by far the majority of such clauses contained an overt *that*. The breakdown of declarative complements is as shown in table 4: 3.

TABLE 4: 3. *Presence and absence of 'that' in declarative complements*

	No.	%
That obligatorily present	5	1
That optionally present	647	96
That optionally absent	20	3
That obligatorily absent	4	1
Total	676	100

The complementizer is not deletable with non-extraposed subject complements and is obligatorily deleted when the mood subject of an object complement is shifted into the matrix – by relativization, interrogative-*wh* fronting or thematization, as in:

(19) the reduction product depended not on the current (the factor which Faraday's laws teaches [*sic*] us is so crucial to electro-chemistry) but on the voltage. (39057)

The 20 optional deletions were all in object complements; no fewer than 6 were after imperative *suppose*:

(20) Suppose we have a semi-infinite superconductor with a plane boundary, and a magnetic field applied parallel to the boundary. (18254)

and in 10 of the remainder the constituent clause subject was a pronoun. Notice that in the following example *that* is deleted from the first member of a coordinate complex, but not from the second:

(21) Assuming the $v''' \gg v''$ and that the vapor behaves like an ideal gas, show that the 'expansivity at constant saturation' is [R]. (29104)

I have included in the figures of tables 4: 1/2 a few examples of complements which are strictly speaking non-finite, for example:

(22) Corpuscular radiation thus seems to be the only possible explanation [...]. The only requirement is that the radius of the particles' spirals *exceed* that of the moon, and measurements of interplanetary magnetic fields indicate that this would be the case for protons of sufficiently high energy. (38398)

In other respects such clauses are more like finites than the non-finites to be discussed in the next section – in particular they take the *that*-complementizer and a nominative subject. Some speakers use finite forms where others have non-finites, so that with a plural subject as in (23) we cannot tell whether a finite or non-finite form was intended:

(23) It is essential, if progress is to occur as swiftly as possible, that individual groups co-operate with each other so that mistakes are not repeated (31326)

A variant of *that* + non-finite is *that* + *should* as in:

(24) These laws must apply to any medium, since the method by which the expression for the pressure was found in no way required that the medium should be gaseous. (28281)

4.3.3 Non-finite complements. A preliminary classification of non-finite subject and object complements is given in table 4: 4, the two dimensions of classification being function at the pre-passive level and form of the complement clause verb in surface structure.

TABLE 4: 4. *Preliminary classification of non-finite complements*

	to-form	φ-form	*ing*-form	*en*-form	Total
Pre-passive object	368	56	10	1	435
Pre-passive subject	359	—	14	—	373
Total	727	56	24	1	808

Whereas table 4: 1 showed that with finite clauses object function was almost five times as frequent as subject, with non-finites there is not very much difference in frequency between object and subject complements; or, to put it another way, with object complements the proportion of finites to non-finites is about 4:2, with subject complements it is about 1:3. Table 4: 4 also reveals a striking difference between the *to*- and *ing*-forms: the *to*-complementizer is about 30 times the more frequent.

I shall now consider in turn the various types of non-finite complements found in the corpus, describing them primarily in terms of the syntactic properties and processes discussed in 4.2. Thirty-three patterns will be distinguished, labelled A to GG, though many of them have only one or two occurrences. The main order of presentation is as follows:

Object complementation
 Constituent clause mood subject raised into matrix
  to or zero complementizer (A–G)
  ing as complementizer (H)
 Constituent clause mood subject deleted
  to or zero complementizer
   Deletion under indefiniteness condition (I)
   Deletion under identity condition (J–Q)
  ing as complementizer
   Deletion under indefiniteness condition (R)
   Deletion under identity condition (S–T)
 Constituent clause mood subject retained
  to as complementizer
   No object-raising (U)
   Object of constituent clause raised into matrix (V)

Subject complementation
    Constituent clause mood subject raised into matrix
        to as complementizer (W)
        ing as complementizer (X)
    Constituent clause mood subject deleted
        to as complementizer
            Deletion under indefiniteness condition
                Complement extraposed; no object-raising (Y)
                Object of constituent clause raised into matrix (Z)
                No extraposition (AA)
            Deletion under identity condition
                Complement extraposed; no object-raising (BB)
                No extraposition (CC)
       ing as complementizer
            Deletion under indefiniteness condition
                Complement extraposed; no object-raising (DD)
                No extraposition (EE)
            Deletion under identity condition (FF)
    Constituent clause mood subject retained (GG)

The number in parentheses after the model sentence of each pattern gives the total number of occurrences for that pattern.

Pattern A: We assume this to be the case (82)
    Object complement with *to* as complementizer; subject raised to become matrix object; no passivization.
    Matrix verbs:

allow	13	determine		find		reveal	
assume	8	enable	14	know		show	3
cause	23	estimate		permit	4	suppose	
consider	4	expect	4	prove		take	
define							

(1) If we *assume* the molecules in this region to be free from one another's influence, we have [R]. (26001)
(2) One *expects* the most stable nucleus of all, iron-56, to appear with a high abundance. (39454)

Ideally, further distinctions should be made within this pattern – e.g. according to the underlying tense of the complement: present in (1), future in (2).

Pattern B: This is assumed to be the case (128)
    Object complement with *to* as complementizer; subject raised to become matrix object; passivization then shifts it to matrix subject position.

Matrix verbs:

allow	7	find	17	predict		see	6
assume	8	intend		presume	2	show	11
believe	8	know	12	report	3	suppose	
cause	2	make	5	require	2	take	
consider	3	observe	5	say	15	think	9
expect	9						

(3) The factor $\frac{1}{2}$ on the right-hand side arises from the fact that the light is *assumed* to be generated by a thermal source and hence is un-polarized; (19231)

(4) When a nerve impulse reaches the synaptic knob, some of the vesicles are *caused* to eject the transmitter substance into the synaptic cleft. (33314)

Pattern C: He made them go (6)
   Object complement with *to* as complementizer; subject raised to become matrix object; no passivization; *to* deleted.
   Matrix verbs: *make* (5), *see*

(5) The unique circulation in the Atlantic *makes* the weed accumulate in a large area, (32338)

Pattern D: He let them go (47)
   Object complement with zero complementizer; subject raised to become matrix object; no passivization.
   Matrix verbs: *let*$_1$ (2), *let*$_2$ (45)

(6) When this occurs, the membrane no longer acts as a barrier to the passage of ions but *lets* them flow through in response to the dif-fering electric potential on the two sides of the membrane. (33291)

(7) *Let* us, for example, consider the Raman line due to the vibration of the methyl group with respect to the iodine atom in methyl iodide. (26387)

Let$_2$ is thus the 'ist person imperative' marker: in subsuming these imperatives under pattern D, I am applying the analysis proposed in 2.4.2. The distinction between C and D is a fairly trivial one – an under-lying *to* can be justified in the former, but hardly in the latter.

Pattern E: We see them moving (1)

Object complement with *to* as complementizer; subject raised to become matrix object; deletion of progressive *be*, main verb of complement clause, and consequent deletion of *to*-complementizer; no passivization.

Matrix verb: *see*

(8) In Fig 18–2 we *see* a force **F** acting at a point **r**. (27380)

Pattern F: They are seen moving (2)

Object complement with *to* as complementizer; subject raised to become matrix object; passivization then shifts it to matrix object position; deletion of progressive *be* and consequently of *to*.

Matrix verb: *see* (2)

(9) The development is very rapid and the young embryos are *seen* moving in the uterus of the parent seventy-two hours after the appearance of the eggs. (23102)

(Notice that *they are seen moving* and *they are seen to be moving* involve different meanings of *see*.)

Pattern G: He had a tooth extracted (1)

Object complement with zero complementizer; subject raised to become matrix object; passive auxiliary *be* deleted from complement; no passivization.

Matrix verb: *have*

(10) Incidentally during both my pregnancies he [*sc.* my husband] had to *have* a tooth extracted. (37068)

Superficially similar to this were two examples containing *show*, as in:

(11) Figure 3 *shows* the *a* and *d* sublattice magnetizations individually compared with the predictions of the molecular field and biquadratic exchange models. (17403)

Here, however, the *compared*...is a statal passive functioning as attribute to *magnetizations*: the example is of the same type as *this picture shows her in her wedding dress* with obligatorily deleted lexical *be*. Notice that we do not find **the figure shows it reach*..., and the type with *show* + *to* + verb involves a different sense of *show*. (11) has thus been omitted from the class of object complements (since we excluded all those with a covert lexical *be* as main verb).

Pattern H: We picture them replacing it (1)
   Object complement with *ing* as complementizer; subject raised to become matrix object; no passivization.
   Matrix verb: *picture*

(12) the most plausible hypothesis *pictures* xanthate anions taking the place of sulphide ions in the exposed faces of the PbS lattice. (32565)

This differs from E in that there is no underlying progressive *be*: the *ing*-form is obligatory with *picture,* and may be affixed to 'non-progressive' verbs. This pattern thus differs from A only in respect of its remote complementizer, but while A was one of the most common types H was very rare. Passivization is possible but is not exemplified in the corpus: there is thus no *ing* analogue here of pattern B.

Pattern I: The first step is to collect the data (22)
   Object complement with *to* as complementizer; subject deleted under indefiniteness condition.
   Matrix verb: *be* (22)

(13) The problem *is* to determine what fraction of the incident radiant energy hv_1, can be converted into kinetic energy under the most favourable conditions. (26142)

Pattern J: Our task is to explain this fact (24)
   Object complement with *to* as complementizer; subject deleted under identity with *part* of matrix subject.
   Matrix verb: *be* (24)

(14) My purpose *is* to present the background and current position of organ transplantation from the points of view of experiment and clinical application to man. (31014)
(15) The prime function of the pigment *is* to shield the cells by absorbing the ultraviolet rays of the sun. (35223)

In (14) the understood subject of *present* is *I*, in (15) that of *shield* is *the pigment.* In all the corpus examples the 'antecedent' of the deleted subject was related to the head of the matrix subject NP by *of* as in (15) or the possessive case, as in (14), but more complex types can be constructed, e.g. *the task we have set ourselves is to*...It is not clear that explicit rules can be formulated for the location of the antecedent, and this last example will perhaps have to be treated under pattern I. It is certainly difficult to draw a sharp and well-motivated line between I and J.

Pattern K: We hope to resolve this problem (79)
Object complementation with *to* as complementizer; subject deleted under identity with the matrix subject; no passivization.
Matrix verbs:

agree	2	decline		manage	2	refuse	
aim	2	endeavour		mean		serve	15
attempt	3	expect	2	plan		try	12
begin		go on		pretend		want	2
choose		hope	3	proceed		wish	5
decide	2	like	5	propose	2		

(16) Little is known about these imperfections, but one would certainly *expect* to find the far greater range of cavity sizes reflected in the width of the optical absorption band. (14462)
(17) In social animals sounds may be produced when a pain stimulus is applied and the sounds may *serve* to warn other individuals and in the case of man to bring others to the rescue. (22535)

Matrix adjectives:

adequate 2	free 2	sufficient 2
equipped	ready 2	willing
fit		

(18) We are *free* to choose the 1 and 2 axes in any direction in the plane perpendicular to H_0. (18147)
(19) Substituent effects are never *sufficient* to show that a reaction necessarily proceeds through the preliminary formation of a complex. (24041)
(20) The problem of finding terminology *adequate* to describe the actions of the sense organs is obviously especially difficult (22117)

It might be argued that in (20) the understood subject of *describe* is *someone/us*, but this would be to understand subject in too deep a sense: the element deleted under the identity condition is the mood subject. *Describe* allows either 'agentive' or 'instrumental' to be mapped onto the pre-passive subject: *we can describe the actions satisfactorily with this terminology – this terminology can satisfactorily describe the actions.* (20) thus has an instrumental-type subject; it contrasts with *terminology which is adequate (for us) to describe the actions of the sense organs with,* which is an object-raising construction (see pattern Z).

7

As noted earlier, the pre-passive object is a fairly superficial function and there are clearly differences in deep function among the objects of the verbs and adjectives in the above lists.

Pattern L: *It is hoped to return to this problem* (2)

Object complement with *to* as complementizer; subject deleted under identity with matrix subject (pre-passive); passivization shifts *it* to matrix mood subject position, the matrix pre-passive subject being deleted.

Matrix verbs: *hope, propose*

(21) It is *proposed* to deal separately with each organelle and region of the cell, comparing details of their fine structure. (12053)

This is the passive counterpart of K, though very few of the verbs occurring in the latter allow passivization. This example shows that, whether or not *it* is introduced in the base, it must be present in the structure at the stage when passivization applies.

Pattern M: *He determined what to do* (1)

Object complement with *to* as complementizer; subject deleted under identity with the matrix subject; no passivization. The complement clause is interrogative.

Matrix verb: *determine*

(22) Less sensitive apparatus, including index tubes, have been used with considerable success in many other countries for 'screening' purposes – that is, for assisting the police to *determine* whether to bring in a motorist for blood examination. (36341)

This type differs from K only in the mood of the complement (unless we claim that there is also a covert 'obligational' modal on the basis of finite clause paraphrases). It was the only non-finite interrogative among the subject and object complements of the corpus. The subject of interrogative infinitival clauses is obligatorily deleted – either under the identity condition, as here, or the indefiniteness condition, as in *can you suggest what to do?*

Pattern N: *This led us to question the theory* (12)

Object complement with *to* as complementizer; subject deleted under identity with the first object of the matrix; no passivization. (The object complement is probably governed by a preposition in remote structure: *into*, etc.)

Matrix verbs:

assist	force	invite
empower	help 2	lead 6

(23) In some cases the changes are very small, *leading* us to believe that a discontinuous change in all three quantities is a necessary property of a second-order transition. (29021)

(24) Already man-made spare parts – artificial valves and pacemakers – *help* thousands of people to lead normal lives. (31574)

Pattern O: He was tempted to go (3)

Object complement with *to* as complementizer; subject deleted under identity with the first object of the matrix, which is shifted to mood subject position by passivization.

Matrix verbs: *pledge, stimulate, tempt*

(25) one is *tempted* to conclude that the planar bath model is the correct one. (26585)

Pattern P: This helped to solve the problem (13)

Object complement with *to* as complementizer; subject deleted under identity with the first object of the matrix, which is then itself deleted under the indefiniteness condition.

Matrix verb: *help* (13)

(26) Measurement of the strength of this magnetic field in interstellar space will *help* to resolve this problem. (34153)

(27) The bushy eyebrows and the eye-lashes *help* to shield the vulnerable eyeballs. (35304)

The identification of the understood subject in the complement of *help* does raise some difficulty. Rosenbaum (1967a: 116) has this to say: 'Intuition can be a dubious guide in the matter of determining exactly what the subject of the underlying embedded sentence is. Chomsky (personal communication) points to such sentences as *John helped Bill solve the problem* or *John helped write the book*. On the reading that "John neither solved the problem nor wrote the book but helped to do both" the selection of *John* as the subject of the underlying sentence seems inconsistent. So similarly would be the selection of *Bill* or *someone* since neither solved a problem nor wrote a book, but collaborated with

7-2

John to do these things.' Where the 'direct object' of *help* is expressed, I do not think there is any doubt but that this is the antecedent of the deleted constituent subject. This is particularly clear when the subject and direct object of *help* differ in animateness, as in (24), where the subject of *lead normal lives* can only be understood as *thousands of people*, not *man-made spare parts*; but it also applies to examples like Chomsky's *John helped Bill (to) solve the problem*: notice that this can be roughly paraphrased as 'Bill solved the problem with the help of John'. It is when there is no overt direct object of *help* that the difficulty arises. Where the complement expresses an agentive process (especially one involving a human agentive) the subject is understood to be identical with an unexpressed object: *John helped write the book* = 'someone wrote the book with the help of John', and similarly in (26). But when the complement clause is non-agentive, such an analysis is not necessarily very plausible; can we really say in (27) for example that there is an indefinite NP understood as object of *help* and subject of *shield*? A more natural interpretation, I think, would take *the bushy eyebrows and the eyelashes* as the understood subject: the sentence occurs at the end of a paragraph dealing with 'a few special protective functions of hair', the preceding context being as follows:

(28) The hairs inside the nostrils slow incoming air currents, trap dust particles, keep out insects and prevent the nasal mucus from pouring down over the lips. The hairs in the outer ear and around the anogenital orifices act as barriers against the entry of foreign matter and small invaders such as insects.

Pattern Q: This helped solve the problem (3)

Like the preceding, except that there is no *to*-complementizer. It seems simpler to have the introduction of *to* optional with *help* than to introduce it and then optionally delete it.

Matrix verb: *help* (3)

(29) Exploratory trials *helped* define suitable conditions for the definitive run, which was conducted for 65 hr. (15433)

Pattern R: This involves measuring the change (3)

Object complement with *ing* as complementizer; subject deleted under the indefiniteness condition; no passivization.

Matrix verbs: *include, involve* (2)

(30) One technique which has been used *involves* measuring the extent to which the individual spectral features of neutral hydrogen are split in the interstellar field. (34156)

Pattern S: We anticipate saving money (2)
Object complementation with *ing* as complementizer; subject deleted under identity with the matrix subject; no passivization.
Matrix verbs: *anticipate, resent*

(31) designers *anticipate* being able to save power, or increase speed with the same power output. (34429)
(32) women often envy men and *resent* having been born female, (37284)

With *resent* the deleted subject cannot, I think, have an agentive role with respect to the complement verb: we do not find **he resents telling her that*, though *he resents being told that/having to tell her that* are grammatical. Pattern S is the *ing*-form analogue of K.

Pattern T: He arranged for us to go (2)
Object complement with *to* as complementizer; no deletion or raising of subject or object; active matrix.
Matrix verbs: *arrange, call*

(33) The way of overcoming the problem is to *arrange* for as much as possible of the vessel to ride above the surface and for its weight to be substantially less than that of conventional ships. (34311)

Here *for* is taken as the complementizer rather than the preposition, though it may well be that there is a covert prepositional *for* as well, since *arrange* and *call* characteristically combine with *for* + NP; as Rosenbaum has observed, there is a general rule deleting prepositions before finite or *to*-form complement clauses.

Pattern U: They are sufficient for us to measure (1)
Object complement with *to* as complementizer; subject retained in constituent clause but object deleted under identity with matrix subject.
Matrix adjective: *sufficient*

(34) a square centimetre column through the disc of the Galaxy contains about 10^{22} atoms of neutral hydrogen – quite *sufficient* for present day radio techniques to measure. (34050)

Sufficient can take subject complementation, as in *it is sufficient for us to measure the hydrogen,* but it is clear on semantic grounds that (35) does not derive by object-raising from any such structure as this; *sufficient* does not belong to the class of adjectives allowing object-raising from within a subject complement (see pattern Z).

Pattern V: They appear to be unrelated (243)

Subject complement with *to* as complementizer; complement extraposed and subject raised to become matrix subject.

Matrix verbs:

appear	59	come	3	have ('must')	35	seem	42
begin	14	commence	2	need	3	start	5
be going	3	continue	6	prove	6	tend	14
cease		fail	8	remain	4		

(35) However, with the availability of modern light detectors and electronic circuitry of very short resolving time, other types of correlations in optical fields *began* to be studied. (19040)

(36) Because it is so free of blemishes [...] baby skin has *come* to be regarded as the epitome of skin beauty. (35156)

I have chosen examples with passive complements to emphasize the voice-neutrality which is criterial for this construction, but the majority of the complements were of course active. Two of the items in the list deserve comment. *Go* takes a split subject only if it is itself in the progressive form, as in:

(37) In other words, the definition of the torque *is going* to be so arranged that the theorem of work has an absolute analog: force times distance is work, and torque times angle *is going* to be work. (27302)

Thus we have *he was going to damage it, it was going to be damaged* but not *he went to damage it,* etc. (except in an unrelated sense): *be going* is probably best regarded as an idiom rather than a genuine progressive.

The inclusion of *remain* in the list may well be an error. This verb is exceptional in that the complement must be passive:

(38) K. Uchida and Y. Shojima [...] have devised a method of collecting clumps of weed which could lend itself well to quantitative studies, yet this *remains* to be done. (32347)[1]

---

[1] The *this* here is presumably meant to stand for something like *applying the method to quantitative studies:* the sentence could not be generated by a pronominalization rule formulated in terms of an identity condition: there is no exact antecedent for *this* in the text.

Remain does occur with clear subject complementation, as in *it remains to determine the value of x*, but it is questionable whether the structure underlying this is a satisfactory source for *the value of x remains to be determined;* notice that with all other verbs in the above list subject-raising is obligatory if *to* is the complementizer.

Matrix adjectives:

able 23	certain	likely 11
bound	liable 2	

(39) The situation for rigid solvents is again different, since the electron will be far less *able* to define the size or the form of the cavities. (14457)

(40) children, the mentally ill, the mentally subnormal andthe simple-minded, are all more *liable* to indulge in magical thinking than mature adults, (37223)

The inclusion of *able* in this class is somewhat problematical: the assignment is correct for some dialects, incorrect for others. It must be admitted that all the textual examples had active complements, but many speakers find sentences like *the problem wasn't able to be solved* quite acceptable, and there were several examples in the corpus of passive complements to the verb *enable* (hence its inclusion under pattern A):

(41) It also [*sc.* the anterior cibarial muscle], with the other cibarial dilators, raises the entrance to the cibarium and creates a wide opening to *enable* food to be pushed into the cibarium. (13211)

It may be that we should allow *able* into both one-place constructions (with subject-raising) and two-place (with deletion of the complement subject). For while we have both *John wasn't able to open the bottle* and *the bottle wasn't able to be opened*, passivization is scarcely acceptable with *John is able to speak ten languages*: *?ten languages are able to be spoken by John*. In the former case we are saying, in effect, that a certain action was possible (and took place), whereas the latter is saying something about John's skill in foreign languages. Near paraphrases are *it was not possible for John to open the bottle* and *John has the ability to speak ten languages*, which have respectively one and two underlying occurrences of *John*. Similar remarks apply to the modal *can*.

Pattern W: The patient requires nursing (1)

Subject complement; I suggested tentatively in 4.2.2 that *to* is the remote complementizer with a subsequent rule replacing *to* plus the passive auxiliary by *ing*; complement extraposed and subject raised to become matrix subject.

Matrix verb: *require.*

(42) During the critical period of six to eight weeks after transplantation the patient *requires* nursing in a unit in which the air is filtered
of all bacteria. (31155)

Pattern X: The gas goes on contracting (5)

Subject complement with *ing* as complementizer; complement extraposed and subject raised to become matrix subject.

Matrix verbs: *continue* (3), *go on, stop*

(43) When gas condenses to make a star, it *goes on* contracting until the
central temperature and density become high enough for hydrogen-
burning to begin. (39378)

As we have seen, *continue* can take *to* in the split-subject construction,
but when *go on* and *stop* are followed by an infinitive the construction
belongs to pattern K – compare (42) with:

(44) Now we shall *go on* to consider what happens when there is a large
number of particles, (27534)

As Palmer (1965: 176) points out in a discussion of *stop+to*, this is
semantically similar to a coordinate construction – *go on and consider.*
The infinitive clause is not one of purpose; notice that it cannot be
thematized without a change in meaning: *to consider what happens...we
shall go on* (compare *he left early to miss the rush-hour ~ to miss the rush
hour he left early*). Whatever deeper function we assign to the infinitive
in (43), it is clear that whereas (42) contains only one occurrence of *gas*
in remote structure (aside from that in the *when*-clause), (43) contains
two occurrences of *we*: the former involes subject-raising, the latter
subject-deletion.

Pattern Y: It is possible to explain this (89)

Subject complement with *to* as complementizer; complement extraposed and subject deleted under indefiniteness condition.

Matrix verb: *suffice*

(45) Prove that it *suffices* to be sure that the sum of torques about any one *axis* [*ital. sic*] (in two dimensions) is zero. (27374)

Matrix adjectives (and other attributive expressions):

appropriate	2	essential	2	necessary	11	useful	2
as well		expedient		plausible		usual	3
convenient	4	hard	3	possible	22	a mistake	
customary		important	2	rash		the custom	
difficult	10	interesting	2	safe	2	the usual practice	
easy	7	irreverent		satisfactory		of considerable interest	
economic		natural	2	tempting	2		

(46) It is perhaps *as well* at present not to try to be too specific, (22111)
(47) It seems probable that both σ-complexes and π-complexes are sometimes formed, although it is not *easy* to show this unequivocally. (24048)

Pattern Z: The membranes are difficult to distinguish (15)

Subject complement with *to* as complementizer; complement extraposed and subject deleted under indefiniteness condition; object raised to become matrix subject.

Matrix adjectives:

easy	5	difficult	7	simple
expensive		hard		

(48) As the damage continued, the chloroplasts clumped together, their outline became quite irregular, and their limiting membranes were increasingly *difficult* to distinguish. (11097)
(49) Although the present designs of hovercraft are *expensive* to buy and operate, a number of unique features turn the economics in favour of the hovercraft in certain circumstances. (34447)

Pattern AA: To obtain this requires careful selection (3)

Subject complement with *to* as complementizer; no extraposition and subject deleted under indefiniteness condition.

Matrix verbs: *be, require* (2)

(50) To obtain a gain of 45 dB per centimetre *requires* careful selection of a suitable cadmium sulphide crystal; (37528)
(51) to remain in a favourable state *is* in general to be inactive (22580)

Pattern BB: It is open to him to give evidence (1)

Subject complement with *to* as complementizer; complement extraposed and subject deleted under identity with object of preposition in matrix.

Matrix adjective: *open*

(52) In other words it is now recommended that when a level of 80 mg per 100 ml is reached it should not be *open* to the accused person to put in evidence of fitness to drive based on his performance under clinical examination. (36087)

Pattern CC: To proceed would provide him with a moral burden (1)

Subject complement with *to* as complementizer; no extraposition and subject deleted under identity with matrix object.

Matrix verb: *provide*

(53) But to proceed with a transplantation in a situation less satisfactory than this would *provide* the surgeon with an excessive moral burden. (31210)

It is perhaps not entirely clear that the subject of *proceed* is deleted under identity with *the surgeon* rather than under indefiniteness: we might understand it to be the transplant team that proceeds, but we certainly interpret the sentence in such a way that the surgeon is responsible for proceeding with the transplantation.

Pattern DD: It is worth hand-netting them (2)

Subject complement with *ing* as complementizer; complement extraposed and subject deleted under indefiniteness condition.

Matrix adjective: *worth* (2)

(54) It is also *worth* noting that, despite the sometimes bizarre manifestations of the couvade syndrome, no-one who undergoes the experience is ever deluded into thinking he is pregnant. (37304)

There are in fact two possible ways of deriving this example from the same deep structure. I have derived it simply by extraposition from *noting that S is also worth*; but it is possible to invoke object-raising, witness the non-extraposed equivalent: *that S is also worth noting*.

Pattern EE: Supplementing the culture medium altered the results (6)

Subject complement with *ing* as complementizer; no extraposition and subject deleted under indefiniteness condition.

Matrix verbs:

allow	cause 2	increase
alter	give	

(55) Supplementing the culture medium *altered* the proportion of sporangia in which meiosis was initiated and the state of the contents when development terminated. (11225)

(56) Bathing, washing or drinking the infected water *allows* the cercaria to enter the final host. (23414)

Pattern FF: Doing this was difficult for him (1)
    Subject complement with *ing* as complementizer; no extraposition and subject deleted under identity with object of preposition in matrix. Matrix adjective: *difficult*.

(57) With a kidney transplant from a living donor the recipient's own risks have still to be assessed, but far more *difficult* for the surgeon is relating these to the risks of the removal of a kidney from a healthy person, even after taking good care to determine that both of the donor's kidneys are functioning efficiently. (31194)

Although extraposition has not applied here (it is in fact comparatively rare with *ing*-subjects and acceptable only with a quite short and simple matrix) the main effect of extraposition – to place the complement after the matrix VP – has been achieved in this example by other means, namely the thematization of the attribute (cf. 8.1).

Pattern GG: It is usual for her to lie upon them (6)
    Subject complement with *to* as complementizer; complement extraposed and subject retained. Matrix verb: *take* (2)

(58) Starting with helium at room temperature, it *takes* only 2 or 3 hr for liquid helium to be produced, (29273)

Matrix adjectives and other attributes: *easy, possible, usual, an offence.*

(59) In the West of Ireland and in some parts of Europe, it is said to be quite *usual* for a woman in labour to wear some of her husband's clothes or lie upon these while in childbed. (37199)

Table 4: 5 shows the frequencies of the above patterns and of the grammatical features into which they have been analyzed. The eight

TABLE 4: 5. Non-finite complements

	A	B	C	D	E	F	G	H	I	J	K	L	M	N	O	P	Q	R	S	T	U	V	W	X	Y	Z	AA	BB	CC	DD	EE	FF	GG	Totals
Pre-passive obj comp	82	128	6	47	1	2		1	22	24	79	2	1	12	3	3	13	3	2	2	1													435 ⎫
Pre-passive subj comp																						243	1	5	89	15	3	1	1	2	6	1	6	373 ⎬ 808
Passive matrix		128				2									3				2															135
Mood subj of comp																																		
Raised	82	128	6	47	1	2	1	1														243	1	5										517
Deleted																																		
Indefinite									22			2													89	15	3	1	1			1	6	140 ⎫
Subj antecedent											79				3				2															84 ⎪
Obj antecedent													1	12		3	13			2	1													32 ⎬ 282
Other antecedent										24																				2				26 ⎪
Retained																		3													6			9 ⎭
Remote complementizer																																		
to	82	128					1		22	24	79	2	1	12	3	3	13			2	1	243			89	15	3	1	1			1	6	737 ⎫
zero			6	47																														51 ⎬ 808
ing					1	2		1										3	2				1	5						2	6			20 ⎭
Be-deletion					1	2	1																											4
To-deletion			6		1	2																												9
To+be+m→ing																							1											1
Comp obj-raising																					1					15								16
Overt it												2													89			1		2			6	100
Interrogative comp													1																					1

Check-list of patterns

A: We assume this to be the case
B: This is assumed to be the case
C: He made them go
D: He let them go
E: We see them moving
F: They are seen moving
G: He had a tooth extracted
H: We picture them replacing it
I: The first step is to collect the data
J: Our task is to explain this fact
K: We hope to resolve this problem

L: It is hoped to return to this problem
M: He determined what to do
N: This led us to question the theory
O: He was tempted to go
P: This helped to solve the problem
Q: This helped solve the problem
R: This involves measuring the change
S: We anticipate saving money
T: He arranged for us to go
U: They are sufficient for us to measure
V: They appear to be unrelated

W: The patient requires nursing
X: The gas goes on contracting
Y: It is possible to explain this
Z: The membranes are difficult to distinguish
AA: To obtain this requires careful selection
BB: It is open to him to give evidence
CC: To proceed would provide him with a moral burden
DD: It is worth hand-netting them
EE: Supplementing the culture medium altered the results
FF: Doing this was difficult for him
GG: It is usual for her to lie upon them

most frequent patterns, V, B, Y, A, K, D, J and I, account for almost 90 % of the complements: the remaining 25 patterns have less than 100 occurrences between them. The mood subject of the complement clause is almost invariably raised into the matrix or else deleted: there were just 9 instances in which it was retained in the complement.

4.4 Complements to nouns

In this section I shall deal briefly with complements occurring in NP's with a noun as head. As before finite complements will be considered first.

Much the most frequent pattern for these involved a declarative clause introduced by the complementizer *that:*

(1) Similarly, results for electrons in hydroxide glasses suggest that the cavities are quite well defined, in accord with *the postulate that* the electrons are trapped at hydroxide-ion vacancies. (14476)
(2) it [*sc.* the particle] accelerates according to *the usual formula that* the *x*-component of force is the mass times the *x*-component of acceleration, etc. (27447)

There were 148 examples of this type, with the following items as head noun:

advantage		effect		impression		proof	
assumption	5	evidence	15	indication	4	reason	
belief	3	fact	51	law		recollection	
chance		feeling	2	misconception		recognition	
concept		finding		notion	3	result	
conclusion	2	form		observation	2	sign	3
condition		formula		phenomenon		statement	2
delusion		hope	3	possibility	4	suggestion	
disadvantage		hypothesis	2	postulate	2	suspicion	
discovery	2	idea	4	probability	8	theorem	
doubt	5					view	4

It is worth stressing that only about half these items are nominalizations.

There were no finite interrogative complements immediately following a noun in this way: all were governed by a preposition, as in:

(3) For a variety of physiological reasons, the assessment of a person's fitness or otherwise to drive a motor vehicle after drinking can be made far more reliably from chemical tests of the amount of

alcohol he has absorbed into his system than from *a knowledge of* how much he has actually consumed. (36001)

(4) *The question* naturally arises *as to* how far we can continue with the exact treatment of molecular systems before the mathematical methods break down under the weight of their own machinery. (26450)

(5) There was *speculation* also *about* what the consequences of drawing the world closer together would be. (36442)

(In (4) and (5) the complement clause is extraposed, but this does not affect the point at issue here.) The noun heads involved were:

guide as to	question as to 2	speculation about
ignorance of	record of	study of
knowledge of		

In some cases the preposition is optional (e.g. *the question whether...*) but more often it is obligatory.

What conclusions can be drawn from this apparent difference between declaratives and interrogatives? It has been suggested that all NP's are governed by prepositions in remote structure: *give*, for example, would be a three-place verb with the three NP's governed by *by*, *to* and *of*; prepositions are deleted under certain conditions (depending partly on general, partly on item-specific rules) and retained elsewhere: compare *Bill gave John the money, the money was given to Bill by John, the giving of the money to John by Bill.* It also seems reasonable to argue that the relation of complements to verbs in clauses is essentially the same as that of complements to nouns in NP's. This seems evident in the case of nominalizations – compare *his assumption that it was so* and *he assumed that it was so*, but can plausibly be generalized to nouns like *fact*, *idea* and so on, that have no verb counterparts. *Fact* would thus be a one-place predicate, *idea* a two-place one (*his idea that...*), 'predicate' being thus extended to include nouns as well as verbs and adjectives. It would follow then that the declarative clauses of (1) and (2) would be governed by prepositions in remote structure in the same way as the interrogatives (3)–(5); whereas prepositions are obligatorily deleted before declaratives, they are frequently retained before interrogatives – cf. *she persuaded John of his error, she persuaded John that he was wrong; this depends on your interpretation, this depends on how you interpret it.* There is even one example of *as to* occurring before an extraposed subject complement:

(6) even in these cases it is still somewhat doubtful as to whether, for example, there is no latent heat or merely an extremely small latent heat. (29009)

If these points are accepted we shall not have a rule of the form NP → N + S for the constructions considered in this section (though I will not speculate on what the rule will be), and this in turn casts some doubt on the appropriateness of this rule for the subject and object complements discussed in 4.2 and 4.3, i.e. on the validity of postulating a base-introduced *it* in such cases.

With non-finite complements, prepositions are retained if the complementizer is *ing*:

(7) The measurement of the temperature dependence of the relative intensities of the two displaced radiations afforded one means of evaluating Planck's constant, *h*. (26173)

(8) the froth flotation process for concentrating valuable minerals is one of the most impressive technical applications of surface chemistry. (32426)

These are taken up in the next section. With *to* as complementizer there is no overt preposition:

(9) Concern for revenue rather than for technical efficiency has been the main motive behind the policy – the desire to protect revenue from the telegraphic service. (36569)

(10) The decision whether or not to use live donors must be an individual one for the surgeons concerned. (31260)

As remarked above, the preposition-deletion rule is obligatory with declaratives, optional (or non-applicable, depending on the items concerned) with interrogatives – *as to* could be inserted after *decision* in (10). Most of the nouns entering into the pattern of (9) were nominalizations, but there were a handful that are not formed from verbs or adjectives: e.g. *condition, effort, opportunity, power, reason:*

(11) A rough elementary derivation of Eq (2.1) may be obtained by decomposing the total intensity pattern into a sum of contributions of different frequency components, and noting the *condition* for the different monochromatic contributions to remain 'in step'. (19160)

(12) In the *effort* to enhance its attractiveness, men and women submit their skin to systematic stretching, scraping, gouging, soaking and burning. (35167)

(13) In Scotland and elsewhere midwives and witches were once thought to have the *power* to transfer labour pains to husbands. (37204)

The full list of nouns taking an infinitival complement is as follows (53 examples):

ability	6	decision		necessity		power
agreement		desire	2	need	2	reason
attempt	10	effort	5	offer		refusal
capability		failure	4	opportunity		reluctance 2
capacity	3	fitness		permission		tendency 4
condition	3	liability				

In all but three cases the complement clause subject is deleted under the indefiniteness or identity conditions: compare (12) and (13), deleted subject, with (11), retained subject, preceded by the complementizer *for*.

Finally we may include under the heading of complements to nouns two cases where the noun is followed by a citation:

(14) Hence the old saw: 'For every child a tooth'. (37094)

(15) The fact that probably no husband has died of it [*sc.* the couvade syndrome] or of anxiety over his wife's condition may well have lent impetus to the obstetrician's well-known saying: 'Don't worry – I've never lost a husband yet'. (37333)

The difference between these and examples (1) and (2) above is clearly the same as that holding in clause structure between *he said: 'John is ill'*, and *he said that John was/is ill*, which lends additional support to the claim that the relation between the noun and its complements is the same as that between the verb and its complements. Notice that the 'direct/indirect speech' contrast isn't confined to nominalizations, as evidenced by (14).

4.5 Non-finite clauses governed by a preposition

This area of the grammar has not been subjected to very detailed study, and I shall attempt here no more than a fairly surface description. I am concerned only with constructions involving an overt preposition. Declarative finite and infinitival complements do not occur in this position and it is unnecessary to add anything here to what has already been said about interrogatives (2.2 and 4.4). There are occasional examples with an *en*-form verb, as in:

(1) The result of applying this procedure is also plotted in Fig. 1, with β again set equal to 0.04. (17383)

but the large majority of clauses governed by an overt preposition have an *ing*-form verb.

As with other types of complement, it is relatively rare for the mood subject to be retained in the constituent clause, as in (2):

(2) In fact the recent BMA Report has recommended that either blood or breath should be taken in preference to urine *in the event of the courts deciding* to accept the blood alcohol concentration as the best scientific evidence of impairment through alcohol of driving ability. (36313)

There were 36 examples (7%) of this overt subject pattern, as compared with 482 clauses (93%) with a covert subject, as in:

(3) Astronomers currently keep close track of solar disturbances *by photographing* the sun and by monitoring its radiations and their secondary effects with instruments on the earth and in artificial satellites. (38373)

The absence of a subject from the complement clause is normally due to deletion (under identity or indefiniteness conditions), but there is one type that might be regarded as subject-raising:

(4) Methods which have been tried so far to prevent transplants from being rejected include preventing antigenic material in the transplant from reaching the defence mechanism of the body and preventing the antibodies and cells from reaching the transplanted tissues. (31086)

This contains three instances of *prevent NP from V-ing*. Are we to say that *prevent* is a three-place verb with the complement subject deleted under identity with the matrix object or a two-place verb with subject-raising? The voice-neutrality test supports the latter analysis: *they prevented transplants from being rejected by the body* is equivalent to *they prevented the body from rejecting the transplants,* and the nominalized object in the following example lends additional support to the analysis of *prevent* as a two-place verb:

(5) The thiopurine Imuran has produced the best results in preventing the rejection of kidney transplants in dogs. (31107)

Subject-raising from a clause governed by *from* is found also with *stop* and *keep* – which are obviously semantically similar to *prevent*. With *stop* we also find constructions without *from* – compare:

(i) *a* He stopped them from playing cricket
   b He stopped them playing cricket
   c They stopped playing cricket

There are two different lexical items here: in *a*, *stop* is equivalent to *prevent*, in the others it is the antonym of *begin* and is syntactically like *begin* (cf. 4.2.2) except that the latter allows either *to-* or *ing*-form verbs in the complement. *Keep* also enters into a paradigm like (i), but again different senses are involved.

I shall now consider the most frequent prepositions in turn: this study is based on an examination of clauses containing an overt *ing*-form other than lexical *being* in parts A and C of the corpus. There were no examples here of complements with an overt mood subject.

By

In almost all cases the antecedent of the deleted complement subject is the pre-passive subject of the matrix clause in which the *by + ing* constituent has instrumental function:

(6) We hope to learn a great deal about baldness *by studying* these animals. (35477)
(7) It may be possible to explain this *by assuming* that, below the surface layer, the animals are dispersed to a greater or lesser extent in depth, (32140)

In (6) the mood subject of *study* is understood to be identical with the subject of *learn*, which is itself deleted under identity with *we* in its own matrix. The cyclical application of the rules, however, means that the (pre-passive) subject of *learn* will be present in the structure at the stage when the (mood) subject of *study* is deleted. In (7) the antecedent of the subject of *assume* (namely the subject of *explain*) is also deleted on a subsequent cycle, this time, however, under the indefiniteness condition. Where *by + ing* occurred in a passive matrix the antecedent was covert (indefinite) and human, as in (8), in all cases except (9), where it is in fact difficult to determine just what pre-passive subject is understood:

(8) The most probable velocity c_0 may be found *by differentiating* equation (8.16) with respect to q and equating the result to zero. (28397)

(9) Each nerve-fibre can carry only one sort of signal and therefore it is clear that response to a wide variety of types of change is achieved only *by having* many different types of receptor, (22412)

There were two examples where the antecedent of the deleted *ing*-clause subject is not the pre-passive subject of the matrix – both involve nominalizations:

(10) The usual method of obtaining TO(Γ),the transverse optical mode at the zone center, is *by analyzing* measurements of the residual ray reflectivity band with the aid of classical dispersion theory. (17014)

(11) we can see some indications that *by using* very large numbers of units, connected at random, there can be registration of the various combinations of afferent impulses that occur (22089)

The first involves equative *be*, and we have already seen (4.3.3, pattern J) that special rules have to be given for locating the antecedent of the complement subject in such structures; in this instance the subject of *analyze* is understood to be identical with that of *obtain*, itself covert. In (11) the subject of *use* is understood to be identical with that of the nominalized *register*.

Of

(a) In many cases the complement subject is deleted under the indefiniteness condition; it is generally understood as human:

(12) The Fries reaction constitutes another practical *method of preparing* phenolic ketones, and a further method is the Hoesch synthesis. (25010)

(13) The method of images as applied here *consists of replacing* a case in which one has one point source and several boundaries between different materials with a case in which one has one material (no boundaries) and several point sources, (17528)

In all such cases except (13) the *of + ing*-clause was post-modifier in a NP, with one of the following nouns as head: *means, method, system, technique, way, cost, difficulty, effect, necessity, problems, result, trauma.*

(b) *Of + ing* may be complement to an adjective such as *capable*: here it is the subject of *capable* in the matrix that is the antecedent of the understood subject of the constituent clause:

(14) But naval strategists would prefer a fast surface ship *capable of carrying* the complex and heavy equipment and weapons of the anti-submarine frigate. (34501)

The subject of *capable* – *which*, or *fast surface ship* – is here later deleted under the relative reduction rule: see 5.5.1.

   (c) *Of* + *ing* may be post-modifier in an NP where the pre-passive subject of the clause containing the NP is the antecedent:

(15) The paper nautilus *Argonauta*, a rather uncommonly caught hyponeustonic animal, has *a curious habit of riding* on the upper surface of the bells of *Scyphomedusae* (32295)

The other expressions occurring in this pattern were: *have the effect of, have the property of, have the idea of, find ways of, go through bouts of,* verb + *to the point of.* Very similar to the *have* + noun + *of* type is:

(16) Before the deodorant and perfume industries usurped *their function of creating* a person's body odor, the apocrine glands no doubt played an important role in human society. (35604)

where it is the possessive determiner of the matrix NP that identifies the covert subject (cf. *they have the function of...*).

   (d) Finally there was one instance where the antecedent is the indirect object of the matrix clause:

(17) Moreover, by dealing with probabilities, such an account gives us some *hope of being* able to speak more satisfactorily in statistical terms about this system with its large number of components. (22107)

In a deeper analysis one would hope to cover this and type (c) with a single generalization: to do so would involve showing that on some level or dimension of structure there is a constant relation between *John* and *hope* in such a pair as *John has some hope of succeeding* and *this gave John some hope of succeeding.*

In

(a) I begin with cases involving some component of 'cooperation': they are somewhat akin to the *help* + infinitival complement constructions discussed in 4.3.3, pattern P.

(18) Thiel emphasized the importance of the fore-gut *in controlling* and regulating the flow of food to the mid-gut, (13488)

(19) The OH absorption spectra are particularly useful here *in distinguishing* between the broadening that indicates the temperatures of clouds and broadening that results from turbulent velocities in the clouds, (34200)

(20) It [*sc.* the skin] plays a major role *in regulating* blood pressure and directing the flow of blood. (35016)

These, or at least the last two, are formally ambiguous. In one reading, not the one intended we may assume, *in* + *ing* is more or less equivalent to *in that* + finite clause: in this sense *the OH absorption spectra* and *the skin* would be interpreted as subjects of the *ing*-clause. It is precisely because the intended readings are not equivalent to the *in that* reformulations that it is necessary to understand the covert subjects as distinct from *the...spectra* and *the skin*. We must therefore say that the subjects of the *ing*-clauses are here deleted under the indefiniteness condition – it is the body, say, not the skin, that regulates blood pressure and so on.

(b) *In* + *ing*-clause is a time or circumstantial adjunct: the antecedent of the deleted subject is generally the pre-passive subject of the matrix:

(21) *in understanding* it [*sc.* the couvade syndrome] more fully we may throw light on a much wider range of human emotional problems. (37343)

(22) Thus the relative velocity of the projected molecule is greater than that assumed *in deducing* equation (8.29), (28559)

In a few instances, however, the subject is deleted under the indefiniteness condition – it is usually interpreted as human:

(23) *In using* kidneys from animals the ethical problems of using live donors no longer apply, (31307)

The transition from (21), where the antecedent is present in surface structure, to (22), where the antecedent is deleted after the identity rule has applied, to (23), where there is no antecedent in remote structure, can be exactly matched in non-prepositional circumstantial clauses with *ing*:

(24) Hass, *using* Moss' value of ϵ_∞, obtained ϵ_0, by fitting the restrahl band in the reflectivity curve with a single frequency oscillator. (17135)

(25) Again the curves calculated from molecular field theory, *using* Anderson's coefficients, have been included for comparison. (17405)

(26) *Using* the single oscillator dispersion relation [R$_1$], the best fit to the experimental curve gave [R$_2$], (17207)

The understood subject of *use* in (24) is *Hass*, in (25) it is the deleted pre-passive subject of *calculate*, in (26) it is indefinite and human.

(c) *In + ing*-clause is complement to an adjectival predicate: the matrix subject is the antecedent, as in:

(27) patients who had chronic kidney diseases with severe uraemia are especially slow *in rejecting* transplanted tissue. (31112)

(d) The *in* is determined by the matrix clause verb; with *consist* the understood subject is indefinite (normally human), with *succeed* it is the matrix pre-passive subject that is antecedent:

(28) A rapid method that affords very pure material though in only 65–74% yield *consists in* passing steam into a mixture of hydroquinone, manganese dioxide, and dilute sulfuric acid; (25399)

(29) High-pressure laboratories have *succeeded in* compacting powdered beryllium into a solid, (38559)

For

(a) *For + ing*-clause is post-modifier in an NP, with the constituent subject deleted under indefiniteness:

(30) *Protosiphon botryoides* is monoecious whilst the desert variety is dioecious, and this fact alone would seem sufficient justification *for regarding* the latter as a distinct species. (21624)

(b) *For + ing*-clause is post-modifier in an NP whose head is the antecedent of the deleted subject:

(31) The blood vessels in the neck and groin can be used as temporary sites *for receiving* the graft, (31524)

(32) it [*sc.* radio astronomy] gives us a tool *for measuring* directly some of the parameters of regions which were previously inaccessible. (34053)

There is some doubt about the analysis of such examples: both *the tool measures*...and *we measure*...(*with the tool*) are possible sources for the constituent clause in (31), and similarly, *mutatis mutandis*, in (30).

(c) *For + ing*-clause is complement to an adjectival predicate: again it may be unclear whether the matrix subject should be taken as the antecedent of the constituent subject or of some instrumental type adjunct:

(33) A large flat area is ideal *for carrying* passengers and motor vehicles, (34442)

(34) It [*sc.* the hovercraft] is particularly attractive to marine task forces *for landing* troops and supplies on hostile shores. (34475)

With some predicates, both subject and object of the *ing*-clause may be deleted; in the following example the object has the matrix (mood) subject as antecedent whereas the understood subject is indefinite:

(35) The main arterial and venous systems in the recipient monkey's chest and abdomen are well suited *for joining* to the vessels of the brain graft. (31522)

In the following, the antecedent is *Miss Nancy Naftel;* the pattern does not seem to be generalizable beyond *indebted* and a few more or less synonymous expressions (e.g. *grateful*):

(36) I am much indebted [...] to Miss Nancy Naftel *for drawing* figures 3 and 4 from photographs of the live animals. (32403)

(d) *For*+*ing*-clause is an adjunct – either of purpose, as in (36), or of circumstance, scope, etc., as in (37); in both, the antecedent is the matrix pre-passive subject:

(37) This is a form of the 'person language' used *for describing* living activities and it may be that for some purposes it is useful. (22123)

(38) For calculating H_{c2} and H_{c3} we can neglect the non-linear term $\beta|\psi|^2\psi$ in equation (3). (18143)

Again there is uncertainty in (37) because of the existence of the pair *we describe it with the person language* and *the person language describes it.*

On (or *upon*)

(a) The *on* is determined by the matrix verb *depend*; here the subject is deleted under the indefiniteness condition:

(39) It *depends* basically *on rendering* selected constituents of an ore floatable, (32430)

(b) *On*+*ing*-clause is a time or circumstantial adjunct; as with *in* the matrix clause pre-passive subject (overt in the active, covert in the passive) may be the antecedent, or else the constituent subject may be deleted under indefiniteness. The following thus match (21)–(23) and (24)–(26) above:

(40) *On eliminating F*, we have [R]. (26027)

(41) *On using* the values [R], it is found that b is 0.994×10^{-8} cm. (26074)

(42) *On using* the values then current for μ, a and α [...] the result is irrational, giving a value of $\cos \theta$ which exceeds unity. (26029)

In three examples, all similar, the structure of the *ing*-clause is unclear:

(43) The gas produced is evolved in part into the capsule during irradiation, and in part *on first heating* to decomposition temperature. (16217)

The analysis is made more difficult by the fact that *heat* is an ergative verb so that while the gas is obviously involved in the heating process it is not clear whether it should be understood as subject (*the gas heated*) or object (*we heated the gas*). The latter is perhaps to be preferred, in which case the subject of the constituent clause will be indefinite. Note finally that *heating* is taken as a verb in surface structure – (43) is distinguished from the nominalization:

(44) Quinone in the solid state has considerable vapor pressure and sublimes readily *on gentle heating* to form large yellow crystals. (25408)

Here *gentle* is a modifier in NP structure, whereas in (43) *first* can be interpreted as an adjunct in clause structure.

After and *before*

In all the textual examples where *after/before + ing*-clause was embedded in a matrix clause, the mood subject of the latter was antecedent for the understood element:

(45) With between 12 and 17 hours of storage, some animals survived if the opposite remaining kidney was left for some weeks *before being* removed. (31286)

Table 4: 6 gives the frequency figures for the various types of constituent clause subject deletion. Three cases are distinguished:

(a) The subject is deleted under the indefiniteness condition as in (42), etc.

(b) The subject is deleted under the identity condition, the antecedent being itself subsequently deleted, as in (41).

(c) The subject is deleted under the identity condition, the antecedent being present in surface structure, as in (40).

Types (a) and (b) are the prescriptivists' dangling participles: it is interesting to note that they account for well over half the total.

TABLE 4: 6. *'ing'-clauses governed by a preposition*

	by	of	in	for	on	after, before	others	Total
Subject deleted under condition of:								
(a) Indefiniteness	1	38	19	20	8	—	1	87
(b) Identity with covert antecedent	69	—	6	5	4	2	1	87
(c) Identity with overt antecedent	51	22	25	9	6	12	19	144
Total	121	60	50	34	18	14	21	318

5 Relativization

5.1 Introduction

The three most basic types of relative clause are exemplified in:

(1) Similar streaks appear on the body of a person *who has gone through repeated bouts of gaining weight and reducing.* (35214)
(2) the mechanism of attachment of the xanthate to the sulphide material *– which is obviously the key to the selectivity of the collector* – remained obscure, (32559)
(3) excitatory synapses produce *what amounts virtually to a short circuit in the synaptic membrane potential.* (33289)

These three types will be discussed in 5.2 and 5.3; other types of relative clause will then be discussed largely in terms of the ways in which they differ from the basic types.

The italicized clause in (3) is traditionally called an 'independent relative clause', those in (1) and (2) by contrast being 'dependent': I shall retain these terms, which have the virtue of familiarity, even though they do not use 'independent' versus 'dependent' in the same way as they are used outside the context of relative clauses. The relative clause in (1) is 'restrictive', that in (2) 'non-restrictive'; independent relatives can only be restrictive.

In general relative clauses are characterized by the presence in their remote structure of an element (which I shall speak of as the 'relativized element') that is co-referential with a preceding element, its 'antecedent'. I shall follow Chomsky (1965) in assuming that this referential identity is matched by linguistic identity in deep structure.[1] Thus in *John, who had overslept, was late for the meeting*, there will be two deep structure occurrences of *John*, the second of which is pronominalized – more specifically relativized – to become *who*. Normally the relativized element and its antecedent are NP's, but there are some types of non-

---

[1] This assumption will doubtless have to be amended in the light of Bach (1970): this and similar recent work is likely to lead to considerable modifications in the transformational treatment of pronominalization and 'identity-deletions'.

restrictive relative where other categories are involved. The pairing of antecedent and relativized element applies to both dependent and independent relatives, but in the latter construction the antecedent is deleted.

In restrictive relatives, the relativized NP and its antecedent are both dominated in remote structure (directly dominated for the latter, indirectly for the former) by a larger NP, which I shall refer to as the 'matrix NP'. Thus in (1) for example the matrix NP is *a person who has gone through repeated bouts of gaining weight and reducing*. In non-restrictive relatives, on the other hand, the antecedent and the relative clause do not, I think, jointly form a constituent in remote structure. Non-restrictives probably derive from underlying coordinate constructions; if so, the relativization rule will be obligatory for restrictives, optional for non-restrictives.

There are two principal types of construction that I include under the general heading of non-basic relatives. There are, firstly, those cases where the matrix NP is the identified element in an equative *be* construction (see 3.8), as in:

(4) What is needed now is a detailed study of series of cases. (37340)
(5) It is only in the last few years, though, that continuous control of voltage to fine limits by electronic means has become possible. (39061)

These differ from basic relatives in that the range of elements that can be relativized is here larger: they thus involve an extension of the normal relative pattern. (4) is often referred to in transformational literature as the 'pseudo-cleft' construction, (5) as the 'cleft-sentence' construction; they are discussed here in 5.4.1 and 5.4.2 respectively.

Secondly there are relatives with a non-finite verb, or no verb at all, in surface structure:

(6) There does not appear to be any cellulose in the material *composing the cell wall.* (21645)
(7) The single species *common in north Europe* grows in damp mud at the edges of ponds, (21596)

These are discussed in 5.5; they may be said to derive by deletion from basic relatives, more specifically from restrictive or non-restrictive dependent relatives. I have not considered pre-head modification in the present study, though many pre-head modifiers doubtless also derive from relative clauses (cf. Smith, 1964) – thus reduction of (the structure underlying) *the carpet which is green* yields *the carpet green*, and this in turn yields *the green carpet* by a transformation which (in this case obligatorily) shifts *green* to pre-head position.

In 5.6 I return to unreduced dependent relatives in order to make a statistical comparison between two registers, based on part A of the written scientific corpus and a corpus of spoken (non-scientific) English analyzed by Quirk (1968).

5.2   Basic dependent relatives

In spoken English the classic distinction between restrictive and non-restrictive relative clauses is marked phonologically. Quirk's account (1968: 99) is as follows: 'Restrictive clauses (as in "you're living in a world which is in the main stream") are linked to their antecedents by close syntactic juncture, by unity of intonation contour, and by continuity of the degree of loudness. In contrast, non-restrictive clauses are characterized by open juncture (recognized, together with the following features, by a comma in written materials), a fresh intonation contour, and a change (especially a diminution) in the degree of loudness. For example:

That's the Haydn *Seven Words from the Cross* – which is an extremely
                        2   24   p3
interesting work   (4 is low; p = "piano")

It is by no means universally the case that all three of these distinctions are present (the closeness or openness of the juncture seems to be especially dispensable), but it is rarely difficult on the basis of these criteria to distinguish restrictive from non-restrictive clauses.'

In written English – or at least in our scientific corpus – punctuation provides a much less reliable guide than is often supposed (cf. Quirk's reference to the comma in the above quotation, or Langendoen, 1969: 93). In general, commas are not used to mark off restrictive relatives (the two clear exceptions to this involve a special type of construction to which I return below) but, contrary to the prescriptions of normative grammarians, many non-restrictive relatives are not preceded by a comma. Among the clearest examples are:

(1) The temperatures in hydrogen clouds vary considerably but the mean value is about − 175 °C *which* represents the equilibrium temperature between the heat gained on collisions between clouds and the heat lost by radiation from the material of the clouds. (34206)

(2) Each antheridium produces one biflagellate colourless antherozoid *which* has been contrasted with the non-motile rhodophycean spermatium. (21272)

(3) Their characteristic shape is brought about by a continual rolling motion over the soil surface under the influence of wave action, and hence the 'ball' forms are found near the shore whilst the 'thread' and 'cushion' forms are to be found farther out in deeper water *where* there is less motion. (21363)

(4) Both samples came from the same ingot *which* was not intentionally doped. (17146)

For this reason the reader has to rely quite heavily on other factors in deciding which type of relative the writer intended. Some of these other factors are grammatical: as we shall see below there are a number of differences in the internal structure of restrictives and non-restrictives, and certain types of antecedent allow only one or other of the two classes of relative – this is why (1) above is unambiguously non-restrictive. But more often the reader's interpretation will be determined by semantic factors – which type of relative makes better sense in the context. The difference in meaning between the two constructions is typically discussed with reference to such a pair as the following, taken from Langendoen (1969: 93):

(i) *a* The Chinese, who are industrious, control the economy of Singapore

  b The Chinese who are industrious control the economy of Singapore

(In all the examples not drawn from the scientific corpus I shall distinguish between non-restrictives and restrictives by the presence and absence, respectively, of surrounding commas.) In (i)*a* the reader will assume (unless there is something in the preceding context to indicate otherwise) that the writer is talking about the Chinese people in general: he asserts of them both that they control the economy of Singapore, and also that they are industrious. In *b* on the other hand he asserts not that the Singapore economy is controlled by the Chinese as a whole, but that it is controlled by a subset of them, namely the industrious ones.

This account is undoubtedly correct as far as it goes, but the examples are to some extent misleading in that they suggest a more striking and obvious difference between the restrictive and non-restrictive constructions than is often found. It is significant that grammarians almost invariably choose definite NP's to exemplify the contrast; with indefinite ones, the semantic difference is frequently less pronounced, and may be largely a matter of 'information structure'. I use this term in the sense of Halliday (1964, 1967c); he distinguishes between such pairs as the following (1964: 147):

(ii) *a* || I saw John yesterday||
      b || I saw John || yesterday ||
(iii) *a* || I'm leaving now to catch the train ||
      b || I'm leaving now || to catch the train ||

(where || marks a tone group boundary: as far as the present discussion is concerned we may say that each tone group contains one and only one nuclear stress). The difference between one tone group and two in such pairs is accounted for at the semantic–syntactic level in terms of one information unit versus two. Thus (iii)*a* is interpreted as conveying a single piece of information, whereas *b* conveys two: I'm leaving now, and the reason is that I want to catch the train. My point is, then, that with indefinite NP's the difference between restrictive and non-restrictive relatives may be no more than that between the pairs in (ii) and (iii).

Consider for example the following sentences from the corpus:

(5) Thus pontellid copepods and one or two species of decapod crustacea possess a pigment which has been extracted and examined spectroscopically. (32258)

(6) *Physalia*, for example, has a large and elaborate float which has been described by A. K. Totton. (32160)

(7) The cushions or plates are frequently lime encrusted and form a tough green stratum with a base that is composed of one or more layers of cells which give rise to dense, erect, branched filaments. (21098)

(8) Fertilization occurs in the water, and the zygote in *H. ovalis* germinates into a branched protonemal thread that in 3 months has developed into a typical *Derbesia* plant with the erect aerial filaments arising from the basal rhizoidal portion. (21655)

(9) Pankratz & Bowen (1963) studied blue-green algae recovering from chlorosis induced by growth under low illumination, and found that remnants of the photosynthetic elements appeared as small vesicles which flattened during recovery to form typical lamellae. (12283)

(10) β is an adjustable parameter which may be approximately identified with the ratio of the biquadratic to bilinear exchange coefficients. (17310)

Both restrictive and non-restrictive readings seem quite plausible in these and quite a number of other examples. The structures of the relative clauses in (5) and (6) are quite similar, but I think that the restrictive reading (one information unit) is marginally more likely in (5) and the non-restrictive (two information units) in (6). This is because it is more informative to say simply that *Physalia* has a large and elaborate float than that pontellid copepods, etc., possess a pigment: to end the information unit at *pigment*, in other words, is to leave it with a rather meagre content. Similarly in (9) it seems to me more appropriate to ask whether the appearance of the remnants as small vesicles and the flattening of the latter are presented as two separate components of the message or as a single joint component than to try to determine whether the flattening 'defines' the vesicles or not.

If this analysis is correct it casts some doubt on the validity of making a rigid distinction between 'stylistic' and 'non-stylistic' phenomena, as is frequently done in transformational-generative grammar. Sentences differing only stylistically are assigned the same deep structure, the stylistic difference between them being handled in the transformational component, or else being regarded as a matter of performance, not competence. But it seems unlikely that a sharp distinction can be made between what is cognitively relevant and what is merely stylistic. In view of the clear cognitive difference between (i) *a* and *b* it is inconceivable that they should be assigned the same deep structure. But if we distinguish in deep structure between restrictives and non-restrictives in these examples, we must surely do so in (5)–(10) as well. Then if we make a deep structure difference in these cases, can we be content to treat the analogous contrast between the pairs in (ii) and (iii) as simply a matter of surface structure, or performance?

Let us turn now to the question of how the difference between restrictive and non-restrictive relatives is to be represented in structural terms. I'll begin with examples containing definite NP's:

(iv) The theory, which was put forward by Jones, is clearly inadequate

(v) The vicar, who gives ferocious hell-fire sermons, rarely sets foot outside the church grounds

(vi) The theory that was put forward by Jones is clearly inadequate

(vii) The vicar who married them rarely sets foot outside the church grounds

What determines the selection of the definite article here? In (iv) and (v) the speaker must assume that the hearer is able to uniquely identify which theory or vicar he is referring to. The hearer may make the identification on the basis of the preceding linguistic context or of his knowledge of the situation or intended universe of discourse – in (iv) the identification will almost necessarily depend on previous mention whereas in (v) it will be enough for the hearer to know which parish is involved: there need not have been any previous reference to the vicar. In (vi) and (vii) the hearer is assumed to be able to identify which theory-that-was-put-forward-by-Jones or which vicar-that-married-them is being referred to. In the latter case they were presumably married by only one vicar, so that the vicar is identified by his role in the marriage ceremony, but there is certainly no implication in (vi) that Jones put forward only one theory – the uniqueness may again derive from the preceding discourse. Thus again the identification may depend upon preceding context or situation/universe of discourse. (vii) does not therefore represent a different use of the definite article: the situational uniqueness of *vicar who married them* is not different in kind from the situational uniqueness (at least in non-technical speech) of *sun*, as in *the sun is shining* (cf. Christophersen 1939: 38). This suggests then a syntactic equivalence between *theory* in (iv), *vicar* in (v), *theory that was put forward by Jones* in (vi) and *vicar who married them* in (vii). This equivalence can be represented by treating them all as constituents of the same type (the question whether the appropriate label is N or NP may be deferred until later).

In (vi) and (vii) *the theory that was put forward by Jones* and *the vicar who married them* are clearly single constituents – NP's – and I have argued that the major constituent cut within them is after *the*. In (iv) and (v), on the other hand, it is doubtful whether *the theory, which was put forward by Jones* and *the vicar, who gives ferocious hell-fire sermons* are single constituents in either deep or surface structure. The reasons for not treating them as such are:

(a) Phonologically the relative clause reads like some kind of interpolation – cf. *the theory, if I may say so, is clearly inadequate*, where one would not take the *if*-clause as part of the subject.

(b) The antecedent of a non-restrictive relative may be a sentence:

(11) The Raman line due to the double bond in methyl methacrylate gradually disappears during polymerisation, and is almost absent in the spectrum of the final polymer, which indicates that linking is due to opening of the double bond. (26399)

In such cases the relative clause can only be an immediate constituent of a sentence, and one might argue from this that all non-restrictive relatives should be treated as constituents of sentences. The coreferentiality of *which* and *the theory* in (iv) has of course no bearing on the constituent bracketing: coreferentiality and anaphora cut right across constituent boundaries, compare:

(viii) This theory was put forward by Jones but it is clearly inadequate

(c) The single constituent analysis is strongly counterintuitive in the case of what Jespersen (1927: 82) calls continuative relatives. Two textual examples are:

(12) After a time it [*sc.* the follicle] forms the germ of a new hair, which then works its way toward the surface, (35355)
(13) The oospore, or *spermocarp*, hibernates until spring when it becomes green and divides into sixteen or thirty-two cells, and these, when the wall bursts, each give rise to a single swarmer. (21282)

Jespersen characterized continuative relatives as those where *who* and *which* might be replaced by *and he, and she, and it* or *and they*. The label 'continuative' suggests he has in mind the 'and then' relation: it is certainly in those where there is an explicit or implicit *then* in the relative that one feels most strongly that the relative clause does not form a single constituent with its antecedent NP. Thus in (12) the boundary before *which* seems clearly to belong higher in the PM than that before *a new hair*, and similarly for *when* and *spring* respectively in (13). I do not thin it would be justifiable to give a radically different constituent analysis to continuatives and non-continuatives (it is not obvious that a sharp line can be drawn between them). It seems best then – in spite of the fact that non-restrictives tend to immediately follow their antecedents – to analyze them as immediate constituents of sentences, rather than of NP's (cf. Halliday, 1964: 149–50).

Let us return now to the structure of NP's containing restrictive relatives. The bracketing I suggested for the matrix NP in (vi) was [[the] [[theory] [that was put forward by Jones]]], so that the structure will be of the shape shown in PM(1), where NP_r stands for the relativized NP.

PM(1)

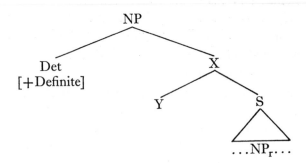

What labels should be given to the constituents X and Y? It would seem unsatisfactory to treat *theory that was put forward by Jones* as a noun, since morphologically and phonologically it is quite different from the normal type of compound word. Moreover we shall want to have X and Y belonging to the same category, since the construction is recursive: the antecedent of a relativized NP may itself contain a relative clause, as in *I'm looking for a book that's suitable for 5-year-olds which isn't too expensive.* (It is comparatively rare for two such relatives to remain unreduced in surface structure, but the deep structure pattern is clearly freely productive.)[1] And since Y is the antecedent, this means that it, like the relativized element, will be an NP if the linguistic identity condition is to hold. These arguments suggest then that both X and Y in PM(1) should be NP's. How can such a structure be generated? If we attempt to generate it by phrase structure rules, we shall have to postulate two recursive rules, NP → Det + NP and NP → NP + S; but the first of these is obviously incorrect, since it could lead to arbitrary strings of determiners as in *the the the boy*. As far as I can see it is impossible to generate PM(1) by means of satisfactory phrase structure rules, if X and Y are NP's. We must therefore either revise our decison about the categorial classification of X and Y, or else derive PM(1) by means of a transformation. This can be done if we follow Postal (1966) in deriving determiners from deep structure features rather than constituents; a partial remote structure for our example would then be as in PM(2) (where NP_a is the antecedent of NP_r).

---

[1] This recursiveness is a property of the restrictive construction only. Such an expression as *John, who had just returned from Rome* cannot be the antecedent of a relative pronoun (or any other kind of pronoun) – this lends some additional support to the claim that the quoted expression is not a constituent, thus not an NP.

PM(2)

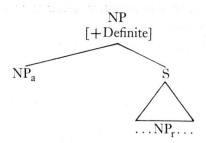

PM(1) would then derive from PM(2) by the determiner segmentalization rule. Notice, however, that this solution is possible only if we allow syntactic features to be assigned to non-terminal constituents – for, as I insisted above, the definiteness is a property of the matrix NP as a whole.

Now the very fact that it is the matrix NP that is definite suggests that the constituent NP's, or at least the antecedent, are indefinite: I take [– Definite] to be unmarked *vis-à-vis* [+ Definite]. The early transformational treatment of relative clauses derived sentences like (ix) *a* by a generalized transformation operating on the strings underlying *b* (the matrix sentence) and *c* (the constituent sentence):

(ix) *a* The man who came to dinner stayed all night
 b The man stayed all night
 c The man came to dinner

and the spirit of this analysis was retained when generalized transformations were abolished in favour of a phrase structure treatment of recursion. But where does the *the* come from in (ix)*b*? The speaker does not presuppose that the hearer can identify the man referred to independently of the information that he came to dinner. To treat the antecedent as indefinite thus seems more satisfactory from a semantic point of view, and also enables us to explain certain differences between restrictive and non-restrictive relatives. It is frequently pointed out that proper nouns can take only non-restrictive relatives: the absence of restrictive relatives would follow automatically from the above suggestion that the antecedent in the restrictive construction is always indefinite. That this constraint on the antecedent does not hold in the non-restrictive construction is due to the fact that here there is no matrix NP: in *the man, who came to dinner, stayed all night* the definiteness is a property of *the man*, not of the expression *the man, who came to dinner*.

Smith (1964) observes that restrictive relatives do not combine with possessive genitives either:

(x) *the man's car that he bought last year

and it seems likely that this constraint is also explicable in terms of definiteness. Smith has argued that genitives like *the man's car* are transformationally derived from structures like *the car of the man's*. The rule is obligatory, since the latter expression is not a well-formed NP; but we do find well-formed NP's like:

(xi) the play of Molière's that is performed most frequently in England

The structure of (xi) is approximately as shown in PM(3), where the transformational arrow notation indicates that the S node dominates a string which is transformed into *of Molière's*. PM(4) gives the structure of *the man's car* before the application of the rule deriving it from *the car of the man's*.

PM(3)

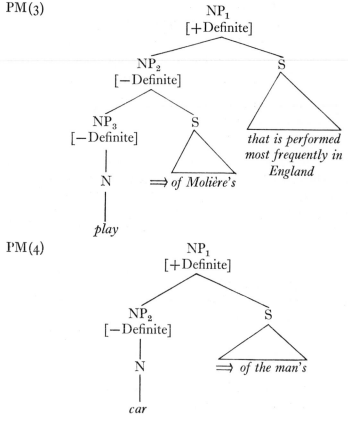

PM(4)

The rule for forming possessive-genitive determiners is conditional on the matrix NP being definite – *John's friend* clearly does not derive from *a friend of John's*. In PM (4) the matrix NP, i.e. NP₁, is [+ Definite], so that the rule applies to give *the man's car*. In PM (3), however, NP₂ is marked [– Definite] in accordance with the suggested constraint on the antecedents of restrictive relatives; since it is NP₂ that dominates *of Molière's* the possessive-genitive determiner rule cannot apply, and hence we get (xi) (where *the* marks the definiteness of NP₁).

Smith also points out the difference in grammaticality between the following pair:

(xii) *a* *Any book, which is about linguistics, is interesting
   b Any book which is about linguistics is interesting

This is not directly relevant to the question of definiteness, but it does lend support to one aspect of the analysis I have suggested. In (xii) *a any book* is non-specific and such NP's cannot be antecedents – for relatives, or deletions under the identity condition: note that in *anyone wanting to leave* the understood subject of *leave* is not *anyone*. (xii) *b* is not an exception to this rule, precisely because the antecedent of *which* is not *any book*: just as *the* in the earlier examples marked the matrix NP as definite, so here the *any* marks the matrix NP *any book which is about linguistics* as non-specific.

Restrictive relatives occasionally occur with personal pronouns. The construction exemplified in the proverbial *he who laughs last laughs best* does not conflict with the proposed constraint on antecedents, for there is no reason to say that the antecedent of *who* is definite. To claim that *he* is the antecedent is to interpret this notion much too superficially; such a claim is to be rejected for the same reasons as the claim that in *the man who came to dinner stayed all night* the antecedent of *who* is *the man* (cf. *the one who laughs last laughs best*). Thus *he* marks the definiteness of the matrix NP, not the antecedent. Much more difficult to explain, however, is the type found in:

(xiii) I who have heard him lecture on this subject know that that isn't what he means

This can be read with either restrictive or non-restrictive intonation, but in the former case the relative clause does not have limiting function and there can be no doubt that the antecedent is definite. The meaning of the relative is different from that of a normal restrictive occurring in a definite matrix NP – a paraphrase might be 'by virtue of the fact that I have heard him lecture on this subject'. But I know of no non-*ad hoc* way of expressing this difference, and at present I must simply concede that my analysis does not account for (xiii).

Let us consider now the internal structure of the relative clause, in particular the form and function of the *wh*-word itself. In the most straightforward cases – by far the majority – the relative word is a pronoun (or pro-form, to use a term that will cover *when, while, where* and *why* as well as *who, which*, etc.) functioning as mood subject or object, or adjunct of time, duration, place or reason. There were no examples in the corpus of *while* in a dependent relative (as in *the time while we were in France*); textual examples of the other five functions are, respectively:

(14) He found that the chromatophore was surrounded by an 85 Å membrane *which* was continuous with the plasma membrane (12420)

(15) We therefore decided to investigate the luminescence of actual specimens of meteoritic material, *which* we borrowed from the British Museum. (38209)

(16) photosynthesis takes place only at times *when* the light intensity is low (32396)

(17) in cultures *where* nutrient conditions are favourable one may obtain branched thread-like growths. (21605)

(18) There are several reasons *why* $V^{(r)}$ fluctuates. (19327)

When, while, where and *why* are interesting in that the antecedents are NP's, not adverbials of time, duration, place or reason. Thus the structure for the relevant part of (16), for example, is as shown in PM(5).

PM(5)

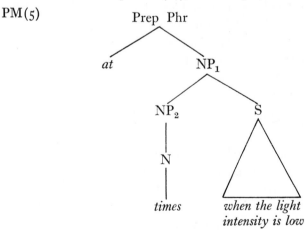

This must be so, since the *at* preceding *times* is not a necessary part of the construction – compare *the times when the light intensity is low are more frequent than might be imagined,* or example (18), where there is no *for* preceding *several reasons.* If we are to maintain the generalization about relative clauses that they contain an element – I've been calling it the relativized element – that is identical (and co-referential) with an antecedent, then the relativized elements will be NP's in these examples, so that *why* in (18) will be the spelling of *for + wh + reasons* (not *wh + for + reasons*) where *wh* is attached to the immediate left of the relativized NP (cf. Katz & Postal, 1964). Only unmarked prepositions are incorporated into these *wh*-words; compare such examples as *I saw him last Christmas, since when I've heard nothing from him* or *he climbed to the top of the hill, from where he had a clear view of the city.*

Consider now other cases where the relativized NP is object of a preposition, leaving aside temporarily those where the prepositional phrase is itself embedded within a larger NP. There are three subvarieties of this construction:

(a) The Prep Phr constituent is retained intact in surface structure, occupying initial position in the relative clause:

(19) the rapidity *with which* gas molecules diffuse indicates that they are in a state of rapid motion. (28139)

(b) Only the relativized NP itself is shifted to initial position, the preposition remaining where it was; in surface structure therefore the preposition is the only constituent of the prepositional phrase. This type was very infrequent in the corpus, the normative grammarian's strictures against 'ending sentences with a preposition' doubtless having more influence in this register than in informal conversation; in the following example the relative pronoun has been deleted at a later stage in the derivation (see below):

(20) I have never seen any signs of crawling or swimming among the specimens *I have looked at.* (32218)

The alternation between types (a) and (b) is discussed in detail in the standard handbooks (e.g. Jespersen, 1927: ch. 10).

(c) The third type is somewhat marginal in all contemporary registers, except perhaps legal writing and the like: the preposition is adjoined as a suffix to the *wh*-word, yielding such forms as *whereby, wherefrom,* etc., as in:

(21) Before the telephone was invented in 1876, F. M. A. Dumont, in the early age of telegraphy (1851), had taken out a patent for 'a particular combination of electric wires for the conveyance of intelligence in the interior of large towns *whereby* a central station has connected with it a certain number of houses in order that each house or subscriber may communicate privately with the central station'. (36475)

Where the Prep Phr is itself a constituent of a larger NP, the options are as follows:

(a) Firstly, the whole of the larger NP may be shifted to initial position in the relative clause:

(22) The maxillary articulation lies near the posterior end of the triangular cardo, *the condyle of which* fits into a socket a short way in front of the posterior rim of the maxillary fossa. (13002)

This type is more characteristic of non-restrictives than of restrictives, though it cannot be entirely ruled out from the latter. The only textual examples involving a restrictive relative were:

(23) In the Tricladida the uterus and the bursa copulatrix are replaced by organs, the *homologies of which* are doubtful. (23015)

(24) Let us consider a diatomic molecule, *the nuclei in which* vibrate about their equilibrium positions with a constant frequency, v_R. (26184)

I do not think the comma should be interpreted as marking an information unit boundary here, for such a reading would lead one to suppose, incorrectly, that the uterus and bursa copulatrix are not themselves organs and that there are no diatomic molecules in which the nuclei do not vibrate in the way specified. However, in such cases as:

(25) In *Yungia* there are some papillae also containing diverticula of the gut, *some of which* open to the exterior. (23217)

that is, cases where one of the pronominal forms *some, each, one, any, none*, etc., is head of the NP dominating *of which*, the relative is necessarily non-restrictive; it is of course reasonable that a set be not definable by properties of a subset of its members.

(b) Secondly, the Prep Phr may be detached from the NP dominating it and shifted on its own to initial position in the clause:

(26) In the Rhabdocoelia, *of which Mesostoma is an example*, there open out from the genital atrium on either side the paired *uteri*, (23003)

(27) Sir William Preece, Chief Engineer of the Post Office, *to whom Marconi was given an introduction in 1896,* had visited the Philadelphia Electrical Exhibition in 1884 (36511)

(28) All the Heterocotylea are ectoparasites with the single exception of *Polystomum* which occurs in the bladder of the common frog, *of which from 3–10 per cent are infected by it.* (23282)

In this last example the antecedent and relativized NP do not appear to be strictly identical, the former being singular, the latter plural, for we cannot have *3–10 per cent of the common frog* (or at least we cannot have it in the intended sense, namely 3–10 out of a hundred frogs, as opposed to 3–10 per cent of each frog). The number discrepancy is due of course to the fact that singular or plural NP's can be used to express genericness: the writer of (28) might equally have said... *which occurs in the bladder of common frogs.* If (28) is to be regarded as grammatical – and there certainly seems no doubt that it is acceptable – we shall have to assign the same deep structure to the generic expressions *the common frog* and *common frogs* or else qualify the generalization about the identity of antecedent and relativized NP's.

(c) Finally, the object of the preposition may alone be shifted to front position, as in the constructed example *he hopes to visit the Pope, who he's writing a biography of.* This type can certainly be regarded as ungrammatical as far as written scientific English is concerned, and is quite marginal even in colloquial English. In no register is type (c) allowable if the NP dominating the relativized NP is subject of the clause: **the Pope, who a biography of is appearing next year,...*

The construction exemplified in (22)–(28) is recursive: the NP dominating the Prep Phr containing the relativized NP may itself be the object of a preposition, and so on. In two examples in the text, the depth of recursion was as in:

(29) Similar fine structures have been found for the Raman spectra of oxygen, *the lines in the spectra of which* are of nearly equal intensity, (26326)

Rather similar is the construction where the Prep Phr is dominated by an Adjective Phrase: again we have different subvarieties according to how large a constituent is shifted to front position – compare:

(30) The many varieties of mammalian skin secretions, some odorless and some extraordinarily malodorous, some fatty and some watery,

some colorless and some strikingly pigmented, perform a wide range of functions, *prominent among which is sexual attraction.* (35496)

(31) With one exception the hydrated ions (ions bound to water) *to which the cell membrane is permeable* under the influence of the inhibitory transmitter substance are smaller than the hydrated ions *to which the membrane is impermeable.* (33448)

There are no examples in the corpus of the type where only the relativized NP itself is shifted: *?which the cell membrane is permeable to.* The type with the whole of the Adj Phr shifted, as in (30), is confined, I think, to non-restrictive relatives, and almost obligatorily has the subject moved to post-verbal position (cf. 8.1). Thus the difference between (xiv) *a* and *b* is the same as that between the non-relatives (xv) *a* and *b*:

(xiv) *a* prominent among which is sexual attraction
     b among which sexual attraction is prominent
(xv) *a* Prominent among these functions is sexual attraction
     b Sexual attraction is prominent among these functions

Finally, the relativized element may be contained within an embedded sentence functioning as some kind of complement within the relative clause:

(32) the evil spirits which a primitive man fears may harm his pregnant wife or new-born child are a projection of his own buried negative or hostile feelings. (37231)

(33) It is an exercise in nuclear physics under the extreme conditions prevailing in the interior of stars, for these are the furnaces in which we suppose the familiar elements of the Earth were 'cooked'. (39285)

(34) The first thing we would like to know is how much the distance *x* changes and how much the distance *y* changes. (27247)

(I mentioned in 2.2.2 some of the restrictions on this construction, with particular reference to Chomsky, 1968.) In (32) the relativized NP functions as mood subject in the sentence embedded as object of *fear.* The structures before and after the rule shifting it to front position are thus as in PM's (6) and (7) respectively.

PM(6)

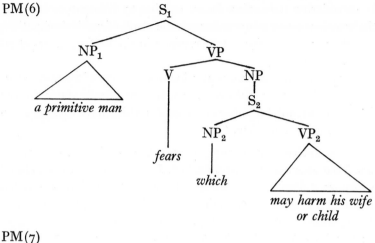

PM(7)

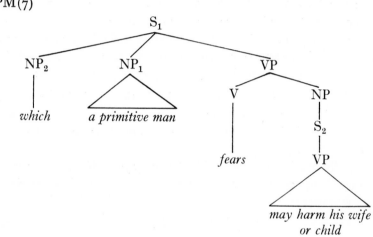

This explains the uncertainty as to whether *who* or *whom* is the socially 'correct' form of the relative in this type of construction when the relativized NP is human. In PM(6), before the shift, the relative is subject of S_2; in PM(7), after the shift, it is a non-subject constituent of S_1 — the *who/whom* variation would thus appear to be due to variation in the ordering of the case-marking and *wh*-fronting rules.

In all the constructions considered so far the relative word has been the head word of a nominal or adverbial phrase. In other cases it may function as determiner in NP structure; the items concerned are *whose* and *which*. *Whose*, the genitive form of *who* or *which*, occurs in both restrictive and non-restrictive relatives:

(35) In considering the surface fauna, one has to differentiate between the transient fauna *whose presence* is the result of vertical migration, and the permanent fauna that remains in the surface layers at all times. (32126)

(36) Under Δx is given the range of velocities in terms of the most probable velocity, *whose value* is taken as unity, and under Δy the fraction of the total number of molecules which have velocities corresponding to this range. (28413)

Which, as a determiner, occurs, however, only in non-restrictive relatives. Two uses may be distinguished. In the first – not exemplified in the corpus: it does in fact appear to be somewhat register-restricted – the noun following *which* is identical to the head noun in the antecedent NP, the repetition removing any doubt as to what the intended antecedent is: *I enclose a prospectus, time-table and application form, which form should be completed and returned as soon as possible.*

In the second use, the noun determined by *which* belongs to a small class of items including *case, time* and one or two others. In all five textual examples the relativized NP is object of a preposition:

(37) Peak concentration is reached in brain tissue within 30 seconds when alcohol is injected into the marginal vein of the ear of a rabbit, *by which time* the concentration in muscle is only half-way to equilibrium. (36166)

(38) Usually one is concerned with *stationary fields* [*ital. sic*], *in which case* all our ensemble averages are independent of the origin of time; (19427)

This construction differs from the other relatives we have been considering in that there is here apparently no identical pair of elements, antecedent and relativized NP. I referred earlier to the suggestion that non-restrictive relatives be derived from coordinate constructions and the present pattern lends some support to this view, for the expressions *by which time, in which case*, etc., are paralleled by *and by this time, and in this case*, etc. It is likely that there are two stages in relativization: a definitization process changing indefinites into definites (note the unacceptability of **a man and a woman appeared; a man was wearing a bowler hat* where the two instances of *a man* are co-referential: definitization must apply here too) and a pronominalization process. Normally both stages apply, but in the type exemplified in (37) and (38) only the first stage does. This doesn't of course solve the problem of (37) and (38) since we haven't stated the conditions for definitization, but this problem clearly goes well beyond the relative construction, embracing definite determiners like *the* and *this* as well as *which*.

We have been discussing the function and internal structure of the relativized NP: this accounts to a considerable extent for the form of the relative word used, but there remains the choice between *wh* (a cover term for *who, whom, which, where,* etc.), *that* and 'zero' (the case where the relative word is deleted). *Wh* is unmarked – there are practically no constraints on the occurrence of the appropriate *wh*-form (recall that we are here discussing basic relatives: there are additional constraints in the type discussed in 5.4), while there are limitations on *that* and zero. Moreover, *that* is unmarked *vis-à-vis* zero: wherever we have zero, *that* could be inserted. This suggests that the simplest way to deal with the variation between the types might be to take the *wh*-forms as basic, formulate a rule that optionally replaces *wh* by *that* under certain conditions, and add a second rule that optionally deletes *that* under certain other conditions.

The most obvious constraint on the distribution of *that* is that it must occupy the initial position in the clause, save only for a coordinating conjunction. Thus *that* could not be substituted for *wh* in (19), (22)–(31), and so on. Relative *that* may function as mood subject, object, attribute and adjunct; in the latter case it occurs freely with an antecedent of time (*by the time that he had finished*), reason (*the reason that he was late*) 'way' (*the way that he did it* – but not **the manner that he spoke*) but hardly with a locative antecedent (*?the place that he was born,* **the town that he lives*). The construction with *way* as antecedent noun is the only one where we can have *that* (or zero) but not a *wh*-form as adjunct **the way how he did it.* (We can of course say *the way in which he did it,* but *which* here does not correspond to *that,* since the latter incorporates the preposition *in.*)

In present-day English *that* is almost wholly confined to restrictive relatives. There was only one example in the corpus that was not clearly restrictive:

(39) One of the most important recent developments in neutral hydrogen studies of our Galaxy has been the discovery of high velocities in the centre and in regions away from the plane, *that* I have mentioned. (34280)

This example is complicated by the long post-modifier to *discovery* preceding the relative clause: this presumably explains the presence of the comma and the fact that any acceptable reading must have a tone group boundary to show that the antecedent noun is not *plane.*

Zero, on the other hand, is wholly confined to restrictive relatives: the *that* in (39), for example, could not be deleted. Intuitively deletion seems less likely the further removed the relative clause is from the head noun of the antecedent NP, but this will doubtless be at most a matter of statistical correlation, not hard and fast rules. In basic relatives *that* cannot be deleted if it has the function of mood subject: **he hadn't invited the man came with Jill.* This rule does not exclude the deletion of the relative in (32) and its like, of course, since the relativized NP is not subject of the relative clause here, only of the clause embedded as object of the latter – and at the stage when *that*-deletion occurs the relativized NP will have been shifted into the pre-subject position in the matrix – i.e. the deletion applies at the stage corresponding to PM(7), not PM(6).

Table 5: 1 shows the distribution in the corpus of the various relative items correlated with the distinction between restrictive and non-restrictive, and with the function of the relative pronoun – subject, as in (14), object, as in (15), adjunct, as in (16)–(18), object of a preposition, as in (22) – or (20): I also include the few cases where the relativized NP is detached from the governing preposition. Where the relative word is a determiner, as in (35)–(38), the classification depends on the function of the NP containing *whose* or *which* as determiner, so that (35) and (36) count as subject relatives, (37) and (38) as objects of prepositions. I have not included in the count clauses where the relative pronoun is deleted by the coordination reduction transformation. Thus for the purposes of table 5: 1 the following contains only one relative clause:

(40) the terminal cells often bear a pectose cap or series of caps which are periodically shed and replaced by new ones. (21153)

The comparatively large number of non-restrictive *where*-clauses is due mainly to a pattern characteristic of the register under consideration: the antecedent is a formula or equation of some kind, and the relative *where*-clause explains the values of the symbols used therein, as in:

(41) From this equation are derived the laws of *perfect gases*, the well-known formula for perfect gases being written

$$pV_0 = R_m T, \tag{8.5}$$

TABLE 5: I. *Dependent relative clauses*

	zero	that	which	who(m)	whose	when	where	whence	whereby	why	Total	
											No.	%
Restrictive												
S	—	296	320	27	28	—	—	—	—	—	671	69
O	41	16	20	1	—	—	—	—	—	—	78	8
A	16	13	—	—	—	3	33	—	1	6	72	8
p+o	—	—	142	—	2	—	—	—	—	—	144	15
Total No.	57	325	482	28	30	3	33	—	1	6	965	
%	6	34	50	3	3	0	3	—	0	1	100	—
Non-restrictive												
S	—	—	287	12	12	—	—	—	—	—	311	56
O	—	1	9	—	—	—	—	—	—	—	10	2
A	—	—	—	—	—	15	142	4	—	—	161	29
p+o	—	—	71	—	—	—	—	—	—	—	71	13
Total No.	—	1	367	12	12	15	142	4	—	—	553	
%	—	—	66	2	2	3	26	1	—	—	100	—
All												
S	—	296	607	39	40	—	—	—	—	—	982	65
O	41	17	29	1	—	—	—	—	—	—	88	6
A	16	13	—	—	—	18	175	4	1	6	233	15
p+o	—	—	213	—	2	—	—	—	—	—	215	14
Total No.	57	326	849	40	42	18	175	4	1	6	1518	
%	4	21	56	3	3	1	12	0	0	0	100	—

where T is the absolute temperature and R_m the gas constant re-ferred to one *gram-molecule* [. . .] (28230)

(See 5.6 for a comparison with spoken English using the same para-meters.)

Table 5: 2 shows the distribution of *wh, that* and 'zero' relatives. correlated with definiteness and the restrictive/non-restrictive opposi-tion. In the context of restrictive relatives definite and indefinite here apply to the matrix NP, with non-restrictives they apply to the antece-dent. The figures are based on a study of part A of the corpus only, leaving out the 44 instances of non-restrictive *where* in the pattern of (41). (The inclusion of these would in fact have strengthened the correlation that emerges from the table.)

TABLE 5: 2. *Relative clauses and definiteness*

(a) Number of occurrences

		wh	*that*	zero	Total
Definite matrix or antecedent	Restrictive	59	33	20	112
	Non-restrictive	82	—	—	82
	Total: definite	141	33	20	194
Indefinite matrix or antecedent	Restrictive	135	84	—	219
	Non-restrictive	58	—	—	58
	Total: indefinite	193	84	—	277
Total		334	117	20	471

(b) Percentages

	Restrictive	Non-restrictive	Total
Definite	34	59	41
Indefinite	66	41	59
Total	100	100	100

	wh	*that*	zero	Total
Definite	42	28	100	41
Indefinite	58	72	0	59
Total	100	100	100	100

Attention may be drawn to two points here. Firstly definiteness seems to correlate with the choice between *wh, that* and 'zero' – in particular all the zero relatives were in definite NP's. Of the 57 instances in the whole corpus only one was in an indefinite NP:

(42) But this [*sc.* that the tangential velocity times the radius is a constant] is something we already knew for the motion of a planet. (27520)

Secondly, the majority of non-restrictives (about 3 in 5) have definite antecedents: I suggested earlier that the antecedent of restrictives is necessarily indefinite, but the table shows a further association between restrictives and indefinites in that about two-thirds of the matrix NP's containing restrictive relatives were indefinite.

5.3 Basic independent relatives

The most obvious difference between independent and dependent relatives is that the former have no overt antecedent. There are, however, compelling reasons for claiming that there is an antecedent in deep structure, so that at this level the structures of independent and (restrictive) dependent relatives are very alike: the striking differences in surface structure result mainly from the different transformational derivations of the two constructions. Thus the underlying structure for (1) can be represented schematically along the lines of PM(1).

(1) When a nerve impulse has been triggered in some way, *what can be described as a gate opens* (33199)

PM(1)

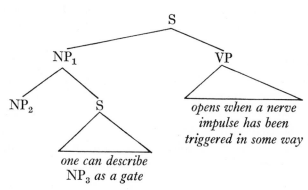

Here NP$_2$ is the (covert) antecedent and NP$_3$ the relativized NP.

The main reason for positing an antecedent in deep structure is that it is needed to account for the selectional restrictions which apply to the matrix NP. Compare, for example:

(i)   What she held in her hand was green and sticky
(ii) *What she told John was green and sticky

The first of these is acceptable, because we can say *she held NP in her hand* and *NP was green and sticky*, where the two NP's are identical. There is no conflict between the selectional restrictions applying to the NP's here: both sets require that the NP have the feature [+Physical Object]. But there is of course a conflict between *she told John NP* and *NP was green and sticky*, since the direct object of *tell* (in the relevant sense) cannot be marked [+Physical Object]: this is why (ii) is unacceptable. There are thus two sets of selectional restrictions to account for – one within the relative clause itself, the other in the matrix clause; they can both be naturally accounted for if we recognize two deep structure occurrences of the relevant NP, whereas without a covert antecedent the matrix clause's selectional restrictions would have to be handled in an *ad hoc* and uneconomic way, since there is no direct grammatical relation between the relativized NP and other elements in the matrix sentence.

A second point is that an independent relative may take either a singular or a plural verb in the matrix:

(iii) *a* What money she has is in the safe
       b What books she has are in the bedroom

If the matrix NP dominating an independent relative can be plural, it is clear that the relative clause cannot be the remote structure head of that NP.

The presence of an antecedent makes the remote structure of independent relatives quite different from that of (dependent) interrogatives, although in surface structure they are quite similar – let us briefly contrast the two constructions to see whether their differences are compatible with the postulated remote structures.

It is easy to construct examples that are ambiguous according as the embedded sentence is interrogative or relative:

(iv) I told him what you told me to tell him
(v)   What John says is of marginal interest is of marginal interest

The two readings are in each case quite distinct in meaning. Suppose you told me to tell him you were ill, then the interrogative reading of (iv) is equivalent to 'I told him that you told me to tell him that you were ill' while the relative reading is equivalent to 'I told him that you were ill'. In the interrogative interpretation of (v) the speaker is expressing his lack of interest in John's views, whereas in the relative interpretation he is on the contrary supporting them: the former we can gloss as 'it hardly matters what John says is of marginal interest', the latter as 'if John says something is of marginal interest, it *is* of marginal interest'. In the relative construction *what* can be replaced without change of cognitive meaning by *that which* (i.e. by a construction with overt antecedent and a dependent relative), but no such substitution is possible in the interrogative.

The difference in meaning is equally clear in the following textual examples:

(2) Thus, our present knowledge of the fine structure of bacteria has been built up from studies of what Murray (1963 a) refers to as 'the scientifically ubiquitous *Bacillus megaterium* and *Escherichia coli*'. (12038)

(3) At one time the study of what happens to materials subjected to very high pressures was conducted in the spirit of alchemy. (38520)

(4) the energy flux required to explain what they had seen called for a proton density that seemed to be out of the question. (38456)

(5) basic work in this field has long been occupied with the problem of explaining, first of all, why the existing process works so well. (32464)

In (3) the study is concerned with finding out ('resolving the indefiniteness', in the sense of 2.2.3) what happens, and the *what* is thus interrogative, while in the relative (2) the studies are concerned with the properties, etc., of *Bacillus megaterium* and *Escherichia coli*, not with finding out what Murray refers to by the quoted expression. (4) is again relative: the flux didn't resolve the indefiniteness, but provided an explanation of the (definite) thing(s) which they had seen. (5) is unambiguously interrogative – *why* cannot be the relative word in basic independent relatives (but see 5.4.1) – compare:

(vi)   *a* *Why he did it was sound

    b The reason why he did it was sound

    c Why he did it was a mystery

Where the wh-word is how the difference in meaning between the two constructions is a good deal less apparent. It seems to matter little whether we interpret:

(6) A study of how hair grows helps to explain some of the superstitions about it. (35400)

as a relative ('a study of the way in which...') or an interrogative ('a study aimed at resolving the indefiniteness'). Yet (6) must surely be regarded as structurally ambiguous since, firstly, *a study of* can take either a relative or interrogative as complement, as we have seen from (2) and (3); and, secondly, *how* can occur in interrogatives or relatives:

(vii) *a* How does hair grow?
      b How she answered his questions was very impressive

(The latter is necessarily relative because *impressive* does not take an interrogative sentence as subject: *who came was very impressive.) Moreover it is possible, I think, to see some semantic difference between the two readings of (6). Interrogative *how* means, as I have said, that the study was aimed at finding out how hair grows, resolving the indefiniteness, whereas relative *how* is definite – it's not a question of finding out, since this may be presumed to be known, but of studying the mechanism involved.

A further syntactic difference between relatives and interrogatives is that the extraposition rule applies only to the latter – compare:

(viii) *a* What he found there was very useful
       b *It was very useful what he found there
  (ix) *a* What he found there was incredible
       b It was incredible what he found there

Pronoun apposition, on the other hand, can apply to relatives (and also to interrogatives), so that (viii)*b* is ungrammatical only in the extraposition reading (see 4.2.1 for the distinction between extraposition and pronoun apposition).

Finally, we noted above that relatives functioning as mood subject in a matrix clause could take either singular or plural concord, as in (iii)*a* and *b* respectively; interrogatives on the other hand are necessarily singular: *who she invited are a puzzle is ungrammatical however many people there were involved.

Let us turn now to the structure of the relative clause itself, concentrating, as with dependent relatives, on the form and function of the *wh*-item. I deal first with the contrast between the presence and absence of *ever*:

(x) *a* She quickly spent whatever he gave her
   b She quickly spent what he gave her
(xi) *a* She stood up whenever the anthem was played
   b She stood up when the anthem was played

The *a* examples imply that there was more than one gift, more than one anthem-playing: that she spent each gift, stood up each time the anthem was played. The forms without *ever* are neutral as to whether there was one or more gifts, anthem-playings. *Ever* doesn't necessarily imply plurality, however; thus in:

(xii) They'll accept whoever she marries

there is no suggestion that she'll marry more than once – the meaning is that they'll accept her husband without conditions as to who he is. Sonnenschein (quoted by Jespersen 1927: 54) equates *whoever* with *anyone who*, and Kuroda (1968) relates *any* and *ever* in deep structure. We could for example paraphrase (x)*a* as 'she quickly spent anything he gave her'; this suggests that in the proposed remote structure of (x)*a*, shown schematically in PM(2),

PM(2)

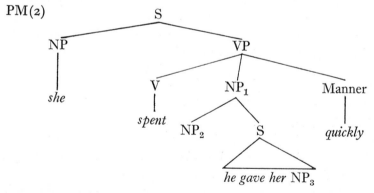

NP_1 should be assigned the features [−Definite, −Specific] (which I take to characterize *any*); NP_2 and NP_3, as with dependent relatives would be [−Definite]. But there is not always a straightforward paraphrase with *any*: there is not, for example, in the textual sentence:

(7) Whatever it is that glows on the moon seems to be localized, (38495)

or, to choose one without the cleft-sentence complication: *whoever told you that was wrong*. This doesn't really mean 'anyone who told you that was wrong' – the meaning is more like 'I don't know who told you that, but he was wrong'. For this reason I do not think we can be content to give the same deep structure to independent relatives with *ever* as to the corresponding dependent relative construction with *any* as determiner in the matrix NP – though I don't know what deep structure we should assign to the former.

There is reason to think that in certain circumstances *ever* may be optionally deleted. In present-day English *who* and *which* normally occur in independent relatives only with *ever*:[1]

(xiii) *a* Whoever she spoke to misunderstood her
      b *Who she spoke to misunderstood her
(xiv) *a* Take whichever book is the most appropriate
      b *Take which book is the most appropriate

But in certain environments *who* and *which* can occur without *ever* – cf. Jespersen (1927: 62): 'It is possible to say "Tom may marry whom he *chooses (pleases, likes)*", but if *likes* is the verb used, it means the same thing as the two other verbs, and has no reference to Tom's personal feelings, for it is impossible to say, for instance, "He is going to marry whom he dislikes".' The simplest statement would thus seem to be that *who* and *which* occur only when the matrix NP has whatever properties are marked by *ever* and that when the relativized NP is contained within a clause functioning as complement to a small class of verbs including *choose, want, please, like,* etc., *ever* may be optionally deleted.[2]

The difference between *which* and *what* is the same as that between these items when they occur in interrogative clauses: *which* involves an implicit or explicit definite domain – the distinction is discussed in some detail in 2.2.2. *Who* and *what* differ, obviously, in respect of the features [± Human]. The adverbial *when, while, where* and *how* involve antecedents with *time, place* and *way/manner* respectively as pro-form heads. As with dependent relatives, unmarked prepositions of time, duration, place and manner may be incorporated – but this time this applies to prepositions in the matrix clause as well as the relative clause. Consider, for example:

---

[1] Thus, *pace* Langendoen (1969: 75) the *wh*-clause in such a sentence as *moneylenders generally know who(m) they can trust to pay* cannot be a relative: it is unambiguously interrogative.

[2] The *ever* suffix cannot combine with *while*, which may therefore be considered a somewhat marginal member of the relative class. Some support for the *ever*-deletion rule can be found in the ungrammaticality of sentences like **do it while you like* in the sense 'do it during the time during which you would like to do it'.

(xv) *a* He lives where he has always lived
  b He climbed up the hill to where there was a clearing
  c He climbed up the hill to where he could see the city from

In (xv)*a* there is an underlying *at* in both matrix and relative clauses –
cf. *at the place at which*; in *b* only the relative has a covert preposition.
c is hardly grammatical – it seems that only unmarked covert prepositions are permissible in the independent relative construction. *How* does
not allow for the incorporation/deletion of a matrix clause *in* – the gap
in the paradigm is filled by *as* (see 6.3):

(xvi) *a* I admired how she did it
  b She did it as/*how she had always done it

With independent relatives, the *wh*-word is always clause-initial – in
this respect they differ from both dependent relatives and interrogatives:

(xvii) *a*   She left what she had once been so keen on in the attic
   b *She left on what she had once been so keen on in the attic

Consider finally the contrast between *what* as head and as determiner:

(xviii) *a* What he had given her was on the desk
   b What money he had given her was the desk

The obvious difference between such a pair is that in *a* the head noun of
the relativized NP is a pro-form, while in *b* it is *money*. But there are
other differences which cannot, I think, be regarded as following
automatically from this first point. We have noted that *what* in *a* can
be replaced without change of meaning by *that which*, and it is plausible
to suggest that *what he had given her* and *that which he had given her* have
the same remote structure – something like that shown in PM(3), where
NP$_2$ and NP$_3$ are identical.

PM(3)

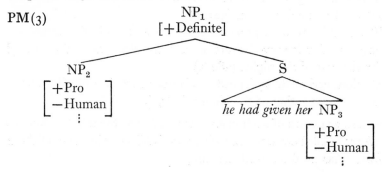

If NP$_2$ is deleted we get *what*; if it is retained we get *that which*. But *what money he had given her in* (xviii)*b* is not a paraphrase of *the money that he had given her*, because the former suggests that he hadn't given her very much money. (Cf. Zandvoort, 1950: 189 'In some cases its meaning [*sc.* the meaning of *what* used attributively] is more or less depreciatory'.) Notice that whereas we can say *what little money/few friends she has* the corresponding forms with 'multal' rather than 'paucal' quantifiers are anomalous: **what much money/many friends she has*. Indeed determiner *what* cannot precede a cardinal numeral (**what five books she's got are in the bedroom*) and can scarcely occur with a count singular noun (**she sold what car he had given her*). We could account both for the meaning of *what* +noun and also for the above syntactic constraints if we postulated an obligatory paucal quantifier in the underlying structure of such expressions: it would be realized as *few*, *little*, etc., or else be purely abstract with no overt realization. The paucal or depreciatory meaning and the syntactic constraints do not apply to *whatever* – cf. the textual example:

(8) therefore the net result is only those forces which arise from other particles which are not included in whatever object we decide to sum over. (27094)

It is likely that Zandvoort's qualification 'in some cases' in the above quotation is needed to exclude some cases where *ever* is deleted, for of the two examples he cites one has the depreciatory meaning (*I gave him what help I could*) while the other has, in terms of the analysis suggested above, an underlying *whatever* (*I shall receive what letters I please*). If the non-depreciatory meaning is confined to examples containing *please*, etc., this provides additional support for the *ever*-deletion rule.

The great majority of the independent relatives in the corpus had the function of adjunct of time, duration or place, as in:

(9) The float [...] is retained at one side of the foot *when* the animal is attached to a substratum. (32200)

(10) Then, *while* we were processing the latest plates in the darkroom, cumulus clouds moved overhead and the sky remained obscured for the rest of the night. (38255)

(11) Calcium carbonate is deposited *wherever* there is a mucilage layer and an aggregation of the chloroplasts, (21528)

There were 254 cases of such clauses with *when* as the *wh*-item and 36 with *where*; in all there were 127 with *while/whilst* but in many of them *while/whilst* has no durational meaning:

(12) There did not appear to be a gradient in the severity of the damage from one cell to another. One cell may be severely damaged with the cell contents completely massed together, *while* an adjacent cell may show no damage or only early signs of the damage. (11125)

While is here more or less equivalent to *whereas*, and I can see no justification for treating it as a relative in such cases.

Of the remaining 33 independent relatives, 11 were mood subject, 10 direct object and 12 object of a preposition. There were 12 cases where the matrix NP was the identified element in an equative *be* construction – i.e. more than half those with subject or direct object function (see next section). It is perhaps also worth noting that of the 21 basic independent relatives with *what* as the *wh*-item 12 had one of the following, semantically somewhat similar, verbs in the relative clause: *call* (5), *appear* (2) (in the sense of 'seem'), *describe as, consider (to be), refer to as, amount to, must* (logical necessity):

(13) At the end of the nineteenth century, A. R. Wallace, the aged evolutionist, produced a balance sheet of *what he called* 'successes' and 'failures' in the nineteenth-century record of achievement. (36455)

Cf. also (1) and (2) above.

The forms with *ever* were very rare: just three examples in all – (11), (8) and (7).

5.4 Relative clauses within an identified matrix NP

5.4.1 Independent relatives: the 'pseudo-cleft' construction.
Where the matrix NP is the identified element in an equative *be* construction (see 3.8) the range of patterns for the relative clause differs in a number of respects from that discussed so far. I shall consider first the case of independent relatives. Of the three textual examples:

(1) What happens at the anode is probably the conversion of chloride ions into hypochlorite and hydrogen ions (39216)
(2) What happens at the cathode, however, is itself a powerful argument for installing the process. (39230)
(3) The simplest 'complicated' object to analyze [...] is what we call a *rigid body* [*ital. sic*], (27019)

only the first has an identified matrix NP: (2) contains the intensive, not the equative *be*, and in (3), where the *be* is equative, the independent relative is the identifier, not the identified (note that it is not equivalent to *we call the simplest 'complicated' object to analyze a rigid body*.)

The main differences that I have been able to find between the present construction and basic independent relatives are as follows:

(a) The *ever*-forms cannot occur within an identified matrix. Thus such a sentence as:

(i) Whatever she wrote was a novel

will not be interpreted as an identified–identifier construction: there would be a contradiction between the identification and the meaning of *ever*, that the identity is not known. We may note in passing that *any* cannot occur as the determiner of an identified NP: *anything she wrote was a novel*, like (i), cannot be identified + identifier (cf. the inconclusive discussion of *ever* and *any* in 5.3).

(b) *Why* may occur as the relative item only with an identified matrix:

(ii) Why he was late was because he had overslept

(c) As Halliday (1967*c*: 233) points out, *who* may occur as the relative item only with an identified matrix and only if the identifier is an ana-phoric or deictic demonstrative: *that's who I meant*. The same double constraint applies, I think, to *how* + infinitive and *how* as modifier of an adjective or adverb – except that *which* is also an acceptable identifier:

(iii) *a*   That's not how to do it
       b   ...which is how old he is, too
       c   *Tactfully is how to do it
       d   *How old he is is 6

It may be that for some speakers the same holds true for *why* as well: there are probably some speakers who find (ii) unacceptable, but there are surely none who reject *that/which is why he was late*. (The *which* here and in (iii)*b* can only be non-restrictive.)

The effect of these differences is to make the *wh*-clauses more like interrogatives than are ordinary independent relatives: this applies most obviously to points (b) and (c), but I think it can also be said to apply to (a) too, for although *ever* does occur in interrogatives its meaning (as least as far as question-interrogatives are concerned) is quite different from that of the *ever* we find in independent relatives. There is moreover a certain semantic resemblance to interrogatives, since the identification structure could be thought of as providing the answer to the question corresponding to the *wh*-clause – compare:

(iv) *a* What he said was that he wouldn't arrive till Tuesday

    b What did he say? – That he wouldn't arrive till Tuesday

There is thus a 'serial relationship' (in the sense of Quirk, 1965) between interrogatives, identified relatives with demonstrative identifiers, other identified relatives and basic independent relatives. Nevertheless, as the terminology I have used in this formulation implies, I think the major division is between interrogatives on the one hand and the other three types on the other – that the *wh*-clause of (iv) *a* for example is a relative, not an interrogative. One piece of evidence is that there is no identification construction giving the answer to a disjunctive interrogative:

(v) *a* *Whether John or Peter saw her was that John did/saw her

    b *Whether John or Peter saw her was John

Secondly the semantics favours the relative analysis. I tried to show in 2.2.3 that *wh*-interrogatives were concerned with resolving an element of indefiniteness, but this interpretation is not valid for the identification construction. This does not involve the resolution of an element of indefiniteness, but the identification of a definite element: the subject of (iv)*a* is definite. Compare for example the two readings of:

(vi) What he was making was a puzzle

In one, the subject is interrogative, and *a puzzle* is attribute; in the other the subject is relative, and *a puzzle* identifier – the definiteness of the subject in this latter case is apparent from paraphrases using a dependent relative: *the thing* (not *something*) *he was making was a puzzle.*

What, finally, is there to be said about the relation between equative constructions with the relative clause as the identified element and the corresponding simple sentence? – between, for example, the pair:

(vii) *a* What he was reading was 'Daniel Deronda'

    b He was reading 'Daniel Deronda'

The main point I would make is that we cannot regard these as deriving from the same deep structure, with *b* as the basic form. Even if we consider only the cognitive meaning, leaving aside matters of discourse structure, the above examples are not paraphrases. This can be seen by embedding them within a larger matrix clause:

(viii) *a* *She watched what he was reading be 'Daniel Deronda'

     b She watched him reading 'Daniel Deronda'

If (vii)*a* and *b* were paraphrases the pair (viii) should be too, and we would expect them to be equally grammatical. But in fact the ungrammaticality of (viii)*a* is explicable in terms of the meaning difference between (vii)*a* and *b*: the latter expresses an action, the former an identification (in the static, non-dynamic sense – thus not an action) and while actions can be watched, identifications cannot. (viii)*a* will thus be excluded from the grammar by the same constraint as excludes:

(ix)   *She watched an equilateral triangle be one whose three sides are of equal length

It would be unsatisfactory therefore to say that the *be* of (ix) was present in deep structure whereas that of (viii)*a* – and (vii)*a* – was introduced transformationally; it is a deep (semantically significant) not a surface phenomenon that (viii)*a* and (ix) both contain *be*.

Simplified deep structures for (vii)*a* and *b* will thus be as shown in PM's (1) and (2) respectively.

PM(1)

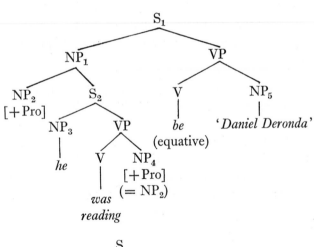

PM(2)

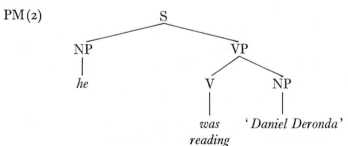

Admittedly these do not express the relationship between the sentences in any direct way, since even the S_2 of PM (1) is different from PM (2) – but the discussion of (viii) showed, I would claim, that the relationship between them is not as straightforward as is sometimes assumed. And notice that the analysis I have proposed for independent relatives is quite capable of explaining the deviance of (x)*a* without our having to derive it from *b*.

(x)   *a* *What he was frightening was sincerity
    b *He was frightening sincerity

The phrase-marker for (x)'*a* will be like PM(1) except that *frighten* replaces *read*, and *sincerity* '*Daniel Deronda*'. As argued in 5.3, there are two sets of selectional restrictions here, both involving a proform: one between *be sincerity* and NP_1, the other between *frighten* and its object, NP_4. If we adopt the proposal of Katz & Postal (1964) and others for dealing with pro-forms, we shall say that the relation with *be sincerity* imposes certain features on NP_1 – and thus on its head, NP_2: in particular, it must be [−Animate], since such sentences as *John/John's cat is sincerity* are deviant, at least as an identification construction. Similarly, the relation with *frighten* imposes certain features on NP_4: in particular it must be [+Animate], since such sentences as (x)*b* are deviant. But NP_2 and NP_4 must be identical (or at least non-distinct) because of the condition on relativization, for NP_2 is the antecedent of NP_4. The ungrammaticality of (x)*a* thus follows from the contradiction between this identity and the antonymous features they must have to satisfy the selectional restrictions they enter into. (x)*a* will thus be handled in essentially the same way as:

(xi) *a* *That which he was frightening was sincerity
    b *The person he was frightening was sincerity

– or example (ii) of 5.3.

5.4.2 Dependent relatives: the 'cleft-sentence' construction.

The argument just advanced for the 'pseudo-cleft' construction with independent relatives applies equally to the cleft-sentence construction with *it* plus a dependent relative. Thus in the following pair of textual examples:

(1) it is only the tangential component of the force that counts, (27384)
(2) Only the tangential part of the momentum counts for angular momentum. (27479)

the *be* in (1) must be present in remote structure for the same reasons as that of (vii) *a* and (viii) *a* in the previous section – compare **she watched it be 'Daniel Deronda' that he was reading.* The structure for such a sentence as *it was John who came* will thus be essentially as shown in PM(1), where NP_2 (the antecedent) = NP_3 (the relativized element).

PM(1)

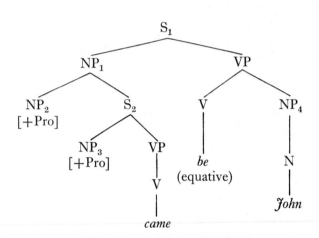

NP_1 is [+Definite] and its head is realized by *it*, whatever features are imposed upon it by its selectional relations with the VP. S_2 is obligatorily shifted to the right of the VP of S_1 by extraposition. Thus in spite of its position in surface structure the antecedent of the relativized NP is not of course *John*, but NP_2. Such a sentence as *it's money that I need* is in fact ambiguous according as it is an example of the cleft-sentence construction or a non-cleft sentence, with *money* the antecedent of *that*. In spoken English the two readings will differ intonationally, as pointed out by Lees (1963); in the phonological notation of Halliday (1963) typical pronunciations would be:

(i) *a* // ˄it's/money that I/**need**//
    b // ˄it's/**money** that I/need//

(**bold face** marks the nuclear stress). (i) *a* answers an implicit 'what money is that?' – *it* is anaphoric, and the matrix NP is *money that I need*; other things being equal the tonic or nuclear stress will fall on *need* in this construction. *b* answers 'what do you need?', or rather 'what is it that you need?' – *it* is non-anaphoric, and the matrix NP is *it...that I need*; other things being equal the tonic will fall on *money*, the unmarked place for the tonic in identification structures being on the identifier.

The relative clause in the cleft-sentence construction differs in the following respects from basic dependent relatives:

(a) The relative item may be deleted even when it has the function of subject, as in *it was John did it*. The omission of a subject relative in this pattern is probably characteristic of informal registers; there were no examples in the corpus. This omission is possible also in certain *there*-constructions, e.g. *there's a man wants to see you*, and for this reason these too should be registered as 'non-basic' relatives: they are considered briefly in 8.2.

(b) The range of elements that can be relativized is apparently very much greater, including many adverbial elements, for example:

(3) It is however only with relative values of $\overline{X}$ that we are concerned, (26372)
(4) It is to these weak bending motions that acetylene owes many of its properties, (26546)

I argued in 5.2 that in basic restrictive relatives only NP's are relativized, though an 'unmarked' preposition governing the relativized NP might be said to be deleted or alternatively incorporated; we noted such alternations as that between *the place at which* and *the place where* or *the reason for which* and *the reason why*. In the present construction the situation is different, for (3) does not alternate with **it is however only with relative values of $\overline{X}$ with which we are concerned*. We can of course say, *it is however only relative values of $\overline{X}$ that we are concerned with*, but here we have changed the identifier element. What are relativized in (3) and (4) are thus clearly Prep Phr's, not NP's, so that this type represents a significant extension of the basic relative construction. It is difficult to determine precisely what can be relativized in a cleft-sentence; among the elements that can *not* take on the function of identifier we may mention conjunctions, prepositions, 'sentence adverbs' (*however, obviously, perhaps*, etc.), and several types of subordinate clause:

(ii) *a* *It was whereas John was a Londoner that Peter was a Parisian
    b *It was although it was raining that he went out

(but one can say *it was in spite of the rain that he went out*).

(c) The *wh*-items *when* and *why* do not occur in cleft-sentence relatives, *that* being used instead:

(iii) *a* It was because of the rain that/*why he stayed at home
    b It's tomorrow that/*when he's coming

In general *that* is much commoner than the *wh*-items, but *who* and *which* are certainly possible. Lees seems to suggest that *where* is not used in cleft-sentence relatives, since he derives (iv)*a* from *b*:

(iv) *a* It is Chicago where they hold the meetings
      b Where they hold the meetings is Chicago

(iv)*a* is thus intended as an example of what I have been calling pronoun apposition, so that the intonation will be:

(iv) *c* //13 ‸it is Chi/**cago**/where they/hold the/**meetings**//

But (iv)*a* can also be read with falling intonation, which is not compatible with a derivation by pronoun apposition from the structure underlying *b*:

(iv) *d* //1 ‸it is Chi/**cago**/where they/hold the/meetings//

Contrast the following, where the tone 1 reading is not acceptable:

(v) *a* //13 ‸it's a/**whiskey**/what he **needs**//
     b *//1 ‸it's a/**whiskey**/what he needs//

where (v)*a* derives by pronoun apposition from *what he needs is a whiskey* (a pseudo-cleft construction). It seems then that we should allow two interpretations of (iv)*a*. In the pronoun apposition reading, (iv)*c*, the *where*-clause is an independent relative; in the reading (iv)*d* it is a dependent relative with *it* the head of the matrix NP.

Of the textual examples of the cleft-sentence construction 11 had the relativized element in subject position, as in (1) above and:

(5) These observations suggest that it is a portion of the vegetative shoot of the plant which must be attached for meiosis to occur (11546)

In the remainder, the relativized element is in all cases an adjunct (realized by *that*). Apart from (3) and (4) above, the identifiers were:

(a) Time expressions: *in only the last ten years or so, only in the last few years, (not) until 1892, (not) until after the end of the First World War, since 1945.*

(b) Reason expressions: *because of this difference, for this reason.*

(c) Place, as in:

(6) It is in the neck that asexual reproduction occurs, fresh segments being continually cut off and, as they grow larger, pushed by the formation of new segments away from the scolex. (23514)

5.5 Non-finite relatives

5.5.1 Participial and verbless constructions. I shall deal first with participial relative clauses – those marked by the verbal suffixes *ing* or *en*:

(1) These [*sc.* pieces of evidence] were: (1) the morphological similarity between colourless blue-green algae and some bacteria, and (2) the existence of so-called 'intermediate forms' (bacteria *possessing several blue-green algal features*). (12016)
(2) The plasma membrane appears in thin sections as two electron-opaque layers *separated by a less dense layer* to give a total thickness of 70–80 Å (12192)

This type occurs not only in restrictive relatives, as in the above examples, but also in non-restrictives:

(3) The strongest glow, *amounting to about 10 percent of the total light*, was emitted by a bright 'ray' of lunar material that crosses the Mare Serenitatis through the crater Bessel; (38143)
(4) In addition, there was 2% of an allylic alcohol (*tentatively believed to be 9a*) and 2% of α,β-unsaturated ketonic material [...] *believed to be largely 10*. (15115)

In this construction the relativized NP is deleted, its function prior to deletion being that of subject (*mood* subject, not pre-passive subject, of course: in (4), for example, the relativized NP belongs in deep structure within the sentence embedded as object of *believe*).

Where the relative clause is passive, the contrast between the *ing*- and *en*-forms is simply one of aspect, the former being progressive, the latter non-progressive. Compare:

(5) Such an argument is without foundation as the same methods when applied to higher organisms reveal structures totally different from those seen in the blue-green algae and bacteria, and more typical of the particular group *being examined*. (12047)
(6) The fine structure of the capsule in the few bacterial forms *examined* show [*sic*] similarities with the sheath of blue-green algae. (12086)

In the active, only the *ing*-type was found in the corpus; the construction exemplified in *those arrived at old age* is rare and only marginally acceptable. The *ing*-form here does not carry any necessary implication of the progressive, so that there is no overt marking of aspect in the active – we cannot for instance have a double *ing* construction: **the man being walking down the street was wearing morning dress*. In general, therefore, we shall have to say that active *ing*-relatives are grammatically ambiguous between the two aspects. In some cases there may be other reasons for ruling out the progressive interpretation – it is for example not very plausible in (1), for we shall hardly attest *bacteria are possessing several blue-green algal features*. In such a phrase as *those now living in Chelsea*, on the other hand, it is quite likely that there will be nothing in the context to resolve the ambiguity between the interpretations 'those who now live in Chelsea' and 'those who are now living in Chelsea'. Where there is an underlying progressive the relative reduction rule simply deletes the subject plus progressive *be*: the *ing* is the complementizer inserted into the complement of *be* (see 4.2.2 and 4.2.5); where there is no underlying progressive the rule must delete the subject and introduce *ing* as a special marker.

With *be* as lexical verb the situation is rather more complex. There are no examples of *being* in the corpus, but acceptable ones can be constructed:

(i) All those being uncooperative were sent out

This is undoubtedly progressive: the meaning is 'those who were being uncooperative'. Moreover the pattern is not found with 'stative' attributes – those which do not allow a progressive form of *be* in finite sentences:

(ii) *Those being illiterate were not allowed to vote

Non-progressive *be* may be itself deleted under certain conditions, and in such cases the relative clause will contain neither subject nor verb:

(7) From these and other studies a unitary concept is beginning to emerge concerning the basic organization of the organelle *responsible for the photosynthetic process*. (12307)

This derives by deletion of relativized subject + *be* from *the organelle which is responsible for the photosynthetic process* (cf. Smith, 1964).

The marking of progressive and non-progressive aspect in reduced relative clauses is thus as shown in table 5: 3.

It is difficult to state precisely the conditions under which lexical *be* may be deleted without obligatory shifting of the attribute to pre-head position, as in *the carpet which was green* ⇒ **the carpet green* ⇒ *the green*

TABLE 5: 3. *Aspect, voice and reduced relatives*

	Progressive	Non-progressive
Passive	*being taken*	*taken*
Active		
be	*being*	(zero)
others	*taking*	

carpet. The relationship between the present category of reduced, verb-less, relatives and the traditional notion of apposition is also a matter of some obscurity: the following remarks will therefore be more than usually tentative. Recent work in transformational grammar has tended to use the term 'appositive' in the sense of 'non-restrictive' (e.g. Smith, 1964; Langendoen, 1969, etc.), but traditional grammar used 'apposition' for both restrictive and non-restrictive constructions – Curme (1931: 89–92), for example, applies the term to both *the preposition 'in'* and *Mary, the belle of the village*: it is the traditional usage that I am adopting here.

I'll begin with the most straightforward case: a noun post-modified by a restrictive Adj Phr, as in:

(8) Parallel and adjacent to this unit membrane system is a thinner electron-opaque membrane *about 50 Å thick*. (12336)

(9) The measurements were made with a grating spectrometer with a resolution *better than 1 cm^{-1} throughout the region* [R]. (17049)

(10) The energies and densities of these protons are sufficient to account for luminescence *visible on the dark side of the moon* but not for the daytime phenomena; (38489)

These stand in a straightforward and systematic relationship to relative clauses containing a relativized subject plus *be*: *membrane which is about 50 Å thick, resolution which was better than...*, *luminescence that is visible*...*, and so on*: they are thus best derived by reduction from underlying relatives. In general the adjectival attribute can remain in post-head position only if the resultant post-modifier is complex – if it consists simply of a one-word Adj Phr it must be shifted to pre-head position (as in the *green carpet* example). The complexity may involve pre- or post-modification within the Adj Phr itself, as in (8) and (9) respectively, or the presence of some adjunct, such as *on the dark side of the moon* in

(10). The textually most frequent type was that where the adjective was a 'two-place predicate', one place being the covert subject, the other following the adjective and governed by a preposition whose selection depends on the particular adjective concerned: *available for, capable of, characteristic of, common to, consistent with, different from, perpendicular to, responsible for, similar to,* and so on. There are two exceptions to the constraint that the post-modifier must be complex. In the first place the rule shifting simple adjectival post-modifiers to pre-head position cannot apply if the determiner and pro-form head of the matrix NP coalesce into a single word – *somebody, anybody, nobody, something,* etc.:

(11) The first pair of plates to show *something unusual* were exposed between 22:35 and 22:45 U.T. on November 1. (38243)

Secondly, there are a few adjectives that may remain in post-modifier position, whatever the head of the matrix NP: e.g. *available, obtainable, present,* as in:

(12) From the limited *data available* I feel that, in general, live donors should not be used at present. (31264)

The non-restrictive analogue of the pattern exemplified in (8)–(10) did not occur in the corpus; a constructed example might be *John, angry at this deceit, determined to rely on his own judgment henceforth.* The reduced relative derivation is probably satisfactory here, though there is the added complication that the Adj Phr may be shifted to the left of the 'antecedent', and may also be interpreted as having some kind of causal meaning.

Let us now leave adjectival expressions and turn to nouns, NP's and clauses: it is these that are traditionally regarded as appositional constructions. We need to distinguish three main types of apposition: characterizing, identifying and narrowing.

(a) Characterizing apposition. This is exemplified in:

(13) The whale, *a completely naked mammal,* is adapted to living in polar waters by a thick layer of insulating blubber, (35289)

The relationship between *the whale* and *a completely naked mammal* – which may be referred to respectively as the superordinate and subordinate members of the appositional relation – matches that holding between them in an intensive *be* construction: *the whale is a completely naked animal.* As *which is* is systematically insertable into this type of construction we can regard characterizing apposition as deriving from an underlying relative. There is normally no restrictive analogue of this type: *the man who was a teacher spoke first* cannot be reduced to **the man a teacher spoke first*. However, certain measure nouns can occur in a restrictive relation:

(14) By contrast, mechanical artificial kidneys that can perform the same functions require apparatus *the size of a large washing machine*, a powerful electric motor, blood transfusion and two or three personnel. (31036)

We shall in any case wish to distinguish for selectional and semantic reasons between *the man was a teacher* and *the apparatus was the size of a washing-machine*, so the exception here does not involve any *ad hoc* categories.

(b) Identifying, or equative apposition. Clear examples are the following:

(15) The glands that actually produce sweat are of two general kinds: the apocrine glands, which are usually associated with hair follicles, and the eccrine glands, which are not. (35584)

(16) Stanier & van Niel (1941) enumerated three features common to bacteria and blue-green algae: absence of nuclei, absence of plastids and absence of sexual reproduction. (12013)

The subordinate member may be not an NP as in (15) and (16), but a clause, as in:

(17) there are two conditions for equilibrium: that the sum of the forces is zero, and that the sum of the torques is zero. (27370)

(18) This phenomenon too [*sc.* corpses growing a beard in the days after death] has a simple explanation: after the skin of a dead person dries and shrinks it may expose a millimeter or two of hair that was below the surface before death. (35424)

In this type the relation between the superordinate and subordinate terms is one of identification: the latter identifies the former. For this reason we might again wish to postulate an underlying relative – this time, one containing the equative *be*. Some support for this proposal comes from the fact that when the identifier is a clause it may have the form of a dependent clause, as in (17), or an independent one, as in (18): as we have seen earlier, this choice also applies to identifying clauses in the equative *be* construction – compare:

(17′) The two conditions for equilibrium are that the sum of the forces is zero and the sum of the torques is zero.

(18′) The explanation is, after the skin shrinks it may expose a millimeter or two of hair...

(With declaratives, the dependent form seems more likely than the independent in the overt *be* construction; with interrogatives the independent form seems more likely than the dependent in the appositional construction.) The derivation of identifying appositions from underlying relatives does, however, run up against some serious difficulties. Firstly the apposition may be marked by one of a small class of expressions like *that is, viz., namely* and so on, which would scarcely be found in the overt relative construction:

(19) the total force, i.e. the rate of change of momentum, acting on the area a_1 is [R], (28220)

(20) In this connection Cameron pointed out that in all instances of intense luminescence the moon has been close to full; that is, it has been on the side of the earth away from the sun. (38470)

(In the latter the superordinate term is also a clause.) Secondly, there is the problem of distinguishing between relativization and complementation. Consider, for example:

(iii) *a* This idea/belief, that he was being followed, tormented him
      b This idea/belief that he was being followed tormented him

These apparently differ simply as non-restrictive versus restrictive, and *that*-clauses can of course occur as the identifier in an equative *be* construction where *idea* or *belief*, etc, is head of the identified NP. Yet to say that there is an underlying *which was* in (iii)*b* conflicts with the analysis of the *that*-clause as a direct complement to the noun – an analysis put forward, with supporting evidence, in 4.4. The insertion of *which was* is possible in (iii)*a* but not in *b*, and this leads Langendoen (1969: 72–4) to suggest that only the former involves relativization: this may well be the best solution.

(c) Narrowing, including exemplificatory, apposition. Examples:

(21) Man, although he lacks the blood-filled sacs around the follicles, possesses nerve endings around many of his hair follicles, particularly those that surround the mouth. (35324)

(22) While they last they emit enough energy, both electromagnetic and corpuscular, to disturb the inner precincts of the solar system for hours and days afterward. (38370)

(23) However, this account takes into consideration the facts that we do know about the cortex, for instance that there are great numbers of input channels, leading to great numbers of cells, among which there are vast possibilities of interconnexion. (22101)

Here there is no question of postulating a deleted *which + be*. Note that (22) does not of course mean 'energy which is both electromagnetic and corpuscular' but rather 'energy, both electromagnetic energy and corpuscular energy'. It is unclear what the deep structure source is of this type of apposition. It bears some relation to coordination and it may be that the process of coordination reduction is applicable here too, so that (21) for example might derive from the structure underlying *man...possesses nerve endings around many of his hair follicles; man possesses nerve endings particularly around the hair follicles that surround the mouth.*

5.5.2 Infinitival constructions. There remains the class of infinitival relative clauses, as in:

(1) for some experiments it [*sc.* the basal nutrient medium] was supplemented in various ways *to be described later* (11287)

(2) Let us [...] draw from this point a system of lines of length *C to represent, in magnitude and direction, the velocities of the different molecules of the gas.* (28197)

(3) The first pair of plates *to show something unusual* were exposed between 22:35 and 22:45 U.T. on November 1. (38243)

The last of these differs syntactically and semantically from the first two. The italicized clause in (3) is dependent upon the pre-modifier *first*, for we could not say **the pair of plates to show something unusual were exposed*...I would argue therefore that (3) derives from the structure underlying *the pair of plates which were (the) first to show something unusual...*, where the infinitival clause is complement to *first*. (1) and (2) are paraphrasable, respectively, by 'in various ways that will be described later' and 'a system of lines which shall represent...'. On the basis of the range of permissible time adverbials we would be justified in analyzing the infinitival clauses here as containing some future component, but I know of no syntactic evidence that would support an analysis involving an underlying *will* or *shall* here. Note that reformulation with *will* or *shall* seems less appropriate in the case of such an example as:

(4) In this beetle, the mandibles are already equipped with well developed setal fringes *to aid in semi-liquid feeding.* (13540)

Semantically, there is an unmistakable element of purpose in this last example – the purpose of the setal fringes is to aid in semi-liquid feeding.

In the above infinitival relatives (1), (2) and (4), the function of the relativized NP prior to deletion is mood subject. Consider next cases where the relativized element is object of a preposition:

(5) May 1965, therefore, provides a good vantage point *from which to survey past and future.* (36400)
(6) The surface of the moon, unprotected by any atmosphere *to speak of*, is exposed not only to visible radiation from the sun and to high-energy ultra-violet and X radiation but also to corpuscular radiation: (38012)

Whereas with relativized subjects, deletion is obligatory, in the present case there is a choice between retention, as in (5), or deletion, as in (6). (5) thus alternates with ...*point to survey past and present from*, though for reasons which are not clear to me the overt relative form of (6) seems rather unlikely: *?any atmosphere of which to speak.* The relative item may be retained only if it is non-initial in the clause (more precisely if it follows the preposition) and if there is no overt mood subject:

(i) *a* *a good vantage point which/that to survey past and future from
   b *a good vantage point from which for us to survey past and future from
   c a good vantage point for us to survey past and future from

The subject is preceded by the complementizer *for*, so that the ungrammaticality of (i)*b* is due to the presence of two different subordinators in the one clause.

The same range of options is available when the infinitival clause is dependent upon a pre-head adjectival modifier, as in:

(7) A fresh solution of quinine sulphate cuts out the undesirable 4,047 line, while slightly diminishing the intensity of the 4,358 line, which is a convenient monochromatic radiation to work with. (26231)

Here the paradigm is:

(ii) *a* a convenient monochromatic radiation to work with
   b a convenient monochromatic radiation for us to work with
   c a convenient monochromatic radiation with which to work

The last of these raises considerable difficulties in analysis. If we accept the usual accounts of pre-head modification in the transformational literature we will derive (ii)*a* and *b* from *a monochromatic radiation which is convenient (for us) to work with*. The relative clause here involves subject complementation and object-raising, so that in terms of the analysis of 4.2.4 the derivation will be:

(iii) *a* (It) for us to work with NP is convenient
    b It is convenient for us to work with NP
    c NP is convenient for us to work with
    d which is convenient for us to work with

Here *b* derives from *a* by extraposition, *c* from *b* by object-raising, *d* from *c* by relativization, and (ii)*a* from (iii)*d* by *which + be* deletion followed by front-shifting of the adjective. Object-raising is optional, so that relativization could apply to (iii)*b* to give:

(iv) a monochromatic radiation with which it is convenient for us to work

But (ii)*c* cannot be derived from this except by a wholly *ad hoc* transformation – yet what other derivation is available for it? It seems in some sense to be a back-formation from (ii)*a* on the analogy of the alternation between such types as the earlier *point to survey past and future from* ~ *point from which to survey past and future* – but current formulations of transformational grammar do not apparently provide for this kind of phenomenon.

    Where the relativized NP is object of a preposition, the latter may also be deleted in some cases, for example:

(8) They [*sc.* artificial hearts, etc.] also provide a means of resting their natural counterparts and thus allow them time *to make good any damage*. (31569)

which has the variant form...*time in which to make good any damage*.
    Consider finally cases where the relativized NP is direct object:

(9) Electrolysis takes place in specially designed cells, and both anode and cathode have *parts to play* in the sterilizing process. (39213)

(10) *What* then, have we *to offer* chemical engineering? (39045)

(11) the hovercraft has *some way to go* to compete with ship ferries on a mileage basis, (34424)

The relative item is obligatorily deleted in these cases, so that we can formulate the general rule that in infinitival relatives the relativized NP must be deleted unless it is non-initial in the clause, more specifically, unless it is preceded by a preposition. Examples (5)–(11) confirm what was said earlier: that it is difficult to find an exact paraphrase with a finite verb. Except where the infinitival clause is originally complement to an adjective, i.e. (3) and (7), there is some future time component involved and, semantically, there is also an implicit but varying modality in certain cases – thus 'a vantage point from which we *can* survey...', 'parts which they *have* to play', etc. At present the precise underlying structure of the infinitival construction remains unclear.

Of the 36 infinitival relatives in the corpus only two were non-restrictive, as in:

(12) In the uncomfortable region from 10 to 4°K, helium gas thermometry is often used, and below 1°K magnetic methods, to be explained later in this chapter, are employed. (29314)

The non-restrictive type is possible, I think, only when it is the subject that is relativized: thus the restrictive *the man to see is Smith* is grammatical, but not the non-restrictive **the man, to see, is Smith*.

5.6   Dependent relatives: a comparison of registers

The distribution of *wh*, *that* and 'zero' relative forms in a sample of spoken (non-scientific) English has recently been investigated by Professor Quirk, who used as his material 'the tape-recorded contributions of some fifty adults to what would amount to about sixteen hours of continuous impromptu talk (equivalent to between three and four hundred printed pages). The speakers were English men and women, educated to university standard, and mainly between the ages of 25 and 50' (1968: 96). The corpus consisted of (a) 'impromptu conversation surreptitiously recorded under friendly and informal conditions'; (b) impromptu discussion with groups of participants who 'knew that the proceedings were being recorded and that it was the intention that a shortened and tidied version should ultimately be broadcast;' (c) 'impromptu discussion on a platform in front of an audience and simultaneously broadcast': there were no significant differences between the subvarieties as far as relative clauses were concerned. In order to obtain comparable statistical data on written scientific English I examined part A of our corpus using the same parameters as Quirk. For the present comparative purposes the *wh*-category covers only *which*, *who(m)*, and *whose*, since *when*, *where*, *why*, etc., are outside the scope of Quirk's study.

TABLE 5: 4. *Register comparison:*
restrictive and non-restrictive relatives
(a) Number of occurrences

	Conversational speech				Scientific writing			
	wh	*that*	zero	Total	*wh*	*that*	zero	Total
Restrictive	520	370	228	1118	183	117	20	320
Non-restrictive	171	1	—	172	145	—	—	145
Total	691	371	228	1290	328	117	20	465

(b) Percentages

	Conversational speech				Scientific writing			
	wh	*that*	zero	Total	*wh*	*that*	zero	Total
Restrictive	47	33	20	100	57	37	6	100
Non-restrictive	99	1	0	100	100	0	0	100
Total	54	29	18	100	71	25	4	100

Table 5: 4 shows the relative frequencies of *wh,* *that* and 'zero' correlated with the distinction between the restrictive and non-restrictive construction.[1] The zero form is considerably less frequent in the more formal register, the percentage of *wh*-forms being correspondingly higher. (Cf. the infrequency of *that*-deletion in complement clauses, 4.3.2.) There is little difference in the relative frequency of *that*. As one might expect, there are more non-restrictive relatives in the written material: 31 % as against 13 % in Quirk's corpus. His study also confirms what was noted in 5.2: that *that* is almost wholly excluded from non-restrictives.

[1] In this and subsequent tables I have left out of account the six 'incomplete' relative clauses in Quirk's data.

Table 5: 5 deals with the position of the relative clause within the matrix clause. Two positions are distinguished, final and non-final, as in (1) and (2) respectively:

(1) They [*sc.* free-floating anemones of the family *Abylidae*] are quite distinct from the anemones *that are frequently found on flotsam,* although they can assume a sedentary existence on occasions. (32197)

(2) The sky was exceptionally transparent and our plates, *which we developed as they were made,* revealed a remarkable sequence of events. (38239)

TABLE 5: 5. *Register comparison: medial and final relatives*
(a) Number of occurrences

	Conversational speech				Scientific writing			
	wh	*that*	zero	Total	*wh*	*that*	zero	Total
Medial	102	80	70	252	77	19	14	110
Final	589	291	158	1038	251	98	6	355
Total	691	371	228	1290	328	117	20	465

(b) Percentages

	Conversational speech				Scientific writing			
	wh	*that*	zero	Total	*wh*	*that*	zero	Total
Medial	15	22	31	19	23	16	70	24
Final	85	78	69	81	77	84	30	76
Total	100	100	100	100	100	100	100	100

'Final' is relative to the matrix clause, not to the orthographic sentence. In both registers over three-quarters of the relative clauses were in matrix final position. In the majority of cases the relative was in this position because the NP containing it was clause-final, so that relatives are more often found within object NP's (direct object or object of a preposition) than within the subject. It is also possible for a relative to occupy final position as a result of the application of the extraposition transformation, as in:

(3) The plants are composed of one or more branched interwoven threads from which vertical filaments arise *that bear clusters of stalked sporangia very like those of Trentepohlia.* (21113)

but this pattern accounted for only 16 of the 455 final relatives in the scientific material. The figures show that the relative pronoun is more likely to be deleted in non-final relative clauses than in final ones – with Quirk's data about twice as likely, with mine about seven times. But with only twenty zeroes this latter figure cannot be taken as statistically reliable: in the whole scientific corpus just under half the zero relatives were in non-final clauses – this still means that deletion is here more likely, but less markedly so than would appear from the data in part A of the corpus.

TABLE 5: 6. *Register comparison:*
function of relativized NP
(a) Number of occurrences

	Conversational speech				Scientific writing			
	wh	*that*	zero	Total	*wh*	*that*	zero	Total
Subject	455	171	2	628	249	115	—	364
Complement	132	157	156	445	13	1	17	31
Adjunct	—	9	28	37	—	1	2	3
Prep + NP	86	—	—	86	66	—	—	66
NP...Prep	18	34	42	94	—	—	1	1
Total	691	371	228	1290	328	117	20	465

(b) Percentages

	Conversational speech				Scientific writing			
	wh	*that*	zero	Total	*wh*	*that*	zero	Total
Subject	66	46	1	49	76	98	0	78
Complement	19	42	68	34	4	1	85	7
Adjunct	0	2	12	3	0	1	10	1
Prep + NP	12	0	0	7	20	0	0	14
NP...Prep	3	9	18	7	0	0	5	0
Total	100	100	100	100	100	100	100	100

Finally, table 5: 6 deals with the function of the relative pronoun. The following types are distinguished:

(a) The relative element is subject.

(b) It is complement, where this term subsumes both object and attribute. I include here cases where the relativized NP is subject within a complement of the relative clause, as in:

(4) They also found elaborations of the plasma membrane which they believed contributed to the lamellar elements of the cytoplasm. (12290)

(see the discussion of example (32) of 5.2).

(c) The relative pronoun is an adjunct, as in:

(5) The lunar phenomenon therefore cannot be caused by electromagnetic radiation such as X rays, since any such radiation from a flare would have its effect on the moon at about the same time that the flare was observed. (38391)

(d) The relative pronoun is governed by a preceding preposition.

(e) The preposition governing the relative element in remote structure is not shifted to the front of the clause, and is thus left with no surface structure object: see example (20) of 5.2.

Where the relative element is a determiner – *whose* or *which* – the relevant function is that of the NP in which it is determined.[1]

In terms of the analysis of 5.2 *that* (both the overt *that* and the one that is deleted to yield the 'zero' form) can only occur as an immediate constituent of the relative clause – it cannot be governed by a preceding preposition. In basic relatives, *that* cannot be deleted if it is mood subject: Quirk's two zero subjects involve the *there*-construction as in *I don't think there's any fighting-service in any element is any good* (p. 98).

The figures reveal quite striking differences between the two registers. In the spoken corpus the occurrence of a preposition in clause-final position is much more frequent: the influence of the prescriptive grammarian is clearly greater in the more carefully constructed written language. A less expected difference is in the proportions of subject and complement relatives: in the spoken corpus the former outnumber the latter by 4 to 3, whereas in the written scientific material the proportion is nearly 12 to 1. This feature of the corpus will be taken up again in the discussion of theme (8.1.)

[1] This accounts for the slight discrepancy between Quirk's and my figures for the spoken material; in his table the adjunct category includes six instances of *whose*, which I have redistributed under subject (4) and complement (2) (e.g. *a lady whose name I certainly won't mention to the public*). I am grateful to Professor Quirk for giving me access to his data.

6 Comparison

6.1 General discussion

I shall bring together in this chapter a variety of constructions having to do with the general notion of comparison, without however attempting anything like an exhaustive coverage. It will be convenient to begin by establishing the main outlines of the basic comparative constructions; I shall then fill out some of the details by reference to the patterns found in the corpus. In this chapter the textual study was confined to parts A and C of the corpus.

The verb *compare* itself was one of those listed in 3.2 as inherently reciprocal or symmetric, and the contrast that was made in that section between thematically undifferentiated and thematically differentiated constructions is relevant to the present area of the grammar. Comparison may thus be said to involve two or more 'terms'; with some comparative items (or 'predicates') the terms may be expressed either in a single phrase (often consisting of a coordination of smaller phrases), or in two separate phrases:

(i) *a* John and Peter are different (differ)
  b John is different (differs) from Peter

In the undifferentiated construction, (1)*a*, there may be any number of terms in the comparison, in the differentiated one, (i)*b*, there are just two (at least inherently: it is not always necessary that they both be overtly expressed). The terms in this second type I referred to earlier as thematically superordinate (*John* in (i)*b*) and subordinate (*Peter*); within the present context the latter may be replaced by 'standard (of comparison)'.

Comparative items which are semantically asymmetric naturally occur only in the thematically differentiated construction. These include expressions like *more, less, rather, before, after*, etc., which are obviously asymmetric, and also *as*, whose meaning is not the symmetric 'equally' but the asymmetric 'equally or more' – thus *John is as bright as Peter*, but not (with the same meaning) **John and Peter are as bright* (compare *John* *and Peter are equally bright*).[1] Most of what I have to say will concern the differentiated pattern. Within it, a further distinction must be made according as the standard is overt, as in (i)*b*, or covert as in (ii):

(ii) *a* (John is tall) but Peter is taller
      b Taller students are asked to use the top shelves

In the first of these the standard is recoverable from the preceding text: we understand that Peter is taller than John, and it is reasonable to say that the standard is present in the remote structure of (ii)*a*, being deleted under conditions of identity with preceding material. (ii)*b* is adapted from a notice in a university library: the students have to leave their brief-cases, etc., on the shelves outside the main part of the library. The meaning is just about the same as that of *tall students are asked to use the high shelves*, since gradable adjectives like *tall* necessarily involve some kind of comparison (cf. Sapir, 1944; Katz, 1967; Lyons, 1968: 465–7). I shall not speculate about the underlying structure of this type, but it is clear that if there is a standard in remote structure, its deletion is not effected under any condition of identity as it is in (ii)*a*.

Let us consider next the following examples with overt standards:

(iii) *a* John is similar to Peter
       b John is as tall as Peter

Superficially these look to be syntactically very alike, but they represent in fact very different kinds of comparison. For whereas in (iii)*a* the terms in the comparison are simply *John* and *Peter*, those in *b* are something like 'how intelligent John is' and 'how intelligent Peter is'. A simplified remote structure for (iii)*b* is given in PM(1).

The main transformational processes applying in the derivation of (iii)*b* from PM(1) are:

(a) The shifting of S_2 so that it becomes the rightmost constituent of the matrix clause Adj Phr.

(b) The attachment of the 'standard marker' *as* to the abstract Degree element in the constituent clause.

---

[1] Thus, *pace* Horn & Morgan (1969), the factive nature of *realize* does not conflict with a semantic analysis of *John is taller than he realizes* as: 'John is tall to extent x, John realizes he is tall to extent y, x exceeds y'. Their argument involves saying that because John is *asserted* to be tall to extent x and is *presupposed* to be tall to extent y, x must equal y. This is a fallacy, for in asserting or presupposing that John is, say, 6 foot tall, one does not necessarily assert or presuppose that he is *exactly* 6 foot – only that he is *at least* 6 foot. Notice similarly that *you can't join the Guards unless you're 6 foot tall* does not exclude those of 6 feet 6 inches.

PM(1)

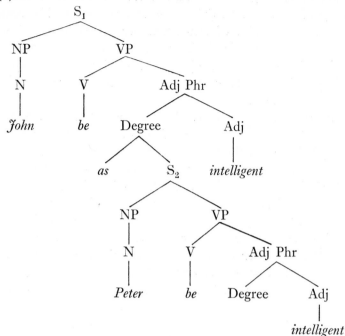

(c) The shifting of *as* to the leftmost position of S_2.

(d) The deletion from S_2 of *intelligent* and *be* (or *is*) under the condition of identity with elements in the matrix (more strictly under the non-distinctiveness condition – cf. Chomsky, 1965: 178–84).

With comparisons of inequality, the standard marker is of course *than*. Rules (b), (c), and (d) apply in that order; I do not know where in the order rule (a) occurs.

This analysis is, in essence, the same as that proposed in Huddleston (1967), which in turn drew heavily on Lees (1961). Lees dealt more or less exclusively with constructions like (iii)*b*, where *as* (or *more*) $+ S_2$ modifies the predicative adjective; I attempted to extend the description to cover a wider range of patterns, including those exemplified in (iv):

(iv) *a* Mary bought more records than Peter
    b Mary achieved more than Peter
    c Mary talks more than Peter
    d Mary is more talkative than Peter
    e Mary bought a more expensive car than Peter
    f Mary talks more rapidly than Peter

These differ according to the function in remote structure of the element consisting of *more + S:* in (iv)*a* it is an ordinator in NP structure ('ordinator' being a kind of post-determiner, the element realized also by cardinal numbers, etc.); in *b* it is the head of an NP; in *c* the head of an Adv Phr; in *d* – which is like (iii)*b* above – it is modifier of a predicative adjective; in *e* the modifier of an attributive adjective; and in *f* the modifier of an adverb.

The generalization that holds about the remote structure of all of these is that the abstract element to which the standard marker is attached by rule (b) above has the same function in the constituent clause as *more + S* has in the matrix – thus in (iv)*a* a *than* is attached to an ordinator in NP structure, in *b* to the head of an NP, and so on. After the application of the *than*-attachment rule, but before that of *than*-shift, the constituent sentences in the above examples are therefore respectively *Peter had than records, Peter achieved than, Peter talks than, Peter is than talkative, Peter bought a than expensive car, Peter talks than rapidly.* It may be that at a deeper level of structure there will be shown to be a single function filled by *more* in the six patterns of (iv) – presumably *more* would be a two-place predicate – but I shall not pursue this point here.[1]

There are two main points about PM(1) and the corresponding remote structures for (iv) that need justifying: the presence of an underlying constituent sentence, S_2, and the presence within it of an abstract Degree element (or abstract ordinator, etc., as the case may be). The most obvious argument for saying that there is an underlying sentence dependent on *more/as* is that these may be followed in surface structure by a constituent having the internal structure of a sentence:

(v) *a* John is taller than he was (last year)
     b The lake is deeper than the river is wide

There are no grounds for saying that (iii)*b* and (iv)*d* are fundamentally different types of construction from these: the surface structure dif-

---

[1] There have been several attempts in the transformational literature to derive the attributive adjective type, (iv)*e*, by relativization of a comparison involving a predicative adjective, as in (iv)*d* – i.e. to derive *a more expensive car than* ...from *a car which is/was more expensive than*....The reason this is difficult to achieve is that *a taller girl than Kim* and *a girl taller than Kim* cannot be equated in deep structure because the former, but not the latter, presupposes that Kim is a girl (cf. Chomsky, 1965: 180, 234). Two very different attempts to overcome this difficulty are to be found in Doherty & Schwartz (1967) and (more promising, it seems to me) Stanley (1969).

ference can be accounted for quite straightforwardly in terms of the identity deletion rule – which is obviously needed to explain the absence of a predicative adjective in (v)*a* or of a verb in *Mary speaks Greek better than Peter German*, and so on. Campbell & Wales (1969) reject this argument: while accepting that certain comparative constructions have underlying constituent sentences (e.g. *I like Peter better than Bill* and presumably (v), etc.) they claim that the construction of (iii)*b* and (iv)*d* is quite different and does not involve a pair of sentences in remote structure. Their main reason for wishing to make this radical distinction between (iv)*d* and (v)*b*, say, is that the former is intuitively simpler, and should therefore have a simpler transformational derivation – in the analysis I have proposed it has a more complex one in that the identity deletion rule applies to it but not to (v)*b*. But the reasoning here is surely quite faulty. I accept that (iv)*d* is intuitively simpler than (v)*b*, but this greater simplicity can be accounted for in terms of the remote structures: (iv)*d* is a 'one-variable' comparison with only one element in the constituent sentence contrasting with a matrix sentence element (*Peter* versus *Mary*) while (v)*b* is a 'two-variable' comparison, with two contrasts, that is (*river* versus *lake, wide* versus *deep*) – the question of the number of variables in a comparison is discussed further in 6.2. Campbell & Wales give no reason for believing that it should be just one aspect of syntactic structure, namely the transformational derivation, that reflects intuitive feelings about the simplicity/complexity of a sentence.

A second powerful argument for the twin-sentence analysis has to do with selectional restrictions. Lees (1961: 172) observes that the deviance of (vi)*a* is related to that of *b*:

(vi) *a* *The boy is more amazed than the table
     b *The table is amazed

If the remote structure of the standard in (vi)*a* is *the table is than amazed* the deviance of the two sentences is shown to be due to a violation of the same selectional rule; Lees' analysis can reasonably be said to *explain* the deviance of (vi)*a*.

The justification for positing an abstract degree element in PM(1) and corresponding abstract elements in the remote structures of (iv), etc., is as follows:

(a) This enables us to account for the systematic absence of sentences like (vii)*a*, as opposed to those like *b*:

(vii) *a* *Mary has more records than Peter has ten books
       b   Mary has more records than Peter has books

The former is ungrammatical because the abstract ordinator is mutually exclusive with *ten*: NP structure does not permit a combination of two ordinators. This is the main syntactic argument; it applies, *mutatis mutandis*, to the other patterns of (iv).

(b) Semantically, it accounts naturally for the fact that *John is taller than Bill* does not entail that Bill is tall – it entails only that Bill has some degree of tallness, that he is ranged somewhere on a scale of tallness. For the underlying constituent sentence is claimed to be, not *Bill is tall*, but *Bill is 'Degree' tall*.[1]

(c) I might add, finally, that the analysis enables us to express the generalization made above concerning the likeness of function of the abstract element to which *than/as* is attached, and of the *more/as*, etc., $+S$ in the matrix.

6.2 'More', '-er' and 'less'

These items occur only in the thematically differentiated construction. In the majority of examples in the corpus (see table 6:1 at the end of this section) there was no overt *than*; in very many of these cases the standard was recoverable from the preceding text or from the general meaning of the passage and a *than*-expression could be inserted without affecting the grammaticality:

(1) *More recent studies* by Fuller (1963) and Fuller, Conti & Mellin (1963) corroborate the findings of *earlier workers*. (12318)

(2) The disease cannot be controlled by spraying with poisons, but the bushes can be made *less susceptible to attack* by treating the soil with potash. (21129)

In (1) we could insert *than these* after *studies* (i.e. than those mentioned in the preceding two sentences), and *than Fuller and Fuller, Conti &*

---

[1] Lees, writing in 1961, be it remembered, has *that* as degree modifier in the constituent sentence; Smith (1961) and Chomsky (1965: 178) have no such element. Campbell & Wales think that this 'widespread disagreement' about the internal structure of the constituent sentence 'suggests that the analysis has got off on the wrong foot at an early stage' – but in discussing these entailment relations they find it convenient to consider only the Smith–Chomsky analysis. The facts of entailment are relevant to a choice between the Smith–Chomsky and Lees–Huddleston analyses, but they are quite compatible, *pace* Campbell & Wales, with the twin sentence approach.

Mellin after *workers.* Similarly in (2), after *attack* we could insert *than they would otherwise be,* and so on.

There are, however, a number of constructions where a *than*-expression cannot occur:

(a) Where *more* (or *less*) is ordinator, or modifier to an attributive adjective, in a *definite* NP: **Mary bought the more expensive car than Peter.* In a very few examples some other means of expressing the standard was used:

(3) Also the convenience of the hovercraft outweighs its higher running costs *compared with* ships. (34460)

(4) this ring-inversion factor did not block the reaction, although it may have been responsible for the lower reactivity of the 5β-olefin *relative to* that of the 5α-olefin. (15270)

Normally, however, there is no standard expressed in definite NP's. The range of patterns is exemplified in the following:

(5) The strong mesal cardo-process projects into the head cavity just dorso-mesal to the cardinal articulation, whilst *the longer and more slender lateral cardo-process* extends across the head floor just lateral to the articulation. (13006)

(6) the proportions of enones formed in the present study are higher than those encountered with ring B steroid olefins under comparable experimental conditions. It may be that *the greater conformational flexibility of ring A* has some influence (15152)

(7) [In] experiments conducted in the normal way (one desk lamp) [...] 6 underwent slightly less than 60% conversion in 120 hr. About the same conversion was obtained in 50 hr. when the light intensity was increased (two desk lamps), and so *the higher intensity* was used for the definitive run. (15498)

(8) Unfortunately, *the higher primates* are rare and expensive, (31312)

(9) During pregnancy the skin of *the lower trunk of a woman* is highly stretched. (35207)

In (5) the lateral cardo-process is compared with the mesal cardo-process mentioned in the main clause; if we take the source of the comparative adjectives to be a relative clause, it can only be a non-restrictive one, so that the underlying form might be, roughly, *the lateral cardo-process, which is longer and more slender than the strong mesal cardo-process.* (6) is perhaps similar in that the standard is derivable from the preceding sentence: the comparison is between the conformational flexibility of ring A and ring B steroid olefins, but here a better paraphrase than one with a non-restrictive relative would be 'the fact that the conformational flexibility of ring A is greater than that of ring B'; it is doubtful, however, whether there is syntactic evidence for distinguishing between (5) and (6). In (7) both intensities had been mentioned in the preceding part of the text – one desk lamp versus two; the example is thus equivalent to *the higher intensity of the two*, the closest analogue among *more/less* comparisons to the thematically undifferentiated construction. In (8) the primates are not being compared with any others mentioned earlier in in the text; the assumption is that primates are ranged on a scale from high to low, and it is those at the high end of the scale that are said to be rare and expensive. This is essentially the same as (iii)*b* of 6.1 (*taller students are asked to use the top shelves*), so that this type is not confined to definite NP's. (9) is very similar, except that here the trunk of a woman is conceptually divided into two parts, on a high/low dimension, and the comparison is between these two parts: the meaning is clearly 'the lower part of the trunk', not 'the lower of the trunks'. There are a few forms which enter only into the patterns of (7) and (8) (or (9)): *inner*, *outer* and *upper*, as in:

(10) The inner edge of the maxilla of *Philonthus* moves in a plane tilted about 45° to the horizontal. (13037)

Thus we do not find expressions like **this edge is in but that one is inner* or **that edge is inner than this one*. In spite of these restrictions, *inner*, *outer*, and *upper* should be regarded as genuine synchronic comparatives, I think – both because of the morphology and because of the meaning: (10) does imply a comparison between the edge under consideration and some other edge. What distinguishes these items from ordinary comparatives like *taller*, *higher*, etc., and accounts for their inability to take an overt standard, is this: normally the adjectives, adverbs, and so on, occurring in *more/less* comparisons involve continuous scales rather than dichotomies,[1] whereas the antonyms *inner* and *outer* refer to the terms in a dichotomy, and not in a gradable scale (and similarly *upper* and *lower*, though the latter is not confined to this use).

(b) A second construction where there can be no overt standard is exemplified in:

---

[1] Cf. Bolinger (1967*b*: 9): 'Comparability answers not to a class of adjectives but to a kind of adjective meaning: scalability. An either-or meaning, one that must be totally present or totally absent, is not comparable.'

(11) The harder the floor the more regular is the shape of the balls, (21367)

The meaning here, clearly, is that there is co-variation between the hardness of the floor and the regularity of the shape of the balls; the writer is not comparing one floor with another mentioned in the preceding or following linguistic context, but is rather concerned with the (varying) place of the floor on a scale of hardness.

(c) *Than* cannot occur with the coordinate expressions *more and more, -er and -er, less and less*, or *more or less, greater or lesser, sooner or later*, etc.

(d) Finally, *more* meaning 'additional' or 'again' cannot combine with *than*:

(12) When it [*sc.* the sky] cleared the next evening, we made more filter photographs, (38259)

Let us turn now to comparatives containing an overt standard introduced by *than*. The general constraint on the structure of the underlying *than*-clause was stated in 6.1: here I shall be concerned with the options allowed. The first distinction I would make is between what may be called 'bound' and 'free' standards, as in (13) and (14) respectively:

(13) The surface layers are exposed to much more light than the deeper layers, (32376)
(14) They [*sc.* dense webs of blood vessels] transport through the skin a great deal more blood than is needed to nourish the skin itself; (35237)

I think the clearest way to express the difference is to say that in the bound type, but not in the free, it is relevant to ask how many variables there are in the comparison. The notion of variable can be clarified by the following series of constructed examples:

(i) *a* Peter earns more than John
    b Peter earned more this year than John did last year
    c Peter earned more this year than John spent last year

In (i)*a* the terms in the comparison are 'how much *Peter* earns' and 'how much *John* earns', which contrast in respect of a single variable, *Peter* versus *John*. In *b* the terms are 'how much *Peter* earned *this* year' and 'how much *John* earned *last* year', so that there are two variables

Peter versus *John*, *this* (*year*) versus *last*. Finally in *c* the terms are 'how much *Peter earned this* year' and 'how much *John spent last* year', with three variables, *Peter* versus *John*, *earn* versus *spend*, *this* (*year*) versus *last*. In a bound comparison all the material in the underlying *than*-clause is either new and contrastive with respect to the matrix (*John*, *last*, *spend*) or else given in the matrix: the given material may be deleted (*earns* in *a*), replaced by a pro-form (*did* for *earned* in *b*) or repeated with weak stress, as in *Peter earns more than John earns*, with nuclear stress on *John*. The notion of variable in this sense does not seem to apply to such comparisons as (14), and a free standard like this may contain material that is both new and non-contrastive. An alternative formulation would be to say that the free type are single variable comparisons where the variable is the whole clause, not individual phrases (or words) within it. Thus in (14) the terms in the comparison are 'how much blood the webs transport through the skin' and 'how much blood is needed to nourish the skin itself': these contrast as wholes. It may be that the distinction between free and bound comparisons is not as clear-cut as this account suggests; nevertheless all the textual examples fit clearly into one or other of the categories, with the marginal exception of a type to be discussed below.

In free standards the passive auxiliary *be* may be optionally deleted, as in:

(15) Microscopic examination of pre-irradiated oxalate has confirmed the formation of an ill-defined substructure on a finer scale than found in virgin material. (16231)

Similarly, lexical *be* may be deleted, as in:

(16) It would be impossible to make *a stronger analogy than this* because the structure–function relationship of the various layers has not yet been established with any degree of certainty. (12263)

(17) we shall find that the phenomena associated with the mechanics of *a more complex object than just a point* are really quite striking. (27004)

After the application of *than*-attachment, the clauses expressing the standard here are respectively *this is a than strong analogy* and *just a point is a than complex object*, where *is* in both cases represents the characterizing use of *be* (in the sense of 3.8). This raises the question of whether we should postulate a deleted *be* in such examples as:

(18) Furthermore, the total number of nuclei present during the cubic period increases with dose apparently to a slowly increasing value for doses greater than 40–50×10^{16} n cm^{-2}. (16260)

(19) These experiments demonstrate that the symmetry of the field-cooled crystals cannot be higher than orthorhombic and that the orthorhombic axes are the $\langle 100 \rangle$ directions; (18575)

These differ from (16) and (17) in two respects. Firstly there is no possibility of inserting an overt *be* in surface structure in (18) and (19), whereas it seems just possible to do so in (16) and (17): certainly *a stronger analogy than this is* is more acceptable than *doses greater than 40–50×10^{16} n cm^{-2} is.* Secondly, if there is an underlying *be*, it is the equative one, not the characterizing one: this is why (18) and (19) are certainly not single-variable bound comparisons – we clearly need to distinguish between *John is taller than six feet* (which is like (18) and (19)) and *John is taller than Peter* (which has a bound standard). Rather than say that there is a deleted equative *be*, it might be better to treat the standard in such cases as a phrase, not a clause. This makes sense semantically, for although *John is taller than Peter* compares 'how tall John is' with 'how tall Peter is', *John is taller than six feet* simply compares 'how tall John is' with 'six feet' – it is doubtful whether we gain anything by saying that the second term is 'how tall six feet is' (with equative *be*).

All the bound comparisons in the corpus were of the single-variable type. In the majority of cases the variable was the mood subject, as in (20) (where the head noun of the subject has been deleted), though there were also quite a few with an adjunct as variable, (21), and one or two with object, (22), or main verb, (23):

(20) transplants from live related donors have been more successful than from unrelated donors, (31220)

(21) We can speak much more precisely about weights, movements, or light changes if these are measured in c.g.s. units by instruments than if they are assessed only by the human receptors. (22164)

(22) The secretion [...] is toxic to living tissues, produces skin blemishes and in general seems to do more harm than good. (35518)

(23) we can, for example, compute the entropy of the benzene molecule with greater accuracy than we can measure it. (26460)

Where the variable is an adjunct, there need not be a contrasting adjunct present in the structure of the matrix: it may simply be given in the context, as in:

(24) The walls are far less muscular than in *Nebria*, (13469)
(25) But when we change the moment of inertia by putting the two masses *m* much farther away from the axis, then we see that *M* accelerates much less rapidly than it did before, because the body has much more inertia against turning. (27619)

In (24) the adjunct contrasting with *in Nebria*, namely *in P. decorus*, occurs two (orthographic) sentences earlier in the text; in (25) the time adjunct contrasting with *before* belongs not to the clause immediately containing the comparative (*M accelerates much less rapidly than*...), but to a clause higher up the constituent hierarchy.

Than may be attached to an element operating in a clause which itself is embedded as subject or object of the clause expressing the standard:

(26) the fathers-to-be are shown to suffer more frequently from the symptoms than can be explained by chance. (37039)
(27) Analysis of our plates with a microdensitometer reveals that the red light in the Kepler region was about 80 percent brighter than normal, (38280)
(28) the diminution of light during these phases was less than would be expected simply on the basis of the geometry of the disks of the sun and the earth. (38096)
(29) Its [*sc.* the couvade syndrome's] significance may well be much greater than first appears (37343)

This is the type mentioned above whose classification on the free/bound dimension is not wholly clear. After *than*-attachment, the standards are:

(26′) that the fathers-to-be suffer than frequently from the symptoms can be explained by chance
(27′) for the red light in the Kepler region to be than bright is normal,

and so on.[1] These are typical of 'bound' standards in that they include a lot of material that is identical with material in the matrix and thus deleted, but there is not the simple contrast between matrix and constituent clause that we had in (20)–(23): it is difficult to give a precise statement of what the variable is. Speaking quite loosely and informally we might say that there are similar clauses in the two terms of the comparison, and either or both of these may be embedded as subject or object of a larger clause. This gives the three possibilities exemplified in:

[1] In this type of complementation extraposition (in the sense of 4.2.1) may not apply: we could not insert *it* as mood subject in (26)–(29).

(ii) *a* Bill is taller than I thought he was

    b Bill thinks it is better than I think it is (than I do)

    c Bill thinks he is taller than he is

In the first the terms are 'how tall Bill is' and 'how tall I thought Bill is' – only the standard has a matrix verb; in *b* they are 'how good Bill thinks it is' and 'how good I think it is' – both terms have a matrix verb;[1] and in *c* they are 'how tall Bill thinks he is' and 'how tall Bill is' – only the first term has a matrix verb. There are a number of unsolved problems here. Firstly what are the restrictions on the matrix verbs? Why for example can we say *John is taller than he realizes*, but not *John is taller than he knows* (cf. Horn & Morgan, 1969)? Secondly there is the point raised by Ross & Perlmutter (1970): how can we express in structural terms the fact that the comparison in (ii)*c* is not part of the content of Bill's thought? – the sentence does not report his thinking 'I am taller than I am'. I don't know the answer to this; but it is clearly just one aspect of a more general phenomenon, for, in such a sentence as *Bill thinks that devastating blonde is quite plain* we assume may that *that devastating blonde* is not Bill's description of the person in question.

If (26)–(29) are 'bound', the following must nevertheless be treated as free:

(30) This [*sc.* the fact that the hovercraft's shape is not particularly critical for the craft's performance] has given designers much greater flexibility than usual for producing vehicles which meet the needs of passengers and freight. (34438)

For the most plausible reconstruction of the remote subject of *usual* here is not *for this to give designers than great flexibility* but *for designers to have than great flexibility;* the deletion of *have* here provides further evidence supporting a semantic–syntactic connection between *give* and *have* (cf. 4.5).

One type of construction that cannot apparently be accounted for in terms of the analysis sketched in 6.1 is exemplified in:

(31) the magnetic fields in neutral hydrogen are less than 10^{-5} gauss. (34160)

(32) the psychological trauma of losing a twin might more than offset the disadvantages of removal of a kidney from the healthy twin (34217)

---

[1] There is a second sense of (ii)*b* where the comparison is within Bill's thought, as it were: i.e. Bill thinks: 'It is better than John thinks it is' (where John is the speaker of (ii)*b*). In this second sense, *I think it is* cannot be reduced to *I do*.

I do not know what the structure of these is; as far as surface structure is concerned I have tentatively taken *more than* and *less than* as single constituents here.

Table 6:1 shows the distribution among the above categories of the *more, -er, less* comparatives in parts A and C of the corpus.

TABLE 6: 1. *Comparisons of inequality*

Without *than*, as in (1)–(9), etc.		484
With *than*:		147
(a) Free standard, as in (14)–(17)	10	
(b) Phrasal standard, as in (18)–(19)	8	
(c) Bound standard, single variable:	98	
(i) Subject variable, as in (20)	68	
(ii) Adjunct variable, as in (21)	27	
(iii) Object variable, as in (22)	2	
(iv) Main verb variable, as in (23)	1	
(d) *More than* or *less than* as a single constituent, as in (31)–(32)	20	
(e) Others, including (26)–(29), (33)	11	
Total		631

Of the 631 examples, 46 had *less*, the remainder *more* or its variant *-er*. In 69 out of the 98 single variable bound comparisons the verb in the matrix clause was *be*.

The 'others' category contains one example which must be regarded as ungrammatical (at least until there is developed a satisfactory way of generating syntactic blends):

(33) This is a more useful way to start than by saying that 'sense organs respond to stimuli'. (22145)

This seems to be a blend of *it is more useful to start this way than by saying*...(manner adjunct variable) and *this is a more useful way to start than saying*...(subject variable).

6.3 'As' and 'so'

The categories established above apply also to 'comparisons of equality', with *as* or *so* instead of *more, -er, less*, and *as* instead of *than*. There are, however, a number of constructions involving *as* and *so* which have no counterpart in comparisons of inequality.

(a) Firstly, there are such compound subordinating conjunctions as *inasmuch as, as far as, in so far as, as long as,* and possibly *as soon as.* These may be regarded as comparatives historically or morphologically, but from the point of view of contemporary syntax it seems preferable to treat them as unanalyzed wholes, unit 'substitution counters' – this is particularly so with *inasmuch as* and *in so far as* (the unitary nature of the former being sometimes partially reflected in the orthography). Thus in:

(1) The gain figures given in Figure 4 are misleading in as much as they take no account of the inefficiency of the transducers used at each end. (37521)

(2) As long as the region of interest is between the band edge and the TO(Γ) resonance, the dispersive effect of the band edge is to increase n near it, (17214)

we will not postulate any identity deletions in the subordinate clauses; and in (2) the *as long as* clause is not a duration adjunct expressing how long the effect of the band edge is to increase n. As so often, however, it is difficult to draw a sharp line between 'fossilized' or idiomatic syntax and ordinary productive constructions. One factor which supports the treatment of the above items as compound conjunctions is that they occur freely in negative clauses, whereas in comparatives proper the negative is subject to stringent constraints – the element to which *than* or *as* is attached may not come within the domain of a negative (cf. Huddleston, 1967: 96–7).

(b) Similar to the above is the expression *as well as* – as used in (3) and (4), but not (5), which is an ordinary manner comparative (a bound comparative with one variable: the subject):

(3) Elution as well as inspection and assay of individual and pooled fractions were carried out (15532)

(4) As well as operating at comparatively high speeds on water, hovercraft can also accomplish useful tasks on land. (34376)

(5) semi-conductors do not conduct electricity as well as metals. (37392)

As well as is serially related on the one hand to coordinating conjunctions like *and* (notice the plural concord in *were* in (3)), and on the other to prepositions, as in (4).

(c) An interesting non-correlative use of *as* is exemplified in:

(6) In fact, as we shall see later, the energy is least when the two sets
of axes coincide. (18325)

The *as*-clause in this type bears some resemblance to a non-restrictive
relative with a sentence as antecedent: the *as*-word, like the relative
wh-word, is a pro-form substituting for a sentence – compare *there was
a good deal of discontent, which/as was only to be expected*. The *as*-con-
struction is positionally much freer than the *wh*-one: it may occur before
or after the antecedent or it may interrupt the latter, whereas relatives
usually follow the antecedent. More interesting is the fact that it is not
often that *which* and *as* can be freely interchanged as in the above constructed example. Notice that to replace *as* by *which* in (6) (with appropriate reordering) would produce the scarcely acceptable:

(6′) In fact the energy is least when the two sets of axes coincide, which
we shall see later

(though I do not know whether rules can be formulated to exclude such
sentences). The constraints on the *as*-construction are perhaps stronger:
**he came late, as caused her some annoyance* is certainly ungrammatical,
though *which* would be quite normal here. The *as*-construction does
indeed indicate a comparison; the problem is to characterize the effect
this has on its structural possibilities. One general point we can make is
that the *as*-clause must be positive (cf. the earlier remarks about comparison and negative/positive polarity): *he lost the match as we had/
hadn't expected. (The generalization in fact needs slight modification
to allow for such double negatives as *as no-one would deny*.) For the rest,
I can only describe the patterns found in the corpus. They were of four
main types.

In the most frequent pattern, *as* functions as pronominal substitute
for a (pre-passive) object clause, as in (7), active, and (8), passive:

(7) As Dr Medawar has explained, there are no rejection problems for
identical twins: (31066)
(8) As was found previously with lithium ferrite, the sublattice magnetizations are significantly higher at temperatures between 0.5 T_c
and 0.9 T_c, where T_c is the Curie temperature, than those predicted
by molecular field theory. (17258)

In the passive, the auxiliary *be* may be retained, as in (8), or deleted, as in
(9):

(9) When the nucleus concentration is low, as indicated by the lower values of α_i (t_0) observed at the higher temperatures, the fractional decomposition at which coalescence occurs is deferred, (16204)[1]

The verbs in the corpus taking *as* as object in this way were:

demonstrate		find		point out	2	state
describe		imply		remark	3	stress
evidence		indicate	6	see	3	suggest
expect		mention		show	2	surmise
explain	2					

These all occur with ordinary clauses as object (*evidence* does so more readily in the passive than in the active). *Describe* differs from the others in that it takes not declarative but interrogative complements; for this reason there may be some doubt as to the grammaticality of the example concerned:

(10) As Dr Medawar has described, total irradiation of the body with X-rays in sufficient quantity destroys the cells' defence mechanism (31122)

Certainly verbs like *ask* and *wonder*, which can take a *how*-complement but not a *that*-one (except in a different sense of *ask*) do not occur in the present construction. We may also include here *make clear*, since after *be*-deletion the subject of *clear* becomes object of *make*.

In a second pattern, *as* substitutes for a clause functioning as subject of an adjectival predicate; there were just two examples, both having *usual* as attribute. In (11) lexical *be* is retained, in (12) deleted:

(11) Some diversity of results are [*sic*] obtained as to the exact type of transition, but, as is usual in the equivalent Ising model problem, this is very critical on the approximation used. (18013)
(12) Let us take the 3 axis in the direction of the magnetic field as usual, (18258)

Thirdly, the *as*-clause may differ from the superordinate term in the comparison in respect of one variable, given material being replaced by substitute forms, (13), or deleted, (14):

---

[1] In this example the deletion of *be* is obligatory, in other cases it is optional – compare *as* (*was*) *indicated above, the values are lower at the higher temperatures*. The obligatoriness of the deletion in (9) is related to the fact that the *as*-clause is within the domain of *when* – there is not just one 'act' of indicating, as there is in my constructed example.

(13) To calculate H_{c2}, we could choose the axes with $\mu_{12} = 0$, as we,
did in I. (18224)

(14) As before, we choose the gauge so that A $= (0, H_0 x_1, 0)$ where
H_0 is the applied field. (18336)

Finally, the *as*-clause may consist simply of *as* plus an adjunct
typically an *in* or *with* Prep Phr, specifying place or 'scope':

(15) It is improbable that the forces exerted between triatomic molecules can be represented by a spherically symmetrical field. If such
were true, the constant, *B*, in Mie's equation [...] could be
evaluated, *as in the case of diatomic molecules*, by taking $m = 6$, and
by adding the orientation, induction and dispersion contributions:
(26091)

(16) toothache was sometimes construed by a married man as a sign of
his wife's infidelity. It was also regarded, *as in the case of Benedick in
'Much Ado About Nothing'* as a symptom of being in love. (37087)

Although apparently identical in all relevant respects these two examples
are semantically quite different. (15) can be regarded as belonging to the
same type as (13) and (14), where the single variable in the comparison
is 'the case of *diatomic* or *triatomic* molecules'. The *as* in (16), on the
other hand, introduces an exemplification rather than a contrast (this
type of *as in* construction is of course a characteristic feature of much
descriptive linguistic writing). Both examples, however, involve a good
deal of deletion from the subordinate clauses (under identity with material
in the superordinate ones): 'it could be evaluated in the case of diatomic
molecules by...', 'it was regarded in the case of Benedick as a symptom
of...'.

(d) A second construction involving non-correlative *as* is that where
the *as*-clause functions as a manner adjunct:

(17) Each of these fractions was individually brominated *as described
below*. (15346)

(18) The olefin [...] in pyridine (6 ml.) was oxygenated and irradiated
as before (65 hr.) except that the sensitizer was omitted. (15558)

There is a clear distinction between the *as before* of (14) and that of (18).
In the latter it is said that the *manner* in which oxygenation and irradiation were performed was the same as before, whereas (14) can be glossed
as 'we choose the gauge so that A $= (0, H_0 x_1, 0)...$, which is what we
did before': the writer is not concerned with the manner in which the

choice was made. The manner type of *as*-clause tends to follow the matrix verb: this is one reason why I have not analyzed (10) as a manner clause – though to do so would remove the anomaly noted above (compare (10) and (17)). The structure of such manner clauses is difficult to account for. In (17) we can treat *as* as a pronominal subject, substituting for a *how*-interrogative clause – compare:

(17′) How each of these fractions was individually brominated is described below.

The verb of the *as*-clause must here be one that can take a *how*-interrogative as object complement; besides *describe* (4 occurrences), the only verb found in this pattern was *report*. However, no equivalent derivation is applicable to (18); it is tempting to postulate a covert *in the same manner/way* (in which case it would be handled by the general rules applying to *same* – see 6.4), but it is difficult to find convincing justification for this *ad hoc* solution. The same applies to:

(19) This result [...] shows that H_{c3} is related to H_{c2} just as it is in the isotropic case, (18299)

This is in fact ambiguous, formally, between a manner and a non-manner interpretation – compare, for example:

(20) we have three formulas for angular momentum, just as we have three formulas for the torque: (27490)
(21) Just as the total *momentum* [*ital. sic*] of an object is the sum of the momenta of all the parts, so the angular momentum is the sum of the angular momenta of all the parts. (27549)

In (19), as I understand it, it is the type, not simply the fact, of the relation that is constant – i.e. H_{c3} is related to H_{c2} in just the same *way* as it is in the isotropic case. It is far from clear what the analysis of (20) and (21) should be. The *just as* clauses are here not genuine manner constituents: the comparison does not involve the *manner* but rather the *fact* of our having three formulas for the torque, of the angular momentum being the sum...Nor can (20) and (21) be subsumed under the relative-like construction discussed under (c) above, for the *as* cannot be taken as a pro-form substituting for some element, and the relative-like construction does not exhibit the contrast between (20) and (21): in the present type, if the *just as* clause precedes the main clause, the latter begins with anaphoric *so*. There is some syntactic resemblance here to the alternation between such patterns as *John's going to the Sorbonne although he doesn't speak French very well* and *although he doesn't speak French very well, nevertheless John is going to the Sorbonne.* I shall refer to the construction of (20) and (21) as the 'pseudo-manner' construction, leaving the problem of its remote structure unresolved.

Although there are no textual examples I might mention here a construction very similar to the manner *as*-clause, namely that where the *as*-clause is attribute: *the outcome was as described below* or *the situation is as before.* As far as the internal structure is concerned, there does not appear to be any difference between the manner and attribute clauses. Manner and attribute are also the two functions that may be filled by the expression *as follows*, which is probably a further example of fossilized syntax:

(22) The law of distribution may be deduced as follows: (28597)

(23) That is called the theorem of the center of the mass, and the proof of it is as follows. (27058)

As if we took as a compound conjunction, rather than a manner

TABLE 6: 2. *Comparatives with 'as' and 'so'*

Covert standard, textually recoverable		8
Overt standard:		36
(a) Phrasal standard	13	
(b) Free standard	1	
(c) Bound standard, single variable	20	
(d) *as...as possible* (cf. (27) of 6.2)	2	
Relative-like construction:		60
(a) *as* substitutes for object, as in (6)–(10)	30	
(b) *as* substitutes for subject, as in (11)–(12)	2	
(c) Single variable comparison, as in (13)–(14)	8	
(d) *as in.../as with...*, as in (15)–(16)	20	
Manner:		14
(a) Genuine manner construction, as in (17–(19)	9	
(b) Pseudo-manner construction, as in (20)–(21)	5	
Fossilized syntax:		39
(a) Compound conjunctions, as in (1)–(2)	12	
(b) *as well as*, as in (3)–(4)	12	
(c) *as follows*, as in (22)–(23)	11	
(d) Others, as in (24)	4	
Total		157

adverbial with extensive deletion; it occurs both in finite and infinitival constructions, the latter being exemplified in:

(24) she recounted that when she had a headache he would place his hands on her head as if to transfer this ailment to his own head. (37154)

The frequencies of the various *as* (*so*) constructions are shown in table 6: 2. Causal and temporal *as* clauses are not included, nor is the *so...that* construction (*it was so hot that he collapsed*). I have also excluded the following example, whose underlying structure is quite obscure:

(25) The McLeod gauge was read at 3–5 min. intervals as convenient. (16045)

6.4 'The same'

Unlike *more* and *as*, *the same* enters into the thematically undifferentiated type of comparison:

(1) All human beings, regardless of race, have about the same number of melanocytes; (35232)
(2) the total translational energy before and after collision must be the same. (28153)

In the differentiated construction, the standard may be covert, in which case it is normally recoverable from the preceding text, as in (3), or overt, as in (4):

(3) Moreover, there is no substantial difference between men and women with respect to the number of hair follicles: a woman has about as many hairs on her body as a man, but many of them are so small and colorless that they escape notice. Indeed *the same observation* holds for the comparison between man and his furrier relatives – the gorilla, the orangutan and the chimpanzee. (35143)
(4) at present hovercraft fall within the same cost brackets as aeroplanes. (34382)

The remote structure of the standard in (4) and its like is, after the application of *as*-attachment, *aeroplanes fall within as cost bracket*. Thus *as* is attached to an abstract element that has the same function in the constituent clause as (*the*) *same + S* has in the matrix – some kind of determiner; this constraint is the analogue for the present construction to that discussed in 6.1 in the context of comparisons of inequality.

Again, we can distinguish between bound and free standards. An example of the former that involves *two* variables is:

(5) Let us inquire whether we can invent something which we shall call the *torque* [...] which bears the same relationship to rotation as force does to linear movement. (27274)

After *as*-attachment the standard is *force bears as relationship to linear movement*. In free standards the only 'given' material, obligatorily deleted, may be the head of the NP containing *the same* as determiner, together with any preposition there may be governing this NP:

(6) Equation (18) is the same as was solved for the isotropic case by Saint-James and de Gennes; (18292)
(7) If at the same time as the cardinal adductor contracted the stipital adductor maintained a weak pull on the stipes, the tip of the lacinia would be pushed forwards in the midline. (13343)

Underlying standards here are *as equation was solved*...and *the cardinal adductor contracted at as time*.

I have also interpreted the following as having free standards – formally they are ambiguous, I think, between the free and bound types:

(8) We can reduce equations (23) and (24) to the same form as the isotropic equations; (18342)
(9) If the *a-a* and *d-d* interactions are neglected but the biquadratic correction is introduced with $\beta = 0.04$, the same value as in lithium ferrite, the fit with the experimental data is greatly improved. (17271)

As a bound standard, (8) would mean '...to the same form as we (can) reduce the isotropic equations to'; I understand it rather as '...to the same form as the isotropic equations have'. Similarly the most plausible reconstruction of (9) is '(which is) the same value as it has in lithium ferrite'. These examples suggest, then, that we must allow for the deletion of *have* from a free standard.

One final point to be made about *the same* is that instead of a following *as*-clause we often find a relative (reduced or unreduced):

(10) The same balding process that occurs on the forehead also takes place elsewhere on the body; (35442)

(11) If a hydrogen electrode containing the same solution used to dissolve the organic reactants is used as the reference half-cell, normal potentials can be determined even in alcoholic solutions of unknown hydrogen-ion concentration, (25487)

This construction is, without question, wholly acceptable. It seems to be a blend between ordinary relativization and *the same + as* type of comparison – compare the paradigm:

(i) *a* He made the mistake that I made
   b He made the same mistake as I made
   c He made the same mistake that I made

It is difficult to see how we can avoid giving a fairly *ad hoc* description to this last type. It would be *ad hoc* to derive the structure underlying (i)*c* from that underlying *b* by a rule substituting *wh* for *as*, but this is probably preferable to treating *c* as unrelated to the comparative construction – which would involve saying that *same* can occur in the ordinary range of comparative constructions, or in a non-comparative provided that the NP containing it also contained a relative clause.

TABLE 6: 3. *'The same'*

Thematically undifferentiated, as in (1)–(2)		46
Thematically differentiated:		86
(a) Covert standard, textually recoverable, as in (3)	36	
(b) Overt standard:	50	
(i) Bound, single variable, as in (4) 34		
(ii) Bound, double variable, as in (5) 2		
(iii) Free, as in (6)–(9) 5		
(iv) Relative clause, as in (10)–(11) 8		
(v) Ungrammatical, as in (12) 1		
Total		132

The figures for the various uses of *the same* are shown in table 6: 3. The example I take to be ungrammatical is:

(12) On the other side of the equation, we get the same thing as though we added before the differentiation: (27077)

As though and *as if* are interchangeable as compound conjunctions, but (12) is a genuine comparison – underlying the standard is *we would have as thing if we added before the differentiation*; where *if* does not form a single constituent with *as* it is not replaceable by *though*.

6.5 'Such' and 'other'

I am concerned here only with that use of *such* where the standard of comparison, if overtly expressed, is introduced by *as*: I thus exclude the *such that* construction. In more than half the cases studied the standard was covert, being recoverable from the preceding context:

(1) the initial discharges die down and are replaced either by inactivity or perhaps by discharges that lead the organism to remain in the condition it has reached. *Such impulses* could be called those of 'pleasure', (22752)

The *as*-clause standards were of the 'free' type:

(2) For example, electronic computers can calculate the probable outcome of the progress of a series of partially correlated events, such as are involved in making forecasts of future weather conditions. (22016)
(3) The responses of organisms differ from those of non-living systems in that they are in the main such as will lead to a continuation of life; they are adaptive. (22199)

Following the principles put forward earlier, I would take the remote structure of the standard in (2) to be, after *as*-attachment, *as events are involved in making forecasts of future weather conditions*, with *as* attached to an abstract element with the same function as *such* in *such events*. (3) is more problematical: *such* is not modifying any substantival head in the matrix, and hence it does not seem plausible to postulate any identity-deletions from the *as*-clause; note that this use of *as* as a pronominal subject is matched by an equivalent use of *such*: *if such were the case* (cf. (15) of 6.3).

For the most part *as* was followed simply by an NP:

(4) Colloidal solutions are easily changed by such factors as stirring, shaking, heating, illumination, or the actions of small amounts of other chemicals. (22197)
(5) It is possible that unpaired vital organs such as the heart or liver could also be transplanted. (31310)
(6) on surfaces that get a good deal of wear, such as the palms of the hands, it [*sc.* the horny layer] is thicker and more rugged. (35057)

The first two examples have restrictive *such*, the last non-restrictive (in the sense in which these terms are used with relatives); the former requires an indefinite NP, whereas the latter can occur with either a definite or indefinite one – thus we could insert *the* before *surfaces* in (6), but not before *such* in (4) or *unpaired* in (5) (unless we also changed the intonation to that which marks the non-restrictive construction). It is questionable how much structure we should postulate in these cases: it is tempting to treat *such as* in the last two examples as a fixed unanalyzed expression, functionally analogous to *like* or *for example*. If we treat them as underlying comparatives the standards will contain *be: stirring, shaking,…are as factors*, and so on.

Of the 108 examples examined, 60 had no overt standard, like (1), 44 had *as* + NP as in (4)–(6) and just 4 had overtly clausal standards, as in (2) and (3).

The great majority of the 236 instances of *other* had textually recoverable covert standards, as in:

(7) by dietary and other restrictions it is hoped to protect the new born child from evil influences. (37194)

There were 15 examples of the reciprocals *each other* and *one another*, leaving just seven cases with an overt standard, the marker being *besides* (twice) or *than*:

(8) The afferent impulses differ in other respects besides velocity, for instance, in duration. (22457)
(9) In instances other than the specific one cited, the quinhydrone may not be easily obtainable, (25480)
(10) Pankratz & Bowen (1963) demonstrated finger-like invaginations of the plasma membrane at places other than at the site of cell division. (12510)

In surface structure the distribution of *other than* is very like that of *such as* in (4)–(6): there is the same choice between restrictive and non-restrictive patterns, and in the former, *other* may either precede the head noun (*other instances than the specific one cited*), or else follow it, as in the textual examples. The structure of the standard is highly constrained: there can never be an overt verb (and if we posit a covert one, it can only be *be*) – there can in fact only be a single phrase after *than*, usually an NP as in (9), occasionally some other type as in (10).

6.6 'Rather'

I deal here only with comparative uses of *rather*, excluding its use in the meaning of 'quite' or 'somewhat'. There was just one example of a covert, textually recoverable standard:

(1) He concluded that it is not the constant light of the sun that causes observable luminescence, and that the luminescence must rather be related to solar activity. (38165)

There were 13 examples of overt standards with *than* as marker, as in:

(2) In this organism the chromatophores, although connected to the plasma membrane, are tubular rather than vesicular (12438)
(3) The specific effects of the discharge of the nerve-fibre connected to a given receptor surface therefore depend on the central connexions rather than on any particular quality of its impulses. (22449)

Rather here seems to be some kind of degree adjunct, 'to a greater extent', so that the remote structure of the standards will be *the chromatophores are than vesicular* and *the specific effects...depend than on any particular quality of its impulses*, where *than* has been attached to a like-functioning abstract degree adverb. This function of *rather* can be matched with one of the uses of *more*:

(4) In *Merismopedia glauca* [...] the characteristic cyanophycean lamellae are replaced by a series of peripherally arranged vesicles, giving the appearance more of the photosynthetic bacteria than blue-green algae. (12276)

One difference between *more* and *rather*, however, is that only the former has a non-comparative form, namely *much*. This is probably why the above sources seem intuitively less explanatory than the corresponding reconstructions for comparisons with *more*: because *rather* cannot be analyzed into a free morpheme + *er* there may be a tendency for speakers to regard *rather than* as a single unit. It is relevant in this connection that in many cases, such as (2) and (3), *rather than* can be replaced by *not* with little, if any, change in meaning. I would certainly wish to take *rather than* as a single constituent in:

(5) it is much easier to examine the input in the form of electrical rather than acoustic signals! (37483)

There is just one comparison here, not two – the terms are 'how easy it is to examine the input in the form of electrical signals' and 'how easy it is to do so in the form of acoustic signals': *rather* could be simply omitted. It seems best to take *rather than* as a compound standard marker here; it is of course very much more restricted distributionally than the simple marker *than*.[1]

(2) and (3) are bound comparisons with just one variable; *rather* does not permit two-variable comparisons, hence the ungrammaticality of **John's a painter rather than Peter a scientist*. The following, in contrast would seem to be free comparisons:

(6) These thick, maxillary brushes allow the crushed food to be held and pushed dorsally during mandibular action, rather than raked towards the mouth as in *Nebria*. (13049)

(7) The flexible materials already in use go a long way towards this goal since their lower edges slide over the surface and conform to the shape of the waves rather than try to push the waves aside like the prow of a ship. (34368)

Where *rather than* is followed by a verb, as here, the subject must always be identical to the matrix clause subject and consequently deleted.

6.7 'Similar' and 'different'

The thematically undifferentiated construction for *similar* is exemplified in (1), the differentiated one in (2), where the standard is covert and textually recoverable, and (3), where it is overt:

(1) A cylindrical vessel is maintained full of a liquid to a depth of 20 cm., and has protruding from it three similar horizontal capillary tubes, each 45 cm. long, (28070)

(2) She finds that the cytoplasm is filled with 500 Å chromatophores. A similar situation is found in a species of *Thiocapsa* grown in low light (12371)

(3) It is clear that this layer grows by a similar mechanism to that of the monomolecular layers. (16519)

Similar can be derived here from a reduced relative clause: *three horizontal capillary tubes which are similar, a situation which is similar to this,*

---

[1] *Rather than* is also a single constituent in such constructions as *rather than see her again he slipped out the back way*, where it functions like a compound preposition except in taking a verb in the 'zero' form.

a mechanism which is similar to that of the monomolecular layers. If relative *wh* is to be attached to just one term in the comparison, then of course the thematically differentiated construction must be selected.

Where the standard is overt, it is normally simply an NP introduced by *to*; the following examples however, are clearly very different from (3):

(4) This air cushion acts in a similar way to the lubricating oil which separates two surfaces in a machine. (34325)

(5) However, *Nebria* and *Notiophilus* apparently capture very similar prey to *Elaphtus* and *Loricera* (13523)

It would violate the meaning to derive these from *a way which is similar to the lubricating oil...*, and *prey which are very similar to Elaphtus and Loricera*. If we take the thematically undifferentiated pattern as basic the remote structure of (4) and (5) will be:

(4′) This air cushion and the lubricating oil...act in similar ways

(5′) *Nebria* and *Notiophilus* and *Elaphtus* and *Loricera* apparently capture similar prey

(where the second *and* in (5′) is higher in the phrase-marker than the first and third). Assuming that *similar* derives from a reduced relative clause, we find that we have an embedded clause *the ways are similar* where *similar* has a plural subject, together with a matrix clause containing phrasal conjunction (in the sense of G. Lakoff & Peters, 1969; see 3.2). This means that the conjoined NP's are not subject of *similar*, although it is clearly because of the *similar* that (4′) must be taken as phrasal rather than sentential conjunction. This seems to me highly suspect, and we would do well to reconsider (4′) in the light of the distinction I have been making between terms and variables. Semantically the example can be analyzed into three components:

(i) *a* this air cushion acts in way$_i$
     b the lubricating oil...acts in way$_j$
     c way$_i$ and way$_j$ are similar

The *terms* in the comparison are thus 'the way in which the air cushion acts' and 'the way in which the lubricating oil acts': *the air cushion* and *the lubricating oil* are simply the contrasting *variables*. (4) is, moreover, analogous both semantically and syntactically to constructions with *more-than* or *as-as* comparisons, for example:

(4″) This air cushion acts in a more efficient way than the lubricating oil which can likewise be analyzed semantically into:

(ii) *a* this air cushion acts in a way which is efficient to extent$_i$
    b the lubricating oil acts in a way which is efficient to extent$_j$
    c extent$_i$ exceeds extent$_j$

I made the point earlier that the standard in *similar* comparisons is an NP, whereas that in *more* or *as* comparisons is (normally, at least) a sentence. The facts we have been considering here suggest that this may be a relatively superficial difference – that at a deeper level of analysis all comparisons will have NP's as their terms. Deeper structures for (4) and (4″) would thus be something like *the way in which this air cushion acts and the way in which the lubricating oil acts are similar*[1] and *the extent to which the way in which this air cushion acts is efficient exceeds the extent to which the way in which the lubricating oil is efficient.*[2] But such sources must remain in the realm of speculation until rules are devised which will transform them into the shallower structures I have been dealing with in this chapter.

The following example must, I think, be regarded as ungrammatical, to be explained properly in terms of blending:

(6) This basic rotatory movement of the maxillae can probably be explained in a similar way to that attempted for *Nebria*, although the arthrodial hump is not so obvious. (13392)

Here *attempted for Nebria* is a reduced relative clause, the full version being *(the way) that was attempted for Nebria* – but there is no corresponding independent sentence **this way was attempted for Nebria*.

Of the 75 examples of *similar*, 4 occurred in the thematically undifferentiated construction, 41 had a covert but textually recoverable standard and 30 had an overt standard. Corresponding figures for the 69 examples of *different* were respectively 46, 13 and 10. In all the thematically differentiated examples *similar* and *different* were in indefinite NP's – contrast the definite determiner in the undifferentiated example:

---

[1] Likewise the remote structure of *the earth is identical to the moon in its chemical composition* (G. Lakoff & Peters, 1969: 126) would be *the earth's chemical composition and the moon's chemical composition are identical*: the non-contrastive part of the compared terms is put in the restrictive *in*-phrase. Compare *John works in as efficient a way as Peter* and *John is as efficient as Peter in the way he works.*

[2] As R. Lakoff (1970) points out, such a source overcomes the problem mentioned above in connection with examples like *John thinks he is taller than he is.* She shows that certain difficulties remain, but they do not seem to me to be such as to invalidate the approach.

(7) It is apparent that much of the uncertainty concerning the structure of the photosynthetic apparatus in the photosynthetic bacteria has arisen from the different growth conditions employed by the various workers. (12452)

With *different* the standard was in all cases introduced by *from*, though *than* is an alternative marker in some dialects. There were no examples analogous to (4) and (5), but they can be readily constructed: *I do it in a different way from/than John.*

6.8 'Before' and 'after'

Finally let us consider very briefly the syntax of *before* and *after*. These items are obviously connected semantically with the general field of comparison (cf. their near-equivalents *earlier* and *later*), but there are also syntactic grounds for including them in the present chapter: several of the categories and rules discussed above apply to these items too.

Because of their asymmetric meaning, they do not occur in the thematically undifferentiated pattern; within the differentiated one the standard may be covert and textually recoverable, as in (1), or overt, as in (2):

(1) We found that phenomena of this type had been reported before, (38297)
(2) Pains in his stomach had started when he left hospital and continued until after nine o'clock (37058)

When the standard is covert, we normally find *afterward(s)* rather than *after*. (Traditional grammar treats these items as adverbs when the standard is covert, as prepositions or conjunctions when it is overt.)

In (2) the standard is a phrase – we shall not postulate a deleted *be* here; in (3) and (4) it is, in remote structure, a sentence:

(3) The metallic minerals were thus, in turn, rendered hydrophobic, and therefore floatable, before the gangue of siliceous minerals. (32492)
(4) Before we calculate H_{c2} and H_{c3}, we shall show that we get the highest values of these fields by choosing a wave function which does not vary in the x_3 direction. (18183)

The latter is a free comparison, the former a bound one with a single variable: *was rendered hydrophobic* is deleted from remote structure under the identity condition. There were no two-variable comparisons in the corpus; a constructed example might be *John finished 'Silas Marner' before Peter 'Emma'*.

One way in which (3) and (4) differ from the constructions dealt with in earlier sections is that the rule of *as/than* attachment does not apply in their derivation. I would nevertheless wish to say that the underlying constituent clauses contain abstract time elements, though mainly on semantic grounds: (3) means, essentially, 'the metallic minerals were rendered hydrophobic at time t_1; the gangue of siliceous minerals was rendered hydrophobic at time t_2; t_1 precedes t_2'. An alternative analysis would be to say that there is an underlying *the time when* after *before* in these examples, but I don't know of any real syntactic evidence for this.

7   *The modal auxiliaries*

7.1   General characteristics

The modal auxiliaries are defined by Ehrman (1966: 9) as 'that closed class of verbs which may occupy the first position of a verb phrase, which may not be immediately preceded by another verb, which may invert with the subject in interrogation, and which are negated directly by *not*'. A fifth characteristic that might be mentioned is their use in what Palmer (1965: 24), following Firth, calls 'code' – substitute forms, as in the second clause of *I can swim and so can John*. The second point in Ehrman's definition distinguishes the modals from the tense, aspect and voice auxiliaries *be* and *have* (and also from 'lexical' *be* and *have*).

I claimed in 4.2.2 that the modals are ordinary verbs as far as deep structure is concerned: for the most part (indeed in all the uses discussed in this chapter) they are one-place verbs taking non-finite subject complementation. The syntactic properties listed in the above definition relate, in this view, to the modals' distribution in surface structure – though the class is not any the less interesting for this fact.

The descriptions of the modals in Joos (1964) and Palmer (1965) offer a striking contrast in approach. Palmer is concerned with formally distinguishing between various uses of the individual modals, whereas Joos attempts to find a unified meaning for each modal such as will distinguish it from all other members of the class. Joos postulates three binary contrasts (casual versus stable, adequate versus contingent, assurance versus potentiality) such that there are eight different possible combinations of terms: these combinations constitute the meanings of the eight modals *will, shall, can, may, must, ought, dare* and *need*. Elegant though such a semantic componential analysis undoubtedly is, I find it quite unjustified empirically – it will be clear from the following sections, I think, that there is often a greater difference between two uses of a single modal than between one use of one modal and a similar use of another modal: this is particularly apparent in the case of *can* and *may*. Palmer's analysis thus seems to me much the more valid and useful, and my own owes a good deal to it. Like him I shall consider the modals in turn, distinguishing various uses for each one, but my criteria will often be more semantic, less 'formal' than his, and my study, unlike his, is of course corpus-based.[1]

The nuclear members of the modal class are *can, could; may, might; shall, should; will, would; must;* and *ought* (this last differing from the others in that it takes *to* as complementizer). *Need* and *dare* are generally regarded as marginal members of the class: in some uses they have the distributional properties of the modals, in other uses they have those of non-auxiliary verbs: we must simply recognize that they belong in both classes (without any corresponding difference in meaning). With *used* there are dialectal differences: some speakers treat it as a modal, others not. Finally there is the *be* that takes *to* as complementizer, as in *you're to leave immediately.* Neither Ehrman nor Joos include this with the modals and Jespersen (1940: 238) gives a number of examples of its use in non-finite constructions, such as *I heard reports of my being to be married to two or three different young men* – but I would not regard any of those he cites as fully acceptable in contemporary English. In the obligation sense of *you're to leave immediately* it would seem to pattern just like a modal (and is so classified by Palmer); however, the use exemplified in *worse is to come* cannot be regarded as modal, for this *be* need not occupy the initial position in the verb phrase (in Ehrman's sense), witness *worse may be to come.*

Could may be analyzed as *can* + the past tense morpheme, and similarly, *mutatis mutandis*, for *might, would* and *should* (though in some of their uses there is little, if any, synchronic connection between *would* and *will, should* and *shall*). In discussing these past tense forms I shall adopt the distinction made in Huddleston (1969*c*) between deep and surface tense. The surface tense system has two terms, past and present, the former being marked by the presence of the past tense inflectional morpheme *ed* (in one of its various manifestations), the latter being unmarked, or marked in the third person singular by the concord morpheme *s*. Surface tense in this sense is a property of finite verbs only. Deep tense has three terms, past, present and future and every deep structure clause has a deep tense feature; 'past', 'present' and 'future' are to be interpreted as 'before', 'simultaneous with (or including)' and 'after' some point or axis of orientation; this may be the time of the speech act itself, or else it may be established in a clause higher in the constituent hierarchy of the sentence. In remote structure

---

[1] I have discussed Ehrman's analysis of the modals in Huddleston (1969*a*).

we need also to recognize a distinction of 'mode' contrasting real and unreal or tentative (I leave open the question of whether unreal and tentative should be regarded as separate modes or as semantic variants of a single mode: there is no difference in the way they are realized in surface structure.)

The relations between deep and surface tense are quite complex. In particular, a surface past may realize:

(a) A deep past, as in *John was born in France.*

(b) A deep present relative to an axis of orientation that is itself past, as in (*John thought*) *the world was flat.*

(c) A deep present combined with unreal or tentative mode, as in the *could* of *I wish I could swim* or *could you come earlier tomorrow please.*

Conversely deep tense may be realized or 'signalled' by:

(a) Surface tense, as in *John lives in London* (present) versus *John lived in London* (past).

(b) The auxiliary *have* (a marker of deep past), as in *John may have left yesterday* or *you needn't have bothered.* In the first of these the remote structure matrix clause – the one with intransitive *may* as main verb – has present tense, while the constituent clause embedded as subject complement to *may* has past tense (compare *it is possible that John left yesterday*). In the second example *have* realizes the past tense feature of the matrix clause: the complement clause is not past (compare *you didn't need to bother*).

(c) Temporal conjunctions, as in *John left before Bill arrived,* where *arrived* is future relative to the axis of *John left.*

(d) Temporal 'specifiers' (or adverbial expressions of time), as in *John may be in London now* versus *John may be in London tomorrow.* In the first the complement clause is present, in the second, future. The optionality of temporal specifiers means that there are frequent formal ambiguities between present and future.

(e) The class of verb in the matrix clause: many (probably most) verbs taking subject or object complementation impose some constraint on the deep tense of the complement clause – *continue* for example requires that its subject complement have present tense (present relative to the axis established by *continue* itself, of course), while *promise* requires that its object complement have future tense (more precisely this constraint applies to the *promise* + infinitive construction, as opposed to *promise* + *that*).

Table 7:1 shows the number of occurrences in the corpus of the various modal auxiliaries; the percentage of finite clauses containing such a modal was 17.

TABLE 7:1 *The modal auxiliaries*

| | Surface tense | | Total | |
	Present	Past	Number	%
may	380	49	429	27
can	464	109	573	36
will	187	152	339	22
shall	38	62	100	6
must	116	—	116	7
need	5	—	5	0
ought	2	—	2	0
used	—	2	2	0
be	17	9	26	2
Total	1209	383	1592	100

The remainder of this chapter is based on a study of part A of the corpus (to which all subsequent figures refer). There were no instances here of *ought* or *used*, and nothing further will be said about these items.

7.2 'May' and 'might'

I distinguish as many as six uses of *may*: the trouble with the familiar binary division into 'permission' and 'possibility' is that *possible* and its derivatives have themselves quite a wide range of meaning.

(a) Qualified generalization.

(1) The cells do not necessarily form a continuous layer and are frequently restricted to the basal region where they *may* develop rhizoids, whilst in other species they are nearer to the apex where they *may* give rise to proliferations. (21469)

(2) One of us has evidence which agrees with the earlier hypothesis of Chapman & Salton (1962) that the lamellae *may* arise *de novo* from the middle of the cell and migrate to the periphery. (12295)

These can be paraphrased with sentences containing *possible*, but it is not the *possible* reflecting uncertainty: (1) does not mean that the author is uncertain whether or not the cells develop rhizoids, but rather that they sometimes do. Similarly it is more plausible to interpret (2) in such a way that the earlier hypothesis was that the lamellae sometimes arise in the way described rather than that this is possibly the way in which they (always) arise. The gloss 'qualified generalization' is intended to suggest, then, that the generalization expressed in the clause operating as remote structure subject to *may* is said to apply to at least some members of the relevant population, but that it is not guaranteed to hold for all members. The link between 'qualified generalization' and 'uncertainty' is that for any individual member of the population the generalization may hold in the uncertainty/possibility sense. The following example shows clearly the need to distinguish semantically the present use from that of uncertainty:

(3) The reproductive cells *may* encyst themselves, and it has been suggested on this evidence that the plant is a colonial aggregate of coenocytic individuals resulting from the retention of cysts which have developed *in situ*. (21486)

If *may* expressed uncertainty here, the first clause could hardly be said to constitute 'evidence'.

As might be expected, the qualification to the generalization may be expressed in more than one place in the clause:

(4) The sessile forms are attached by means of branched septate rhizoids, but some of them (e.g. *C. fracta*) *may* become free-living later, (21316)

Here the *some* and the *may* are performing essentially the same role; *some* is probably a stronger qualification than *may*, since there is a greater implication that the generalization definitely does not hold for all members of the population.

Where a negative such as *not* follows *may* in this use, it applies to the generalization, not to the modality:

(5) The hairs are there all the time, although they *may* not grow noticeably before puberty. (35142)

Here the meaning is, approximately, 'sometimes they do not grow...' – the negative belongs in the complement sentence functioning as remote structure subject to *may*.

(b) Exhaustive disjunction.

(6) These anemones *may* be blue or dull green in colour. (32203)

(7) The sessile and stalked sporangia *may* occur on the same plant or else on separate plants. (21202)

The *may* here is, in a sense, redundant – (6) is just about synonymous with *these anemones are blue or dull green in colour.* This use is very similar to the 'qualified generalization' one and should possibly be subsumed under it: assuming that disjunctive coordination derives from deep structure coordination of sentences (cf. 2.2.1), *may* will be present with the qualified generalization sense in each of the disjuncts – the anemones may be blue or they may be dull green, though they must be one or the other, blue and dull green constituting an exhaustive list of the alternatives. In (8) the disjunction is not reduced to surface structure phrasal coordination; the 'redundancy' of *may* is evidenced by the fact that it is expressed in the second disjunct but not in the first:

(8) The zygote either germinates immediately to give a new plant or else *may* remain dormant for some time. (21631)

One reason for distinguishing use (b) from use (a) is that if we inserted a *not* after *may* in such examples as (6) and (7) the modal would be within the scope of the negative, in contrast to the situation of (5). The reason is that in:

(6′) The anemones may not be blue or dull green

not cannot negate *be blue or dull green* to the exclusion of *may* because there is a *may* understood in (deleted from) the second disjunct. Thus whereas *the hairs may not grow noticeably before puberty* has roughly the structure shown in PM(1), (6′) has the structure PM(2).

PM(1)

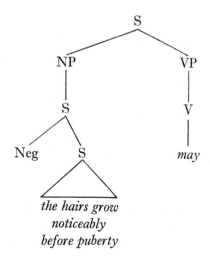

PM(2)

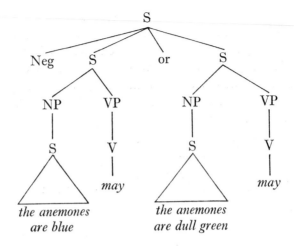

(c) Uncertainty (possibility).

(9) The study of luminescence, by leading to the identification of the luminous materials, *may* provide a valuable tool for long-distance geological prospecting in the moon's outer crust. (38498)

(10) Cohen-Bazire thinks that the chromatophores *may* be structural artifacts which have resulted from a selective breaking of the bacterial membrane system at 'weak' points. (12393)

(11) The plant is probably haploid, and morphologically is of great interest in indicating how the more advanced Siphonales *may* have arisen. (21635)

This corresponds largely to the traditional category of 'possibility' – (9) may be paraphrased with 'will possibly provide...', (10) with 'are possibly structural artifacts', and so on. The deep tense of the clause embedded as remote subject of *may* can be future, (9); present, (10); or past, (11). As with use (a), the *may* of uncertainty is outside the scope of a following *not* – the latter does not change the uncertainty into certainty, the possibility into impossibility:

(12) Recent evidence suggests that a lamellate structure of a chromatophore *may* not be necessary for the capture of light energy. (12461)

(d) Concession.

(13) The spots Greenacre and Barr saw *may* have been as intense but the area they covered – a few square miles in all – was minute compared with the bright area of our photographs, (38286)

The meaning is, roughly, 'I concede that the spots were as intense'; such a *may* is characteristically followed by *but* – or equivalently the *may*-clause is introduced by *although*, and we should doubtless also include under the present heading the *may* that frequently occurs in concessive interrogatives (2.2.3):

(14) Whatever the relations *may* be, the present order is clearly demarcated from the other groups and any affinities would seem to be somewhat distant. (21309)

Where *may* is in an independent clause, as in (13), it is the chief, or only, marker of the concessive meaning, whereas when it occurs in an *although*-clause or an interrogative clause like (14), this meaning is conveyed primarily by the type of dependent construction, so that *may* merely emphasizes the concession and could be omitted with little changes in meaning (cf. *whatever the relations are*).

(e) Legitimacy.

(15) For example, in the case of an atom, which we *may* regard as a rigid body, its [*sc.* the system's] position can be fixed when x, y, z, the co-ordinates of the centre of gravity of the body, and three angles θ, β, ψ determining the orientation of the body, are given. (28430)
(16) This lacuna in our knowledge of the sea *may* be attributed in a large part to the use of the conventional tow net. (32036)

This corresponds to the traditional category of permission – I have avoided this term as a label in order to emphasize that the 'permission' need not be granted by any human authority: in the textual examples it is rather a question of 'the facts' allowing the prediction, so that a suitable paraphrase will often begin 'it is legitimate, valid to...'. The only example of permission in the normal sense of human-given permission is (17), taken from a section consisting of problems for the reader to solve:

(17) Calculate the time taken for the pressures to become 12 and 13 cm. of mercury respectively. The viscosity of oxygen *may* be taken as 0.000199 C.G.S. (28069)

All the textual examples were positive, a *not* after the *may* will normally negate the modality (*you may not go* = 'you are not permitted to go'), but if the *not* is stressed the modal may be outside its domain (*you may ʹnot go*, may mean 'you are permitted not to go').

(f) Ability.

(18) It *may* be shown that the value of each of these terms is RT, so that the mean kinetic energy of translation of a molecule is given by [R], (28456)

(19) The sample is mounted in a movable holder so that the electron beam *may* be directed onto any spot on its surface. (17447)

The meaning here is '(we) are able to show...', '(we) are able to direct the electron beam...'. All the examples have human subjects at the pre-passive level – they are deleted in all passive clauses. This *may*, unlike the corresponding use of *can*, cannot fall within the domain of a negative.

The number of occurrences of *may* in each of the above uses is given in table 7: 2; since the same categories apply to *can* as to *may*, a single table is provided: it is to be found on page 304.

The majority (10 active, 7 passive) of the occurrences of *might* are 'present tense relative to past axis' or 'unreal' counterparts to the *may* of uncertainty/possibility:

(20) Earlier observations had suggested [...] that transient lunar phenomena *might* be connected with corpuscular radiation from the sun. (38201)

(21) It seemed quite possible that this red glow *might* occur on the moon in regions where meteoritic material is exposed on the surface. (38216)

(22) When Bridgman's methods were finally used to make industrial diamonds, he spoke of the development with the enthusiasm another man *might* have had for the making of gems. (38541)

The remaining two instances (both passive) are unreal/tentative versions of the *may* of legitimacy:

(23) An example of what *might* be called 'science in pursuit of technology' is provided by the classic flotation system (32471)

7.3 'Can' and 'could'

All the uses of *may* except the concessive one can be matched by a more or less synonymous use of *can*. There are some uses of *can* (e.g. Palmer's 'willingness' and 'sensation', 1965: 117–18) where *may* could not replace *can*, but these were not exemplified in the text. For the rest the main differences between the two modals are syntactic: the surface past tense form *could*, unlike *might*, can express (for some of the uses) a deep past tense as well as 'present relative to past axis' and 'unreal'; and secondly *can* is able to fall within the domain of a negative in more of its uses than *may*. For the most part it will be enough in this section simply to exemplify the various uses established in 7.2.

(a) Qualified generalization.

(1) In a later paper Drews & Giesbrecht (1963) clearly show that a similar situation *can* occur in *Rhodopseudomonas spheroides.* (12437)

(2) They [*sc. Abylidae*] are quite distinct from the anemones that are frequently found on flotsam, although they *can* assume a sedentary existence on occasions. (32199)

In some cases, as in (2), this use is rather close to Palmer's category of 'characteristic'.

(b) Exhaustive disjunction.

(3) v_R *can* be greater than, equal to, or less than zero according as to whether the scattered light is displaced towards the red end of the spectrum, is unaffected, or is displaced towards the violet end of the spectrum. (26163)

We might also include under this heading:

(4) In the *Aegagropila* group the species *can* exist as (a) threads, (b) cushions and (c) balls. (21354)

(5) The capsule, where present, *can* vary in thickness from the large structure in *Pneumococcus*, which may be detected in the light microscope by negative staining, to the 50 Å-thick microcapsule in *Nocardia calcarea.* (12082)

(4) expresses an exhaustive list of alternatives but uses a conjunction not a disjunction to do so: *or* could replace *and* with no perceptible change in meaning here. In (5) the alternatives are not discrete but form a continuum; as in the *or*-disjunctions, the *can* could be omitted.

(c) Uncertainty/possibility.

(6) Jeans has pointed out that this equation *cannot* be accurate since it does not take into account the persistence of velocities after collision, (28570)

All the examples were negative, with *can* within the domain of *not*, so that the uncertainty of a positive predication is changed into the certainty, necessity of a negative one.

(d) Legitimacy.

(7) Although it is still not possible to trace each lunar enhancement to a specific solar event, one *can* say that the lunar flares are probably caused by protons emitted in solar flares. (38486)

(e) Ability.

(8) If we take Maxwell's Law for the distribution of velocities into account, it *can* be shown that the mean free path becomes [R]. (28566)

(9) Nets used in this way catch the plankton that is common in the upper part of the whole zone in which green plants *can* live, (32050)

Table 7: 2 shows the number of occurrences of these uses in active and passive clauses for *may* and *can* (present tense forms only). Although the uses are the same for the two modals, the relative frequencies are very different. It will also be noticed that there is a marked variation in the proportion of actives to passives: it is in the legitimacy and ability uses that the pre-passive subject of the complement clause is normally human.

TABLE 7: 2. *The uses of 'may' and 'can'*

	may			can		
	Active	Passive	Total	Active	Passive	Total
Qualified generalization	32	5	37	5	1	6
Exhaustive disjunction	10	—	10	5	—	5
Uncertainty/ possibility	30	4	34	2	1	3
Concession	2	—	2	—	—	—
Legitimacy	1	16	17	2	17	19
Ability	4	20	24	29	32	61
Total	79	45	124	43	51	94

There were 41 examples of *could*. Twenty-three of them were in the 'unreal' mode – one exhaustive disjunction (10); four uncertainty/ possibility, (11); four legitimacy, (12); and fourteen ability, (13).

(10) This discrepancy *could* be due either to the fact that intrasublattice interactions have been neglected or to the fact that the formula of Eq. (1) is not an adequate approximation to the biquadratic correction at the lower temperature. (17396)

(11) The function of this widespread blue coloration is not known. It *could* be due to one particular group of strongly pigmented animals, such as the Pontellid copepods, being a key food organism for a number of other animals. (32268)

(12) The difference between the frequencies of the incident and emergent radiation is termed the Raman frequency. It *could*, more logically, be called the Raman shift: (26161)

(13) The hands and feet need rough surfaces; if they were perfectly smooth, they *could* not get a good grip. (35096)

It is the presence of *either* in (10) that makes the exhaustive disjunction interpretation very much more plausible here than uncertainty/possibility – compare (11).

The 18 examples of 'real' *could* (expressing deep past tense or present relative to a past axis) all involved the ability sense:

(14) As no reports of measurements of this resonant frequency, or that of other III–V compounds *could* be found, our choice of 3920 cm^{-1} is based entirely on the above. (17121)

7.4 'Will' and 'would'

The 49 examples of *will* can be distributed among the following three uses:

(a) Futurity, relative to present (10 active, 7 passive).

(1) Someday the lunar flares that result from this process *will* be monitored systematically, under an international cooperative program, (38515)

This is a straightforward prediction about the future. The fact that the infinitive expresses an agentive process does not necessarily make the *will* volitional, so that examples like the following have been included under the present heading:

(2) These granules will be discussed in more detail later. (12520)

There were in fact no examples of volitional *will*, assuming that we use the voice-neutrality test for distinguishing between the futurity and volitional uses of *will* (see 3.1 and 4.2.2).[1] In:

(3) It remains to be seen whether a similar basic concept *will* apply to the holochrome particles of certain photosynthetic bacteria, (12500)

what is future is not so much the concept's applying to the particles but the discovery that, or whether, it does; *will apply* could be replaced here by *applies* (since the future is implicit in *remains to be seen*) or *will prove/turn out to apply*.

(b) Induction (24 examples, all active).

(4) Under certain conditions the cells *will* also produce aplanospores. (21297)
(5) If a longer rope is used, the weight of the net ring *will* take the net below the surface. (32045)

'Induction' is Palmer's term (1965: 111): '*will* is used for 'general' timeless truths, that may be proved inductively, of the kind illustrated by *oil will float on water*.' He points out that such examples are semantically equivalent to the corresponding clauses with a non-modal simple form of the verb in its habitual use, compare *oil floats on water*. Earlier (p. 86), in discussing the non-modal form, he distinguishes between inductively known facts (like *oil floats on water*) and 'general' truths (like *the Severn flows into the Atlantic*), where the latter has no equivalent form with *will*. As far as I can see, what determines whether *will* can be used in clauses of this type is whether the process is a conditional one or not. Thus we can say *if you pour oil onto water it floats/will float, if you heat water to 100° it boils/will boil* (cf. Palmer's *water boils/will boil at 100°*); *the Severn flows into the Atlantic, the sun rises in the east*, on the other hand, do not describe the activity of the Severn and the sun under certain conditions. Relating the inductive *will* to the notion of condition helps to explain its use in this type of clause and also the equivalence of *will* and the non-modal form. In a patently conditional construction like *if you pour oil onto water it will float*, the floating is future relative to the pouring, i.e. the pouring happens first; if we used the non-modal *floats* here we would simply be leaving this temporal

---

[1] Palmer (1965: 110) uses occurrence in an *if*-clause as a criterion: he claims that the *will* of volition, but not that of futurity, can occur in conditions: *if he'll come tomorrow*, but not *if it'll rain tomorrow*. But a *will* of futurity can occur in an *if*-clause where the meaning is 'if it is the case that'—e.g. *well, if the match will probably be over by tea-time let's get going immediately.*

relation between *pour* and *float* implicit and selecting a tense for *float* on the basis of its relation to the speech act. Most of the textual examples included under the present heading contained an overt conditional phrase or clause, as in (4) and (5). The following is slightly different and perhaps represents an intermediate use between uses (a) and (b):

(6) the reason [*sc.* why the stubble feels rough after shaving] is simply that the soft, tapered ends of the hairs have been cut off; the new hairs that will succeed them later *will* still have soft tapered ends. (35418)

The new hairs succeeding the old hairs is future relative to the process of cutting off the tapered ends of the latter – but the whole compound process of cutting and new hairs arising is iterative, so that again the modal forms could be replaced by non-modals ones: *the new hairs that succeed them later still have soft tapered ends.* I have thus limited use (a) to cases where the futurity is, in effect, relative to the speech act.

(c) Deduction (8 examples, all active).

(7) Thus of the N molecules per c.c., the number, dN_q, having a resultant velocity between q and $q + dq$ is [R]. Hence the mean, or average, velocity of all the molecules *will* be the average value of q, (28382)

(8) If we regard the atoms as points, each atom *will* have three degrees of freedom, corresponding to the x, y, z co-ordinates: (28434)

The *will* here expresses the 'it follows that' relation. There is a clear semantic difference between the *if*-construction of (8) and that of (5); yet in this use, as in the last, the modal form is normally replaceable by a non-modal one (alternatively we could replace *will* by *must*). Palmer's *will* of probability, as in *that'll be the postman*, can, I think, be regarded as a special case of this deductive use.

All but three of the 39 examples of *would* were in the unreal mode; there were two distinguishable uses:

(a) Tentativeness (11 examples).

(9) This is a feature of its metabolism that *would* seem to require further investigation. (21146)

In all cases but one the verb was *seem*, *appear* or *expect* (passive), the first two of which have tentativeness as part of their meaning: the *would* reinforces this component – compare the series *it requires/seems to require/would seem to require further investigation.* This tentative *would* cannot, I think, be related synchronically to any use of *will*, and is probably best regarded simply as a marker of unreal/tentative mode, so that we would have the proportion *seems* : *would seem* :: *can* : *could*.

(b) Prediction (25 examples).

(10) Without them [*sc*. these specialized nerves] the human body *would* be almost as out of touch with the outside world as it *would* be if it lacked the major sense organs. (35273)

(11) Physiological investigations into the adaptations to this environment [*sc*. the surface layers] *would* be most interesting, but the animals have not so far proved any more tractable to living in captivity than those from greater depths. (32382)

Here we are concerned with making predictions about 'unreal worlds'. In the simple cases the unreality of the world being talked about is established by an *if*-clause expressing an unreal condition or by some equivalent adjunct, such as the *without them* in (10) (= 'if it did not have them'). In other cases it is established implicitly from the context, as in (11); in several examples the writer uses *would* in investigating the consequences of a hypothesis. The distinction between this use and the tentative one is not always easy to make; the following I put under (a) though it bears a good deal of resemblance to (11):

(12) There has been no cytological work to show whether there is any alternation of generations and such an investigation *would* be highly desirable. (21204)

(11) predicts that the investigations would be interesting if they could be carried out – the real mode counterpart is *will be most interesting*, but (12) can scarcely be interpreted as making predictions about the desirability of the investigation – it is, rather, a tentative way of saying that it *is* desirable.

The three real mode *would*'s were;

(13) it [*sc*. a surface living fish] 'rose' to these like a trout feeding on the imagos of Ephemerids, and *would* even eat dried plankton providing it floated. (32308)

(14) C. L. Perkins in 1919 had the idea of using as collectors, in place of complex oils, sparingly soluble organic compounds that *would* be relatively easily oxidizable. (32514)

(15) It is known that light of short wave-length is more readily scattered than light of long wave-length – a result which Rayleigh showed *would* account not only for the Tyndall effect but for the blue colour of the sky. (26115)

The *would* of (13) is past in deep as well as surface tense; the corresponding present tense, *it will eat dried plankton*, belongs under the 'induction' type (note the conditional 'if there is any dried plankton floating, it will eat it'). It differs from Palmer's *pigs will eat anything* in being obviously less general a statement, but this difference may be simply attributed to the contrast between the specific and generic subjects.

The *would* of (14) is present relative to a past axis; the corresponding *will* form, *compounds that will be relatively easily oxidizable*, is a straightforward example of use (a) above, futurity relative to present.

In (15) the *would* is likewise due to the presence of a past tense in the matrix clause (*showed*). *This result will account for the Tyndall effect* does not fit into any of the categories suggested above for *will*, and I am not sure how to characterize this use in general terms – it could perhaps be handled with the *will* of submission discussed in 3.1, for notice that we could say *we can account for the Tyndall effect with this result*.

7.5 'Shall' and 'should'

There is little to be said about *shall* on the basis of the textual examples. In 7 of the 9 cases, *shall* had *we* as mood subject and expressed 'futurity relative to present':

(1) After dealing with a dozen or so molecular models, we *shall* discuss the principles underlying the scattering of short wave radiation and of electrons, and *shall* compare some of the experimental data with those of spectroscopy. (26464)

None of the *will*'s of futurity had first person mood subjects, so that the data fit the traditional paradigm of *I/we shall, you/he/she/it/they will*: *shall* and *will* are to be regarded in this futurity use as a single item in remote structure. The remaining two *shall*'s were in clauses embedded as complement to the noun *probability*:

(2) The probability P_x, that a molecule moving with a velocity c *shall* describe a free path at least equal to x is $f(x)$, and the probability that it *will* pass over the path $x + dx$ is, therefore, [R]. (28600)

Shall here matches *will* in the later clause of the example: there is presumably no difference in meaning between them; this use of *shall* seems to me somewhat unusual – we would not expect to find it in complements to the adjective *probable* (*?it is probable that the molecule shall describe a free path*).

The 21 examples of *should* were of the following types:

(a) Obligation (8 examples).

(3) This assignment *should* be regarded as tentative until measurements have been made on a number of different samples to insure the absence of impurity effects. (17159)

(4) It has been suggested that a thin layer of high-conductivity material on the face of the sample might conduct heat away from the hot spot well enough to keep temperatures in the sample at a tolerable level. The question is, how thick *should* this layer be? (17459)

(b) Logical expectation (9 examples).

(5) This luminescence *should* be brightest when the sunspots are near the solar equator and the plane of the earth's orbit; when the sunspots move to higher latitudes, the excitation they cause *should* decrease in intensity. Danjon's finding of just such a pattern provided indirect support for the idea of corpuscular excitation of lunar luminescence. (38089)

The distinction between these two uses parallels that between the obligation and logical necessity senses of *must* (see below): in both cases *should* expresses a weaker element of compulsion/necessity than *must*. In the first use the pre-passive subject of the infinitive is typically human and agentive, but examples like (4) show that this is not an absolute rule. (4) clearly differs semantically from such a clause as *you should be more careful*, inasmuch as in the latter the obligation is on you to be more careful, whereas in (4) the obligation is not on the layer to be so thick – we understand (4) to mean something like 'how thick should we make this layer?'. There is little syntactic motivation for regarding the *should* of obligation or logical expectation as the unreal/tentative mode version of *shall*.

(c) First person form of tentative *would* (2 examples).

(6) Before discussing the pictures we made I *should* like to explain how we came to make them. (38194)

This may be regarded as the same remote structure item as the *would* of tentativeness discussed in 7.4, the difference in surface realization being accounted for by the person category of the mood subject. However, the proportion *it would seem*: *it seems* does not hold for *I should like*:

I like, since *I like to explain* cannot be used for a single act of explaining – it implies habit, iteration, etc. The closest non-tentative analogue to *I should like* is *I want* (which does not have the tentative form *I should want*).

(d) In complement clauses (2 examples).

(7) It is curious that this dramatic loss of hair *should* take place on the scalp, (35455)

This cannot be subsumed under any of the uses of *should* in independent clauses (except perhaps Palmer's *who should I see but Bob* type) and *ad hoc* provision must be made for it. There are severe limitations on the class of predicate taking *should* in the complement. The other example, perhaps a little different, was in the object complement of *require* – it was discussed earlier as example (24) of 4.3.2.

7.6 'Must' and 'need'

The 37 examples of *must* belonged under one or other of the familiar two uses mentioned above:

(a) Obligation (10 active, 14 passive).

(1) it is now clear that the luminescence of the moon [...] *must* be accepted as a fact. (38479)
(2) As a wrapping that *must* accommodate itself to changes in the shape and size of the body, the skin is highly elastic. (35200)

(b) Logical necessity, conclusion (12 active, 1 passive).

(3) Any change in the frequency of light due to its passage through the medium *must* accordingly be due to a change in the internal energy of the scattering molecule. (26158)
(4) The large enhancement we photographed in 1963 [...] indicated that the energy flux of the incident particles *must* have been some 100,000 ergs per square centimeter. (38411)

The semantic difference between obligation and logical necessity is for the most part clear. The meaning of *must* in the latter use is that the proposition expressed in the clause embedded as subject complement in remote structure is necessarily true, whereas with obligational *must* the complement clause does not normally have a truth value. There are, however, certain cases where the distinction is not easy to apply; these typically involve an element of condition (one might even set up conditional *must* as a third use), as in:

(5) One of the conditions for the stability of a molecule so constituted is that it resists small deformations inwards or outwards, i.e. that $du/d\theta$ *must* be zero. (26040)

(6) Calcium carbonate is deposited wherever there is a mucilage layer and an aggregation of the chloroplasts, but apparently both these conditions *must* be fulfilled before lime can be laid down. (21528)

(7) For these two sets of data to be consistent one must postulate a low rate of increase with dose of wholly independent nuclei which can sustain cubic growth to high values of α, accompanied by an initially more rapid increase in numbers of nuclei in crystallite face boundaries, which saturates at about 40×10^{16} n cm^{-2}. A limiting crystallite size *must* exist for this to be true. (16263)

These express necessary conditions: unless $du/d\theta$ is zero, the molecule cannot be stable; unless the conditions are fulfilled, lime cannot be laid down; unless a limiting crystallite size exists, 'this' cannot be true. I have taken the first two as obligation, the third as logical necessity, since with the last the necessary condition is a condition for the truth of a proposition – but it is something of a borderline case.

Nor are there, as is sometimes suggested, clear-cut syntactic differences between the two uses of *must*. The verb *must* itself occurs only in the present tense, but the subject complement clause may vary in tense. With obligational *must* the complement is very often future (*you must work harder next term*) but I would not agree with Palmer (1965: 119) that the complement of the *must* of logical necessity cannot be future – for many speakers at least such sentences as *look at those clouds: it must surely rain before we get home* are quite acceptable. Nor is it the case that the complement can have past tense (marked by *have*) only with logical necessity (as in (4) above) – compare *you must have been born British to get a job in MI5* (one of the 'necessary condition' type). With either use of *must* the complement may be positive or negative: *you must/mustn't go, the match must/mustn't be over.* But *must* itself (again in either use) cannot fall within the domain of a negative – the meaning 'not-must' is expressed by *needn't*; the one textual example has the logical necessity sense:

(8) All known examples of lunar luminescence seem to be directly or indirectly related to some activity of the sun, but the relation is not simple and *need* not be based on overall sunspot activity. (38483)

but examples of the other use can easily be constructed (e.g. *you needn't come tomorrow*).

As a modal, *need* occurs only in negative and interrogative clauses (and one or two other 'affective' environments, in the sense of Klima, 1964; e.g. after restrictive *only*). Like *must*, *need* has no surface past tense form, but unlike *must* it can occur with deep past tense, realized by *have*, as in *he needn't have come*.

7.7 'Be'

I have distinguished the following uses:

(a) Instruction (4 examples).

(1) It *is* to be observed that the distance between the carbon atoms in cyanogen [...] is almost the same as the interatomic distance in the diamond lattice. (26533)

These are semantically equivalent to imperatives: *observe that...*; this use is very similar to the *should* of obligation, and as with the latter the pre-passive subject of the complement clause is typically human and agentive.

(b) Potentiality (5 examples).

(2) According to Hammerling the immature plant contains only one nucleus, which *is* to be found in one of the rhizoids, (21572)

All five examples contained *is/are to be found*; the heading 'potentiality' is intended to suggest a rough paraphrase with *can*. The modal status of *be* is somewhat doubtful here, and indeed the structure as a whole is quite obscure. One difficulty is that it is not possible to change the voice of *find* from passive to active: *which we are to find in one of the rhizoids* cannot be regarded as an ordinary active counterpart of (2). The expression *is to be found* is semantically similar to *is located* or *is situated*; it differs grammatically from them in that the *is* cannot be replaced by a non-finite form of *be* (which is why I have treated it as a modal auxiliary) – compare *it may be located*, **it may be to be found...*

(c) I offer no heading for the following, whose syntax is also rather obscure and idiomatic:

(3) The assignment seems to be consistent in that a $TO_1 + TO_2$ band is not observed which *is* to be expected if the TO_1 and TO_2 come from high density-of-states regions at different wave vectors. (17165)

This can be paraphrased approximately as 'which (is what) we would expect...', but such a paraphrase offers no real clue to the syntactic analysis. As with (2), there is no active counterpart, the *is* is necessarily finite, and the pattern is of very limited productivity.

(d) Marker of unreal conditions (1 example).

(4) If this process *were* to occur among the atoms of the lunar surface, they could of course emit radiation that would penetrate the earth's atmosphere, namely visible light. (38033)

This is very similar to *if this process occurred*...(with unreal mode, not real mode and past tense), and this use of *be* is restricted to unreal conditions: there is no real mode counterpart of (4) containing *be*, for *if this process is to occur* means something quite different. I would say therefore that in conditional clauses unreal mode may be realized either by a surface past tense form (*occurred*) or by the *were*+infinitive construction. (There is a similar use of *should*, though this is not exemplified in the corpus.)

8   Theme

8.1   Marked theme

Following Halliday (1967*c*, 1969) I shall use 'theme' to name the grammatical function of the leftmost element, or group of elements, in the clause. More specifically we can adopt his contrast between clauses with marked theme and those with unmarked theme, where a marked theme is any element (or group) preceding the mood subject other than *wh*-items and conjunctions. (I shall here be considering only declarative clauses: the formulation would have to be amended slightly if it were to cover non-declaratives too, cf. Halliday, 1967*c*: 222). Thus in:

(i) *a* John was reading yesterday
    b Yesterday John was reading
    c when John was reading

(this last being a relative clause), the themes are respectively *John*, *yesterday* and *when*. (i)*b* has marked theme inasmuch as a special rule is needed to account for the presence of *yesterday* in the theme position – this rule may be called the marked theme transformation. In this brief section I shall examine the kinds of marked themes found in the corpus.

There was only one example where this position was filled by a (post-passive) object:

(1) *This sum* we might call the total torque, τ. (27342)

In independent clauses there are two ways in which an element functioning as object at the pre-passive level may come to occupy the theme position: by means of the marked theme rule as in (1), or by passivization as in:

(1') This sum might be called the total torque, τ.

As far as the scientific corpus is concerned, we can say that thematization of the pre-passive object is effected just about exclusively by this second method. In dependent clauses there are further ways of thematizing an object, such as relativization, but we have already had occasion to note (5.2) that there were only a handful of examples where a post-passive object was relativized: it is thus very rare in this register for a post-passive object to occur as theme, whether marked or unmarked.

Hardly less rare than marked object theme was marked attribute theme: there were just seven clear cases, including:

(2) *More effective and certainly more interesting*, however, is a structure recently demonstrated by the team at the Bell Telephone Laboratories, using magnetostrictive materials. (37595)

(3) Nevertheless, *such* was the heat of the controversy that some surprising distortions of the law of mass action were invoked, (32575)

In all of them the subject and verb were inverted, the verb (*be*) being presumably too 'empty' to occur in the position which normally carries the focus of the information unit; but this inversion is effected by a separate rule and is not obligatory in principle (cf. *young he may be, but...*). No fewer than 5 of the 7 examples had as attribute a comparative Adj Phr with the standard of comparison deleted under identity with material in the preceding text, as in (2).

One might perhaps regard the six examples like the following as also having marked attribute theme:

(4) *Surrounding the liquid helium* is liquid hydrogen, the intervening space being evacuated. (29509)

(5) *Evenly scattered deep in the epidermis* are the melanocytes, cells that produce the dark pigment melanin. (35222)

(Again the subject followed the verb in all cases.) These all involve the extensive rather than intensive use of *be* (see 3.8), and there may be some doubt as to whether the participial clauses are correctly analyzed as attributes, though in 3.7 we did see other examples of attributive extensive clauses, and one of the six cases had an Adj Phr as theme:

(6) Beneath the cell wall, which is typical of that seen in most Gram-negative organisms, there are two layers of unit membranes. *Parallel and adjacent to this unit membrane system* is a thinner electron-opaque membrane about 50 Å thick. (12333)

Nevertheless the italicized phrase here has a certain locative meaning, as indeed do the participial clauses in (4), (5) and the other examples; notice that *there* could be readily inserted before *be* in all these examples (see 8.2). A further difficulty is that it is scarcely possible to interchange the theme and subject phrases (without completely changing the structure of the sentence) – (4), for example, is not simply a thematic variant of *the liquid hydrogen is surrounding the liquid helium* (if it were it would be an example of Halliday's 'marked predicator theme' like his *standing outside the door he was* from *he was standing outside the door*).

There are two other constructions involving a thematic attribute which need special provision. One is exemplified in:

(7) Successful as these treatments were in supporting continued development of cells already in division, they were not successful in initiating meiosis, (11560)

This is a marked theme version of *though these treatments were successful* . . . ; in (7) *as* may be replaced by *though*, whereas with unmarked theme *as* cannot occur (except with a different meaning). (7) cannot be handled by the ordinary marked theme rule since the construction is unique in having the theme precede the subordinating conjunction.

The second construction is the double comparative:

(8) The stronger his conscience the stronger the guilt and anxiety which may be evoked. (37256)

Again special rules would seem to be needed. (8) is a compound sentence consisting of two clauses, the order of elements within the clauses being determined in part by the order of the clauses within the compound sentence, in part by the nature of the construction. The only other possible order is:

(8′) The guilt and anxiety which may be evoked are the stronger, the stronger his conscience.

(The verb *is* could be inserted after *conscience* in both examples.) *The stronger his conscience* is the subordinate clause, the other the superordinate one (notice, in support of this analysis, that the subject of the latter, but not of the former could be relativized – . . .*guilt and anxiety, which are the stronger, the stronger his conscience*). Within the subordinate clause the order is fixed: attribute + subject + optional *be*; within the superordinate one the position of the attribute is adjacent to the subordinate clause.

The occurrence of an adjunct as marked theme, as in (9), was quite frequent:

(9) In view of the variety of these achievements one must now distinguish between the goals of the investigator and those of the industrial technologist. (38564)

Of clauses with an overt mood subject and a finite verb 19 % had marked adjunct theme: 1959 out of 10382; the total number of clauses with such a theme was 2304.

Like the relative *-wh* preposing rule, the marked theme transformation may shift to initial position an element from within an embedded sentence:

(10) If I is the molar magnetization of the gas at temperature T and in an external field of magnetic intensity $\mathscr{H}$, Brillouin showed that [R], (29433)

(11) Until such legislation is forthcoming the BMA has suggested that evidence based on clinical examination should be limited to determining whether the suspect's behaviour was due to any other factor such as illness or injury. (36081)

Before the application of the marked theme rule the *if-* and *until*-clauses belong in the object complements of *show* and *suggest* respectively. The rule is cyclic, so that we have such a paradigm as:

(ii) *a* He said he would stay in if it rained
      b He said if it rained he would stay in
      c He would stay in if it rained, he said
      d If it rained he said he would stay in
      e If it rained he would stay in he said

In (ii)*a* the rule hasn't appled to either matrix or constituent (object) clause; in *b* it has applied to the constituent clause only; in *c* and *d* it has applied to the matrix clause only, in the one case shifting the object, in the other an adjunct from within the constituent clause; in *e* the rule has applied on both cycles.

The marked theme position may also be filled by the post-modifier of an NP, as in:

(12) Of the species so far investigated the chromosomes appear to be present in multiples of 4, and this probably indicates polyploidy. (21414)

The structure prior to thematization is *the chromosomes of the species so far investigated appear to be present*...; in this respect too, therefore, the marked theme rule resembles relative-*wh* preposing – compare *species of which the chromosomes*...(see 5.2).

Normally clauses with marked adjunct theme have the order subject followed by verb. There are, however, two kinds of inversion that may be triggered by the selection of marked theme. Firstly, there is the subject–auxiliary inversion that applies to independent interrogative clauses: this kind of inversion also takes place in declaratives with a negative marked theme, as in:

(13) The sporogenous tissue developed to the spore-mother-cell stage, but *in no case* was meiosis initiated, (11510)

(14) Because the skirts of the hovercraft are light and flexible the drag they cause is small; *neither* is air resistance serious at present day speeds of between 60 and 80 knots. (34433)

The order here is used by Klima (1964) as one criterion for distinguishing 'sentence negation' from 'constituent negation', for the above examples contrast with ones like *in no time he had solved the problem*, where the clause as a whole is positive. It should be added, however, that the inversion applies also when the marked theme contains restrictive *only*, which is not a sentence negator:

(15) Only then can some of the explanations put forward be adequately tested. (37341)

Secondly the subject may be shifted to the end of the clause, as in:

(16) In this Chapter will be found a partial answer. (26453)

(17) The scolex is usually buried in the intestinal mucosa of the host. *Behind the scolex comes the neck*, the most slender portion of the body, which may or may not be sharply marked off from the scolex. (23510)

This is the type of inversion that we found with the marked attribute themes above, (2)–(6). The effect is to put the subject in the position where, other things being equal, it will carry the nuclear stress of the tone group, this making it the focus of new information (cf. Halliday, 1967c) – notice that in the italicized clause of (17) *the scolex* is informationally given, *the neck* new. I am not able to state explicitly the conditions under which this inversion, which seems in general to be optional, may take place with marked adjunct theme. The breakdown of the 19 examples in the corpus was as follows:

(a) Locative theme + extensive *be* (9 examples).

(18) the cells in the tongue that are responsible for 'taste' have no nerve-fibres themselves, but *around them* are the endings of nerve-fibres whose cell bodies lie in the cranial ganglia. (22284)

(b) Locative theme + some verb other than *be*, as in (16) and (17) (4 examples).

(c) 'Direction' or 'source' as theme (4 examples).

(19) *Through each proglottis* runs [*sic*] the excretory canals and the nervous strands which are common to all. (23522)

(20) *from this simple concept* has developed a sophisticated technique that is both versatile in scope and sensitive in discrimination. (32430)

(d) Others.

(21) *With adolescence* comes an enlargement of the hair follicles and a more active growth of the hair. (35160)

(22) to such thermometers are [*sic*] attributed the accuracy of much of the work done in low-temperature physics since 1951. (29365)

Perhaps one can say that in all cases but (21) there is some component of 'place', physical or metaphorical, with or without movement. Again we may note a similarity between marked theme and relativization: this shift of the subject to clause-final position also occurs in relative clauses – compare *this chapter, in which will be found a partial answer,* or example (30) of 5.2 (*prominent among which is sexual attraction*). In (19) and (22) the verb agrees for number not with the mood subject but with the NP immediately to its left, suggesting the concord rule has applied *after* thematization (cf. also (2) of 8.2).

So far I have been concerned with clauses containing just one adjunct as marked theme; there were 148 examples where the theme position was filled by a sequence of two (or, in a couple of cases, three) adjuncts. All but 15 of these clauses occupied the initial position in the orthographic sentence.

The breakdown of the 'complex theme' clauses was as follows:

(a) In 130 cases one of the thematic adjuncts was a 'discourse sentence adverb' (Halliday, 1967c; see also Greenbaum, 1969, for a detailed study of sentence adverbs and related matters):

also	2	for instance		in other words		similarly	
consequently		further		moreover	2	so	7
conversely		hence	6	nevertheless	3	then	5
finally		however	45	now	8	therefore	8
first	2	indeed	3	on the other		thus	15
for example	8	in fact	2	hand	3	yet	4

(23) Now because of the high frequency of optical vibrations, V cannot be measured as a function of time with any presently available optical detectors. (19391)

Generally these items occupy the first thematic position, as in this example, but *however* (27), *therefore* (7) and *for example* (3) were also found in second position, as in (24) and (25) (where both thematic elements are discourse adjuncts):

(24) In *Philonthus*, however, each comb is united to the lateral wall of the base of the ligula anterior to the hypopharyngeal fold, and thus could be considered as a paraglossa. (13160)

(25) Thus, for example, the typical lines (1,632 and 1,725 cm^{-1}) of the ethylenic link are present in the spectrum of ethyl acetoacetate, but are absent from that of ethyl dimethylacetoacetate, (26398)

(b) There were 11 examples where one of the thematic elements was a modal or a comment adjunct:

clearly	incidentally	perhaps	2
evidently	interestingly	presumably	
importantly	of course 3		

(26) Of course if we want to find the magnitude of the velocity, we just write [R]. (27262)

(c) There were only 9 examples with two 'lexical' adjuncts as theme:

(27) On October 5, 1963, near 5,450 angstroms in the green region of the spectrum, he observed strong luminescence ranging as high as 30 percent of the total light. (38156)

(28) In this arrangement, when the incident polarization is parallel to the magnetization direction of the second cobalt–iron crystal, only neutrons whose polarization is unchanged on scattering by the chromium will reach the counter. (18519)

8.2 'There'

In this section I shall be concerned with the unstressed *there* of such constructions as:

(1) The species grow as epiphytes or on stones in damp tropical and subtropical regions, but they will also grow under temperate conditions if *there is an adequate supply of moisture.* (21135)

This *there*, which is to be distinguished from the deictic locative adverb *there* (they are normally distinct phonologically, the former being rhythmically a 'weak' syllable, the latter 'strong' in the sense of Halliday, 1963), may be assumed to be introduced transformationally, so that the structure of the italicized clause in (1), prior to the application of the *there*-transformation, will be *an adequate supply of moisture is*. The effect of this rule is to move the subject to the post-verbal position where, other things being equal, it carries the nuclear stress and is the focus of 'new' information, and to insert dummy *there* into the subject position. As noted earlier this rule precedes the subject–auxiliary inversion which applies in interrogatives, etc. (cf. *is there an adequate supply?*). The NP moved into post-verbal position functions as a kind of object; if relativized the relative-*that* deletion rule may apply, as in *everything (that) there was*.

It is difficult to state precisely the conditions under which the *there*-transformation may (or must) apply. In examining the examples in the corpus I shall initially leave aside those where there is a finite relative clause or a participial clause following the head noun of the NP shifted to post-verbal position.

In the majority of cases the rule applies to clauses with extensive *be* as main verb; there were six examples containing some other verb, as in:

(2) There remains [*sic*] the unpleasant side effects like the low-tide smell, often called 'decaying seaweed', and the oily slick on the sea. (39164)

The rule cannot apply to clauses containing an object at the post-passive level. Thus five of the examples were intransitive clauses with the verbs *emerge, lead out, occur, open out* and *remain*; and the sixth was an agentless passive:

(3) During the course of evolution *there has been produced* from the responses of simple living systems an amazingly sensitive arrangement by which minute changes occurring perhaps at a great distance from the surface of the animal, are measured and lead to readjustments that ensure its continuance. (22202)

In discussing the passive rule earlier we saw that it has two principal effects. Firstly it moves the pre-passive subject to adjunct position, where it can be retained as the carrier (in the unmarked case) of nuclear stress, i.e. as the focus of new information, or else deleted; (3) is one of those where it is difficult to say what a plausible pre-passive subject might be, and this may be assumed to have favoured the selection of passive voice. Secondly passivization shifts the object into subject position, where it will be (in the unmarked case) theme, but not the focus of new information (unless contrastively stressed). The use of *there* in (3) has enabled the writer to achieve the first of these effects without the second, which would be contextually inappropriate (notice, for example, the length of the pre-passive object): passivization moves the object into pre-verbal position, the *there*-transformation then moves it back into clause-final position.

Normally the NP moved out of the subject position is indefinite, but this cannot be said to be an absolute constraint. The following examples of definite NP's are unquestionably wholly acceptable:

(4) Therefore, there is the possibility of forestalling the onset of the reaction. (31352)

(5) Sewage-contaminated water can carry a whole range of pathogenic bacteria – typhoid, bacterial dysentery, cholera, tuberculosis and viruses for infective hepatitis and polio, for example. Then *there are the parasitic worms, threadworms and tapeworms,* (39175)

(6) Meiosis takes place at the segmentation of the zygote so that there is only the haploid generation. (21289)

(4) represents quite a productive pattern: the NP is an ominalization of a subject complement + adjectival predicate construction – cf. *there is the possibility, probability, certainty that . . .,* etc. (5) too exemplifies a quite normal pattern of listing, classifying, etc. – cf. *What is there in the suit-case? – There's my jacket, your shoes, a couple of handkerchiefs . . . ;* compare also (2) above and (10) below. (Thus, *pace* Postal, 1966: 180, 200, questions of the form *what is there* + locative can have definite NP's in the answer.) Of the 198 *there*-clauses (I still exclude the relative and participial constructions) all but 5 had indefinite NP's.

Perhaps surprisingly, only 39 of the 198 contained a locative adjunct:

(7) the 'thread' and 'cushion' forms are to be found farther out in deeper water *where there is less motion.* (21365)

(8) Many hyponeuston animals are herbivorous, and *there must be a permanent flora in the surface layers* in spite of the very high light intensities. (32395)

The corresponding clauses without *there* would be scarcely acceptable, especially in the case of (7).

A further 20 examples had an NP containing an embedded clause as complement:

(9) there is no doubt that, although man still has as many hair follicles as his primate cousins, his hair growth is gradually declining, (35335)

It is perhaps worth adding that over a quarter of the *there*-clauses were negative, although the percentage of negative clauses in the corpus as a whole was less than 5.

Let us now turn to the difficult construction where the head noun of the shifted NP is followed by a finite relative clause. In discussing the cleft-sentence construction in 5.4.2, I made a distinction between:

(i)   *a* // ˌit's/money that I/**need**//
      b // ˌit's/**money** that I/need//

where the relative clause in (i)*a* is post-modifier to *money*, and *b* derives by extraposition from *it that I need is money*. An equivalent intonational distinction is to be found in *there*-clauses:

(ii) *a* // ˌthere's a/film I/want to/**see**//
      b // ˌthere's a/**film** I/want to/see//

The first might be an answer to 'What's on at the Odeon?', the second to 'What shall we do this week-end?' Of the following textual examples I interpret (10)–(12) as being of the first type, (13)–(15) as being of the second:

(10) The permanent surface fauna [...] may be divided into two main components. There are, firstly, those animals which are adapted entirely to a surface existence, partly in air and partly in water, which A. I. Savilov has called the Pleuston, and secondly those animals, the Hyponeuston, which inhabit the immediately sub-surface layers. (32146)

(11) Yet even after the telephone had been invented, there were people who believed that its main use would be to enable mistresses of households to communicate with their domestic servants more efficiently than by speaking tube. (36480)

(12) Today there are presses that can attain more than 3,000 tons per square inch. (38545)

(13) TRENTEPOHLIACEAE. A genus which lives on stones and the shells of gastropods that are to be found in fresh and salt water, although there is one species that is terrestrial. (21094)

(14) But *something* [*ital. sic*] goes in a parabola, there is an effective 'center' which moves in a parabola. (27052)

(15) There is one important difference between mass and moment of inertia which is very dramatic. (27627)

(Notice that (13) and (15) have *one* rather than *a* as determiner: this suggests strongly a reading with stress located here.) Examples (10)–(12) (and (ii)*a*) can be handled straightforwardly by means of the *there*-transformation that we have been discussing – the shifted NP just happens to contain a relative clause, so that (12), for example, will derive from *today presses that can attain more than 3,000 tons are* (application of the *there*-rule being obligatory). But such a derivation will not do for (13) –(15) (and (ii)*b*), if we are right in our claim that the relation between the sentences in (ii) is essentially the same as that between those in (i). The fact that a proper noun could occur in type (ii)*b* supports this position, cf. *Who might be able to help? – There's John you could try.* We cannot analyze *you could try* as post-modifier to *John* since the latter cannot take a restrictive relative. These considerations argue strongly that we should treat the relatives here as extraposed, so that prior to extraposition the structure of (13) would be *there that is terrestrial is one species.* Following Halliday (1967*c*: 238) this may be regarded as a subvariety of the cleft-sentence construction: he distinguishes the *it* and *there* types in terms of the definite/indefinite contrast. This certainly makes sense semantically, witness the difference between the above *there's John you could try* (= 'one person you could try is John') and *it's John you should try* (= 'the person you should try is John'); the textual example (14) might almost have been coined specially to support this hypothesis, for *a center* in the second clause identifies the indefinite *something* mentioned in the first clause. In both subvarieties of the cleft-sentence construction extraposition of the relative clause is obligatory, and contrary to the rules for basic relative clauses a subject-*wh* may be deleted (*there was a man came to see you*).

A final problem concerns the participial construction exemplified in:

(16) in any given area *there are always some follicles growing and some resting*, so that normally there is no wholesale shedding and the total hair growth remains constant in all seasons of the year. (35373)

(17) we shall suppose that there is a system of particles on which *there are some forces acting* (27440)

(18) *There have been many observations made* on the weed and its fauna from the time of Columbus to the present day, (32344)

(I am not concerned with cases where the participial clause is a reduced relative operating as post-modifier to the noun it follows – these can be handled in the same way as (10)–(12) above.) It might be thought that these are simply cleft-sentences with reduced relatives – compare *it was John who was speaking* and *it was John speaking*. But such an analysis is difficult to reconcile with the relativization in (17): if *acting on the particles* is a reduced relative clause we should not be able to relativize *the particles* – compare **the book which it was John (who was) reading*. It may be best therefore to revise the *there*-transformation so that it will derive examples like (16)–(18) from *many observations have been made on the weed*..., etc. Instead of shifting the concord subject to the right of the whole verbal group as in the first examples we considered, it could shift it to the right of the auxiliary *be* in complex verbal groups. This is in effect to say that there are two partially similar *there*-transformations – compare (18) with (3) above. Unlike the one considered first, this new one is not restricted to intransitive (or passive) clauses:

(19) There may well be other animals utilizing this rather special food supply. (32310)

Appendix: Sources of the corpus

The selection of the corpus is described by Hudson in Huddleston *et al.* (1968); here I simply give the bibliographical details of the 27 texts.

PART A

Text 12, High stratum biology
Echlin, P. & Morris, I., 'The relationship between blue-green algae and bacteria', *Biological Reviews* 40.2 (May 1965), 143–55.

Text 16, High stratum chemistry
Dominey, D. A., Morley, H. & Young, D. A. 'Kinetics of the decomposition of nickel oxalate';
Fleischmann, M., Pattison, J. & Thirsk, H. R., 'Electrocrystallization of thin films of thallous chloride on thallium amalgam'; *Transactions of the Faraday Society* 61.6 (June 1965), 1246–63.

Text 17, High stratum physics
Lorimor, O. G. & Spitzer, W. G., 'Infrared refractive index and absorption of InAs and CdTe';
Prince, E., 'Sublattice magnetization of yttrium ion garnet as a function of temperature';
Almasi, G. S., Blair, J., Ogilvie, R. E. & Schwartz, R. J., 'A heat-flow problem in electron beam microprobe analysis'; *Journal of Applied Physics* 36.6 (June 1965), 1841–9.

Text 21, Mid stratum biology
Chapman, V. J., *An introduction to the study of algae*, Cambridge, Cambridge University Press (1941), pp. 65–87.

Text 26, Mid stratum chemistry
Moelwyn-Hughes, E. A., *Physical chemistry*. London, Pergamon Press (1957), pp. 466–86.

Text 28, Mid stratum physics
Newman, F. H. & Searle, V. H. E., *The general properties of matter*. London, Arnold (5th ed. 1957), pp. 249–65.

Text 32, Low stratum
David, P. M., 'The surface fauna of the ocean';
Fleming, M. C. & Kitchener, J. A., 'Development of the theory of the flotation of sulphide ores'; *Endeavour* 24 (May 1965), 95–103.

Text 35, Low stratum

Montague, W., 'The skin', *Scientific American* 212.2 (February 1965), 56–65.

Text 38, Low stratum

Kopal, Z., 'The luminescence of the moon';

Zeitlin, A., 'High-pressure technology'; *Scientific American* 212.5 (May 1965), 28–38.

PART B

Text 11, High stratum biology

Thomson, W. W., Dugger, W. M. & Palmer, R. L., 'Effects of peroxyacetyl nitrate on ultrastructure of chloroplasts';

Clutter, M. E. & Sussex, I. M., 'Meiosis and sporogenesis in excised fern leaves grown in sterile culture';

Bell, T. A., Etchells, J. L. & Smart, W. W. G., 'Pectinase and cellulose enzyme inhibitor from Sericae and certain other plants'; *Botanical Gazette* 126.1 (March 1965), 66–78 and 40.

Text 14, High stratum chemistry

Lidgett, R. A., Lynch, E. R. & McCall, E. B., 'The direct phthalidimidation of the aromatic nucleus';

Blandamer, M. J., Shields, L. & Symons, M. C. R., 'Unstable intermediates, Part xxx. Solvated electrons: line shapes of electron absorption bands';

Catterall, R. & Symons, M. C. R., 'Unstable intermediates, Part xxxi. Solvated electrons: solutions of europium in ammonia'; *Journal of the Chemical Society* (June 1965), 3754–64.

Text 19, High stratum physics

Mandel, L. & Wolf, E., 'Coherence properties of optical fields', *Reviews of Modern Physics* 37.2 (April 1965), 231–40.

Text 23, Mid stratum biology

Borradaile, L. A. & Potts, F. A., *The Invertebrata*. Cambridge, Cambridge University Press (1932), pp. 186–204.

Text 24, Mid stratum chemistry

De la Mare, P. B. D. & Ridd, J. H., *Aromatic substitution*. London, Butterworths Scientific Publications (1965), pp. 45–59.

Text 29, Mid stratum physics

Zemansky, M. W., *Heat and thermodynamics*. New York, McGraw-Hill (4th ed. 1957), pp. 332–54.

Text 33, Low stratum

Eccles, J., 'The synapse';

Sager, R., 'Genes outside the chromosomes'; *Scientific American* 212.1 (January 1965), 56–71.

Text 36, Low stratum
Havard, J. D. J., 'Recognizing the intoxicated driver';
Briggs, A., 'The communications revolution'; *New Scientist* 26.443 (13 May 1965), 422–8.

Text 39, Low stratum
Goodridge, F., 'Electrochemical engineering';
De Walley, C. H., 'Chlorination of sewage';
Pagel, B., 'Origin of the elements'; *New Scientist* 26.438 (8 April 1965), 98–107.

PART C

Text 13, High stratum biology
Evans, M. E. G., 'A comparative account of the feeding methods of the beetles *Nebria brevicollis* and *Philonthus decorus*', *Transactions of the Royal Society of Edinburgh* 66.5 (1963–4), 91–106.

Text 15, High stratum chemistry
Nickson, A., Schwartz, N., Di Giorgio, J. B. & Widdowson, D. A., 'Reactivity in allylic systems, IV. Stereochemical factors in the photosensitized oxygenation of 5α- and 5β-cholest-3-enes', *Journal of Organic Chemistry* 30.6 (June 1965), 1711–17.

Text 18, High stratum physics
Burley, D. M., 'A first-order transition in a plane lattice gas with rigid repulsions', *Proceedings of the Physical Society* 85.6, no. 548 (June 1965), 1173–88.

Text 22, Mid stratum biology
Young, J. Z., *The life of mammals*. Oxford, Clarendon Press (1957), pp. 459–73.

Text 25, Mid stratum chemistry
Fieser, L. F. & Fieser, M., *Organic chemistry*. New York, Reinhold (1944), pp. 709–29.

Text 27, Mid stratum physics
Feynman, R. P., Leighton, R. B. & Sands, M., *The Feynman lectures on physics*, *I*. Reading, Mass., Addison–Wesley (1963), 18.1–8.

Text 31, Low stratum
Calne, R. Y., 'Organ transplantation';
White, R. J., 'Isolating the brain';
Sen-Gupta, A. & Kolff, W. J., 'Synthetic substitutes for internal organs'; *Discovery* 26.3 (March 1965), 28–38.

Text 34, Low stratum

Davies, R. D., 'A new look at our Galaxy';
Bingham, A. E., 'Hovercraft—the versatile vehicle'; *Discovery* 26.6 (June
1965), 30–9.

Text 37, Low stratum

Trethowan, W. H., 'Sympathy pains';
Gibson, A. F., 'A new method of amplifying sound'; *Discovery* 26.1 (January
1965), 30–7.

References

ANDERSON, J. (1968). 'Ergative and nominative in English', *Journal of Linguistics* 4, 1–32.

AUSTIN, J. L. (1962). *How to do things with words.* (Oxford: Clarendon Press.)

BACH, E. (1970). 'Problominalization', *Linguistic Inquiry* 1, 120–1.

BOLINGER, D. L. (1957). *Interrogative structures of American English.* (Alabama: University Press. Publications of the American Dialect Society.)

(1961). 'Syntactic blends and other matters', *Language* 37, 366–81.

(1967a). 'Imperatives in English', in *To honor Roman Jakobson*, 335–62. (The Hague: Mouton.)

(1967b). 'Adjective comparison: a semantic scale', *Journal of English Linguistics* 1, 2–10.

(1967c). 'Adjectives in English: attribution and predication', *Lingua* 18, 1–34.

(1968). 'Entailment and the meaning of structures', *Glossa* 2, 119–27.

CAMPBELL, R. N. & WALES, R. J. (1969). 'Comparative structures in English', *Journal of Linguistics* 5, 215–51.

CHOMSKY, N. (1957). *Syntactic structures.* (The Hague: Mouton.)

(1965). *Aspects of the theory of syntax.* (Cambridge, Mass.: M.I.T. Press.)

(1968). *Language and mind.* (New York: Harcourt, Brace & World.)

(Forthcoming). 'Remarks on nominalization', in *Readings in English transformational grammar*, edited by R. A. Jacobs & P. S. Rosenbaum. (Waltham, Mass.: Blaisdell.)

CHRISTOPHERSEN, P. (1939). *The articles: a study of their theory and use in English.* (Copenhagen: Munksgaard.)

CLARKE, D. C. & WALL, R. E. (1965). 'An economical program for limited parsing of English.' In *Proceedings of the Fall Joint Computer Conference.*

CRYSTAL, D. & DAVY, D. (1969). *Investigating English style.* (Longmans.)

CURME, G. O. (1931). *A grammar of the English language, Vol. 3: Syntax.* (Boston: Heath.)

DOHERTY, P. & SCHWARTZ, A. (1967). 'The syntax of the compared adjective in English', *Language* 43, 903–36.

EHRMAN, M. (1966). *The meanings of the modals in present-day American English.* (The Hague: Mouton.)

FILLMORE, C. J. (1963). 'The position of embedding transformations in a grammar', *Word* 19, 208–31.

(1967). 'The grammar of "hitting" and "breaking"', *Working Papers in Linguistics, No 1*, 9–29. (Computer and Information Science Research Center, Ohio State University.)

(1968a). 'The case for case'. in *Universals in Linguistic theory*, edited by E. Bach & R. T. Harms. (New York: Holt, Rinehart & Winston.)

(1968*b*). 'Lexical entries for verbs', *Foundations of Language* 4, 373–93.

(1968*c*). 'Types of lexical information', *Working Papers in Linguistics, No 2*, 65–103. (Computer and Information Science Research Center, Ohio State University.)

FODOR, J. A. (1970). 'Three reasons for not deriving "kill" from "cause to die"', *Linguistic Inquiry* 1, 429–38.

FRIES, C. C. (1952). *The structure of English.* (New York: Harcourt, Brace & World.)

GREENBAUM, S. (1969). *Studies in English adverbial usage.* (Longmans.)

HALLIDAY, M. A. K. (1961). 'Categories of the theory of grammar', *Word* 17, 241–92.

(1963). 'The tones of English', *Archivum Linguisticum* 15, 1–28. This and the next paper are republished, slightly adapted, in *Intonation and grammar in British English.* (The Hague: Mouton, 1967.)

(1964). 'Intonation in English grammar', *Transactions of the Philological Society for 1963*, 143–69.

(1967*a*). *Grammar, society and the noun.* (London: H. K. Lewis.)

(1967*b, c,* 1968). 'Notes on transitivity and theme in English, Parts 1, 2 & 3', *Journal of Linguistics* 3, 37–81 & 199–244; 4, 179–215.

(1969). 'Options and functions in the English clause', *Brno Studies in English* 8, 81–8.

HORN, L. & MORGAN, J. (1969). 'Why comparatives are more complicated than you realize', *Phonetics Laboratory Notes* (University of Michigan) 4, 38–42.

HUDDLESTON, R. D. (1967). 'More on the English comparative', *Journal of Linguistics* 3, 91–102.

(1969*a*). 'Review of M. Ehrman, *The meanings of the modals in present-day American English*', *Lingua* 23, 165–76.

(1969*b*).'Predicate complement constructions in English', *Lingua* 23, 241–73.

(1969*c*). 'Some observations on tense and deixis in English', *Language* 45, 777–806.

(1970*a*). 'Two approaches to the analysis of tags', *Journal of Linguistics* 6, 215–22.

(1970*b*). 'Some remarks on case-grammar', *Linguistic Inquiry* 1, 501–11.

HUDDLESTON, R. D., HUDSON, R. A., WINTER, E. O., & HENRICI, A. (1968). *Sentence and clause in scientific English*, Dept. of General Linguistics, University College London (mimeographed). Lodged with the U.K. National Lending Library for Science and Technology as O.S.T.I. Report No. 5030.

JACKENDOFF, R. S. (1968). 'Quantifiers in English', *Foundations of Language* 4, 422–42.

JESPERSEN, O. (1924). *The philosophy of grammar.* (London: Allen & Unwin.)

(1927, 1931, 1940). *A modern English grammar on historical principles, Parts 3, 4 and 5.* (Copenhagen: Munksgaard.)

(1969). *Analytic syntax.* (New York: Holt, Rinehart & Winston. First published in 1937.)

JOOS, M. (1964). *The English verb.* (Madison: Wisconsin University Press.)

KANDIAH, T. (1968). 'Transformational grammar and the layering of structure in Tamil', *Journal of Linguistics* 4, 217–45.

KATZ, J. J. (1967). 'Recent issues in semantic theory', *Foundations of Language* 3, 124–94.

KATZ, J. J. & POSTAL, P. M. (1964). *An integrated theory of linguistic descriptions.* (Cambridge, Mass.: M.I.T. Press.)

KIPARSKY, P. & KIPARSKY, C. (Forthcoming). 'Fact' in *Progress in linguistics*, edited by M. Bierwisch & K. E. Heidolph. (The Hague: Mouton.)

KLIMA, E. S. (1964). 'Negation in English', in *The structure of language*, edited by J. A. Fodor & J. J. Katz. (Englewood Cliffs, N.J.: Prentice-Hall.)

KOUTSOUDAS, A. (1968). 'On wh-words in English', *Journal of Linguistics* 4, 267–73.

KURODA, S. Y. (1968). 'English relativization and certain related problems', *Language* 44, 244–66. Republished in Reibel & Schane (1969).

LAKOFF, G. (1966). 'Stative adjectives and verbs in English', in *Mathematical Linguistics and Automatic Translation, Report NSF-17.* (The Computation Laboratory of Harvard University, Cambridge, Mass.)

(1968). 'Instrumental adverbs and the concept of deep structure', *Foundations of Language* 4, 4–29.

(Forthcoming). 'On generative semantics', in *Semantics*, edited by D. D. Steinberg & L. A. Jakobovits.

LAKOFF, G., & PETERS, S. (1969). 'Phrasal conjunction and symmetric predicates', in Reibel & Schane (1969). First published in 1966.

LAKOFF, R. T. (1968). *Abstract syntax and Latin complementation.* (Cambridge, Mass.: M.I.T. Press.)

(1970). 'Another non-source for comparatives', *Linguistic Inquiry* 1, 128–9.

LANGACKER, R. W. (1967). *Language and its structure: some fundamental linguistic concepts.* (New York: Harcourt, Brace & World.)

LANGENDOEN, D. T. (1969). *The study of syntax: the generative-transformational approach to the structure of American English.* (New York: Holt, Rinehart & Winston.)

LEES, R. B. (1960). 'A multiply ambiguous adjectival construction in English', *Language* 36, 207–21. Republished in *The English Language, vol. 2*, edited by W. F. Bolton & D. Crystal, Cambridge University Press, 1969.

(1961). 'Grammatical analysis of the English comparative construction', *Word* 17, 171–85. Republished in Reibel & Schane (1969).

(1963). 'Analysis of the "cleft sentence" in English', *Zeitschrift für Phonetik* 16, 371–88.

LEVENSTON, E. A. (1969). 'Imperative structures in English', *Linguistics* 50, 38–43.

LYONS, J. (1966). 'Review of J. J. Katz & P. M. Postal, *An integrated theory of linguistic descriptions*', *Journal of Linguistics* 2, 119–26.

(1968). *Introduction to theoretical linguistics.* (Cambridge: Cambridge University Press.)

MCCAWLEY, J. D. (1969a). 'Semantic representation', read at Cognitive

Studies and Artificial Intelligence Research, 2–8 March 1969, The University of Chicago Center for Continuing Education, Chicago.

(1969*b*). 'Tense and time reference in English', read at the Ohio State Semantics Festival, 14 April, 1969.

MIHAILOVIČ, L. (1967). 'Passive and pseudopassive verbal groups in English', *English Studies* 48, 316–26.

PALMER, F. R. (1965). *A linguistic study of the English verb.* (Longmans.)

POSTAL, P. M. (1966). 'On so-called "pronouns" in English', *Monograph Series on Languages and Linguistics* 19, 177–205. Republished in Reibel & Schane (1969).

(1970). 'On the surface verb "remind"', *Linguistic Inquiry* 1, 37–120.

QUANG PHUC DONG (1969). 'Phrases anglaises sans sujet grammatical apparent', *Langages* 14, 44–51.

QUIRK, R. (1965). 'Descriptive statement and serial relationship', *Language* 41, 205–17.

(1968). 'Relative clauses in educated spoken English', Paper 9 of *Essays on the English Language* (London: Longmans.) First published in *English Studies* 38 (1957), 1–13.

REIBEL, D. A. & SCHANE, S. A. (eds.) (1969). *Modern studies in English.* (Englewood Cliffs, N.J.: Prentice-Hall.)

ROSENBAUM, P. S. (1967*a*). 'Phrase structure principles of English complex sentence formation', *Journal of Linguistics* 3, 103–18.

(1967*b*). *The grammar of English predicate complement constructions.* (Cambridge, Mass.: M.I.T. Press.)

(1968). 'English grammar II', Section 1 of *Specification and utilization of a transformational grammar*, Scientific Report 2. (Yorktown Heights, N.Y.: I.B.M. Corporation, Thomas J. Watson Research Center.)

ROSS, J. R. & PERLMUTTER, D. M. (1970). 'A non-source for comparatives', *Linguistic Inquiry* 1, 127–8.

SAPIR, E. (1944). 'Grading: a study in semantics', *Philosophy of Science* 11, 93–116. Republished in *Selected writings of Edward Sapir in language, culture and personality*, Berkeley: California University Press, 1949.

SEARLE, R. (1969). *Speech acts: an essay in the philosophy of language.* (Cambridge: Cambridge University Press.)

SMITH, C. S. (1961). 'A class of complex modifiers in English', *Language*, 37, 342–65.

(1964). 'Determiners and relative clauses in a generative grammar of English', *Language* 40, 37–52. Republished in Reibel & Schane (1969).

STANLEY, R. (1969). 'The English comparative adjective construction', in *Papers from the Fifth Regional Meeting of the Chicago Linguistic Society, April 18–19, 1969*, edited by R. I. Binnick *et al.* (Chicago: Dept. of Linguistics, University of Chicago.)

SWEET, H. (1891). *A new English grammar, vol. 1.* (Oxford: Clarendon Press.)

THORNE, J. P. (1966). 'English imperative sentences', *Journal of Linguistics* 2, 69–78.

ZANDVOORT, R. W. (1950). *A handbook of English grammar.* (4th ed. Groningen: Wolters.)

Index